The Big Book of
CANADIAN
HAUNTINGS

Other Books of Canadian Mysteries by John Robert Colombo

"They are the best collections of their kind being produced
by anyone, anywhere, as far as I can see."
— Hilary Evans

The Big Book of Canadian Ghost Stories (Dundurn, 2008)
Strange but True (Dundurn, 2007)
More True Canadian Ghost Stories (Prospero, 2005)
Terrors of the Night (Dundurn, 2005)
The Monster Book of Canadian Monsters (BSDB, 2004)
True Canadian UFO Stories (Prospero, 2004)
The Midnight Hour (Dundurn, 2004)
True Canadian Ghost Stories (Prospero, 2003)
Many Mysteries (C&C, 2001)
Ghost Stories of Canada (Dundurn, 2000)
Ghosts in Our Past (C&C, 2000)
Weird Stories (C&C, 1999)
The UFO Quote Book (C&C, 1999)
Mysteries of Ontario (Dundurn, 1999)
Singular Stories (C&C, 1999)
Three Mysteries of Nova Scotia (C&C, 1999)
The UFO Quote Book (C&C, 1999)
Closer than You Think (C&C, 1998)
Marvellous Stories (C&C, 1998)
Haunted Toronto (Dundurn, 1996)
Ghost Stories of Ontario (Dundurn, 1995)
Strange Stories (C&C, 1994)
Singular Stories (C&C, 1994)
Ghosts Galore! (C&C, 1994)
Close Encounters of the Canadian Kind (C&C, 1994)
Voices of Rama (C&C, 1994)
The Mystery of the Shaking Tent (C&C, 1993)
Dark Visions (Dundurn, 1992)
The Little Book of UFOs (Pulp Press, 1992)
UFOs over Canada (Dundurn, 1991)
Mackenzie King's Ghost (Dundurn, 1991)
Mysterious Encounters (Dundurn, 1990)
Extraordinary Experiences (Dundurn, 1989)
Mysterious Canada (Doubleday, 1988)
Windigo (Western Producer Prairie Books, 1982)
Colombo's Book of Marvels (NC Press, 1979)

The Big Book of
CANADIAN
HAUNTINGS

JOHN ROBERT COLOMBO

DUNDURN PRESS
TORONTO

Editor: Jason Karp
Design: Erin Mallory
Printer: Webcom

Library and Archives Canada Cataloguing in Publication

Colombo, John Robert, 1936-
    The big book of Canadian hauntings / John Robert Colombo.

ISBN 978-1-55488-449-0

    1. Ghosts--Canada. 2. Haunted places--Canada. I. Title.

BF1472.C3C576 2009   133.10971   C2009-902466-7

I   2   3   4   5   13   12   II   IO   O9

 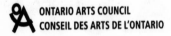

Conseil des Arts   Canada Council   ONTARIO ARTS COUNCIL
du Canada   for the Arts   CONSEIL DES ARTS DE L'ONTARIO

Canada

We acknowledge the support of **The Canada Council for the Arts** and the **Ontario Arts Council** for our publishing program. We also acknowledge the financial support of the **Government of Canada** through the **Book Publishing Industry Development Program** and **The Association for the Export of Canadian Books**, and the **Government of Ontario** through the **Ontario Book Publishers Tax Credit** program, and the **Ontario Media Development Corporation**.

Care has been taken to trace the ownership of copyright material used in this book. The author and the publisher welcome any information enabling them to rectify any references or credits in subsequent editions.
                                                            J. Kirk Howard, President

Printed and bound in Canada.
Printed on recycled paper
www.dundurn.com

Dundurn Press   Gazelle Book Services Limited   Dundurn Press
3 Church Street, Suite 500   White Cross Mills   2250 Military Road
Toronto, Ontario, Canada   High Town, Lancaster, England   Tonawanda, NY
M5E 1M2   LA1 4XS   U.S.A. 14150

CONTENTS

INTRODUCTION

Miss Seward (with an incredulous smile): "What, Sir! about a ghost?"

Johnson (with solemn vehemence): "Yes, Madam: this is a question which, after five thousand years, is yet undecided; a question, whether in theology or philosophy, one of the most important that can come before the human understanding."

— James Boswell, quoting Dr. Samuel Johnson on
April 15, 1778, *The Life of Samuel Johnson* (1791)

D id you ever wonder whether the place where you are now dwelling is haunted?

Here is a big book about such matters, about ghosts and hauntings, a book that is calculated to make you pause and wonder about the world of spirits, about haunted sites and places, and about the interconnections that may exist between the world of the living and the world of the dead or unborn. The accounts in this tome raise questions about the extent and limit of human knowledge and the reliability of human experience. In many ways it is an entertaining book; in other ways, a sobering collection of riveting accounts of "what should not be." In other words, here are one hundred or so of what I call "Canadian mysteries."

For the last forty years, I have been an assiduous collector of "Canadian mysteries." Perhaps I should explain this term because there are not too many collectors of mysteries, Canadian or otherwise, in this or any other country. What I mean by "Canadian mysteries" is accounts of events or experiences that are neither explicable nor inexplicable, but at present are unexplained. Hence I have in mind the operations of powers or abilities that are above and beyond the capacity of human beings to entertain or perform, as well as of events that seemingly defy rational explanation. Such occurrences have been reported in the past, continue to be reported by Canadians in the present, and, I have no doubt, will continue to be reported in the future.

I collect such accounts but I specialize in the ones that are expressed in the words and phrases of the witnesses themselves, rather than in the words and paraphrases of interviewers, reporters, or commentators. First-person statements convey a sense of immediacy that is lacking in second-hand or third-hand accounts. There is a fair amount of interest in these statements and I am pleased to devote time and energy to collecting them — which means I enjoy encountering people — and setting down their memories in readable form.

Many people enjoy reading about the unexplained, the mysterious, and the fantastic, and there are various reasons why this is so. Perhaps the main reason is simply the wonder of it all. Most of us at one time or another has pondered the mysteries of life and death — about such matters as extensions of the mind, body, or spirit in time and space and about access to minds other than our own. Indeed, we have often worried about the state after life as well as the state before life, and here is a place to shelve our apprehensions, at least for the time being. Are powers greater than human fictions? We may soberly ask ourselves, can such things be?

Accounts of psychical and other activities are "wonder tales" and come in one of two kinds — narrative accounts and personal accounts. The narrative accounts are basically objective reports of peculiar events, like acts of prophecy, reports of mysterious disappearances, instances of telepathy, et cetera. The personal accounts, on the other hand, are subjective reports that take the form of first-person descriptions of experiences that have occurred to that person. Both kinds of accounts are "told as true," — that is, they record events and experiences that defy rational expectation, supposedly true reports that elicit disbelief. Such stories — the word *story* is something of a misnomer here because it involves fiction, but here it is being used in its non-fictional meaning — characteristically involve encounters with ghosts and spirits. Far from being rare, such stories are quite common! I like to say that extraordinary experiences are extraordinarily common. They are widely reported from coast to coast, even in Canada!

The subject of the paranormal is a vast one and it is surveyed in dozens of books that I have written or compiled, many of them of limited distribution, but most of them commercially available. For instance, I compiled *The Big Book of Canadian Ghost Stories*, which brought together almost two hundred such accounts. One reviewer compared the book's jumbo form to that of the telephone directory of a middle-sized city! And it is large, for it contains some 175,000 words — the same number of words as the present volume, *The Big Book of Canadian Hauntings*, which is the size and format of another city's telephone directory!

The majority of the accounts in these two volumes consist of reports of the first-person variety — that is, they are told by the witnesses themselves. These are not "told-to" stories, nor are they third-person stories — that is, experiences related to a third party, like a journalist, who records them, adding a few frills and possibly chills in the process. Nor are these accounts imaginative fiction like the ghost stories of M.R. James or Robertson Davies or Stephen King. Instead they are "stranger than fiction," being "told as true," with nothing irrelevant included and with nothing relevant excluded.

How truthful are these accounts? The reader will have to decide. Some of the prose from the nineteenth century is certainly overwritten, and the newspapermen who contributed these columns are given to embroidery and drollery in equal proportions. Conversely, some of the prose from the twentieth century is underwritten, in the sense that many of the witnesses, lacking some of the structures available to writers of earlier centuries, simply recount their experiences in the ways in which the incidents and the impressions occurred, perhaps with a nod to familiar formulas from horror programs on television or horror movies on the big screen. There is really no way to prove that any of the incidents recorded in these accounts actually occurred, or occurred in the ways that they are being described, so it is expedient to keep a critical eye open.

I like to say that there are three areas of deception — foolishness, fraud, and fantasy — and that each of these is worth a pause. Many people are foolish and find it difficult to distinguish between what they feel and what they think, between what they sense and what they know. Rigorous thinking is difficult for foolish people, who listen to what other people say all the time and hence are deceived — unlike the fraudster, who knows exactly what he is doing. Fraud is outright deception, generally for commercial gain or social power over other people, and there are certainly many celebrated deceptions in the field of psychical research and parapsychology, ranging from peasant mediums who engaged in outright deception to distinguished statisticians, psychical researchers, and parapsychologists who were uncovered fiddling with the records to make a point or two. Finally there is fantasy, basically wishful thinking, and psychologists have suggested that there is a part of the population that is what they call "fantasy prone" — that is, given to mixing imagination with reality. Foolishness and fantasy have characteristics in common, but the main difference between the foolish person and the fantasy-prone person is that the former has no idea what she is doing or saying, whereas the latter knows quite well that her ideas and deeds are not quite right. Foolishness, fraud, and fantasy are areas of deception. But over and above these pitfalls there are areas of knowledge — fields of experience or realms of insight, intuition, and imagination — that exist on their own and that are part of the life of man and woman. These are our mysteries and they inspire our sense of wonder.

The title of the present volume is *The Big Book of Canadian Hauntings*, but I am of the opinion that its title could be reduced from six words to one word. That one word is *fear*. This is a book that is all about fear — fear of the unknown, fear of what is outside ourselves, fear of what is inside ourselves, fear of what is above us, what is below us, what is far beyond life itself ... fear of what is beyond death. Indeed, we feel those very fears (the limbs quivering, the skin crawling, the hair standing on end, the body shivering, the pulse quickening, the attention wavering, the perspiration forming, the cheeks flushing, the eyes watering, the stomach trembling, the bowels loosening) in the face of the unknown! We feel ourselves to be threatened, and often the appearance of a ghost or a spirit will initially amplify and then eventually allay that fear. We may then feel a sense of relief, a feeling of completion, or a realization that "we have come full circle." This is currently called "a sense of closure." So the present volume is a collection of human stories about fear, about inhuman threats to human beings which may, paradoxically, leave us feeling more human than ever.

As Marshall McLuhan once observed, "The most human thing about man is his technology." Instead of the word *technology*, he might have substituted the word *ghosts*. "The most human thing about man is his ghosts." Only human beings know anything at all about ghosts and spirits, though it is true that in folklore and literature there are many descriptions of animals responding to appearances and disappearances of spiritual entities. (But this folklore and these works of fiction were written by human beings.) There are many people who are critical of ghost stories and accounts of the unknown, and these people may be sceptics (who doubt rather than believe in the existence or operation of mysterious powers or abilities) or they may be believers (who want to limit such powers or abilities to their own conception of a Holy Spirit, a Holy Ghost, a Saviour, a Devil, a Satan, an angel, et cetera). The truth is nobody knows anything at all for sure about such matters, though sacred scriptures and scientific works of psychology and books of imaginative literature help us along the way. They at least raise great questions. So it is best to maintain an open mind and to accept whatever evidence is at hand.

This book deals with our principal primordial fear, and that is the fear of the dark. This is the sense of fear and the sense of foreboding that we face when we are lost in the dark, beginning when the sun begins to set at dusk, continuing through the darkness of midnight and the wee hours of the morning (sometimes called the "hours of the wolf") until the sun begins to rise at dawn, when once again we know what is happening to us. Here night is a metaphor for the "inner night" that alternates with the "inner day" that dawns upon all of us. *The Sleep of Reason Produces Monsters*, Spanish painter Francisco Goya titled one of his demonic etchings. The critical faculties do fall asleep and the associative and imaginative faculties sometimes wake up and "come into their own," most directly in dreams and the dreams we call nightmares because they are so shocking or so discomforting. The present book is a collection of accounts of how we face the world of darkness and its shadows, how we confront our own fears and experiences (what is "in there") with what we find in the world (what is "out there"). Many of the experiences reported in the pages of this book will remind its readers of half-formed dreams and half-recalled episodes of real life. Who is to say, along with the ancients, that dreams do not convey knowledge and information? The great psychologists of the twentieth century, notably Sigmund Freud and C.G. Jung, held strong views on man's half-remembered, semi-dream life. Freud felt the world of dreams to be "the royal road to the unconscious." Jung conducted dream analyses in which dreams were treated like *mandalas*, images to be pondered.

Here is a book of impressions and experiences — the physiological responses of the body, the emotions of the heart, and the thoughts of the mind. They beg the question: what is it that sends us into a state of apprehension, even of shock? It may be many things, but since childhood we are conditioned to worry about imaginary beings. Many children begin to play with their own imaginary companions. Other children fear the "monster under the bed." Indeed, youngsters are introduced to imaginary beings — good fairies, bad fairies, Peter Pan, Winnie the Pooh, et cetera — which then take the form of inscrutable figures, some of them companions or guardians, others of them scarecrow-like figures, stern and even destructive. Witness these horrible synonyms for *ghosts* and *spirits*, which I corralled from a thesaurus:

aliens, apparitions, banshees, beasts, beings, bogeymen, brownies, chimeras, demons, devils, doppelgangers, doubles, elves, entities, fairies, forerunners, ghosts ghouls, goblins, gremlins, haunts, imps, incubi, kelpies, leprechauns, manes, monsters, phantasms, phantoms, pixies, poltergeists, revenants, shades, shadows, souls, spectres, spirits, spooks, sprites, succubi, sylphs, trolls, vampires, visions, visitants, visitors, wraiths, zombies

There are many more of these where these were found, but I think forty-six synonyms are enough for now!

While checking the thesaurus, I came up with an even greater number of synonyms for *fear* and *dread*. Here are sensations, affections, and notions that overcome people from time to time in real-life situations and are recalled when they read accounts like the ones in this book:

agitation, alarm, amazing, anguish, anxiety, apprehension, astonishing, astounding, awesome, baffling, bewildering, bizarre, concern, confounding, confusing, cryptic, curious, disquieting, distress, dread, dumbfounding, elusive, enigmatic, extraordinary, fabulous, fanciful, fantastic, fear, foreboding, fright, ghastly, grotesque, hallucinatory, horror, illusory, imaginary, incomprehensible, incredible, inexplicable, marvelous, mysterious, mystifying, outlandish, panic, paradoxical, perplexing, puzzling, quaking, quivering, scare, shakes, shivers, shocked, shudder, startled, strain, strange, stress, suspense, sweats, tension, terrifying, terror, tremble, trepidation, troubled, unfathomable, unusual, upset, weird, wondrous, worry

That list consists of seventy-two descriptors, but I am sure there are many more such words.

Here in these pages there are more than one hundred "told-as-true" accounts of eerie events and weird experiences. In the main these episodes are *anomalous occurrences* — that is, any attempt to explain them or at least to account for the fact that they have happened in the past and will happen again in the future makes for "heavy lifting." An experience that is *anomalous* may be simply unconventional, or it may be really strange, odd, peculiar, or eccentric. It may also be abnormal in the sense that such events and experiences are not easily explained, difficult to account for, and hence lead to unease and sometimes worse. I would call them *supernatural states* except for the fact that there is a better way to describe them, and that is to refer to them as *preternatural states*. They are not "super" anything, but they are beyond normal states. The Canadian psychologist Graham Reed labelled them *anomalous experiences*, thereby liberating them from the last pages of textbooks on psychology and psychiatry where they used to be herded together and regarded as *abnormal experiences*.

I cannot account for the persistence, the variety, or the intensity of these experiences. What I can attest to is that my informants — the men and women who sought me out to recall their experiences for me and for my readers — believe that these psychological and sometimes physical events occurred as they are described, factually and fully, and that they are as puzzled by these experiences as I am. There is no doubting the immense power of such encounters and the dramatic need to recall them and then relate them to sympathetic souls. A psychological event that took place thirty years ago, which lasted for thirty seconds at the most, leaves an indelible impression on the tablets of memory, on the chalkboard of the heart, and in the pit of the stomach. I wish I could account for such experiences, though I believe, by now, most of the informants have given up expecting an explanation for them. Some correspondents wish confirmation that they are not alone in experiencing such episodes; others wish to add their descriptions to the ever-widening pool of *anomalous experience*, what psychical researchers in the late nineteenth century called their "census of hallucinations," using the latter word in the sense of disorientation rather than illusion.

I am an author and anthologist by profession, and an editor and writer by training, who, ever since he can remember, has been fascinated by — and bewildered with — accounts of *anomalous events and experiences*: reports of ghosts and spirits, apparitions and spectres, the poltergeist and the entity experience, prophecies and predictions, legends and myths, strange gifts and wild talents, visions and revelations, clairvoyance and precognition, psychokinesis and extrasensory perception, psychical research and parapsychology, psychometry and precognition, alternate states of consciousness, reincarnation and past-life regression, cryptozoology, miraculous cures, occult organizations, near-death and out-of-body experiences, conspiracy theories, unidentified flying objects, alien beings and hybrid creatures ... you name it!

Once I began in earnest to collect and publish accounts of such episodes and occurrences in this country, I was dubbed "Canada's Mr. Mystery." I have now published some three dozen collections of such encounters with the irrational and each one includes introductory and often explanatory notes. Since I am interested in the past as much as I am in the present, with each book I try to offer readers some historical material, largely in the form of columns reprinted from nineteenth-century newspapers and books. But in the main readers are offered new, never-before-published accounts that I have gleaned from my own explorations and investigations, inquiries and interrogations, and correspondence on paper and via email. I encourage readers of my books to communicate with me directly and to share with me, and then with future readers, accounts of their own experiences, no matter how bizarre.

The question must be asked: as a reader, should I trust that these accounts are truthful? Let me attempt to answer that question. In the past I would request each person contributing an account to one of my collections to sign a statement that affirms that the account to be published is truthful, accurate, and complete — the truth, the whole truth, and nothing but the truth. No one ever refused to sign this statement, though the occasional contributor requested anonymity or subsequently developed cold feet and asked that nothing at all be published. All such requests have been honoured. Subsequently I dispensed with that statement. But I do, in my own way, keep my eyes open for what I call the "three Fs." These are fraud, foolishness, and fantasy. But we discussed those earlier.

Over the four decades that I have been collecting these accounts, I have come to a number of conclusions about "told-as-true" stories in general, and about the ones that appear in these pages in particular. I call these accounts *memorates*, employing the term used in folklore studies to refer to first-person accounts of experiences that are confided to friends and family members. These are originally oral in nature and are not meant for broader distribution, as they are shared to bear witness, not argue or convince anyone of anything. When I use the folklorist's term, I do not argue that the accounts themselves are folklore, or that they are "fakelore," only that they bear some of the characteristics of folklore, the two principle ones being repetition and variation. The accounts are quite often quite similar with incidental differences.

Typically the *memorate* will begin, "You won't believe me when I tell you what happened to me the other day." Typically it will end, "And that's what happened. I don't know what to make of it." In between, a standard account will be a straight-forward description of an odd happening that is objectively described and subjectively validated. So the *memorate* comes in three parts, with the beginning and the ending stressing a modicum of belief, a quantum of disbelief, and a fair amount of not knowing what to think.

The key factor of the *memorate* is that the witness himself is at a loss to explain what has happened, what is going on, and what it could possibly mean. When I have asked witnesses about their belief systems, I am quite often surprised to learn that they have none, at least none that will make sense of the experience that they have had and have described. Some people subsequently become knowledgeable about New Age matters, and UFO sighters typically know all about "mother ships" and "aliens," "contact," and "hybrids." Indeed, they seem well informed. I myself am at a loss to explain what has been occurring, and all I can do is suggest the dynamic or organic mechanisms involved. So what I do fall back on is my own familiarity with descriptions of such experiences, so I assure witnesses that far from being extraordinary, such experiences are surprisingly commonplace!

I am regularly asked about my own beliefs. People directly ask, "Do you believe in ghosts?" Over the years I have perfected a reply that runs like this: "I do not believe in ghosts. I do not disbelieve in ghosts. I am *interested* in ghosts." I will often add the following admission: "What I do believe in is *ghost stories*." I find these narratives to be convincing in and of themselves. Depending on the interest of the questioner, I might reply, "Ghosts and spirits do not belong to the category of belief. They belong to the category of experience." Yet the question that I keep asking myself is, "Why are these accounts so riveting? Why do people recall in such detail the sight of a spectral figure that appeared for ten seconds before vanishing so many years ago, even decades ago? Why are they compelled to tell and retell their experiences to people like myself who ask them about their encounters and are prepared to listen to them?" In some ways the witnesses are like the Ancient Mariner or the Flying Dutchman, burdened with fabulous memories.

Those are questions to ask, but not of everyone. Some people have no time at all for ghosts and spirits; other people are held spellbound by these subjects. At receptions I enjoy asking people, "Have you ever seen a ghost?" The usual answer is no. I then ask a supplementary question: "If you have never seen a ghost, do you know someone whose judgment you respect who has told you that he or she has seen a ghost?" There is usually a pause here, followed by the hesitant answer, "Well, yes. My brother / sister / uncle / cousin / best friend told me he saw a ghost."

It is frequently said that ghosts and spirits are illusions and delusions and that we would be better off if we simply forgot about them. Then it is sometimes added, rather mysteriously, "This way leads to madness" or "These are works of the Devil." That does not make much sense. There are no good reasons to ignore this dimension of the human personality. Ignoring such experiences guarantees continued ignorance. In fact, I am prepared to argue, and have done so on many an occasion, that ghosts and spirits are good for us. They are good for us because they require us to open our minds to the *possibility* that such things exist. They require us to think about the ultimate mysteries, about life and death, about destiny and fate, about grace and disgrace, about mystery and goodness, about evil and goodness, about madness and sanity, about the nature of life and reality. Responding to such possibilities prompts us to be more thoughtful, more impassioned, and more accommodating to the prospects and expectations that exist in our society, the world, and the universe in which we live.

This is not my opinion alone, but the considered opinion of William James, the great psychologist (who developed the theory of Pragmatism) who was known in his day as a psychical researcher. He devoted twenty-five years of his life to psychical research in the United States and Great Britain. In a letter to a fellow researcher, dated January 1, 1886, he ventured the following conviction about this field of interest and inquiry to which I subscribe:

> It is a field in which the sources of deception are extremely numerous. But I believe there is no source of deception in the investigation of nature which can compare with a fixed belief that certain kinds of phenomenon are *impossible*.

I

HAUNTINGS OF THE PAST

1

SPIRITS OF THE
NATIVE PEOPLES

The reader will find in the first section of this book descriptions of the psychical and spiritual practices of the Native people, as they were recorded in the columns of the newspapers of their day. Prior to the 1960s it was customary to refer to the Native people who occupy the polar regions of Canada as "the Eskimo" and "Indians." The tone of these accounts is by turn quaint and condescending. But they do preserve a sense of surprise and mystery as they describe shamanistic or pagan principles and practices, and they do prepare the reader for the final account, a memoir, which is much longer than all the rest combined. It is included here because it brings everything up to date. It suggests that the Native mysteries, far from being relegated to the past, are very much part of the present and will positively be part of the future, too!

FEASTS FOR THE HAPPY SPIRITS

In the 1960s, as if to mark the coming to political power of the Native people, the word *Eskimo* was dropped in favour of the word *Inuit* (which means "people" in Inuktitut, the language the Inuit speak). Since articles like this one predate the 1960s by almost a century, the word *Eskimo* will be maintained. "Spiritism among the Esquimaux" appeared in the *Sarnia Observer*, December 4, 1874. It must have represented a novelty to the readers of that paper. Nothing is immediately known of its source other than what is named in the last line.

Spiritism among the Esquimaux

The religion of the Esquimaux is of all curious systems of theology, the most curious. Nevertheless they are not polytheists, demon worshipers, not even idolaters, in the common acceptance of that term. They believe in one supreme deity, whom they call Toongarsoon, their word for the devil, who is of the feminine gender, but whose proper name, if she has one, I could never ascertain. Their god is supposed to reside in a handsome dwelling situated somewhere in the sea. His occupation, according to their notion, is a very benevolent one, for he is said to keep large herds of seals, sea-horses, etc., for the express purpose of providing entertainment for the souls of the good men, which are transported immediately after death to the apartments assigned for him in the marine palace where his godship resides. A large apartment of this place is said to be fitted up with cooking apparatus, on the most extensive scale; pots and kettles of such dimensions that walruses, sea unicorns, seals, etc., in large numbers are boiled or baked therein every day to furnish a perpetual feast for the happy spirits of deceased Esquimaux hunters, or such of them as behaved themselves with tolerable propriety while in the flesh. Hence it will appear that the Esquimaux heaven consists of a never ending feast of fat things, an eternity of well cooked walrus meat and seal's blubber.

The devil (a female one, remember) is supposed to be an unworthy sister of the divine, Toongarsoon. She resides at some distance from her brother's palace, on an island, where she takes charge of deceased sinners, who, under her domestic management, fare worse if possible than the inmates of some of the cheap boarding-houses in New York. In fact, these delinquent spirits suffer the pangs of starvation, and their cries and shrieks of agony are often heard above the howling of the arctic gales and the angry war of the mountain torrents. — Prof. Sountage's *Narrative*, etc.

INITIATION AND INSTRUCTION

This article exemplifies the habit of non-Native writers of the past for finding Native practices remarkable if also somewhat ridiculous. "Superstitious Indians" appeared in the *Winnipeg Free Press*, January 6, 1894. It was reprinted from the *Boston Transcript*. Although the writer uses the first-person singular, his name is not given.

Superstitious Indians One Reason Why Missionaries Make So Little Progress

North of the Lake of the Woods lies a region which is as yet unpenetrated by the lines of travel. In this section, perhaps, more than any other in British America, the Indians deserve the name which even the Crees about Lake Winnipeg apply to them, "Heathen Indians." During a visit to the eastern shore of Lake Winnipeg I saw some of these Indians, and our inspector of Indian agencies, the Hon. Ebenezer McColl, gave me many particulars concerning their customs.

Among these natives flourishes unabated the superstitious belief in the power of the medicine men. These artful old conjurers, more interested in extorting from the people their living than in their advancement, prejudice them against all inroads of teachers or missionaries, and by their monotonous incantations and weird ceremonies frighten them into following their advice. Into this order both men and women are initiated at any time from childhood to extreme age. A variety of rites attend upon this initiation. In one order it is the custom to demand of candidates certain sacrifices before admitting them into the sacred precincts of the medicine lodge; then food and drink are dealt out. After partaking of these they immediately retire to some secluded place, miles from the village, where fasting and sleeping, they pass from one to ten days according to their powers of endurance. During these protracted fastings the good and evil spirits visit them, showing not only the good and evil they are empowered to do in after life, but designating the object, either animate or inanimate, to which they must look for assistance.

From these visiting spirits they claim to receive instructions in the most commonplace affairs, even in the number and variety of the poles used in the constructing of the conjuring tent are designated. Those who fast the longest are the "biggest medicine," and claim that, in the latest days of their fast, is imparted to them much more information than they received at first, their patient endurance having proved them worthy. These revelations are to be kept secret throughout life. Should they happen to be disclosed, their virtue is destroyed, and all power given is lost. When the initiates return to their lodges, each is given two swallows of a drink in a birch-bark cup, and about the same quantity of food. No more is allowed (although they are starving in sight of plenty), until a half-day has elapsed, when they are at liberty to appease their hunger. — *Boston Transcript.*

RELIGIOUS BELIEFS

W.E.H. Stokes is the author of the strongly argued article "Saskatchewan's Indians and Their Religious Beliefs," published in the *Regina Leader-Post*, May 30, 1906. Stokes's name does not appear in reference books for Canadian folklore or literature. He asserts with an intensity uncommon in newspaper articles that the word *pagan* should not be applied to the Indians of the Northwest. He objects on the basis that the word means "heathen" — that is, a faithless person or a person who worships evil, the Devil. Yet at its core the word *pagan* means "rustic," the opposite of "civic." Still, Stokes is well ahead of his time in stating that the spiritual beliefs of the Indians should be respected and not submerged in the religious beliefs of the white man. In our day there is wide-spread interest in the survival of the principles and practices of shamanism. In the archaic period it was a global phenomenon; in our period its last-surviving remnant is undergoing a revival. It has always been characteristic of the Indians of the Northwest.

Saskatchewan's Indians and Their Religious Beliefs

Perhaps no greater injustice was ever perpetrated by one race of people against another than when the Crees and other Indians of Saskatchewan and Alberta were officially styled "Pagans" by the Dominion Government. After having had a somewhat exceptional chance of enquiring into the obscure subject of Indian religious beliefs, I think it safe to say that the word *Pagan* is not in any sense applicable to these people, and I think that if the missionaries to them would first apply themselves to the study of what the Crees and the Blackfeet believe, their efforts to Christianize them would be attended with a much greater degree of success than they have achieved hitherto.

But no, with scarcely a single exception the missionaries, both Catholic and Protestant, that I have met with approach the Indian they desire to convert thoroughly imbued with the idea that what the so-called Pagan believes in is such a weird, childish tissue of fancies that it is scarcely worthy of the serious attention of any sane man. The Indian's beliefs, as I have been fortunate enough to ascertain, are as sacred, as real as ours are to us, and I have yet after fourteen years' experience in this country to meet with the clergyman who had the least idea of what he had to combat in the minds of the Indians, or had ascertained if there was any mutual belief that he and they both held which might be used as a starting point to work from. As a rule it must be admitted that to the missionary, the Indian's creed is Anathema Maranatha.

This may seem to you to be a rather sweeping condemnation of the methods that have been followed by Protestant and Roman Catholic missionaries in this country for almost two generations, but when I reflect, and, by your leave, when you reflect upon the enormous sums of money that have been expended, upon the loss of life and health, and upon the real devotion and zeal that have been and are even now being displayed by the clergy and other workers for Christianity, it must make us sad. It must give us pause. To what results can we point? The only answer that has been given to this question is "Give us more time, more money, more workers," but I reply, and hope to prove that I am correct, "Your efforts are misdirected, you have started wrong, and in the meantime the good you have accomplished is largely discounted by the tide of civilization which has undoubtedly undone and is pernicious to the races of Indians which you and I are so anxious to elevate."

In what then do the aboriginals of this country believe? The following is what I found, and it cannot be more than a mere outline on account of the short time in point of years that I have devoted to this, to me, extremely interesting subject. They believe in two deities, the Great and the Small, the Great they call Manitou, which has the power for all good, and the Small Matchee-Manitou, which has the power for all evil. The possession of power being to the Indian's mind the greatest and dearest attribute, he will, naturally apply himself to whichever of these two deities will most further his ends for blessing or cursing, but, whereas, he will through another, submit supplications and make great sacrifices through a mediator to the Great Spirit, he will pray, occasionally, to the Small Spirit without any intercessor or formalities or sacrifices. He dare not pray direct to the Great Spirit, but will, recognizing his own innate baseness, go through almost anything in order to secure the interest of a mediator or intercessor, who he trusts will have more influence with the Great Spirit, or Manitou, than has his unworthy self. It is in the selection of this mediator that the influence of dreams, in all ages and climes a great and powerful agent in their operation on men's minds, comes into force. These mediators must themselves be spirits, and only can reveal themselves to man in dreams, or sometimes they have been known to possess the insane, or mentally afflicted. These latter, however, are often possessed by the Matchee-Manitou, and then the evil spirit must be driven out, resulting in the barbarities familiar to us, when a human being is supposed to have a Weh-ta-ko, or Wehtigo. The Indian believes that his own influence with Manitou is as good as anyone's except a Spirit's. What is then his definition of a Spirit? It is hard to define, but the explanation of the term according to the Cree and Blackfoot is this. It is the invisible essence that formerly animated the body of a human being or animal when living, also it is re-flected in and by the shadow cast by inanimate objects when the sun shines. This latter idea appeals to me as a very beautiful and poetic one. We know that all things above ground change and go through their appointed periods of bloom and decay. Nothing in nature is everlasting, the very face of the world itself alters, and that even within a single lifetime, so that when the Indian says, "Must there not be a spirit or soul in inanimate things as well as in those bodies which we deem endowed with life," it is not an extravagant or even a peculiar thing that he should believe that there is a spirit of a stick, a rock, the prairie grass, or the mountains. He will therefore attach as much importance to the revelations conveyed to him by dreams of these objects as he will to those of his dead fellow creatures, dreams of his dead forefathers or relations, or of any animals or creatures which we call living creatures.

All of these spirits alike were called into being by Manitou and are being recalled into his presence as one by one they die or depart from mortal ken.

Now if the Indian dreams frequently on any object dead, or inanimate, that is to say, of any person or animal dead or any object above ground that casts a shadow, he believes that the spirit of that particular person, animal, or thing casting a shadow, as the case may be, has either some power for him, or some message for him or perhaps that the spirit wishes to signify to him that he or it will protect and patronize him by presenting his petitions to Manitou. The spirits themselves have no personal power except only that they are acceptable mediators between the poor Indian and Manitou. Therefore it is to these spirits of which the Indian has frequently dreamed that he will address his prayers, devout supplications and sacrifices in order that Manitou may be pleased to send to the suppliant power to gratify his wishes, whether they be for success in haunting or in the council tent, or for power to work harm to his enemies or for whatever particular thing it may be that at the time is most earnestly desired. Even though he may be dying the Indian will not even presume to make these prayers or sacrifices more than twice a year, as he fears to intrude so unworthy a being as he feels himself to be upon the notice of his patron spirits more often, and is afraid to be so presumptuous as to have a petition from him presented to the Great God more frequently than this, owing to the reverent fear in which he holds his very idea.

Let me go back for a moment. I found that among the older so-called Pagans, the Lesser Spirit, or Matchee-Manitou, is a being that they would hardly consider seriously, although they believed in his existence firmly. They seemed to attach little importance to the power of the Evil Spirit who they thought was held strictly in subjection to Manitou, and they apparently only used Matchee-Manitou as a sort of figure-head on which to lay the blame for any misfortune that might overtake them. In fact they would always try to turn aside my inquiries with a laugh, when I asked them about Matchee-Manitou. I need not perhaps refer to him again, as it is only very rarely that an Indian will pray for power to do evil, to this ideal of everything that is bad, called Matchee-Manitou, and, as already pointed out, they would never invoke the aid of an intercessor, or make any sacrifice to obtain the power he might have to bestow. But their silence and refusal to answer my questions may, nevertheless, be due to fear.

You will observe that the so-called Pagans are great believers in dreams which they regard as an intimation from some spirit which desires the dreamer to make use of it as intercessor or mediator with the God who is so holy in comparison with the suppliant, that he would otherwise be unapproachable. Therefore the Indians relate to one another the dreams that visit them, and when it becomes known that a man or woman often has the same dream, the others recognize that individual as being under the protection of the spirit of the object dreamed of. In this way a large number of them, to us incomprehensible names so common among them, have arisen. They are named after the spirit or thing or person or animal they have dreamed of so frequently. This of course only applies to some of their names, which do not descend from father to son.

If by any chance you should happen to see one of these mis-named Pagan Indians at his devotions (and it is only by chance that you will do so) and should ob-serve that he apparently addresses himself to a tree, a rock or to nothing that is discernible, remember that he is only doing as the Roman Catholics do, that is, asking his patron spirit to approach in his behalf the very same Great God that we believe in, but whom the Indian, so poor and vile a creature does he believe himself to be, dare not, and will not directly address. Protestants believe only in one mediator, one intercessor, one ever-living though once dead, sacrifice — Jesus Christ. The Pagan Indian knows nothing of Him and is inclined to regard the story of His incarnation as a flight of the imagination. There is this to be said, that once the postulate is granted in the matter of the Spirit or immortal essence permeating what we call inanimate things — and this is not a matter that would seem difficult to me — there is nothing in the so-called Pagan's creed which demands the surrender of his reason, or the great and child-like faith which Christians deem necessary. That it is necessary I believe myself, not from any superior knowledge given to me compared to that granted to an Indian, but merely because I recognize in myself so much that is contrary to my reason and yet so much that I accept as true, without anything in the way of evidence.

Though the Christian gospel may not appeal to the Indian's reason, the effect or result of Christianity does appeal to him, and in no attractive light either. For what does he find? Civilization, which must follow Christianity, has been a blight on the Cree, the Blackfoot and on all Indian nations. This is a truism, but the fact remains that civilization has acted and reacted upon the Indians very much as the introduction of a city sewer would do upon a clear and limpid mountain lake, polluting from underneath, insidiously, the various strata of the Indian's life, affecting first the young, the vain, and the foolish and at last, as the older generations die off, slowly obliterating the last trace of the purity and beauty that formerly was its boast.

It may be said, "Is Christianity to blame for this?" but the Indian does not try to draw the distinction between Christianity and civilization, he concerns him-self only with the effect of either, or both, he cares not which, upon his own and his nation's well-being.

All "old-timers" will bear me out when I say that the Pagan Indian is an honest and God-fearing a man as ever lived, that there is less immorality according to the ideas which prevail among them, I mean less personal mean-ness, and almost no petty thievery among the Indians, where they have been fortunate enough to escape the evil influences which the arrival of white men among them has invariably produced. This may seem to some extravagant language, but it is my experience at all events, more partic-ularly among the Mountain Stoneys, who have in a great measure preserved their much-despised Pagan principles of right dealing, honesty and general uprightness. They are Methodists now, and as far as I could see they had but to make a slight change after all in their beliefs, and no change in their daily lives. They believe now in God, the Trinity, and have eliminated the mediation of every spirit but that of Jesus Christ and seem to have found that their old conception of Manitou differs in no important particular with that of their new-found Father Almighty, the same all-good Power that they have always acknowl-edged to be their master. No much of change perhaps; who among the living can say? Formerly they were Unitar-ians, with the very beautiful theory of spiritual intercession added; now they profess with equal sincerity Christianity or Methodism, as you prefer. Whether this result should be attributed to the Rev. John McDougall, or the inaccessibility of their homes and hunting grounds I cannot say. I have not had the honor of meeting this missionary and he is therefore not among the failures alluded to above. Honor to whom honor is due. I have met with Mountain Stonies both at Morley and Lac Ste. Anne, and I would trust one in all matters implicitly, relying on his good principles that I should never regret it.

The forms and ceremonies connected with this religion are really few in number, but as they have been so frequently described and even witnessed both by those who understood and by those ignorant of their meaning, perhaps it is scarcely necessary to describe them fully. It will not be in any sense relevant to the question at issue, which is simply this — why are the Indians of the late North-West Territories called "Pagan"?

If I accomplish anything by what I have said which may awaken a train of thought in the minds of my superiors tending towards the removal of the stigma "Pagan," I hope at all events to see the day dawn when the official name of "Pagan" may be altered to some word more applicable, more true. Call them, I suggest, instead of Christian worshipers, worshipers of God-in-Nature. Jehovah and Manitou, Jew and Indian, not I beg of you, Christian or Pagan, Protestant or Roman Catholic, or Christian and any name except Pagan. Jehovah of the Jews and Manitou of the pure-blood Indian resemble, and in fact, probably mean, one and the same conception of God. Let them then, and that soon, be styled Pagan no more.

WHEN HE CAME TO LIFE AGAIN

Much cultural lore and many of the spiritual traditions of the Ojibwa people, which would otherwise have been lost in time, were preserved in written form by Peter Jones. One of his books which is particularly valuable for the light it sheds on the Native belief system is titled *History of the Ojibway Indians with Especial Reference to their Conversion to Christianity ... With a Brief Memoir of the Writer and Introductory Notice by the Rev. G. Osborn, D.D., Secr. of the Wesleyan Methodist Missionary Society* (1861, 1970).

A Mississauga Indian learned in his people's traditions, Jones was a convert to Christianity. He was converted by Methodist missionaries and, ordained a minister, he preached the social gospel among his own people. He found more comfort in the monotheism of Christianity than in the pantheism and polytheism of his Native religion. "In all my fastings I never had any vision or dream," he confessed, "and, consequently, obtained no familiar god, nor a spirit of the rank of a pow-wow. What a mercy it is to know that neither our happiness nor success depends upon the supposed possession of these imaginary gods, but that there is one only true and living God, whose assistance none ever did, or even can, seek in vain!"

Here is a passage from Jones's book which documents or dramatizes the Native notion of the afterlife, what the white man calls "the happy hunting grounds."

He Came to Life Again

The following story, which was communicated to me by an Indian named Netahgawineneh, will serve to illustrate the source whence they derive their absurd ideas of a future state: —

In the Indian country far west an Indian once fell into a trance, and when he came to life again, he gave the following account of his journey to the world of spirits.

"I started," said he, "my soul or spirit in company with a number of Indians who were travelling to the same spirit land. We directed our footsteps towards the sun-setting. On our journey we passed through a beautiful country, and on each side of our trail saw strawberries as large as a man's head. We ate some of them, and found them very sweet; but one of our party, who kept loitering behind, came up to us and demanded, 'Why were we eating a ball of fire?' We tried to persuade him to the contrary, but the foolish fellow would not listen to our words, and so went on his way hungry. We travelled on until we came to a dark, swollen, and rapid river, over which was laid a log vibrating in a constant wavering motion. On this log we ventured to cross, and having arrived at the further end of it, we found that it did not reach the shore; this obliged us to spring with all our might to the land. As soon as we had done this, we perceived that the supposed log on which we had crossed was a large serpent, waving and playing with his huge body over the river. The foolish man behind was tossed about until he fell off, but he at length succeeded in swimming to shore. No sooner was he on land than a fierce and famished pack of wolves fell on him and began to tear him to pieces, and we saw him no more. We journeyed on, and by and by came within sight of the town of spirits. As soon as we made our appearance there was a great shout heard, and all our relatives ran to meet us and to welcome us to their happy country. My mother made a feast for me, and prepared everything that was pleasant to eat and to look upon; here we saw all our forefathers; and game and corn in abundance; all were happy and contented.

"After staying a short time, the Great Spirit of the place told me that I must go back to the country I had left, as the time had not yet arrived for me to dwell there. I accordingly made ready to return; and as I was leaving, my mother reproached me by all manner of foolish names for wishing to leave so lovely and beautiful a place. I took my departure, and soon found myself in the body and in the world I had left."

A CREATION MYTH

Creation myths and "just so" stories abound in the oral traditions of the Native peoples of Canada. "A Lake Superior Legend" appeared in *The Nor'Wester* (Winnipeg, Red River Settlement), August 24, 1869.

A Lake Superior Legend

In the summer of 1864, while in the Lake Superior country, I took a notion one day to have a swim. So, donning a light bathing dress, I dropped into the water. The plunge almost took my breath away. I had anticipated coldness, but I had not anticipated such icy coldness as this. The Lake Superior Indians never bathe; the reason they assign is, that the water of the lake is never warm.

A great many years ago the waters of the mighty lake were warm in the summer season. The Indians were the sole inhabitants of the land in those days. Manabozho was a great manitou (good spirit), and the Lake Superior tribes were his favourite children. But sometimes Manabozho used to put on his Seven League Boots, and stride away over the mountains on a visit to his mighty brother of the setting sun. He had gone on such a journey one melting day in July, and the Indians lay in their forests, dreaming dreams about the fairy lands of the East.

There was a bad spirit who hated the Indians fiercely. This bad spirit was a monstrous snake. He was very much afraid of the good manitou, Manabozho, and when Manabozho was at home the bad spirit stayed in his fiery lake, away back into the forest.

But now Manabozho was gone on a journey, so the bad spirit resolved to take advantage of his absence to destroy the tribes whom he hated. He had a large number of demons in his service, who were ready for any work he might set them. He dispatched an army of these demons to annihilate the Indians. For his part he set himself to watch for Manabozho, in case that good manitou should return unexpectedly.

The Indians saw the army of demons coming, and knowing that in the absence of their chief they were powerless to fight against them, they gathered their women and children together, and paddled away in their canoes across the lake. The demons could not swim, and had taken a great dislike to the water, and when they saw the

Indians paddling away, they howled in their rage, and belched forth great clouds of flame and smoke.

But as soon as the Indians had safely reached an island, a thick covering of ice suddenly overspread the lake, and the demons yelling with joy rushed upon it. When they were all safely upon the ice bridge, it parted as suddenly as it had appeared, and became an ice-craft, and floated hither and thither. The demons were in great distress, being unable to get to either shore. And now the form of Manabozho rose to view. Manabozho understood the situation at once, and stretching out his mighty arm, larger than a pine tree, roared with a voice louder than thunder, "Sink, sink, and rise no more!"

And the raft sunk, and the demons perished, and the Indians came back and worshipped Manabozho. And this is why the waters of Lake Superior are so cold.

FEATHERS WITHIN

When I began to collect people's accounts of supernatural and paranormal experiences, a fellow writer and editor noted, "John Robert receives the most fascinating mail in the country." I immediately agreed with him. These days, as I continue to collect accounts of people's experiences, including those of a psychical, spiritual, and mystical nature, I feel I receive "the most fascinating *email* in the country."

Witness the present email from Sparrow (or White Sparrow) and some of the accompanying files. The inner narratives described herein took me by surprise. Indeed, from the first lines they surprised me, as I had (automatically) assumed that my correspondent was a male. Why? Who knows? These accounts are certain to raise a bevy of questions (and supply a handful of answers).

I cannot tell Sparrow much, but I can assure her that these accounts of her experiences are at least as astounding as any that I have published. She fears they are "relatively tame." Well, in terms of seeing ghosts or being cursed by ghouls, they are, but as her experiences are those that enlarge the soul rather than assault the spirit, they are germane and genuine. At the same time, they evoke the wisdom and wonder of the spirit of the Native people.

Feathers Within

From: Sparrow
Sent: Friday, May 20, 2005 8:00 PM
To: *jrc@ca.inter.net*
Subject: Purchased your book today!

Greetings John Robert Colombo!

Well, Sir, you may wish to grab yourself a coffee, tea, or something stronger to sip on! The reason being, my connection to you today is becoming as strange as some of the stories that I am in the process of currently reading!

Earlier this afternoon, I purchased a copy of *More True Canadian Ghost Stories*, John Robert Colombo. (I have only read a dozen or so pages and felt compelled to write you!)

I have many books on my shelf, but none of them include full collections of such stories!

Nothing I do is ever simple! Which makes this email to you now rather long and complex! For that, I apologize!

I was in a book store in Owen Sound, Ontario this afternoon. I was browsing for something new to sink my reading teeth into.

First, I immediately picked up a book entitled *Emily Dickinson: Poems*. A book or two away was yours! I don't buy ghost story books. However, I am learning more and more to follow my instinctive hunches or callings, as I call them.

At the time, I could not make the connection between poetry and ghost stories! That is until I type in your web address! So, now I am even more convinced I was meant to contact you!

I'm not sure, Sir, where to begin!

My personal journey is quite a story all on its own. I am right in the middle of a very odd life situation. I am also currently trying to write about it behind the scenes, so to speak!

Let's see!

I am a decade long member of the Canadian Country Music Association. A member of SOCAN [Society of Composers, Authors, and Music Publishers of Canada]. A published songwriter and published poet! I also have a sixty page and growing website which I use as a way to vent some of my creative energy. I am NOT an editor, by any stretch of the imagination! When I am not working at one of the previously mentioned, I am working full time at a private resort!

I turn fifty next month! Two months ago, I JUST completed a long "legal" process with regards to my name!

I am now LEGALLY called White Sparrow!

It is two words ... but only ONE name!

I do not recognize my forename as "White." Nor do I recognize my surname as "Sparrow"! My name is only SPLIT when government, or standard forms insist on requiring me to do so! This is most unfortunate, but such is life! (For the most part, I simply SHORTEN my full name to SPARROW for everyday use! My signature is White Sparrow! Phew!)

To get a tiny glimpse into my story behind the story, make yourself welcome at the following. *www.whitesparrowwigwam.com.* My bio is but a flicker of the journey that I am currently on!

My future plans include doing an e-book from my website, as well as perhaps having it put in regular book form. I haven't decided. I sort of fall into things rather than preplan! One might say that I operate on Indian time! lol!

Basic recap of myself. I am White on the outside, Red on the inside! (Well of course, except for my unusually high cheek bones!) Which probably has something to do with my name, but that's a whole other chapter in my one day book!

Aside from all of the above I have been known to do some out of the ordinary things! What I can clarify for you at this point is that, the older I get, the stronger this talent seems to be growing!

Unlike the many folks that I read about, who are so calm, cool and collected about such experiences ... I can assure you, it is NOT something that I have become comfortable with! Especially in some cases! One as recent as a few weeks ago!

Bottom Line — Mr. Colombo, I have had "several" experiences that seem to fall right in line with the stories that you gather and have published! Many have witnessed these encounters or experiences that I have had! They come to me ... both through Red eyes and White!

My Native encounter I am planning to use in my own book! However, I am at the bottom of the totem pole here. Therefore, it might be of wiser use to also pass it along to you as well, if you feel it might be something that you can use.

I realize that I have given little detail to you at this point about my experiences. Most of them I would have to create files for and email to you. They are only in my memory at this point in time, and, in the memory of those who have been involved! The length of them are as varied as the encounters!

Perhaps, Sir, you would prefer to scan some of the material on my website first! I say scan, because there is a lot of material for a busy person to delve too deeply into!

Should you be remotely interested, you can respond to me at this email address! (I use my email address on my site ... strictly for site related issues!)

In true appreciation of your time and your compiled stories! I will now go back to continue reading them.

Currently, I am wrestling with a good case of laryngitis! So, this is a perfect opportunity for me to get to know more about the stories that interest you!

Once again, thank you for listening!

Sparrow

Feathers Within: May the Great Spirit Watch Over and Bless Us All!
by White Sparrow

1. *The Beginning: My Dream: There's a Buffalo in My Bedroom*
2. *The Middle: The Sacred Circle: Emerging as White Sparrow*
3. *The End: My Calling: One Lost Sparrow and One Great Canadian Chief*

In the year 1905, exactly one hundred years ago, Civilla D. Martin (lyricist) and Charles H. Gabriel (composer) collaborated on the hymn titled "His Eye is On the Sparrow." The refrain:

> I sing because I'm happy,
> I sing because I'm free,
> For his eye is on the sparrow,
> And I know he watches me.

Matthew 10:29–31: "Are not two sparrow sold for a penny? Yet not one of them will fall to the ground apart from the will of your Father. So, don't be afraid; you are worth more than many sparrows."

1. My Dream: There's a Buffalo in My Bedroom

It had been over three years since I had slept in my own bed, in my own bedroom. I had spent three years of sleeping on a living-room couch. There was no logical explanation for this. Nothing that I could say. This is the reason why.

Somehow, there was comfort from the back of the couch when it pressed up against me. I have been on my own for longer than most people stay married. I thought I had a full life. I was working full time, was a published songwriter, and had two grown sons out in the world making their own way.

For a momentary second, I was starting to question the state of my mental health. I mean really! What would prevent a grown woman from sleeping in her own bed?

Then, I began to dig inside myself for some straight answers. Like, when exactly, had I stopped sleeping in my bed, and why?

Three years earlier I decided to change the décor of my sleeping quarters. I decided to undo the Native Indian decorating, but something stopped me from completing this task. So there sat my bedroom, half one way, half the other!

Convincing myself I was on to something, I set my sights on putting the room back the way it was. You know, as an experiment. It still wasn't nearly finished, but somehow with even just a few changes it had already began to give comfort to my restless spirit. So I made up my mind to try camping out in it once again.

That first night, before falling asleep, I prayed for a sign! Not just any old sign, but something big and profound. Something that would unquestionably answer my searching. What I wanted and needed to know was if I was headed in the right direction. Well, I think I may have prayed just a little extra too hard. Here's what happened.

That night, I quickly, calmly, and quietly fell asleep. The next thing I remember was the earth shaking under my queen-size bed. I looked out my large window to the east and could hear what sounded like a freight train headed straight toward me. I looked hard with searching eyes. Nothing was in view, only more rumble and shaking.

Finally, there came the image of a huge black buffalo. It was travelling at an enormous speed, and the dust was swirling under its thundering hooves. All I could think to do was roll myself quickly in towards the window. By doing this, I thought by the time it had reached me it would jump over me, rather than landing right on me. I rolled over once and than twice. Then there was a horrific smashing of glass. As I turned and looked up, I witnessed a full-grown black buffalo leaping above and across my bed and over me! Before it crashed and disappeared into my double closet, it immediately changed colour from jet black to pure white!

I instantly woke from my dream and sat straight up in bed looking over at my closet. "Woe-wah," came spilling out of my mouth soon followed by a wide grin. It was the exhilarating answer to my prayer. Just as I had requested, the Great Spirit had sent a message so large and so life-like that not even I could miss his message!

My answer was "Yes!" I was moving in the right direction, on the right road.

This is by far the most profound and vivid dream I have had to date. Other dreams come close, but this one was definitely over the top! Within days, my bedroom was added to one article at a time — until, it had the look and feel of home for me. Native Indian!

2. The Sacred Circle: Emerging as White Sparrow

Who would ever dream one's rite of passage could or would ever arrive in their mailbox, and for free? Well, I am here to tell you that this is how one of mine came to me. Now, that's just about as close to your own doorstep as life can deliver.

One day, while surfing the Net, I bumped into the website for Alan Greywolf. I didn't know at the time that the event would become a key to my life's journey and would result in my new legal name!

At the time I was researching anything and everything on the subject of Native American Indian history, culture, legends, you name it. This was an obsession. I suppose it still is!

When I began to read through Alan's site, I became engrossed in the subject. I ended up spending the next seven or eight hours there without a break. I read every sentence, every line, and every word! After covering the site from top to bottom and from start to finish, I decided to email him. Actually, it was more like I was compelled to email him.

It was not long after my initial email of self-introduction that Alan mailed out to me one of his own guided and self-produced meditation CDs. More precisely, the CD was *The Sacred Circle*.

For those who may not be familiar with this term, with Alan, or with his CDs, allow me (with his permission) to capture the essence of this CD and the purpose for which he created it. The purpose appears on the back of his CD jacket cover in these words:

> Within your own centre you will create one of the most mystical and powerful symbols for life, your own personal Medicine Wheel, the Sacred Circle of the Native Americans. Here you will connect to elemental spirits, and the Spirit Keepers of the Four Directions.
>
> Through these connections, you will find the power and the means to enhance and change your life. New directions, growth, abundance and prosperity, your own truth and wisdom, all are open to you as are many more possibilities.

Well ... let me clarify this as one of the biggest understatements that I have encountered in my lifetime! If Alan ever needed a testimony for his ability to guide one through a meditation that delivered every single thing that he said it would, then mine is a given!

Neither Alan nor I believe in such a thing as coincidence. Our paths were designed to connect, and they certainly were successful in completing this mission.

Prior to receiving this CD, I had never listened to or read a single article on meditation. Quite honestly, I didn't understand the topic, and I certainly didn't put great stock in it. For the record, so to speak, I have no desire to ever listen to another one. Why would I? Alan's had succeeded in changing my life forever. Forever!

Picture, if you will, me, tearing the shrink-wrap off of the CD. I immediately was drawn to the beautiful photo shot on the front of the jacket cover. This feature alone brought me to a place of solid, solitary grounding. Next, I popped the CD into the player and hit the power button on the machine. Didn't have a clue how one goes about meditating, but I was willing to give it a shot. Then I quickly whipped over to the couch and lay down as if I was getting ready to be transported in a space shuttle! Oh, if Alan could have only seen me then. I'm afraid he wouldn't have believed I would ever gotten through it!

Immediately I hit pause on the CD, and jumped up to light some tea lights. Then I just as quickly lay back down on the couch again and strapped myself into the get ready for lift off position! You know, absolutely board stiff! Cripes, I couldn't have been more tense if I had of planned it out for weeks in advance!

Next, with straining ears, I heard the beginnings of soft music grow slightly stronger and stronger. It was soothing, original, and I liked it! My mind-set had already began to change. I was starting to think that maybe I could be on to something here.

Then, my ears filled with the "warm lavender" voice of Alan Greywolf, a voice with the quality to fill out a microphone without crowding out the listener! For any of you men out there, reading this, his voice isn't just soothing to a woman. His voice is simply soothing, period!

Anyway, just as I was thinking that I had no clue how to go about meditating, Alan began to speak in a voice that beckons you until you follow! He began to tell me step by step "exactly" how to proceed.

Well, how about that? A man who knew "exactly" what to say and when to say it! Sorry guys, just venting here a little! Okay I thought this might be a bit of all right!

What Alan does on this CD is verbally massage your body, mind, and soul into a state of relaxation. How does he do that? Beats the heck out of me; but, ladies and gentlemen, it works! He seems to know every single place to pinpoint to successfully complete this process.

After the first few fits of giddy silliness at my awkwardness with meditation, I found myself getting more serious about the potential it might hold. I began to trust Alan's voice. I knew I was in the comfort and safety of my own home and that he hadn't said to do anything strange or bizarre to cause me to be concerned. It was from this mind set that I surrendered my conscious mind to his direction.

What I really appreciate the most is how he guides! He instructs one on what to do, but at the same time with the freedom of independence to do it in your own individual way. This impressed me, a lot. Perhaps this is the underlying secret to the success of his ability. Then came the real icing on the whole cake. The soft solitude music that is feathered into the background of his voice-over guidance! This entire process I found just as interesting and relaxing as the unwinding and unraveling of my tense and stressed body and mind.

Yes, I had been working a lot of crazy hours and shifts prior to this meditation, and that seemed to strangely add to the potent magic of just how powerful Greywolf's gift really is! Before you know it, you seem to operate on automatic pilot.

Once the relaxation stage is complete, Alan walks you into your Sacred Circle. The name alone drives one to draw nearer and listen closer as he speaks. Now I was getting good and hungry for what he was about to feed me next. I didn't know what to expect or what was coming, but I strongly felt it was going to be something like I had never experienced before, and I was right!

Alan leads you once around the entire Circle. Then into the sacred heart of the Circle via the east arm! There I stood upon a sacred and ancient stone. From this point of the CD, nothing and no one else mattered or entered my thoughts. I was on the inside of myself, and it was quite a trip!

Here Alan warmly introduces you to the Eagle. The Spirit Keeper of the East! To Native Indian peoples, the Eagle represents a heavenly messenger. You see animal medicine is very sacred, very powerful, and very respected medicine. It is not to be taken lightly! Not to take it seriously is unthinkable and a sign of great dishonour! Animal medicine is also part of one's animal totem, but that's a whole other story.

I felt humbled and honoured to be introduced to the Great Eagle. I truly felt as if we had communicated with one another. I would have stayed here longer in visit, but Alan's voice gently nudged me to continue on around the Circle to the next keeper, the Wolf. The Spirit Keeper of the South!

What an incredible visit, this one is. Particularly, because I share wolf medicine! You go one-on-one with the Wolf in this direction. The experience is so real you can all but touch the softness of the Wolf's thick neck fur and coat as he is within only inches away! *Incredible* is the best word that comes to mind to describe this visit.

The greatest reason I think is because there is no fear in this realm, only the purest fascination here for one another. Animal and human, communicating without spoken words between you. It is a truly awesome feeling!

As for anxiety, what anxiety? The furthest thing from your mind at this time is what the heck you were doing, thinking, or stressed about prior to turning this CD on! Ah, but back to the Sacred Circle!

Well, you have only gone half the Circle's distance when in the southern direction. You subconsciously or consciously wonder how this could get any better, but then it does.

Once again, Alan's voice coaches you to follow him further around the Circle. Here you share space with the Bear. The Spirit Keeper of the West! Bear is a true contradiction between strength and gentleness! The power of bear medicine is so hard to define in simple words!

It was at this point on the CD when I realized that I

was weeping a steady stream of tears. They came to the surface of my eyes and spilled over with no prompting on my part. I didn't even realize they were spilling out of me until I felt the salty wetness of them running down out from the corners of my closed eyelids.

It's hard to explain, but these tears seem to come from me as a cleansing of all the toxic and negative thoughts that had dammed up my purest positive beliefs in myself — from a well years hidden and buried deep inside of myself! At no time did I make any attempt to stop them, wipe them, or prevent them from escaping my body!

The Spirit Keeper of the West, he never left my side during this process! This Great Bear just sat watching all the while, mysteriously mothering the resurrection of true belief in my own worth, my own strength in self! He never moved to leave even once, until I had finished washing all the sounds of hurt from my heart away!

It was at this point that I fell into a state of sleep like no other. I could still feel the toxic thing flush itself down the sides of my face. A lifetime full of anger was literally washing itself clean, as I lay motionless on the couch.

From here, I drifted into a deeper state of sleep, for I could no longer hear or identify Alan's voice. It was as if Alan had relinquished himself as my Indian guide and gently passed me over to another guide that seem to pick up the trail without missing a beat.

Now, I was one with the Sacred Circle! Alan Greywolf was nowhere to be heard. Before me now standing on the sacred centre stone was an Indian Maiden. She was younger than I was. You know, with the perfect shaped figure that we women and men fantasize about!

She was dressed in a long, tan-coloured, fringed skirt and long-sleeved, fringed top. Her hair was dark, straight, and lightly blowing in a gentle breeze. My eyes were completely fixed on her. Her energy was calming and peaceful and although I couldn't see her face, I knew she was there to give me answers that I was hungry for and longing to know.

As I was studying her presence and peaceful pose, I noticed a formation starting to appear in front of my eyes. As she stood there with her back turned toward me, I struggled to focus hard on the back of her shirt. Closer and longer I watched.

While this transformation was slowly developing, I was soon able to identify it as a symbol of a white bird. This bird first showed itself as a child-like cartoon drawing. Then it continued to transform and take the shape of a real bird. I witnessed it grow and come to life! I was mesmerized! It magically became and turned into a little sparrow. It fluttered and fluttered its little wings until it broke free from the maiden's shirt and flew up and off toward the Guardian of the East. The direction of the Eagle! The direction of all new beginnings!

I felt as innocent as a child making a first and new and wonderful discovery! The bird quickly and playfully flew around for a moment above the maiden's head and hair. Then it settled and positioned itself back onto the back of her shirt and transformed itself back into the white child-like symbol of a bird. I can't explain how profoundly this affected me. My eyes blinked and wept a flood of happy tears!

Carefully and closely, I watched this Indian Maiden softly retrace the same previous trek that Alan had guided me on, around the Sacred Circle. She spoke no words to me! There was strangely no need. It was clear to me that she knew she had my full concentration. It was also understood that I knew that she had been sent to guide me.

After steadily stepping and completing the circle, her body transformed into that of the little sparrow and resumed and repeated her walk around the Sacred Circle just as before. It was during this particular part of the sleep process that the words *White Sparrow* rang through my sleeping soul. It was clearly but unexplainably understood that this bird was telling me what I was to do. That I was to become "White Sparrow"! That "White Sparrow" was to become me!

No, I was not on drugs! No, I was not intoxicated! No, I was not brainwashed by Alan Greywolf! The gift of my name came from a much greater source, a divine source.

You see, Alan's CD is only forty-five minutes long. However, I awakened four hours later! Alan's CD became a bridge for me. The bridge between my past and my future, and that day, on my couch, I gave myself up and I crossed that bridge!

When I woke and realized the magnitude of what had happened, I anxiously replayed the CD. As it was not a tape, I was unable to rewind it, so I had to let it go through the previous sequence again, until Alan's voice picked up like an unmissed beat and continued to guide me on toward the last Keeper in the Sacred Circle. The Spirit Keeper of the North! The Great White Buffalo!

This was the best of the best for me! I believe this not only because of the spiritual qualities of the Buffalo, but because when I came to the Buffalo, I came to visit it not as who I had been, but I came to visit there as the new me. I came there guided as "White Sparrow"!

It was in the direction of the North that I felt the Great Spirit had baptized my name! That this is the place that I became one with White Sparrow!

Before I left the Sacred Circle, the Indian Maiden reappeared and stopped at each Spirit Keeper to give thanks. Once she completed this cycle, the little sparrow repeated the pattern. It hopped and stopped before the Great Eagle, the Great Wolf, the Great Bear, and the Great Buffalo! From here, the sparrow, the Indian Maiden, and I myself stepped off of the sacred centre stone and exited the arm of the Sacred Circle. It was from here that I took the knowledge that I had emerged — reborn Red, as "White Sparrow." The legal name I wear with greatest honour today!

From this amazing journey developed my website, and from the website grew the dream of telling the true story called "Feathers Within." The story that hopefully you are reading for yourself now!

3. My Calling: One Lost Sparrow and One Great Canadian Chief

"Cape Croker, Cape Croker, Cape Croker!"

On Thursday, April 24th, 2004, these words came profoundly and mysteriously to me, and through me.

At 3:00 or 3:30 that afternoon, I was standing at the front desk of a private resort in Thornbury, Ontario. It was a quiet day, with only a few guests staying with us at the time. I was working my day shift just like any other day. It was near the end of my shift when I was over come and captured with these words. I heard them as a pledge! I heard them as a prayer! I heard them as an answer!

"Cape Croker, Cape Croker, Cape Croker!"

With these words came a great surge of energy and an even greater sense of urgency! My mind was racing with questions as to what was happening and why.

Now, I openly admit here, this was not the first time in my life that I had had strong sensations come over me. On a number of previous occasions, I have been known to receive messages either for myself or for or about other people. What I had never encountered, though, was the strength, intensity, and the speed by which these words were reaching me. I readily knew that something major was about to play out in my life. The only fear that accompanied this experience was the fear of not being able to follow it through, the fear of losing the trail of this sensation before I could make logical sense of it. There was no time to lose!

Working at a resort gave me access to many tour guides, maps, and magazines. I quickly bent down and opened a bottom drawer that contained a full array of them. I had certainly recognized the name Cape Croker, but I didn't even know where it was. Where would I begin?

My hands started sliding and shuffling the magazines around one after another. They finally stopped, when I came to one called Manitoulin Island and on a second one called Bruce County. Something told me to try these two.

So I quickly grabbed them both up and began frantically flipping through their pages.

Like many of us, I have a certain percentage of routine in my life. For instance, every Saturday I dedicated to my mother. Therefore, I definitely knew that I had to contact her to tell her that our plans for the up coming weekend were about to be altered.

Now, there is not much point to looking like a fool if you don't have any onlookers. So, naturally, I had a couple of co-workers witness this frenzy as it played out. It took everything in me to stay and finish my shift that day!

When my shift ended, I quickly said my good-byes, grabbed my purse, and headed to my car. In my hands I was clutching one of the magazines that had an article on Cape Croker. I was extremely pleased and relieved to discover that Cape Croker was located just a little over an hour from where I was.

My butt had hardly touched the driver's seat of my car when this same energy sent me back into the resort on the fly. One of my co-workers asked, "What happened? Didn't your car start?"

"No, my car's okay," I replied, "but something tells me I'm supposed to look in that other magazine again."

Hastily, I headed back to the drawer of magazines and grabbed the one lying on top. I flicked through the pages until I reached the name "The Indian Carver."

I prompted both my co-workers standing next to me to tell me if they had ever heard of the Indian Carver. Both shook their heads and said no. Puzzled, one of them asked me, "Why do you need information on the Indian Carver?"

"I don't know," I snapped back. "I only know that I'm supposed to check it out!"

With that, I picked up the magazine and headed out to my car, which I had left running. Once in my car, I knew that I was about to drive directly to Meaford to my mother's apartment. As anxious as I was, I didn't speed. I needed the driving time to mull over exactly how I was going to explain what was happening to me. You see my mom is a huge skeptic when it comes to stuff like this. So I was trying my best to come up with the words that would be the most convincing: (a) so that we both didn't think I was crazy and (b) to let her know that we might not be able to do our usual grocery shop on the upcoming Saturday.

Mother to daughter and wide-eyed, I quickly spilled my story to her. Then I offered her the opportunity to come with me to Cape Croker, or she could stay put Saturday and I would go on my own. Maw's no dummy, and she clearly got the message I was going to be going, with or without her. She looked me in the eye and said, "Well, I guess it looks like we'll be going then."

"From the way you are speaking, there wouldn't be much point in trying to talk you out of it."

"You're right," I answered her, "there isn't!"

Little did I know that this mystery was only just beginning to unfold.

After I left Mom's, I went home to research the magazines. I practically ran to turn on my laptop to see what I could learn. The only thing I could find under Cape Croker through my magazine tips turned out to be about Wiarton and Wiarton Willie. This made no sense to me! I was clearly past the point of focus.

By now, my body and mind were completely exhausted. All of my energy had been spent! I don't think I even ate supper on this night. My body was on empty so I took the hint and simply crawled into bed. I immediately fell asleep.

Friday morning, I was back at work and sitting in the staff room. Was I spun for fun! I was well rested and strongly charged up and driven to follow up on my mysterious Cape Croker journey. A few of us were sitting around the staff room table talking about the afternoon before enjoying those first few minutes of bliss before starting your morning routine.

While engaged in random conversation, the Assistant Manager appeared in the doorway to ask me if I was expecting a fax from an Indian man.

"What do you mean, Indian man?" I asked her.

I immediately rose to my feet and went over to read what she was holding in her hand. I was stunned! Across the top of the fax I read Cha Mao Zah. It then went on to mention the Indian Carver.

"Where did this come from?" I asked her.

"I just picked it up off the fax machine now," she stared and replied.

Immediately, I began to interrogate everyone in the room, asking if they had requested this information. I knew full well in the back of my mind that there were only two other people, not counting my mother, who knew I was looking for information on the Indian Carver. One of them was home on her day off, when I called to question her. The other one was working for another company and I wouldn't be able to interrupt her until noon hour. We all knew that no one had intervened on my behalf, but I still had to make the rounds anyway. This was just too bizarre and uncanny.

Well, I wasn't for sitting still and doing nothing. And, I certainly wasn't about to wait until lunch-time for answers. They knew it, and so did I. So I took the fax and scurried off into the back office to make a phone call.

There I sat looking at the telephone in front of me, trying to collect myself. Then, I dialed.

"Hello, Cha Mao Zah," came a woman's voice.

I was searching every nook and cranny of my mind for the best words to respond with. Finally, out came, "Good morning, I'm calling from a private resort. I have a strange question to ask, so please bear with me! Do you know who might have been trying to send us a fax today? You see, we seemed to have mysteriously received a two page fax from you folks here this morning. However, we have over forty rooms here, and I can't seem to find a name as to whom it should be directed!"

"Yes, and no," came back the woman's voice.

"I'm sorry," I said. "Now I am confused!"

She then went on to explain, "When we came into

the office this morning, there was a strange kind of phone message left on our answering machine. It was very garbled and all that we could really make out was a number. We tried dialing it, only to find out that it was a fax number and not a telephone number. We took a chance that someone must be trying to reach us regarding information on Cha Mao Zah or the Indian Carver. Therefore, I took one of our brochures and faxed both sides of it to the number that had been left! We didn't have a clue where it would end up. I do hope that it was okay to send it there!"

"I'm sorry, what is your name?"

"My name is —!"

"Well — I think we are suppose to meet," I said. Then I explained what had happened previously at my end and then I sputtered out, "Can I ask you this? Is there really an Indian Carver?"

"Oh, yes," she enthusiastically replied.

"Is he still living?" I almost held my breath at this point, waiting for her reply and hoping that she would say yes.

"Oh, yes," she replied again. "He is still living and he is eighty-three years old."

"Forgive me, but do you work for the Indian Carver, or how may I ask are you connected to him?"

"I am the other half of the Indian Carver!"

"I understand," I answered back.

My heart filled to the top! I can't tell you how relieved I was to hear he was still living. "Well then," I jumped in, "please don't be surprised if I land on your doorstep some day soon. I truly believe that he and I are supposed to meet in person."

"Before you go," she piped up, "there is one thing that you should know! The Indian Carver is not in Cape Croker. We are located just south of Tobermory."

"Tobermory," I exclaimed! "How far is that from Thornbury, would you say?"

"About two hours. I can't be sure."

"Thank you, and please know that you and I will

definitely be in touch again."

After I got off the phone, I did feel pretty foolish. You see, in my haste, I hadn't taken the time to read their location information, which I was holding in my hand! I can't explain exactly what happens when you go through something like this. You just seem to throw logic and caution out the window, and fly by the seat of your pants!

Friday evening I sent an email to Cha Mao Zah. I told them I couldn't wait; I had to meet these folks!

Saturday morning finally came, and the anticipation was killing me! I immediately checked my email. Still, no response was received. It didn't matter. Not to me, not on this day. I was up for going, and nothing short of dying was going to prevent the inevitable from playing out. Believe me, I was up, showered, and over at my mom's in record time! I couldn't have loaded her any quicker into the car unless I had of carried her in my arms.

With a road map stuck in my visor, I was headed north. Along the way, I was only half-listening to the small talk that my mom was making. In my mind, I had bigger fish to fry. I was being strongly pulled toward a man I had never met. More mysteriously, not understanding why, and why with such urgency!

After passing the exit to Cape Croker, my mom spoke up. "We'll, I guess if we were going to Cape Croker, we just missed our cut off back there.

"Ah, Mom, we aren't going to Cape Croker just yet. I haven't told you what happened since Thursday night. So, I hope you had no other plans for today, because we are now headed to Tobermory!"

"Tobermory! What's in Tobermory?"

"We are! Turns out that the Indian Carver lives in Tobermory, not Cape Croker."

"Oh!" was all she replied.

I could tell that Mom was becoming agitated and was starting to squirm in her seat. Nearly everything my mom does is based on logic. What we were doing that day had absolutely nothing to do with logic. I felt compelled to sell her on my notions and beliefs of intuition and simply following one's gut instincts.

On the way there I spotted Cha Mao Zah. I pulled in the lane, but no one seemed to be around. Tobermory was only about three miles away now, so we drove up to the tip of the peninsula. It wasn't long before we found a lovely little place called the Princess Hotel. Nearly as soon as I had Mom seated in the restaurant, I headed for the nearest phone. I dropped my coins in, dialed the number, and it rang. But no one answered. I left a message saying that I was currently at the Princess Motel in Tobermory. I said that my mother and I were planning to have brunch and that I would try once more after eating to reach them before departing.

Once Mom was served, I was much calmer. Knowing that she was enjoying the food and the restaurant, I began to relax because she was. For me, just being closer in proximity to the Indian Carver brought such a settled peace and comfort deep inside. Something wonderful was going to happen that day! I don't know how I knew this, I did. That's just the way I felt!

After brunch, Mom headed to the little girl's room and I headed straight back to the phone on the wall. I dialed again and this time I made a voice to voice connection. I got the Indian Carver himself. He asked if we were staying over night at the hotel. I told him no, I was only up for the day and heading out very shortly to Cape Croker. He asked if I could be back at his shop for 3:00 p.m. He went on to explain that the shop isn't opened up during the month of April. However, he was willing to meet me if I could be there! Of course, I immediately accepted his offer.

I know this sounds even stranger, but this man didn't seem to be thrown off by anything that I said. It was as if he also strangely knew something bigger than the two of us was doing the steering!

It was shortly after 2:00 p.m. and it was a beautiful bright and sunny day. The wind off the water in front of

us sure had a winter's bite still in it, but ask me if I cared!
Mom and I drove just a minute or two away and parked
the car. We got out and went for a stroll and a talk. I
had to walk down to the water's edge and stick my hand
directly into its icy waters, just so that I can say that I had
touched it.

Mom's enthusiasm for the cold icy waters ranked far
below mine. She waited well back and up the bank. For a
brief moment or two while squatted down with my hands
submerged in the water. I prayed and gave thanks in silence
for whatever was about to happen that day. I'm no Einstein,
but I knew it was to be a profound day, and that it might
be many years if ever again that something this wonderful
would be gifted on me. I wanted to show my gratitude,
even if I didn't know what was about to happen. Even if I
clearly understood my mother's uneasiness of being there
this day with me!

My heart was pounding after our walk. Getting back
into my car meant that I was about to head south for three
or so miles and meet a man, meet a great man!

Before going there that day, I had mentioned to a
friend of mine that I hoped I would have the opportunity
to meet with this man, to take his hand and simply to walk
among the woods with him heavily engaged in wisdom
and conversation. Little did I know this was more of a premonition than it ever was simply wishful thinking.

Three o'clock came and as I was pulling into one lane
way leading to his shop, his vehicle pulled into another
lane way, just a few yards away but parallel to me. My car
was dark red. His van was dark red. From that moment
on, until I left, I was pretty much oblivious to the fact that
my mother or anyone else on mother earth existed.

I immediately got out of my car and walked towards
him. He had already gotten out of his vehicle and was
standing silently to the right of and next to the base of a
tall tree in a wooded, yet cleared area. My mind instantly
flashed to a panoramic picture that I had purchased only
a week or so earlier that now hung directly above the

headboard of my bedroom. It was a photo of a lone wolf, standing silently to the right of and next to the base of a tall tree, with nothing surrounding it but the base of other trees. I realized in this moment that photo I had at home had just transformed from a wolf and shaped-shifted into the human-life form that was standing before me. It was a grand confirmation that I had been purposely and divinely led there. No one anywhere could or ever will talk me into believing anything otherwise. I knew I had just witnessed a miracle!

As an extremely private person, it is not my nature to spontaneously open up to anyone, especially within a matter of moments. However, as I was still in movement and walking toward him, I asked him if it was all right if I hugged him. The words weren't even out of my mouth as his arms reached up and extended openly toward me in welcome. I hugged him! I hugged him for dear life! I hugged him as if we had crossed many milleniums to be reunited! I hugged him like I had never hugged my own father! I hugged him as if I had finally found my lost way home!

I could not speak! I had no words! I had no voice! He asked me three times, "What is it my child, what is it?"

He did not let go of me, and I could not let go of him! I could only hug him longer and sob harder! Somehow I managed to pull myself together long enough to peel myself off his knitted sweater coat. Somehow I managed to reach up with one hand and wipe the tears that were seeping, steadily from under the bottom of my sunglasses and dripping from my jaw line. Somehow I had hit God's target squarely and fairly, and I could now feel it in my heart, in my soul, and wetly on the cheeks of my face.

He clearly knew that I was no ordinary guest! Somehow he also knew that this was no ordinary greeting. Then, just as I had spoken of doing earlier to my friend, we instantly took one another's hand and we walked together around his grounds. You could feel a great presence and peace there! It was walking and watching among us! The sun was filtering through the branches of the trees as we walked out into an open clearing. It was like no other moment in my life!

My speech was still broken. I could not recapture my voice. So he spoke for me. He gave me a guided tour of this sacred space that we walked upon. We never for a moment let go of each other's hand.

After I had gained control of my overwhelming emotions, I began to ask many questions. There was synchronicity and harmony between us. There was pleasant humour and great wisdom dispensed from a forever youthful, quiet, and intelligent gentleman.

I asked questions that I'm sure were completely mundane on most accounts, but he showed no boredom. He offered up his answers with generosity and without hesitation. He instinctively seemed to understand my need and hunger to learn as much as possible in a short but given time. I was no regular visitor to this earthy camp-grounds and lands known as Cha Mao Zah!

In that short time, I had learned many things. A lot of Native ways and culture! A lot of this man whom I was stepping alongside! You see, in the course of our conversation, I had learned that he was strongly tied and connected to Cape Croker. He had been born and raised there. He had also been one of the longest running chiefs of Cape Croker. He had been their chief for fourteen years!

It was from that moment on, from that story on, that I continue to this day to refer to him as "The Chief." Now walk backwards, for a moment. From here you will find the words that originated my journey toward: "The Chief" — "Cape Croker, Cape Croker, Cape Croker!"

We spoke of many things, the Chief and I! We spoke of spiritual journeys. We spoke of the people. We spoke of the world. We spoke of the greater plan and the future. We spoke of the past. We spoke of the present. Whatever it was that we spoke of, we both laughed we both learned, and we both enjoyed whichever conversation we found that we had journeyed easily into.

We walked in a circle and made our way back towards his shop, my car, and my mom. My mom, who up until this moment I had completely and utterly forgotten, was there with me! Somehow, as unimpressed as I knew that she would be, I also knew that she was trying to understand this journey that I was on and that she would be okay as long as I was.

As we approached his shop, he gave my hand a gentle squeeze and quickly and softly released it. We were greeted by a woman of my own age. She came up to us and spoke directly to the Chief. She immediately volunteered that she had seen "two eagles" on the way over to the shop. This news delighted the Chief as he smiled when he replied, "You did!" She quickly confirmed it with a "Yes." He then looked directly in my eyes and smiled. It was later on, after this experience, that I learned that a sighting of an eagle can be a heavenly message or a heavenly messenger. Like it or not, for her, I guess, that included my mom as well as me.

It was at this part of the visit that Mom got out of the car and came to join me. With camera in hand, she graciously smiled and asked to take pictures of the three of us. Oh and let's not forget Jessie, the little Jack Russell that didn't wish to be left out of the shot.

From here began the indoor visit, but first came the trip to the rabbit's pen and a stop off to visit the ducks. Inside the shop, which more resembles a museum than a shop, I discovered a wonderful reserved space of Native living past and present.

As soon as I stepped through the doorway, I impulsively gasped, "I could sleep right here!" Everyone laughed, but me! I was serious. I was in Native heaven. I never felt as if I had belonged anywhere anymore than I had here and now this day. My spiritual thirst had been quenched with the Native culture, upon Native land, and among Native history. I felt as if I had found the missing piece of my soul. I recognized I was learning some life-changing answers to questions that had been sleeping inside of myself for spans of years! All of this, topped off with a kind, wise, and strong spirit that was as eager to teach me about them as I was to learn of them. It was a grand day, a profound day, and a day in which I will carry inside of me forever!

Things were turning bittersweet! I felt the rapids of being rushed come over me. I wasn't intentionally wanting to be disrespectful to either my mother, who I knew was anxious to get going, nor to the Chief for taking up so much of his generous time. I was feeling torn between what I wanted to do, and what was expected of me to do. As I continued to study the wonderment around me, I tried hard to battle off the feelings of my inner guilt and simply tried to satisfy what I wanted, what I needed. Which was to stay just a little bit longer and drink in all that was around me.

Throughout my earlier conversations with the Chief, I mentioned to him that I had a website. However, I felt that this was more than just about a paragraph or two on my site. I told him that I wasn't sure why I had been guided to find him. I also mentioned that I was a published songwriter and a poet and that I was convinced that one day I was intended to write a book. I had no idea at the time "Feathers Within" was the story that I was growing inside of me.

While confessing my soul to the Chief, I was also hoping somehow that he might be able to shine a little light on the situation from his side. Perhaps he had been asking for answers or guidance for something that would help add up some answers for me. He didn't seem to be passing any out. I was unsettled by the lack of my ultimate answer. Why was I there? On the other hand, I also hold a deep belief that one is always without their answers, until the universe feels it is the right time for one to know! That being said, it still left me feeling as if I was going to be walking away from something too soon. Although I believe the Great Spirit has a wonderful sense of humour, I don't believe that he just wanted to send my mom and I on an old fashioned, wild-goose chase.

Inside the shop my eyes covered as many objects as they could take in on a short time. One piece that stood out apart from all others was a carving the Chief had done.

It was the carved figure of a woman. She was extremely sad and yet sacred looking. It was not a sadness that repelled me. It was one that drew me towards her. I had to run my hand over the texture of this particular piece of wood, to let her know I could understand her sadness. It made me glad that I had made the trip, that it was for reasons yet to be, and so it seemed it was. For on my website, I wrote a poem called "The Indian Carver," and in that poem I mention this carving that left such an impression on me.

We eventually made our way back outside. I went to my car, opened the trunk, and took out a very large and heavy book called *The American Indian.* It covers the history of the U.S.A. and Canada. I asked the Chief if he would honour me by autographing it for me. Logically speaking, this was pretty presumptuous on my part, considering I didn't even know if I was going to meet him. Yet inside, something greater told me that I would, and I had.

When we hugged good-bye, I hugged him with all my heart, as someone I had known a long time, not as someone I had just briefly met only in passing. We promised each other we would be in touch. I felt torn as I let him go, like a child who wants to cling to a parent and not be left with a strange babysitter. I could feel he felt the same way. It was no easier for me to try to explain to my mother, than it was, I'm sure, for him to have to explain to his mate either. It was time to let go, so we did. I got into my car and waved good-bye!

My heartstrings were still being pulled as I left his laneway. I turned my car south and headed down toward Cape Croker. I couldn't imagine how anything at Cape Croker was going to top anything that I had just experienced. However, I stuck to my plan and struck out to find out.

It was only minutes later, when I had glanced up into my rear-view mirror, I made the pleasant surprising announcement to my mother that the Chief was chasing us. Then, I added, "Ah, actually, Mom, that was the Chief that just passed us!"

There was one more unexpected surprise yet to come.

He blew by us, only to pull over up in front of us. Then, he jumped out of his vehicle and was standing at the passenger's side of my vehicle as I pulled up. Mom was very uncomfortable. As for me, I never even questioned it. I put my car in park, jumped out, and without a word followed in through some trees. Poor Mom, this wasn't exactly her cup a tea. She doesn't drive and she was trying to plan our escape should I get in to something over my head.

On the other side of this treed pathway was a beautiful wood home. He opened the door and asked me to wait there. Quick as a flash, he leapt up the staircase and began to start rooting for something. The house was beautiful, clean, and amazingly built. I could watch as he made his way down the hallway to the right. From the silence of this beautiful home came the sounds that I can only refer to as those of a wolf busily digging up a long-forgotten bone. No sooner had this thought passed through my mind than he was on his return down the stairs and back towards me.

In his hands he held a package that he motioned toward me to accept. I took it into my arms and hugged it closely to my chest. I told him that I would guard it with my life. He immediately responded, "And so you should!"

We both stepped back outside the house again. With this mysterious brown paper package under my one arm, he took my hands in his and made a bridge between us. "Your one story is in there," he said. He looked intensely into my eyes, then smiled and slipped around the side of his house as quickly and as silently as a wolf.

I swiftly made my own way back to my car, glancing over my shoulder to see not another glimpse of him. I opened my trunk, placed the unopened package into it, and drove off toward Cape Croker, feeling like a secretly inspired Nancy Drew on her hottest mystery ever!

My mother's only words as I climbed back into the car again were, "You are very trusting, aren't you?" I did feel for her concern for me, but in the same breath, I had never felt safer in all my life. I tried my best to deliver this message to her as we were driving away.

"Mom, think about it! What would make a man that had never met me before trust me with something that obviously meant so much to him? In all the years he has lived, he has chosen me!"

It is hard for me even now to describe the feeling of deeply knowing that we were simply brought together by divine intervention. What else could one ever call it?

Mom and I did visit Cape Croker's camp-grounds that day. I just drove in far enough to say that I had been there, to see if I felt any strange and profound feelings. What I felt was it was familiar! It brought me peace, quiet, and calmness. It was the end to a very special day indeed.

As I was driving away, I told my mother that I would be back to Cape Croker, that I would return for the pow-wow, that I was intended to have something more unfold for me in this place. I could feel a strong and future con-nection to Cape Croker. One day, I knew I would find more answers there.

On April 29th, my phone rang at my work. It was the Chief, and he was asking if we had reached White Spar-row. I answered yes, and we spoke of things in confidence. Advice and wisdom he wanted me to know; that, above all else, to maintain balance! To never walk too far in any one direction, not even in good times! That I should stay focused and let things unfold in life naturally. Not to be so eager to have all my answers so quickly!

I told him, I had connected with him, that I felt closer to him than to my dad, to my grandfather, or to the man who once raised me. When our conversation ended, I told him that I wished that I could give him a hug. He replied in a very matter of fact tone, "Then just say I love you!" He had read my mind and I answered back, "I love you!"

Then, I set my phone back down and became teary eyed. I just sat there, quietly reliving his voice and calm-ness of voice and words. I prayed for the strength to not shout that he had just called, because I so wanted to share it with someone in hopes they could mirror back my bliss in complete understanding.

At the time of this writing, the Chief and I are still very much in touch. I still bombard him with questions, and he cheerfully supplies the answers. We share great laughter and friendship together. Of all the things he has taught me, one came totally unexpected. He has healed a wound so deeply carved into my childhood heart. Only the Chief could cover over and successfully heal such a wound! I pray I come remotely close to offering something as good a trade in return! Like — truth, spirit, conversation, and love of friendship!

The Chief's spirit is always one with my own! He is one of Canada's natural resources! His work and his carvings are known around the globe! His roads are many! I am ever grateful to be but a pebble on his path!

For the Chief's birthday in 2004, I wrote a poem called "The Indian Carver." He has asked my permission to have it published along with his memoirs! How could I say no to such a great, great honour?

There is so much more to write and speak of about my journey with the Chief! But this is not the time. Perhaps, Mr. John Robert Colombo, you will honour — One Lost Sparrow and One Great Canadian Chief on another path, on another page, on another time!

To you, Chief, until you make camp, the other side of the river, know that I am always and forever with you!

To Wilmer Nadjiwon, Chippewa of Nawash Elder (The Indian Carver), from your little bird friend.

With deepest love, *Meegwich*, (Thank you)
White Sparrow!
May 21st, 2005

From: SparrowSent: Sunday, May 29, 2005 8:27 PM
To: *jrc@ca.inter.net*
Subject: Three Documents!

Greetings Mr. Colombo:

Well, sir, after reading more of your compiled stories, I am teeter-tattering between the value of the ones I am about to enclose to you.

When one is experiencing such events, one has the tendency to feel totally isolated and somewhat out of ones mind!

Then, when one begins to read your books on entire dealings of such strange events, I must admit, my own seem to be relatively tame in comparison with many of the others that I have now read!

What does make them unique, though, is that they happened to me! Some of these I have been able to make later sense of; others remain yet a mystery.

I do, however, admire your patience and persistence to sift though all the submissions that you must get flooded with!

Consider the following three submissions, self-serve style! (Meaning: If you like them, then please help yourself!)

This opportunity is not taken for granted!
In appreciation of your time and efforts,

Sparrow

Body in the Bay

It is important for me to begin this story with the greatest respect for the family and loved ones of this missing body that I make reference to here in this story! It is not my intention to bring sensationalism to what must have been a true living family nightmare. I have had my own personal experience with a loved one who went missing. I can promise you, no matter what the surrounding circumstances are, when you are going through it, it truly is — hell on earth!

It was approximately 8:00 a.m. one April morning in 2004. I was headed east, in the direction of the private resort where I work. I was driving across Highway 26 where it crosses with the old Capitol Theatre. When I arrived at this landmark, I felt a band of current or energy rush through my right side and out my left. It was travelling from south to north. At this same time a strong knowing, feeling, sensation, whatever you wish to call it, told me someone was missing!

As usual for me, I only caught fragments of what this encounter actually meant. What I did know was that someone male or female went missing. The questions that followed went something like this. Had someone on that street lost someone? Was it their energy I was feeling? Would someone on that street find someone who was missing? Was it their energy I felt? Had someone just learned of someone missing? Could it be a child that had gone missing? This last question didn't seem to hold water, so to speak, as it was still April. Generally, children are more apt "in my mind" to go missing in June, after school has let out for the season. For whatever reason, I talked myself back out of this equation. It just didn't seem to be fitting.

Thoughts overcome me when something like this happens. It consumes my thinking and my emotions. It leaves me feeling helpless and frustrated, as I don't have all the required pieces. It also makes me feel different and apart from most of the folks who for the most part seem to be so grounded and practical. You know! Those who have never encountered or admitted encountering anything unexplainable! Somehow, these experiences seemed to have been saved for me in my circle of family and friends.

Anyway, when I arrived at the resort that morning, I immediately told my experience to the Assistant Manager. Just her luck — she usually is the one to end up listening to my tales of the unexplainable. During our conversation, I asked her to write down the date and put missing person beside it. She did as I had asked and then proceeded to put the small piece of paper into her desk drawer.

Weeks and months passed and nothing. No news of a missing person. That was the good news. The bad news was, one begins to feel foolish and out of whack with reality when something so strong and strange ends up going nowhere. You start thinking that everyone around you thinks you may just be over the edge a bit, if you know what I mean. However, life moves on in its own peculiar way and there's nothing we can do about that.

The following April, I heard a helicopter hovering over my home, not once, but many times. It had a pattern of making numerous return trips, concentrating on my area in particular. I told myself this was not the usual military training pattern that often transpires. (You see, the town of Meaford, where I reside, is home to the Meaford training and tank range.) Nor did it look like the typical helicopters that generally whiz by.

I turned on my radio; I haven't been a follower of television in years. I was able to catch a portion of the news that explained that a man somewhere up in his late seventies had been missing for a day or so. Apparently, they had brought out the dogs a day or an evening earlier, but this part of the search had ended unsuccessfully. The next active step was for the community to come together and organize a manhunt.

The military and regular police were already obviously involved. This new search was to be made up of volunteers, and they wanted everyone to meet at the community centre in town. They were inviting all interested parties to please come out and join in the efforts.

My mind immediately flashed back to the previous April. I was already in the process of getting ready to go in and work my shift. I just decided to speed things up a bit and head in a little earlier. I was eager to get to the intersection of the Old Capitol Theatre and Highway 26. When I got there, I craned my neck from side to side to read the street name. It was Collingwood Street. "I knew it," I said out loud. This was the confirmation that I had been unfortunately waiting for.

You see, two blocks to my right, on Collingwood Street, is where the town's people were rallying to set up volunteer search party teams. Of all the streets in Meaford, this was the one where the town's folks were gathering. Of all the years that I have lived in Meaford, this was the first time I ever remember hearing about such an extensive search for any missing person.

This experience for me was bittersweet. It was nice to know that I wasn't crazy for thinking and feeling what I had the April before. The part that really floored me though, once it finally sank in, was — how could I have possibly known this an entire year before it had transpired? By the time I got to work, my Assistant Manager was just getting out of her car a few feet ahead of me. I threw open the door of my car and called out her name. Her head immediately spun around to meet my eyes. She knew something was up.

Seeing her somehow allowed me to let go of the freakish turmoil that was spinning inside of me. I openly admit, I lost it! I began to empty myself through my tears. I remember shaking my hands, as if this would somehow shake off this confirmation. I knew I couldn't walk inside to deal with the guests until I had pulled myself together. Thank goodness for the calmness and candor of this person that was now talking to me. I wish I could explain better the process that I went through, but I simply don't have the words to describe it.

Later that morning, I was still pretty upset. About half an hour after I was officially on the clock, the switchboard rang. Surprisingly, this call was for me and not for one of our guests. It was a female from our community. She was asking about the search. She asked me, if I were there with them, where would I look? After stammering about I had no answers, I finally told her that I would definitely start at the community centre and work my way "toward the water" in a straight line. (This was just the same way and direction that the energy had surged through me a year earlier.)

It was thirty-three minutes after this conversation when she called back to say that the body had been found. She added that although the search party had not found it, all the same the body had been found along the shoreline. When she told me the location, it probably was within a mile or so from where Collingwood Street meets the waterfront.

I never claimed to be nor ever want to be a psychic like Sylvia Browne! I never claimed to say who the missing person was, or who would find the missing person. I never claimed to have known or predicted anything, except that someone had gone missing. That, my friends, was apparently more than enough for my rookie system to handle.

After all of these events had unfolded, I contacted a friend of mine who channels. I'm not exactly sure how one does this, but I do know she has passed out some pretty accurate information to me personally in the past. I turned to her for some kind of comfort for what I had just experienced. Her words brought me reassurance, comfort, and a sort of peace of mind. What she said was this: "You will never be given more than you can handle. You will have to learn to deal with the pain and the emotion that comes with it. You will be fine!"

You will never be given more than you can handle. Boy, I must have repeated her words five or six times out loud and in my head. They seem to bring me immediate comfort, just by saying them! My intuition, as I call it, has travelled from Thornbury to Tobermory in the past. However, this was my first time to ever unknowingly know of something that would or could transpire one year ahead of time!

Mr. Colombo, I would like to thank you once again publicly for allowing me this unique opportunity to vent the unordinary occurrences that I have experienced. It is paramount for me to let you know this! It is also just as important that you receive your due rewards for putting together these self told, original, and compiled experiences. In purest appreciation for these opportunities to share with other liked minds!

Hallway Funeral

Have you ever attended the funeral of a complete stranger ... especially when it was totally and completely by accident?

Well, I have! Leave it to me! I am an original! No carbon copy, that's for sure!

Like many folks, I come from a large family. Truthfully, I am closer to some of them than to others. I have four brothers and two sisters. I am for whatever reasons closer to my two sisters. Lynda is my older sister and Donelda, who prefers to be called Donel, is my younger sister. Although I am smack dab in the middle of them, the two of them are closest to each other. (I have always been the lone wolf of the family.) I used to call myself the black sheep of the family. Now, I refer to myself as the Red sheep!

Anyway, Lynda had just recently moved into her new apartment location on Cedar Avenue in Richmond Hill. My mother had wanted to make the trip down to see her. Mom always likes to be able to visit someone in a new place at least once, so she can later picture it in her mind.

Well, after several failed attempts to co-ordinate schedules, Mom and I were finally able to visit. Donela unfortunately was not able to make the trip. Actually, at the time of writing this story, I don't think she has made it down there yet. It was my first time in Richmond Hill. I had no idea just how memorable it was going to be.

Mom and I got settled in okay, and shortly after Lynda's girlfriend Ruth ended up dropping by to visit as well. We had met Ruth before, so it was also good to hook up with her again. Somewhere during the course of catching up on all our news, Lynda suggested we haul some of her many books downstairs and put them into storage. With all our extra arms to help, why not? She then further suggested that she would like us all to meet her new superintendent. Well, our sole purpose was to come down for a visit so, once again, why not?

We were all up for the little jaunt down to the basement. Books in hand, away we headed. First out the door was my sister, then Mom, then me, and last thoughtful Ruth.

We made our way on and off the elevator in the same order. Ruth and I seemed to be strongly engaged in catch-up conversation, and thereby ended up as the two stragglers in the group. I distinctly remember seeing Lynda and Mom making a right turn up ahead at the end of the corridor. Therefore I was in no rush to catch up as I could see my destination point without any fear of losing track of them.

Seconds after they disappeared from view, I stopped immediately and abruptly in my tracks. I was completely taken off guard by what I encountered. I can't remember if Ruth almost bumped into me, or actually did end up stepping on my heels when I stopped. What I do remember was spluttering, "Oh my God, I just walked into a funeral!"

I didn't wait for Ruth's response. I remember asking, more like interrogating her, "Can't you smell it?"

"It smells like that warm sweet flowery smell that you smell in a funeral home."

At the risk of sounding self-consumed, I don't know if Ruth said or did anything except witness my actions. I guess one would have to ask Ruth if she remembers.

What I remember next is looking up to my right and overhead to see if there was some sort of vent or air duct that could have been pumping the smell in. Nothing! Solid walls, and solid ceiling. There was absolutely nothing to distinguish this portion of the hallway from any other particular spot. Very odd indeed!

At some point, Ruth came up from behind me and stood to my left side. I remember cautioning her, that we should not say anything to my sister, at least until my mom went to sleep that night.

What follows next gets even stranger! Part of me wanted to rush down the hallway and drag my sister back to share this with her, but the bigger part knew that for whatever reason Ruth was the one to experience this encounter with me.

Next, I looked down at the space on the floor where I was presently standing. Nothing looked different to the naked eye. I did, however, feel like I was standing in a 24" x 24" square perimeter. It also felt to be very tall. Like a pillar of energy, or beam, if you will. It seem to extend from the floor to at least my own height and taller. Obviously, I didn't have a tape measure on me, so I can only guesstimate at these measurements.

With Ruth as my witness, I remember stepping repeatedly in and out of this invisible perimeter. As I stepped to the left, I said, "Can't smell it here." Then I would step back into the perimeter and say, "I can smell it here." Then I did and said the same thing, as I moved forward from it and directly back from it. I could not do so to the right of me, as that was where the wall ran.

It was the smell that was so defined, as was the area in which it occurred. I probably looked up at the ceiling a couple of times. I found it incredibly hard to imagine that it was just coming from nowhere.

Shortly after this step-dance of mine, I pulled myself together, and the two of us scooted on down the hallway to join the others in the room on the right. Inside Mom and Lynda were cheerfully chatting innocently away with the new super. Lynda was showing and describing the fitness area, et cetera.

What hit me in this room was how beautiful it was for a superintendent's office. It was none like I had encountered over the fifteen years or so that I had lived in the Mississauga and Brampton areas. I was thinking they must pay the supers a lot better in Richmond Hill than they do elsewhere!

I continued to swivel around in place, looking at the dark wall unit and the wall pictures — the personal homey kind of touches to this office area! It was at that point that I stated how surprisingly nice it was. It was at this juncture that Judy, I believe her name was, softly explained, "Well, you see, years ago we used to have a lot of seniors living here with us. Many of them just like family, so we sometimes ended up using this room to hold wakes."

As these words made contact with my ears, I quickly reached to my right and grabbed a hold of Ruth's arm in an attempt to prevent her from blurting anything out. She and I made instant eye contact, but no words were exchanged between us. I quickly ended my conversation with the super and headed towards the exit.

A sense of anticipation was building even stronger in me now, and I am sure Ruth as well, to spill out our experience to Lynda at the earliest point possible. Lynda, thank goodness, was also ready to make her way back up to the apartment, so we all thanked Judy for her kindness and hastily made our way back down the long corridor. I remember wondering how Lynda was going to take this news, considering that she had just nicely gotten herself moved into her new surroundings.

What I would like to reiterate is the part about the mysterious perimeter. There didn't seem to be any harmful, bad, or hurtful vibes, if you will. It seemed to be a gentle source. Quite possibly, but unfortunately unknowingly, I was unable to confirm female or feminine energy that I was drawing on! For some reason it did seem to fit in line with adult energy and not child-like power. However, I'm not exactly sure what, if any, difference this makes to anyone reading this — except that it rounds off the experience the only honest way I know how.

Perhaps, it may mean something to someone who reads this, if they happen to know of anyone who passed over in an apartment building on Cedar Street in Richmond Hill. Or, perhaps, this encounter was of someone who visited or worked there. How would one ever know the real answer? I learned a long time ago that this world was never intended or designed for us to hold all the answers, only to guess the possibilities of all the "what ifs"!

At the time of writing about this occurrence, I can tell you this detail. My sister is still happily living in this building. To the best of my knowledge, she has never heard or encountered any such stories as the one that I just shared with you!

Raining Intuition

Every once in a while, we seem to notice how life has changed us. I don't just mean how it has changed our body. It does that, but I mean how it has changed our thinking as well. Every experience we have slowly adds up to our own unique process!

I'm not at all sure when my very first unusual encounter was, but for the sake of argument, I will tell you about the first one that sticks out most in my mind!

I was sitting at my mother's kitchen table in Meaford, Ontario. At the time, I was visiting with her from the city of Mississauga. You see, just previous to this visit, I had received a phone call to say that my dad had taken ill and was in the Owen Sound Hospital. Upon sharing the news with my sons, my oldest son decided that he would take my car in for a car wash. In case you hadn't guessed, he had just recently acquired his driver's licence and would be happy to drive at the time for nearly any mundane reason!

On the return from his good deed, I was to learn that the automatic car wash had eaten the driver's-side windshield wiper completely off! There was no time to waste! I explained that I would have to be the one now to drive up North. The reason was it might start to rain and I was supposedly a more experienced driver! My son was disappointed with this news, to say the least, but he also understood it was for the best.

So we loaded up and headed off. Not a raindrop in sight! We had bare roads and clear sailing all the way. We all settled safely two hours later at our destination. The next morning, before heading over to the next town to make our hospital visit, my son Damon asked if he and my youngest son Ryan (Rye as I call him) could borrow the car for a quick road trip to visit briefly with their uncle who lived nearby. This particular uncle is three months "younger" in age than Damon! In other words, his grandmother and I were pregnant at the same time. (This is known as a M.A.C. situation — Middle Age Carelessness!) It seemed to be a fairly clear day. So I told him there was no problem so long as they were back by 1:00 p.m.

Approximately a half-hour later I shared my gnawing concern with my mother. I explained that every time my sons get together with this particular uncle, a twist of fate soon follows, or so it always seemed to me. This day was to be no exception.

Minutes following this comment — intuition rains down on me — and I shot straight up off my chair, causing it to crash against the kitchen wall behind me! I remember spouting out, "Something just happened to the kids! Something's wrong, I can feel it!"

My practical, logical-minded mother began to tell me that I shouldn't be thinking like this! She asked me why I would say such a thing.

The words had no sooner left her mouth than her telephone rang. It was for me. It was the Meaford town police. A lady officer began explaining that my two sons and a third party had rolled and totalled the car! She quickly went on to add that they had been admitted to the Meaford Hospital. She also asked if I had any other transportation. I said no. So she immediately offered to come and pick me up and take me up to see them.

Long story short! Apparently, they picked up their uncle and went out for a short drive on some nearby gravel roads. During this back-road tour, it immediately started to pour down rain! Damon was driving and he did what any other driver instinctively would do. He reached up and hit the windshield wipers, only to be sadly reminded he didn't have one on his side of the car. With no vision, they ended up going around a bend in the road and rolling the car a couple of times down over an embankment.

The police officer did add that they had "not" been

speeding. She said they had only been doing about fifty miles per hour. She explained that, with a passenger in the front seat and a passenger on the same side in the back, when they went around the corner, the weight displacement added to the car flipping over so easily!

I remember getting out of the officer's vehicle. I remember thanking her, but I don't remember seeing her after that. I remember walking into the hospital and asking at the desk to see my sons. I also remember nervously asking, "Who was hurt the worst?" but not really wanting to really hear or know the answer.

In through the doorway I went. First, I spotted my youngest, Rye. I knew in his eyes he was happy to see me, but also at the same time pleading in his brother's defence that he was so worried about the car. I quickly hugged him and said I'd be back after I checked on his brother.

The hospital was keeping him on the opposite side of the room. I could see a doctor with him. He was going over him closely, checking for signs of whiplash and whatever else they look for. I guess, as the driver, Damon had got it the worst.

Upon spotting me, he immediately started apologizing for rolling the car. I told him not to worry about the car, it was insured. I asked the doctor how he thought they medically looked. He told me that both of them were bounced around pretty good, but luckily both had been wearing their seat belts.

I don't remember what happened with their uncle. He wasn't there! At the time that was just as well, I had enough on my plate to deal with. All in all, they had relatively small bangs, bumps, and bruises compared to what could have happened. I think the biggest injury was their minds and naturally their nerves! Damon, especially, felt the responsibility for both his passengers and the car. He didn't seem too concerned for his own physical condition!

The details that hang heaviest over me to this day about the accident are two-fold. Number One, how easily I could have lost both my sons in one easy freak swoop!

Number Two, the feeling of the energy that had shot through my body that day that told me something wrong had happened! How unnerving and helpless I felt, because I was unable to capture any of the details.

The best way I suppose to describe this feeling to others is like this. It is like someone witnessing a dog barking incessantly at something but not being able to see or hear what it is that the dog is barking at. You only sense that it can't be good. All you really know is that common sense tells you to act defensively, to be alert, and to be on guard!

This source of energy has come to visit with me on other occasions as well. For the above-stated reasons, it continues to be both a blessing and a curse. It immediately overcomes me at different speeds, strengths, and lengths of time!

What I have figured out is that the older I get, the stronger it seems to get! Also, that it picks me! I never pick it! I usually end up pacing and my mind racing as it occurs. My mind and my heart do instant battle.

Which one wins? The honest truth? The one I feel the most!

May 26, 2005

2

SOME OLD-FASHIONED GHOSTS

The fact that there are so many words in the English language for *ghosts* and *spirits* argues on behalf of their very existence! Elsewhere in this book I have gathered these words together and arranged them in alphabetical order. Here I have gathered some "ghost stories" of the traditional kind, as I found them in the columns of old newspapers and journals. Not all ghosts, when they appear, need to be swathed in white shrouds or cerements — but many were and still are. It is worth noting that we do not "see" ghosts so much as we do "sense" their presence. Yet these ghosts are as much phantasms or psychical experiences as they are creatures of folklore. Perhaps for that reason they have particular penetrative powers! They haunt us still.

A GHOST STORY

Nova Scotian, Halifax, Nova Scotia, November 7, 1859

Mr. Hector M'Donald, of Canada, was recently on a visit to Boston. When he left home his family were enjoying good health, and he anticipated a pleasant journey. The second morning after his arrival in Boston, when leaving his bed to dress for breakfast, he saw reflected in a mirror the corpse of a woman lying in the bed from which he had just risen. Spell-bound, he gazed with intense feeling, and tried to recognize the features of the corpse, but in vain; he could not even move his eyelids; he felt deprived of action, for how long he knew not. He was at last startled by the ringing of the bell for breakfast, and sprang to the bed to satisfy himself if what he had seen reflected in the mirror was real or an illusion. He found the bed as he left it, he looked again into the mirror, but only saw the bed truly reflected. During the day he thought much upon the illusion, and determined next morning to rub his eyes and feel perfectly sure that he was wide awake before he left bed. But, notwithstanding these precautions, the vision was repeated with this addition, that he thought he recognized in the corpse some resemblance to the features of his wife.

In the course of the second day he received a letter from his wife, in which she stated that she was quite well, and hoped he was enjoying himself among his friends. As he was devotedly attached to her, and always anxious for her safety, he supposed that his morbid fears had conjured up the vision he had seen reflected in the glass; and went about his business as cheerfully as usual. — On the morning of the third day, after he had dressed, he found himself in thought in his own house, leaning over the coffin of his wife. His friends were assembled, the minister was performing the funeral services, his children wept — he was in the house of death. He followed the corpse to the grave; he heard the earth rumble upon the coffin, he saw the grave filled and the green sods covered over it; yet, by some strange power, he could see through the ground the entire form of his wife as she lay in her coffin.

He looked in the face of those around him, but no one seemed to notice him; he tried to weep, but the tears refused to flow, his very heart felt as hard as a rock. Enraged at his own want of feeling, he determined to throw himself upon the grave and lie there till his heart should break, when he was recalled to consciousness by a friend, who entered the room to inform him that breakfast was ready. He started as if awoke from a profound sleep, though he was standing before the mirror with a hairbrush in his hand.

After composing himself, he related to his friend what he had seen, and both concluded that a good breakfast only was wanting to dissipate his unpleasant impressions. A few days afterwards, however, he received the melancholy intelligence that his wife had died suddenly, and the time corresponded with the day he had been startled by the first vision in the mirror. When he returned home he described minutely all the details of the funeral he had seen in his vision, and they corresponded with the facts. This is probably one of the most vivid instances of clairvoyance on record. Mr. M'Donald knows nothing of modern spiritualism or clairvoyance, as most of his life has been passed upon a farm and among forests. It may not be amiss to state that his father, who was a Scotch Highlander, had the gift of "second sight." — *Boston Traveller*.

THE GHOST OF THE DROWNED MAN

Collingwood is located on Georgian Bay in Northern Ontario. Today it is an affluent year-round resort community; in the past it had a profitable ship-building yard. This news story is reprinted from the *Quebec Daily News*, Quebec City, December 22, 1862.

A Collingwood Ghost Spiritually Inclined

A few months ago an old man fell over the railway wharf at Collingwood, and was drowned. — Ever since, the more simple folks of the town have been under the impression that his spirit walks the wharf when churchyards yawn. On Tuesday night, one of the railway officials had occasion to walk along the wharf on business. He carried in his hand a lantern, and to his astonishment he observed what he supposed to be the ghost of the drowned man. In the outstretched hand of his ghostship was a tumbler containing what appeared to be liquor, the deceased having been rather fond of a drop, while an inhabitant of this lower world. While the official stood gazing at the spectre, a voice exclaimed, in deep sepulchral tones, the word "Beware," and the spirit vanished into thin air. He returned to the office and acquainted the other officials with what he had seen, who tried to laugh him out of it, but without effect. He still declares that he saw the ghost of the old man.

A GUARDIAN OR A WARDEN

A spirit is often believed to be the guardian of a person or the warden of a specific site. "A Ghost in Thorold" appeared in the *St. Catharines Journal*, October 23, 1863.

A Ghost in Thorold

Last week the bridge-tender at the bridge over the Canal entering the village from the North resigned his position, and a gentleman of the Irish persuasion from the town took his place. It seems that at some indefinite period a man was drowned near the bridge, whose shade remained perfectly invisible until Thursday night last, when Andy was on duty. On that night Andy saw a man with a lantern, or a lantern without a man, approach the bridge, and apparently inspect it very closely. Andy went toward the object, and said, "It's a fine night then," but received no answer. This incivility on the part of a stranger irritated Andy, who raised his foot and made a kick at the lantern, hitting a shabbing post. He repeated this operation several times, and with a like result each time. Before he would kick, the lantern would seem to be between him and the post, and after doing so, it would appear on the other side. This puzzled him, and caused his toes and conscience both to become sore, and he retired to his shanty, locking himself in. — On Friday night the same interesting programme was performed. On Saturday night Andy swore he would not stop alone, and when three boys came along, he impressed them and detained them until two a.m., and then let them depart, the "Witching hour of night, When church-yards yawn, And graves give forth their dead" being over. On Monday he resigned, and refuses to go near the bridge.

P.S. — Since the above was written, a new version of the ghost has appeared. It now comes in the shape of a dog, with six legs and six lights, one being in its mouth. The story has thoroughly alarmed the boys and women of the village, and they will not pass that bridge alone on any consideration. In our opinion, it is the duty of the Canal Superintendent to suppress this ghost, as it may interfere with navigation. If he would inquire very closely of the remaining bridge tender a solution might be obtained. It may be that somebody is anxious for the situation.

THE SERGEANT'S GHOST STORY

Weekly News, St. Catharines, Ontario, March 6, 1873

Everybody, or nearly everybody, young or old, loves a ghost story. It is not necessary to believe in its truth to derive enjoyment from it. The more inexplicable it appears to our ordinary reason, the greater the charm that it exercises. Incredulity itself is pleased by a flight into the regions of the wonderful and the supernatural, as is evident from the satisfaction derived by people of all ages and nations from fairy tales which nobody accepts for truth. But the fairy tale only appeals to the imagination. The ghost story goes deeper into the mysterious fountains of human nature and touches on the confines of the great undiscovered land of spirits, whose secrets are not to be divulged on this side of the grave. Hence its charm and fascination, and hence everybody who reads or hears a ghost story experiences a satisfaction, either in believing it implicitly, or in explaining it away by natural causes.

A few years ago I travelled in a British colony in America. The governor was absent in England on his holiday visit, and the duties of his office were temporarily performed by the chief justice aided by the prime minister, or secretary of state. I was a frequent guest at Government House, and there became acquainted with an old soldier, one Sergeant Monaghan, who performed the part of orderly or messenger, and sometimes waited at table when the governor had company. The manners of a colony are free and easy, and learning that the old soldier was a thorough believer in ghosts, and one ghost story which he was fond of telling, I invited him to my room, treated him to a cigar and a glass of grog, gave him a seat by the blazing wood fire, and prevailed on him to evolve the story once again out of the coils of memory. I will repeat it as nearly as I can, in his own words.

"You see," said Sergeant Monaghan, "Tom O'Loghlin was a delicate and weak sort of a boy. He had a love affair in Ireland that weighed on his mind. He was a kind of cousin of mine, and served in my regiment as a private. Perhaps he would have risen to be a sergeant if he had lived, but, as he said, he was not strong. You may have noticed that from the gate of Government House, where the sentry box stands, you can see into the burial ground, on the opposite side of the road. Not a cheerful situation for Government House. But, however, all the best rooms look into the garden at the back and the governor need not see much of the burial ground, except when he goes in and out. One foggy night, Tom O'Loghlin was stationed as sentry at Government House. It was full moon at the time, but the light upon the white warm mist that lay like an immense blanket over the earth, shone weak and watery lake. It was not a very thick fog, and did not hide objects at a distance of a hundred yards but only revealed them to make them look larger than they really were. I was in the guard-room smoking my pipe, comfortably as I am now (either a pipe or a cigar, it's all the same to Sergeant Monaghan, if the 'bacey's good.) when who should walk in but Tom O'Loghlin, with a face of such wild, blank, dismal terror, as I never saw before or since on a human being. It was fully an hour before his time to be relieved of duty, and in leaving his post he had committed a very serious offence. I ordered him back to his post, but he sat down by the fire, and doggedly refused to stir.

"What's the matter with you, Tim?" said I. "Are you unwell? And why did you come off duty? And it's I myself that'll have to report you."

"You may report — you must report; but I will not go back again, though I be shot for it. I have seen him."

"Him — and who is him?"

"Him! Why Captain Percival. He came close up to me, and pointed to a man in the burial-ground next to his own."

The Captain had died about a month previously, and Tim, who was very much attached to him — and indeed everybody in the regiment was — had grieved very much about his death. He had acted as the Captain's servant, and had received many favors at his hand, and poor Tim was a grateful creature.

"It's all nonsense, Tim," said I. "Go back to your post, and in reporting you I'll make the best case out that I can for you."

"Never!" said Tim, "if I be shot for it."

To break the ice as luck would have it, the doctor happened to drop in at this moment, and learning the circumstances that had induced Tim to leave his post, questioned him fully on the subject. But he felt Tim's pulse first, and there came over his face an expression that I noticed, but that Tim did not, which said very plainly to me that he did not like the beat of it. Tim was confident that he had seen Captain Percival, and that the Captain pointed out the grave which a man was digging alongside of his own, and had distinctly told him that he was to be buried there as soon as the grave was quite ready.

"And you saw the man digging the grave?" asked the doctor.

"Distinctly," replied Tim; "and you can see him too, if you go immediately."

"Do, you go, sergeant," said the doctor to me, "and I'll sit with O'Loghlin till you return. I think you had better detail another sentry in his place. Is there any brandy to be got? But stay; it does not matter. I have a flask. And O'Loghlin, my man, you must have a pull at it; it is medicine, you know, and I order it."

Tim was taking a pull at the flask as I went out. I thought it possible enough that the grave-digger might be at work, but I did not know what to say about the Captain, except to think, perhaps, that Tim had been dreaming, and fancied he saw things that had no existence. I got into the burial-ground without difficulty — the gate was not fastened — and went straight to the grave of Captain Percival. There stood the gravestone, sure enough, with the Captain's name, age and date of death upon it, and a short story besides, setting forth what a good and brave fellow he was, which was true as the gospel. — But there was no grave-digger there, nor no open grave, as Tim had fancied. I went back, and found Tim and the doctor together, Tim not looking quite so wild and white as before, but bad and ill, all the same.

"Well," inquired the doctor.

"Well," I replied. "There's nothing to be seen. It's just as I thought. Poor Tim's fancy has cheated him, and it's my opinion the poor boy is not well at all. And what am I to do about reporting him?"

"You must report him, of course," said the doctor; "but I don't think much harm will come to him of that. O'Loghlin, you must go into the hospital for a day or two, and I will give you some stuff that will bring you out again right as a trivet, and you will see no more ghosts."

Tim shook his head, and was taken quietly to the hospital, and put to bed. The brandy had done him good; whether it was all brandy, or whether there wasn't a drop of sleeping stuff in it, I can't say, but it's very likely there was, for the doctor told me the longer he slept in reason the better it would be for him. And Tim had a long sleep, but not a very quiet one, for all that same, and tossed about for the matter of a dozen hours or so. But he never got out of bed again. When I saw him at noon the next day he was wide awake, and very feverish and excitable.

"How are you, Tim, my poor fellow?" said I, taking his hand, which was very hot and moist.

"I've seen him again," he replied. "I see him now. He is sitting at the foot of the bed, and pointing to the grave-yard. I know what he means."

"Tim, it's crazy that ye are," said I.

He shook his head mournfully.

"Monaghan," he sighed, rather than said, "ye've been a kind friend to me. Give that to the little girl in Ireland — you know." And he drew a photographic portrait of himself from under his pillow, tied round with a blue ribbon, from which depended a crooked six pence with a hole in it. "In a few days ye'll be laying me in the ground alongside of the Captain. Do ye see him now! He is leaving the room smiling upon me, and still pointing to the graveyard. I am no longer afraid of him. He means me no harm, and it is no blame to him if he is sent to tell me to get ready."

"Tim, you are cheating yourself. What you are telling me is all a walking dream. I can see no ghost."

"Of course, you can't," said Tim. "The spirits never appear to two persons at once. But Patrick Monaghan," he added, "let us talk no more on the subject, but send Father Riley to me, that I may unburden me soul, and die in peace."

"It would have been cruel to me to have argued the matter with the poor afflicted creature, and him such a friend of my own, too, so I left him to go in search of the doctor first, and of Father Riley afterwards. They both came. What passed between Tim and the Holy Father, of course, I never knew; but the doctor told me distinctly. Tim was in a very bad way — stomach was wrong, the nerves wrong, the brain was wrong; in fact, he was wrong altogether, and had a fever which the doctor called by a very grand and night-sounding name, which I did not hear very plainly, and which if I did, I am unable to remember. Tim survived three days after this, sleeping and dozing, and talking in his sleep, and every now and then saying amid words which I could not well put together into any meaning, "I am coming, I am coming." Just before he died, he grew more collected, and made me promise that he should be buried in the grave that had been dug for him by the side of the Captain. I knew that no such grave had been dug as he said, and that it was all a delusion; but what was the use of arguing with a dying man? So I promised, of course, by my honor and by my soul, to do all I could to have his last wish gratified. The doctor promised also and so did Father Riley, and I think poor Tim died happy. His last words were something about the ribbon and the crooked six pence, and the Captain, the very last syllable being, "I come."

"We buried the poor lad in the place assigned by himself, and I was so affected altogether by the sadness of the thing that I could have persuaded myself, in fact I did persuade myself, that I saw Captain Percival in undress or fatigue uniform, just as he had appeared to poor Tim walking past the sentry-fox before the door of the Government House, and stopping every now and then to point at the grave; and the more I closed my eyes to avoid seeing him, the more permanently and clearly he stood before me."

"And are you in any doubt on the subject now?" I inquired.

"And indeed I am," replied the sergeant, shaking the ashes from his cigar with the tip of his little finger. "Tim must have seen the ghost, and must have believed in him, and if I only saw it, after Tim's death, it is but another proof of what almost everybody knows, that two people never saw the same ghost at the same time. And ghost or no ghost, it is quite clear that Tim died of him, and might have been alive at this moment, but for the ghost's extraordinary behavior. But it's one of the questions that all the talk in the world can't settle."

"Do you think Tim would have seen the ghost of

Captain Percival, or anybody else, if he had been sound in mind and limb, if he had been a strong hearty man with a good appetite, and an undisordered stomach?"

"Can't say," replied the sergeant, taking a sip of his liquor. "The doctor thought not; but doctors don't know everything; and if there were no ghosts, why I should like to ask should the spirit of Samuel appear to Saul, and answer his questions?"

"Well, sergeant," said I, "if you are going to the Bible for arguments, I shall shut up. Finish your glass, my man, and let us say good night."

He finished his glass, he said good night, and walked away with the air of a man who thought he had the best of the argument.

GHOSTS AND WITCHES

In the Western Part of Cumberland — Romantic Traditions of Old Time Tragedies — Along the Parrsboro Shore — A Very Racy Story — By S.D. Scott — (Written for the Christmas Herald)

Halifax Morning Herald, December 24, 1887

The person who led the Editor of the Herald's Christmas supplement to suppose that Parrsboro and the regions adjoining are richly supplied with interesting ghosts, should have been called upon to write a paper on that subject — rather than the writer. The western section of the good old county is, indeed, not without its romantic traditions. In several settlements there remained a few years ago a saving remnant of believers, survivors of those richer times, when local tragedies, acted upon the unskepticized minds of men, as seed falling on good ground, brought forth a fruitful harvest of good old-fashioned ghosts. During those fine times, not more than two generations ago in this region, little information came by way of the post office, and few were the travelers who brought accounts of the business of distant climes. Messages from other countries came so seldom that the people naturally turned for society to residents of that Undiscovered Country, from whose bourne they had been led to believe occasional travelers returned. The other world was nearer than the greater part of this, and the affairs of the nation, the strife of political factions, the war of creeds, the new discoveries of science, or the latest inventions in fashions never diverted their attention from supernatural visitors. The early families read few books in those original days. They rather sought light in evening consultation before the big fireplace, and in that solitary meditation from which minds naturally receptive and unbiased by the methodical training of modern school life, come out well stored with theories of natural and spiritual life. Few are the localities where the well authenticated facts of fifty years ago are now received with that faith which alone makes a ghost story prosperous. These things pertaining to the supernatural are in a sense spiritually discerned, and if historian and audience are not for the time in a believing mood the most stirring narratives become in the language of the late Mr. Lennie's "things without life, as milk."

The Cumberland ghosts are of two classes, one of which we may call Real Estate Ghosts, and the other Portable Ghosts. The first class are so designated because they are attached to the realty. They remain near the scene of the tragedy to which they owe their existence, and show themselves to suitable travelers without respect to the connection or want of connection the spectator may have had with the original event. The Portable Ghosts are the personal property of the murderers or other parties connected with the crime. They usually act in lieu of conscience and keep dark deeds from escaping the mind. Several haunted men have lived and died in Parrsboro. Their ghosts have departed with them. The permanent apparitions, as the age degenerates, are the less disposed to be visible, finding the people fewer and fewer to whom a self-respecting ghost would care to appear.

A chapter on Parrsboro ghosts would therefore read much like the famous treatise on snakes in Ireland. At last accounts, however, the Holy Way Brook ghost in the Fork Woods, near Athol, had not yet taken his final leave. The woods themselves, which before the railway was built, stretched without a break a mile each way from the rock whereon the fearful visitor was wont to sit in the quiet evening hour, are now destroyed. The spirit that dwells on the old Etter road has not yet entirely been withdrawn. The change of the name of Maccan mountain to Mapleton has not deprived the two or three disembodied inhabitants of their earthly home. Civilization has not so much as approached the Boar's Back ghost, and though the Haunted Mill at Parrsboro is now no more there, the spot where it stood has still its horror.

Along the shore before reaching Advocate Harbor there are many spots to which the spirits of the departed were of late wont to return, and unless the telephone and other materialistic influences have wrought for evil, the same is true at present. A precipice by the highway down which a carriage rolled with its human freight, has its well known ghost. There is a shipyard where, perhaps twelve years ago, a woman's form appeared almost every evening throughout the summer. Moving lightly and mysteriously about the frame work and stagings, passing securely over perilous places, she ever sang strange wild songs, which were heard by scores of the neighbors and by passers by. There is a spot on the beach where ghosts have been often seen hovering near the foot of the high-arched headland above Spencer's Island, where strange deeds have perhaps been done, and it is said, though on shadowy authority, that the spirit of the sailor whose tomb on the island itself gives the place its name, has been met by the lone tourist. The ghost of one of Capt. Kidd's murdered men, killed and stationed to guard buried treasure, is familiar to those who go to Cape d'Or or "Isle Haunt" to dig for pirate gold. These and a few others are all the ghosts that remain of the grand old company that formerly dwelt in Parrsboro and its neighborhood. Of the ghosts, who are personal attendants of bad men, who can write of them? Those who possess the best information are, for obvious reasons, the least communicative. It is not, perhaps, to the credit of human nature that the belief in witches survives the faith in ghosts. This truth not only reflects upon the spiritual faculties, as indicating the need of a material form wherewith to connect the supernatural manifestations, but it also tells against our disposition, since it leads to the suspicion that the refusal to abandon faith in witchcraft may be due to a lingering desire to believe ill of a neighbor. It is probably safe to say that in this country every rural township which has been long settled has at some time within the century contained a family skilled in witchcraft. Parrsboro and the adjoining region is certainly no exception. Fifty years hence, if we all live and do not change our minds, fuller historic details will be in order. One of the most prosperous communities in the neighborhood of which we are talking, was one day, within the recollection of all elderly, and of many middle-aged persons now living, thrown into great confusion by remarkable and dangerous flights of stones. Pebbles of all sizes were seen hurling through the air, journeying horizontally, perpendicularly, and in all manner of unnatural curves. They changed direction at right angles while moving, doubled back on their track as if thrown from a celestial boomerang. Never were the laws of projectiles so absurdly violated. It was absolutely impossible that the singular storm could be due to human agency. Many of the best citizens of the place saw this wonderful sight, and several had demonstration more painful than that of sight. It was a terrible day, one well remembered and often spoken of. You may believe that this rain of stones was caused by some natural process, but if so it will on the whole be better for you not to say so in the presence of the good people who were there at the time. They will assure you with dignity that they have the testimony of their eyes, ears and sense of feeling, and will regard your questioning as a reflection on their veracity. One thing is certain that the character of the witnesses forbids the assumption that the story is a fabrication. If you will pursue your inquiries you will learn that the ordeal or test known as "boiling for witches," was solemnly applied, and with such success that the human associate of the Prince of Darkness was forced to the scene of inquest, so that any doubt, (not that there was any) must be set aside. Much may be learned of other dark doings of the above-mentioned workers of witchcraft. How domestic animals brought under the spell sometimes died, but more frequently acted in a most unaccountable fashion. The hitherto well-behaved ox no longer followed the furrow, the best of cows either went dry or gave red milk, the staidest of horse kind became coltish and exhibited evidences of terror. For these bewitchings the remedy was the boiling or burning test. The milk of the unfortunate cow thus treated, with the proper solemnities, brought the agent piteously begging, and in awful suffering, to the door — where pledges of total abstinence from witchcraft against the afflicted family were promptly administered. It is said that this remedy eventually reduced the offenders to general good behavior. There is no foundation whatever, for the report that Cumberland has had more than its share of witches. A few families, not more probably than half a dozen, would include all those who have wrought these mysteries west of Spring Hill and Amherst within the lifetime of any but the patriarchs. It is doubtful if there are now more than two or three survivors of the many who have seen the Evil One in any of the shapes which he is wont to assume. Not long ago there were those whose evidently genuine accounts of diabolical visits were calculated to keep small boys from going out at night. It is not necessary to explain these things. But we will understand them better if we keep in mind the fact that in New England over a century ago, when the Cumberland settlers came thence, ghosts and witches were plentiful enough, and that the Yorkshire colonists who located in the country had attended the meetings of John Wesley to whom, as he has himself recorded, the Devil in the form of a beast sometimes appeared. The secluded life of a settlement apart from the outside world, and the home training of the young in the shadows of the forest, by parents bringing their beliefs from over seas, would not be likely to induce scepticism in the second generation.

A GHASTLY APPARITION

A Strange Spectre Daily Haunting Niagara's Lonely Places

Kingston Daily Whig, November 22, 1880

The town of Niagara is in a state of excitement over a ghastly apparition which has haunted the place of late. The experiences are growing more numerous, and even men are chary of going abroad after dark. A farmer leaving town the other night about eleven o'clock, the moon being bright, avers that he saw the thing rise from among the tombs, in the churchyard, and trail toward him. It had the semblance of a woman with long white garments and fair hair, apparently floating, or else with far more than the average length of limb. The farmer closed his eyes, and turning his horse drove back into town at a furious gallop, his animal seeming to share the fright. He never looked round until safely in the heart of the town. Another account states that at one of the lonely crossings in the outskirts of the place the woman was seen crouching beside a low fence. The spectators, two in number this time, did not at first recall the stories of the apparition, and went toward the thing under the impression that some vagrant was crouching there for shelter. As they went near, a peculiar sensation affected them both, and without speaking to each other or exactly knowing why they stopped involuntarily and turned away. As they did so a shuddering thrill went through them, as they say, and they broke into a wild run for the nearest lights.

Other tales have contradictory points, but all agree that the apparition has the form of a woman, and possesses a strange floating motion. There is much speculation in the place over the matter.

Five successful burglaries have been accomplished, and three unsuccessful ones attempted, and the evil deeds are still going on. It is possible that the burglaries have been committed by the ghost, although there is nothing to show this positively.

DR. BRIGGS'S GHOST STORY

Professor De Morgan

Toronto News, April 19, 1883

Dr. Briggs, when quartered in the Hill Country, used to meet once a week with the officers and others; the custom being to breakfast at each other's houses after the sport was over. On the day for Dr. B.'s turn to receive his friends, he awoke at dawn and saw a figure standing at his bedside. Having rubbed his eyes to make sure that he was awake, he got up, crossed the room, and washed his face in cold water. He then turned, and, seeing the same figure, approached it, and recognized a sister whom he had left in England. He uttered some exclamation and fell down in a swoon, in which state he was found by the servant who came to call him for the hunt. He was, of course, unable to join his hunting friends, who, when at breakfast on their return, rallied him as to the cause of his absence. In the midst of the talk he suddenly looked up aghast, and said in a trembling voice: — "Is it possible that none of you see the woman standing there?" They all declared there was no one. "I tell you there is; she is my sister. I beg of you all to make a note of this, for we shall hear of her death."

All present, sixteen in number, of whom Sir John Malcolm was one, made an entry in their notebooks of the occurrence and exact date. Some months after this, by the first mail from England that could bring it, came the news that the sister had died at the very time of the vision, having on her deathbed expressed a strong wish to see her brother, and to leave two young children in his charge.

STRANGE PREMONITION OF IMPENDING FATE

We have been informed by a strange coincidence in the death of the late Alderman McPherson, which involves the mysterious to such a degree as to make it one of those unaccountable illusions which sometimes occur as a prescient to some impending fate. The facts abound so much in the marvellous, that, were they not given on the undoubted authority of the bereaved widow, who now is left to mourn the loss of him whose death was so strikingly revealed to her, we should not attempt to rehearse them. On the Thursday night previous to his death, the deceased gentleman was awakened by the continued sobbing of his wife, whose cries, though asleep, were distinctly audible to several of the inmates of the house. Awakening her he inquired the reason of her incessant moaning, when she informed him that she had had a dream, in which she saw the two gentlemen, who were afterwards the first to tell her the sad news, enter the house and actually inform her of his death. Every circumstance was so vivid, that she remarked it as something peculiar, and besought him on the Saturday morning, when he went away, to be careful of himself, as she felt confident that something unusual would shortly occur. True, in her premonition, he never returned alive, and on the Rev. Mr. Scott and his friend Mr. Lester, entering her house on the same evening, to inform her of his death, she did not wait for their announcement, but holding up her hands in despair, said, "Is he dead?" and without waiting for an answer, fell exhausted on the floor. The sad coincidence of the actual circumstances as they occurred, with the dream, marks it one of the strangest on record. — London C.W. *Prototype*.

A TRUE GHOST STORY

Moose Jaw Times, October 4, 1895

Not many years ago, people used to sneer at ghosts and ghost stories much more than they do now, and one would constantly hear people whisper to one another (while some individual was relating his or her experience): "Ah! it is very odd that these ghost stories should always be related at second or third hand. Now, I want to see a person who personally has seen the ghost, and then I will believe!"

Yes! People are more accustomed to hearing about ghosts now; and yet, even now, should it be a wife, daughter, or sister who ventures to narrate some supernatural experience, she is pooh-poohed, or laughed at, or told to "take a pill."

Now, I have seen a ghost — and am prepared to attest most solemnly to the fact, as well as to the truth of every word here set down. I have, of course, avoided names, but nothing else; so, without further preamble, I will state my case.

Some years ago I became the object of the infatuated adoration of a person of my own age and sex; and I use the word *infatuated* advisedly, because I feel now, as I did at the time, that neither I nor any mortal that ever lived could possibly be worthy of the overwhelming affection which my poor friend lavished upon me. I, on the other

side, was not ungrateful towards her, for I loved her in
return very dearly; but when I explain that I was a wife and
the mother of young children, and that she was unmar-
ried, it will easily be understood that our devotion to each
other must of necessity be rather one-sided; and this fact
caused some dispeace between us at times.

For many years my friend held a post at Court,
which she resigned soon after she began to know me;
and although her Royal Mistress, in her gracious kindness, assigned two houses to her, she gave them both up,
to be free to live near me in B ----- ; indeed, she gave
up relatives, old servants and comforts in order that she
might come and live (and die, alas!) in lodgings, over a
shop, near me. But she was not happy. She "gloomed"
over the inevitable fact that, in consequence of the difference in her home-circumstances and mine, I could
not be with her every day, and all day long. I think she
was naturally of an unhappy disposition, being deeply,
passionately, and unjustifiably jealous, and also painfully
incapable of taking things and people as they were. All
this gave me often much annoyance; but we were all the
same, sometimes very cheerful and happy together, and
sometimes — the reverse.

Later on, she, poor soul, was taken ill, and during
months of fluctuating health I nursed her — sometimes in
hope, sometimes without — and at moments during her
illness she found strange comfort in foretelling to me, after
the most "uncanny" fashion, things which she declared
would happen to me after her death. They were mostly
trivialities — little episodes concerning people and things
over whom and which we had talked and laughed together
for she was gifted with a keen sense of the ridiculous.

Amongst other things, she said to me one afternoon: —

"This bazaar for which we are working" (she had been
helping me for weeks for a charity bazaar, and I can now
see her dainty little hands, as she manipulated the delicate
muslin and lace. Poor, poor L --- !) "I shall be dead before
it takes place, and I shall see you at your stall, and on one

of the days of the bazaar, an old lady will come up to you and say: 'Have you any of poor Miss L --- 's work?' (mentioning me). And you will answer, 'Yes! here is some!' and you will show her this which I am working, and she'll say, 'Have you any more?' and you'll say, 'Yes' again; and she'll carry it all off, and say she buys it for 'poor Miss L --- 's sake.' And I shall know and see it all!"

I remember repeating, wonderingly, "What lady?"

She answered dreamily, "Oh! I don't know — but — some old lady! You'll see!"

And I am bound to say, this is exactly what occurred at the bazaar, months after her death; an old lady, with whom I was not acquainted, did buy all her work, having asked for it, and carrying it away "for her sake!" An old lady, too, whom I had never seen.

One other curious circumstance which attended her death was that, after looking forward with more than usual pleasure to my coming birthday (which she said would be "a more than commonly happy anniversary"), that was the very day on which she died!

I think that one of the sharpest regrets which I ever experienced in my life consisted in the fact that I was not with my dearest friend at the moment that she passed away. She had made me promise that I would be with her at the time, and, God knows, I had the fullest intention of fulfilling her wish, but on that very evening, of all others I was called away, and she died in my absence. I had been sitting by her bed-side all the afternoon, and all that evening I had held her dear hand, and had kept whispering comforting words in her ear; but latterly she had made no response, and was, seemingly, unconscious.

Suddenly a messenger came from my house (not a hundred yards, it was, away), saying my husband wanted me at once, as one of my children was ill. I looked at the nurse, who assured me there was "nothing immediate" impending; so, stooping over my poor friend, I whispered — at the same time pressing a kiss on her forehead — that "half an hour should see me at her side again." But she took no notice, and much against my will I hastily, and noiselessly, left the room.

Throwing a shawl over my head I hurried across the square, and as I passed the church the clock struck twelve, and I suddenly remembered that — to-day was my birthday!

I got back in less than half an hour, and on my return heard, to my everlasting sorrow, that I had not been gone ten minutes before my dear L--- became restless and uneasy, then suddenly starting up in her bed, she looked hastily around the room, gave a cry, then there came a rush of blood to her mouth, and after a few painful struggles, she sank back, gasped once or twice, and never moved again.

Of course, I thought then, and do to this day, that she was looking round the room for me, and that she had died feeling I had broken my faith with her. A bitter, never-failing regret!

I have given this slight sketch of the feelings which existed between me and my poor friend (before narrating the circumstances of her supernatural visit to me), just to emphasize the facts of the alluring fascination, the intense affection, which existed between us during her life-time, and which, I firmly believe, have lasted beyond her grave.

Quite a year and a half after her death, my poor L--- , with what motive I know not (unless it may have been, as I sometimes fondly hope, to assure me that she understood and sympathized with my sorrow at my having failed her at the moment of her extremity), appeared to me the same once — but never again. It occurred thus: —

I had been suffering all day from brow ague, and had gone early to bed — but not to sleep. All the evening I had been kept painfully awake by that same church clock which I have mentioned above. It seemed to strike oftener, louder, and more slowly than any clock I had ever had the misfortune to come across. Of course, my ailment of the moment caused the clock's vagaries to appear peculiarly painful, and I bore the annoyance very restlessly, with my face turned pettishly to the wall; but when the midnight hour began to chime, I felt as though I could bear it no longer. Muttering an impatient exclamation, I turned in my bed, so as to face the room, and looking across it, I saw my poor ---, standing close to a screen between me and the door, looking at me.

She was in her usual dress, wearing (what was then called) a "cross-over," which was tied behind; while her bonnet (which she was always in the habit of taking off as she came upstairs) was, as usual, hanging by the ribbon, on her arm. She had a smile on her face, and I distinctly noticed her lovely little white ears, which were always my admiration, and which were only half covered by her soft brown hair.

She stood — a minute it seemed — looking at me, then she glided towards me, and I, half-apprehensive that she was about to throw herself on my bed, exclaimed, jumping up in a sitting posture: —

"Dearest! what brings you here so late?"

With deep reverence be it spoken; but as soon as these words were out of my mouth I was irresistibly reminded of those spoken (Holy Writ tell us) by Saint Peter at the awful moment of the Transfiguration! Awed and dazed at the sight of the spiritual visitants, we are told he uttered words "not knowing what he said." These words of mine also seemed to leap to my lips, but with little meaning in them — if any.

As soon, however, as my voice had ceased, the apparition disappeared, and I remained some moments motionless.

One of the most curious features of the case is that, although I was very especially restless and awake at the moment of the appearance, I recognized my friend so completely, that I forgot also to recognize the fact that she had died; or, rather, it happened too quickly for me to bring that fact to mind. Indeed, it all took place in such a flash — in such a moment of time — so much quicker than I can tell it — and she looked so exactly like her well-known self, and that till she had disappeared, I really believed I was seeing her in the flesh! Of course, as soon as I had time to reflect, I remembered, and realized what it was I had seen!

I was not frightened, but I felt colder than I had ever felt in my life, and I have never felt so cold since, but the moisture seemed to pour off my body. I called no one to my assistance; all I realized was that God had permitted me to see her once more, and that perhaps He might send her to me again. But He has not done so, and, probably, now, He never will.

I lay awake all night afterwards, hoping for — and, I think, almost expecting — her again, and after the day had dawned I fell asleep.

Before telling my story to anyone, and dreading unspeakably all the doubting and sarcastic speeches which such a narration would inevitably call forth, I sent for my doctor, an old and trusted friend, and after making him talk rationally to me for some time, I asked him whether he considered me in an exalted state, or whether I had ever betrayed any hysterical tendencies. He reassured me heartily on these points, and then asked my reasons for such questionings. I thereupon opened my heart to him, and he neither ridiculed nor disbelieved, but, on the contrary, told me another case of the same kind which had lately happened to a friend of his; but he strongly advised me to keep my own council at present (which I did for some time), and kindly added that he did not look upon me as a lunatic, but simply as a woman for whom one corner of the curtain which guarded the unseen had been lifted.

In conclusion, I repeat I am ready to vouch for the truth of every word here set down, and also, should it be required, to give names — in private — to satisfy those who doubt.

3

SOME OLD HAUNTED HOUSES

Creaky floorboards, phantom footsteps, locked doors, rusty skeleton keys, fusty attics, dank cellars, curtains that billow in the breeze, thunder and lightning, moans and groans! Everyone who has ever been to the movies or watched television has, vicariously, entered a haunted house — and then tried to get out! Then the fun begins. The scary stuff! In this section moviegoers and television watchers will be able to read some stories of old-fashioned houses haunted by some old-fashioned ghosts and spirits.

THE DEVIL AT LARGE

Halifax Daily Reporter, July 15, 1869

To His Satanic Majesty, much has been attributed in days gone by, and at the present moment it appears the inclination of the masses is far from lessening his responsibility. The latest sensation His Majesty is responsible for is the destruction of the peace and harmony of the neighbourhood of Number 294, St. Mary Street, in so far that he has taken possession of the house bearing that number, and both during the day and dark night giving blood-curdling and mysterious proofs of his presence there. "The masses may laugh and jeer and sneer," as the inmates of the house say, "but if they were only here instead of us, they would soon find out the terrible truth we are telling." Upon enquiry, the following is the manner and means whereby His Majesty chooses to indicate his "being there." The house is a small one and under an apartment there is as usual in such dwellings, a small but deep and dark cellar, reached by a trap door through the floor. It is of this cellar the infernal head-quarters have taken possession. The first indication of anything unusual was the flying up of the trap door one day not long ago, and the ejection from the darkness below of a scrubbing brush, a lot of nails, eggshells, etc., etc., all accompanied by a strong smell of brimstone. The eruption done, the trap door closed again, leaving the horror-stricken and trembling inmates speechless, and in a profuse cold perspiration. Of course, the neigh-bours heard of the mysterious indications, and a number of them, boldly declaiming they did not believe it, and were not afraid, were invited to wait and see for them-selves. They did so, and sure enough as midnight drew near, bang-bang opened the trap door, out came nails, egg shells, feathers, etc., and out rushed, wildly scream-ing, the bold neighbours, who at once declared it was the devil, one being ready to swear he saw him sitting in a corner with his tail twisted round his neck. Then it was at once settled that the devil was in possession and no one else. The opening of the trap door and discharges took place at regular intervals. The police were then sent for and one of the number having entered the house, stood with the eldest female awaiting developments. He had not to wait long when up flew the trap door and out came the usual quantity of infernal machines. "Don't you see him? Don't you see him?" screamed the female, and away she rushed to tell that the devil had appeared even before a policeman. "Well," said the policeman, "if it's the devil in the cellar, I'll have you up for hav-ing spirits in the house without licence, that's all." It's but just to say the policeman looked into the cellar, but could see no signs of an infernal presence. Meanwhile, the trap door opens and closes at intervals, accompa-nied by the usual egg shells and iron nail discharges. The neighbourhood are convinced it is the devil himself, and with trepidation await the result of the infernal visit.

A hard-headed unbeliever says that the tenant in the house has for some times found the rent rather high and is desirous to lower it or have it lowered by some or any means surely, surely not. — *Montreal Gazette*.

A GHOST IN WHITBY

The Apparition Seen and Described

Sarnia Observer, August 15, 1873

For some days past the ghost, which, it is asserted, has been seen in the neighbourhood of the Court House, has been the talk of Whitby. The apparition, according to report, is seen under various forms — that of a black dog, which suddenly assumes the shape of a rather tall man, and from whose eyes burning red flames seem to issue, being the most familiar. Others assert that the ghost has been seen leaning with both hands on a staff standing on the Court House steps, or walking slowly between the steps and the entrance gate, at "the witching hour of night." Those who have had the temerity to approach the midnight intruder allege that on their approach it has all at once disappeared as in a flame of fire, sinking, as it were, into the ground. Others say that the most sorrowful moaning has been heard to proceed from where the ghost makes itself at first visible, and in fact all sorts of versions are given as to what has been seen and heard of what people persist in calling the "Court House Ghost." Last night a gathering assembled around the Court House railings, and remained there until nearly twelve o'clock to ascertain what could be seen, but at that hour hurried home to bed, cold and disappointed at the non-appearance of his ghostship. After the departure of the crowd, however, it is stated that the apparition was again seen by respectable and creditable people, that it was a tall figure walking heavily with a cane, and frequently stopping to look up at the sky, and groan while making its round wearily through the grounds in front of the Court House. There are, as may be expected, all sorts of surmises as to what the trouble is, and a determination avowed by many parties to find out all about it, and if it be a trick, to expose those who would impose this latest ghost hoax upon a community. — *Whitby Chronicle*.

FEARFUL SIGHT

The Devil Looking in at Parkhill — through the Bar Room Window — [From a Correspondent]

London Daily Advertiser, July 8, 1870

Allow me a little space in the columns of your valuable paper to describe one of the most fearful sights that ever was seen in this village, as witnessed by six or seven persons.

On the night of Thursday, June 30th, at about eleven o'clock at night, the inmates of a certain hotel in Parkhill were apparently enjoying themselves carousing, singing sacred songs, and having a regular jollification, when suddenly appeared at the bar room window a most fearful-looking object taking a look at them through the window, and more particularly at Mr. Hastings, who generally is styled "the deacon." The size of this unnatural object was about two feet in length, and not quite as broad, covering nearly two large panes of glass; its body was smooth, having four arms or legs extended with long, slender claws, and a fifth leg emanating from its body, upon which it turned backwards and forwards on the window. Its head was rather small, but therein were placed two fiery eyes, which stared like fiery globes at the inmates of the bar room. One would think that the age of such unnatural visions had long ago passed away. The consternation and awe of the beholders of this object cannot adequately be described, particularly that of Hastings's. To his horror he beheld two flaming eyes looking at him through the window. What to do in such a crisis he did not know, imagining that he was the object of pursuit, and feeling himself unprepared to accompany the old gentleman he took to his heels, and bound for the hall door, leading to the stairway; summoning all his strength and courage, the deacon with one or two such strides as he never before in his life had made, found himself at the top of a flight of stairs twenty feet long. But unfortunately for the deacon, he nearly lost his coat tail in his flight, it having come in contact with the railing. A dint of about an inch deep is said to have been left in the post.

The incident is all the talk in Parkhill; though there are those who profess to know that the object purposely placed at the window was much less formidable than the excited imagination of Hastings pictured it.

GHOST STORY

Free Press, Acton, Ontario, March 6, 1879

A stout Yorkshire farmer of the name of James Wreggit, having emigrated to Canada, settled himself and family on a good farm which he rented in one of the townships. He was considered fair-dealing and honourable in all transactions with his neighbours, and in every respect bore a most excellent character. In the farmer's house was a first-floor sitting-room with a large fire-place. In this room the children slept, but from the first night evinced the greatest dislike to going to bed there, screaming with terror, and saying that a man was in the room with them. For a long time the parents paid no attention to their complaints. During harvest time a change was made, and the farmer himself slept in this room, as it was cooler and more convenient. The first night he slept there he was about to rise almost before the break of day, when, glancing towards the fire-place, he saw standing there a stranger of a dissipated drunken appearance. "Ha'lo! What's thee doing there?" was his very natural exclamation. Receiving no reply, "Won't thee speak? I'll make thee speak!" and picking up one of his heavy boots from the bedside he was preparing to throw it at the intruder, when the man, suddenly raising his arm as if to ward off the blow, vanished in a moment from before his eyes. Wreggit, unable to get this matter of his head, brooded over it till the next day, when about noon he entered into conversation with a neighbour who was working with him, and asked him to describe the former tenant of the farm, who had died from excessive drinking. The description so entirely resembled the man he had seen in the room that he at once exclaimed, "I saw him last night!" Wreggit recounted this to some old friends near whom he had lived before taking the farm, and it is from the dictation of one of his auditors that I have written down this remarkable circumstance. At the time neither Wreggit nor his friend had the slightest belief in apparitions.

REMARKABLE PHENOMENA

This account offers a view of a farming community in Ontario. It appeared in *The Globe* (Toronto), September 9, 1880. The incident took place near Crosshill, Wellesley Township, Ontario.

Remarkable Phenomena — The Windows of a Farmer's Dwelling — Repeatedly Shattered to Pieces — And the Inmates Drenched with Water

WELLESLEY, Sept. 6. — A very extraordinary story having gained currency in this section of the country that Mr. George Manser, a very respectable and well-to-do farmer residing near the village of Crosshill, in the township of

Wellesley, had with his family been driven out of his dwelling by the mysterious breaking of his windows and showering down of water in dry weather, your correspondent took occasion to-day to visit the place and interview Mr. Manser and his family in regard to the report in circulation. On approaching the house he noticed the windows, six in number, closed up with boards, which still further excited his curiosity and gave reason to believe that there must be some ground for the report.

The house I found to be a large one-and-a-half story hewed log building, rather old but in a very good state of repair, situated a short distance from the highway on the most elevated part of the farm. On stating the object of my visit Mr. Manser very kindly showed me through the building and gave me the following facts:

About a month or six weeks ago the glass in the windows began to break, several panes bursting out at a time. These were replaced with new ones only to meet the same fate. A careful examination was then made to ascertain the cause. It was at first supposed that the house being old and getting a little out of shape might affect the windows, but the sash was found to be quite easy and even loose in the frames. Then the family are surprised and put to flight with a shower of water, saturating their beds, their clothing, in fact everything in the house, whilst the sun is shining beautifully in the horizon, and outside all is calm and serene. Nothing daunted, Mr. Manser repairs to the village store and obtains a fresh supply of glass, and even tries the experiment of using some new sash, and utterly failing to discover the mysterious cause of either the breaking of the glass or the sudden showers of water, all taking place in broad day light. His neighbours are called in, and whilst they are endeavouring to solve the mystery, a half dozen or more panes of glass would suddenly burst, making a report similar to that of a pistol shot. Mr. Manser states that he inserted more than one hundred new lights of glass and then gave it up, and boarded up the windows, first taking out the sash and setting them aside, but on account of the continued bursts of water, they were compelled to remove all their beds, some to the wood-shed and others to the barn, leaving only those things in the house that are not so liable to be damaged by the showering process to which he has been so repeatedly subjected. He has commenced the erection of a new dwelling, hoping thereby to escape those remarkable tricks of nature, or whatever it may be, which seem to continue their operations to the old house. If these strange occurrences had taken place at night one would suspect that Mr. Manser was the victim of some mischievous people, but occurring in the daytime in the presence of the family and other witnesses, and in fine weather, it seems very difficult of solution. Various theories have been put forward, but none of them seem sufficient to account for the double phenomena of the sudden showers of water under a good roof in fine weather, and the oft-repeated bursting out of the windows. Perhaps you or some of your scientific readers can crack the nut.

A MIDNIGHT APPARITION

A Supernatural Visitor

Ottawa Free Press, June 16, 1882

A respected and jolly hotel keeper on the Perth Road from Kingston, recently at the midnight hour, when silence reigned in the tavern and the noisy bibulists had sought repose, was quietly roused from sleep, and at once recognized something standing near his bed in the appearance of a brother recently deceased, as also a man well known around the country who died some short time ago, who cautioned the landlord to at once give up selling drink, or if he did not stop giving out liquor, ruining the bodies and souls of his fellow men he would surely merit just condemnation; or to use his own words, "go to h -- ll."

So convinced was he of the truth of the apparition and meaning he received, that he got up early next morning, took down his sign board, locked up his bar room and will on no account give liquor to any one. This landlord is well known as a sober, clear-headed, conscientious man, a good neighbor in every way, and a man much respected by all who know him. Would not our temperance friends wish that those midnight visitants may also appear to and tickle the consciences of some other of the publicans who are not yet too hardened to reform.

THE CLARION-SQUARE GHOST

A Christmas Tale of Toronto —
Specially Written for **The World**

Toronto World, December 25, 1883

The natural and proper scene of a ghost story is some lonely old mansion in the country, whose better days have long deserted it, and which is now falling gradually into decay. A ghost is indigenous to such a house, with its long flights of stairs leading nowhere in particular, its gloomy straggling corridors which run hither and thither, and its musty, old-fashioned rooms, not less mysterious and gloomy. The blue room, and the red room, and the room which a hundred years ago was shut up because of some terrible deed committed within it, at the mention of which the gray-headed butler shakes his head solemnly and says nothing, offer attractions which no ghost in the course of my reading has ever been able to resist. The portraits of the periwigged and balloon-skirted ancestors which hang grimly on the walls, seem inanimate enough, but the on-looker secretly feels, as he gazes on them, that there is not one which is unprepared to step out of the frame when the clock strikes at midnight, and proceed at once to play all sorts of unwarrantable and ghostly antics. The wind, too, at night has a fashion of moaning dolorously around the corners and among the nooks and crannies of the old building, while the trees which cower close to its moss-covered sides, bend over and tap with their branches at the windows of the visitor's room, and add fresh horrors to his lot. For, be it observed, it is always a stranger, some guest invited by the family perhaps, who is treated in this shabby way by the inhospitable old place. It is no credit to the house of this kind to have a ghost or two in it. Indeed, as modern advertisements say, it would not be complete without one.

Number 39, Clarion-Square, is not at all a place of this kind, and you would as soon think of looking for a ghost in a baker's shop as inside its walls. Judging from appearances indeed, no building in the whole city of Toronto would be less likely to harbor a supernatural occupants. As everybody who is acquainted with the Square knows, Number 39 is one of the new red brick row of houses, all of which are built exactly on the same pattern, and all of which bear equal testimony to the thriftiness of the builder, who has successfully solved the problem of how to get the maximum of rent in return for the minimum of outlay. True, the walls are not very tight, and the doors not very close, so that a moderately flexible ghost would experience very little difficulty in any of these respects, and as the plumbing is not better than that of the ordinary brick house built to see, his ghostship could, I am convinced, if he found every other means of ingress blocked, obtain easy entrance by way of the waste-pipe. At the time of my story, Number 39 did duty as a genteel boarding-house, and fairly comfortable we were on the whole with Mrs. Rackham. I — that is the secretary and paymaster of a thriving railway company — had a large room which opened off the first landing up-stairs, and immediately above mine were the apartments of Gormes and Johnson, two students of the law, of whom Johnson was a harum-scarum fellow, chiefly noted for his love of mischief and late hours, while

Gormes, on the contrary, was steady and studious, with hopes someday of becoming a Q.C., and in the meantime a regular attendant at the Oak street church. One evening in December, not many years ago, as I was reclining in my easy chair after dinner, in front of a cheerful fire, Gormes tapped at the door, and in response to my invitation entered and took a seat. We lit our pipes, and as I liked nothing better than a chat with my young friend Gormes, who was an earnest, clever fellow, I essayed a conversation on one of our customary themes. Somewhat to my surprise, he made little or no effort to reply, and our talk flagged. I looked at him and saw he wore a perturbed look.

"Gormes," said I, "what's the matter? Have you got the blues? You look as if you had seen a ghost."

"So I have," was the rather startling reply.

"Tut, you're joking," said I, though somewhat disconcerted by Gormes' serious face.

"Not joking a bit," returned he; "I saw a ghost, or something very like one, no longer ago than last night."

"Where?"

"In this very house, and in my own room," said Gormes.

This was coming near home indeed; for, as I said before, Gormes' room was immediately above mine, and if a nocturnal visitor of this kind had called on him I was very likely to receive a similar compliment next.

"Tell me how it was," I said.

"Well," replied he, "you'll laugh at me, perhaps, but I saw something last night that wasn't of this world, or else I'm not Gormes, and I'm not sitting here on this chair looking at you."

As he was certainly both, I could offer nothing by way of objection and Gormes went on.

"I'm not particularly superstitious, and I haven't much faith in ghost yarns as a rule, but last night I was lying in bed reading, after everybody else was asleep, yourself included, and not a soul moving in the house. It was

Taylor's Equity I had, for that's one of the books on the list for our next exam, and I was reading away when suddenly I felt constrained to lift my eyes from the book and raise them to the top of the door opposite the foot of the bed. In doing so, I caught a glimpse of something that looked like a face disappearing quickly from behind the fanlight, just as if somebody were standing on a chair peering in, and drawing away as soon as noticed. I got up and opened the door, but there was nobody there. Only half convinced that I had not dropped into a momentary doze and been deceived by my imagination I went back to bed and took up my book again. Presently I had the same feeling of being obliged to look up, and again I saw the face withdrawing from above the door. Thinking it might be some trick of Johnson's I stole along quietly to his room, but no, his door was locked, and on listening I could hear him snoring inside. Besides, it was not possible for him to have come out of bed and climbed up to the top of my door without making noise enough for me to hear him. I returned to my room and in a little while the same thing occurred again in precisely the same way. I cannot be mistaken. I was fully awake and in possession of my senses, and I say I saw that face three times above my door last night."

"What did it look like?" said I, impressed by the seriousness of Gormes' manner.

"The face," replied Gormes, "was that of a young girl, with a queer, troubled expression. And the strangest thing was that beyond being a little nervous, I didn't feel in the least frightened. But I don't know what to make of it. I always thought ghosts were out of date."

Then after a pause:

"Don't tell Johnson or any one. If I don't see it again I shall think it was all an illusion, though dear knows *Taylor's Equity* is not the kind of book to excite one's imagination."

Next morning I inquired of Gormes if he had seen anything the previous night, but he shook his head and said he hadn't. Nothing occurred in two weeks, and then

Gormes left the house, saying that though he had seen nothing more, he could not any longer sleep comfortably in the room. A few days after his departure, I met Johnson on the stairs in the act of removing his trunk and other valuables, as if he were taking leave of his quarters.

"Hello! Johnson," said I, "going away? I didn't know you intended moving."

"Neither did I," responded Johnson, "until to-day. I wouldn't stay here any longer if I were paid for it."

"What's up now?" I queried. "Had a quarrel with Mrs. Rackham?"

"No," said he, "but I've wanted to change for a long time."

Then seeing his explanation was somewhat contradictory, he drew me into my own room, and having closed the door, said with unusual solemnity:

"This place is haunted, and I've seen it."

"Seen what?"

"Why, the ghost." And Johnson went on to relate in almost precisely the words Gormes had used: how he had been reading in his room late the night before; how he had felt compelled to lift his eyes to the half-open door, and how, as he did so, a face had suddenly disappeared behind it, how he had got up and looked but found nothing; and how the same thing had occurred twice again before he turned out the light. On my pressing him he recalled that the face seemed to be that of a girl or young woman, and had an anxious look, as of a person in fear or perplexity.

"I don't expect you to believe me," continued Johnson, "but that's what I saw, and I don't propose to stay in the house where there's any such nonsense going on."

"Did Gormes tell you why he left?" said I.

"No," returned Johnson, "why?"

"Well," said I, "he said he saw something of the kind, too."

"That settles it," said Johnson; "Number 39 sees me no more. And you had better come too or it'll be your turn next."

"Thanks, I'm pretty comfortable. I guess I shan't move yet. I want to see the ghost," said I.

Nevertheless I was not at all reassured. The accounts which had been given by Gormes and Johnson, whom I had no reason to suspect of being in collusion, agreed so exactly that I was more than half inclined to believe they had both actually seen something. What that something was I was anxious to know, and after a little conflict between my resolution and the misgivings I secretly entertained I determined to stay and see whether as Johnson had predicted "it would be my turn next." This was in broad daylight, and my nerves were correspondingly strong. When evening approached, however, my courage weakened and I began to repent that I had not followed the example of my friends and left too. It so happened that that night — a week or so before Christmas — I had the whole house to myself, Mrs. Rackham and husband having gone out to spend the evening at a neighbor's. I sat before my fire as usual, thinking partly of the strange events that had occurred of late, and partly of the journey which lay before me on the morrow, when I was going along the line to pay the band's their month's wages, for which purpose I had that afternoon drawn from the bank several thousand dollars, and placed the same in the breast-pocket of my overcoat. All was silent — so silent I could hear the ticking of my gold timepiece which lay on the dressing-case close at hand. Outside the snow was falling noiselessly, yet thickly, and once in a while I could see below the half-lowered blind that the wind caught up some of it from the kitchen roof just below my window and dashed it against the panes. Hark! what's that? Only the falling of a lump of coal in the self-feeder downstairs. But listen! isn't that some one walking about in the room above? No, it's the man next door. Pshaw! I'm getting nervous. I sit a little while longer, and at last begin to feel sleepy. All at once I am wide awake, every sense on the alert. I hear nothing; but I feel there is somebody or something behind me. I turn quickly around and lo! the face at the door. 'Tis the ghost! I jerk open the door and rush to the top of the stairs! Again the face! and in some mysterious way moving straight through the glass door in the hall, and turning one beckoning look on me before it disappears. I seize a hat from the rack, and follow impetuously into the street. Is that the drifting snow or a ghostly face at the lamppost a few yards away? When I get there, nothing. Round the Square I go, still looking for the face, and round the next block, and round half a dozen blocks, but finding it not, and at last awake to the fact that I am out in a snowstorm overcoatless, and with nothing on my feet more substantial than a pair of slippers. I make my way back to the house as best I can. Fortunately, I never part with my latch-key, and so get in without trouble, resolved to give Mrs. Rackham notice in the morning, and to leave before night. On entering my room, the first thing that catches my eye is my window wide open, through which the snow is drifting in. Wondering what has happened, I look around. My watch is gone! I rush to my Newmarket. Gone is my wallet! The truth is too clear; during my short absence I've been robbed, robbed of watch and money, and probably thrown out of my situation, to be a suspected man for life for who would believe that I had lost the company's funds in so extraordinary a way? But all these things in a moment appear as trifles, for turning round, I catch sight of something lying on the bed, and realize how narrow is the escape which I have had. There, glittering in the light of the gas jet which is still burning, is a long, sharp, deadly looking knife, a grim and murderous weapon indeed, and a surer and more silent instrument than the noisy revolver. Beyond a doubt, it has been left behind in his hasty flight by a wretch who would have cut my throat with as little compunction as he has shown in robbing me. But I have no time to lose even in reflections of this kind, and so give alarm at once. The neighbors rush in and a policeman is called, who takes possession of the knife and discovers the ladder by which the scoundrel obtained access to the room from the kitchen roof below, but this is all. The miscreant's footsteps are already covered by the falling snow, and there is nothing to show which way he has gone. And though I have reason to believe that every diligence was used by the police, the owner of the knife has never turned up to this day. As for the money, it was in bank bills, and the same has long ago been transferred to the wrong side of the profit and loss account in the railway company's books. It was evident next morning that the rooms upstairs formerly occupied by Gormes and Johnson had also been visited and ransacked, but as they were unoccupied no further booty was obtained. It was doubtless fortunate for these young men that they left the house when they did; otherwise my fate, or even a worse one, might have befallen them. The theory was advanced by the police that I had been seen at the bank during the day drawing out this large sum of money by the villain, who then followed me home and laid his plans for committing the robbery — and murder if necessary — accordingly. But this was mere theory, and the misery which attended the commission of the crime still hides its perpetrator.

As I carried out my intentions of leaving the house next day, I cannot say whether or not the mysterious face has ever reappeared at Number 39. From the fact that a genteel boarding establishment still flourishes there, though presided over by another than Mrs. Rackham, which I understand to be well patronized. I infer that it has not, nor do I think it likely, as I have never heard of any burglaries or attempted murders having since taken place there. I am happy to say that the railway authorities after a fall investigation into the case, unanimously agreed that there were no grounds whatever for attaching suspicion to me, and that they meant this, an increase of salary which the New Year brought me abundantly testified. I have never since that eventful night shortly before Christmas 188— been able to regard ghosts in the same light as previously. Before that time I fully shared in the general disrespect, nay, dislike, in which they are held, but now there is a large corner of my heart which I keep warm on their account, and should like nothing better than an opportunity to personally express my gratitude to one of their number. Indeed, I have come to think that ghosts are a very much reprehended class. However this may be, Gormes and Johnson agree with me in being very grateful to the particular ghost which rendered us such good services at 39 Clarion-Square. If we are ever able to do anything for that ghost by way of return you may be sure we will do it.

BOTHERED BY GHOSTS

Strange Sounds in a Clarence Street House — Occupant Thinks It a Case of Spite

Daily Free Press, Ottawa, Ontario, March 1, 1890

"I'm surprised at your living in this house so long. Ghosts!"

This is the wording of a scrawling epistle received a couple of weeks ago by Mrs. Chenier, of 239 Clarence street, who has been terrorized since the receipt by all sorts of noise every night around the house.

Mrs. Chenier is not inclined to be superstitious nor in any way afraid of ghosts, but the noises she has heard have made her somewhat nervous and have interfered a little with her regular sleep.

She stated yesterday that she thought the whole thing was a matter of spite against the owner of the house. For the past week she heard vigorous knocking at her door. She went out once or twice, but could see no one in the immediate vicinity. She stood this patiently until the last couple of nights, when the "ghosts," to whom she refers as human tricksters, made a peculiar noise on the roof of the house and apparently dangled a chain down the chimney. On one occasion she went out and looked up on the roof, but it being slanted, she thinks a party could avoid being seen by lying down on the opposite side behind the chimney.

Last night the noise became worse, so Mrs. Chenier has asked the policeman on the beat to keep a watch for the ghosts. The request will be complied with, and, if no cause for the noise can be discovered from the outside, the bobby will search inside. The house is a small one and the constable is confident of corralling the "spirits" in some way or another if they continue their pranks.

MY TOWER GHOSTS

King's County News, Hampton, New Brunswick., January 3, 1895

At one corner of my house is a tall, wide tower, rising high above the trees which surround it. In one of the upper rooms of this tower I work and think, and here in the evening and early part of the night, I used to be quite alone except for the ghosts.

Before I had come to this house, I knew that the tower was haunted but I did not mind that. As the ghosts had never done anyone any harm, I thought I should really be glad of their company which must certainly be different from the company of ordinary people. So, when I had arranged an upper room in the tower so that I might pleasantly work and think therein, I expected the ghosts to come to me, and should have been very much disappointed if they had not.

I did not exactly understand these ghosts, of which I had heard nothing definite except that they haunted the tower and I did not know in what way they would manifest themselves to me. It was not long, however, after I had begun to occupy the room before the ghosts came to me. One evening a little before Christmas, after everybody in the house but myself had gone to bed, and all was quiet outside and inside, I heard a knock and was on the point of saying "Come in!" when the knock was repeated and I found that it did not come from the door but from the wall. I smiled.

You cannot come in that way, I thought, unless there are secret doors in these walls, and even then you must open them for yourself.

I went on with my writing, but I soon looked up again, for I thought I heard a chair gently pushed back against the wall in a corner behind me, and almost immediately I heard a noise as if some little boy had dropped a number of marbles, or perhaps pennies, but there was no chair in the corner at which I looked, and there were no pennies nor marbles on the floor.

Night after night I heard my ghosts — for I had come to consider them as mine, which I had bought with the house — and although I could not see them there were so many ways in which they let me know they existed that I felt for them a sort of companionship. When in the quiet hours of early night I heard their gentle knocks I knew they would have been glad to come in, and I did not feel lonely.

Now and then I thought I heard the voices of the ghosts, sometimes outside, under my window, and sometimes behind me in the distant corner of the room. Their tones were low and plaintive, and I could not distinguish words or phrases, but it often seemed as if they were really speaking to me, and that I ought to try to understand and answer them. But I soon discovered that these voice-like sounds were caused by the vagrant breezes going up and down the tall chimney of the tower, making aeolian tones, not of music, but of vague and indistinct speech.

The winter passed, and at last there came a time when I saw one of the ghosts. It was in the dusk of an evening, early in spring, and just outside of an open window, that it appeared to me. It was as plain to my sight as if it had been painted in delicate half-tones against a somber background of tender foliage and evening sky.

It was clad from head to foot in softest gray, such as phantoms of the night are said to love, and over its shoulders and down its upright form were thrown the fleecy folds of a mantle so mistily gray that it seemed to blend into the dusky figure it partly shrouded. The moment I saw it I knew it saw me. Out of its cloudy grayness there shone two eyes, black, clear and sparkling, fixed upon me with questioning intensity. I sat gazing with checked breath at this ghost of the tower.

Suddenly I leaned forward — just a little — to get a better view of the apparition, when, like a bustling bubble, it was gone, and there was nothing before me but the background of foliage and evening sky.

Frequently after that I saw the ghost or it may have been one of the others, for it was difficult, with these gray visions, with which one must not speak or toward which it was hazardous to move even a hand, to become so well acquainted that I should know one from another. But there they were; not only did I hear them; not only, night after night, did my ears assure me of their existence, but in the shadows of the trees, as the summer came on, and on the lonelier stretches of the lawn I saw them and I knew that in good truth my home was haunted.

Late one afternoon, while walking in my grounds, I saw before me one of the specters of my tower. It moved slowly over the lawn, scarcely seeming to touch the tips of the grass, and with no more sound than a cloud would make when settling on a hilltop. Suddenly it turned its bright watchful eyes upon me, and then with a start that seemed to send a thrill even through the gray mantle which lightly touched its shoulders it rose before my very eyes until it was nearly as high as the top of my tower.

Wings it had not nor did it float in the air; it ran like a streak of gray electricity along the lightning rod, only instead of flashing down in, as electricity would pass from the sky, it ran upward. I did not see this swiftly moving spirit reach the topmost point of the rod, for at a point where the thick wire approached the eaves it vanished.

By this time I had come to the conclusion, not altogether pleasant to my mind, that my ghosts were taking advantage of my forbearance, with their mystic knocks and signals in the night and their visits in the daylight and that there must be too many of them in my tower. I must admit that they annoyed me very little and I was not in the least afraid of them, but there were others who came into my tower and slept in some of its rooms and to the minds of visitors and timorous maids there was something uncanny and terrifying in these midnight knocks and scratches.

So, having concluded from what I had seen that day that it was the very uppermost part of the tower which had become the resort of these gray sprites, and from which they came to disturb our quiet and repose, I determined to interfere with their passage from the earth to my tower top. If, like an electric current, they used the lightning rod as a means of transit, I made a plan which would compel them to use it in the conventional and proper way. The rod was placed that the lightning might come down it, not that it might go up, so I set myself to put the rod in a condition that it would permit the ghosts to descend as the lightning did, but which would prevent them from going up.

Accordingly I thoroughly greased the rod for a considerable distance above the ground.

"No," said I to myself, "you may all come down, one after the other whenever you like. You will descend very quickly when you reach the greased part of the rod, but you will not go up it again. You are getting very bold, and if you continue your mad revels in my tower you will frighten people and give my house a bad name. You may become dryads if you like and shut yourself up in the hearts of the tall and solemn oaks. There you may haunt the blue jays and the woodpeckers, but they will not tell tales of ghostly visits, which may keep my friends away and make my servants give me warning."

After that there were no more gray flashes up my lighting rod, though how many came down it I know not, and the intramural revels in the tower ceased. But not for long. The ghosts came back again; perhaps not so many as before, but still enough for them to let me know that they were there.

How they ascended to their lofty haunts I could not tell, nor did I try to find out. I accepted the situation. I could not contend with these undaunted sprites.

One evening in the autumn, outside the same window from which I had seen the first ghost of the tower, I saw another apparition, but it was not one of the gray specters to which I had become accustomed. It was a jet black demon. Its eyes large, green and glaring, shone upon me, and it was as motionless and hard as a statue cut in coal.

For only an instant I saw it, and then in a flash, like the apparition I had first seen from that window, it disappeared. After that I saw the demon again and again and strange to say the ghosts in my tower became fewer and fewer, and at last disappeared altogether. The advent of the black spirit seemed to have exerted an evil influence over the spirits in gray, and like the Indian in the presence of the white man, they faded away and gradually became extinct.

The last time I saw one of my ghosts it appeared to me late on the November afternoon among the brown foliage of an aged oak, just as a dryad might have peeped forth from her leafy retreat wondering if the world were yet open to her for a ramble under the stars. The world was open to my gray ghost, but only in one direction. Between it and me could be seen among the shadows of the ground the dark form of the demon, trembling and waiting. Then away from the old oak, away from my house and tower, along the limbs of the trees which stood on the edge of the wood, slowly and silently, my ghost vanished from my view like a little gray cloud, gently moving over the sky, at last dissolving out of my sight.

Now, in the early hours of the night my tower is quiet and still. There are no more knocks, no more revels in the hidden passages in the walls. My ghosts are gone. All that I hear now are the voices in the chimney, but I know that these are only imaginary voices, and, therefore they produce in me no feeling of companionship. But my ghosts really existed.

4

STRANGE EVENTS
AND STRANGER PEOPLE

In this section will be found phenomena that are not readily explained. The blind seemingly see, the deaf apparently hear. Events that occur in distant parts of the world might be accessible to people living far, far away. Even the future may be "seen" or foretold. Prophecies are fulfilled! All through the ages there have been reports of such powers, and these reports, when not anecdotal, are quite often well-attested by reputable people, professionally trained observers, et cetera. Yet such powers, if and when they are manifested, exert themselves sporadically at best. It seems that they cannot be recreated in laboratories. Carl Sagan, the astronomer and advocate of the scientific method, nourished a sense of awe and wonder about man and the natural world, especially the cosmos. He was attracted to mysteries, yet all the while he kept foremost in his mind Marcello Truzzi's maxim: "Extraordinary claims require extraordinary evidence."

THE OLD WOMAN'S ACCOUNT

A Native woman predicts the outcome of a battle fought elsewhere between her people and the English forces based on a vision. This instance of successful "jugglery" (the term used by Europeans to describe the work of medicine men or shamans) among the Mississauga Indians of that region was reported by Pierre Pouchot, a French officer at Fort Niagara in 1756. His account appears in *Memoir upon the Late War in North America, Between the French and English, 1755–60* (Roxbury, Massachusetts. Printed for W. Elliott Woodward, 1866), a two-volume work translated from French and edited by Franklin B. Hough. (For knowledge of this reference I am grateful to Donald Smith of the Department of

History of the University of Calgary.) Pouchot's circumstantial account, although sketchy in the extreme, is interesting in at least one way. It states that an unnamed officer took notes and "confirmed" the Native woman's account. In other words, the account is not simply hearsay or rumour but fact, and although brief, represents centuries of "jugglery."

> At the end of six or seven days, they [the French officers at Fort Niagara] enquired why they [the Mississauga Indian women] made no more medicine, when an old woman replied that their people had beaten [won]; that she had juggled and that they had killed many people. An officer who knew these juggleries, wrote down the spot, the day that she designated, and when the party returned, he questioned the Indians and prisoners whose answers confirmed the old woman's account.

A REPUTED CANADIAN WITCH

"A Reputed Canadian Witch" appeared in *The Bathurst Courier* (Bathurst, New Brunswick), April 7, 1854. The account is apparently reprinted from the *Bytown Gazette* (Bytown, now Ottawa, Ontario).

> We find the following singular statement in the *Bytown Gazette*: —
> GROSS SUPERSTITION. — Incredible as it may appear, there are still persons to be found in Canada, who believe in the existence of witches, and of the practices formerly ascribed to them. In the neighbouring country of Russell lives an aged dame, whom the superstition of her neighbours has from some cause or other invested with the character of a witch, and to whose malevolent agency are ascribed all the causes of mental malady, and lingering sickness that have occurred for some years in the neighbourhood. On the principle, we suppose, that there is no poison to which Providence has not provided an antidote,

the neighbourhood has also furnished a person of the opposite sex, who has for some time followed the lucrative and pious occupation of exorcising the witch, at the rate of six dollars per victim. A clergyman from Bytown, hearing of the absurd stories that were afloat, remonstrated with the man, and so far apparently with success, that he promised to forego his calling in future, although we have not heard of his having restored any of the fees previously received by him for his supposed mastery over the Black Art. To argue the enlightened persons from the supposed witch's vicinity, out of their belief in her supernatural league with the powers of darkness, seems so far a hopeless task, and it is even at this moment believed that a person labouring under disease of the liver is the victim of her diabolic machinations. An instance came under the personal knowledge of the writer two years ago in which the sickness of an individual was ascribed to her agency. Nor is it possible to reason persons, otherwise apparently intelligent, out of the belief, the Witch of Endor being appealed to as an unanswerable argument that such things can exist.

THE VERY POLE ITSELF

"Mrs. Denton was a psychometrist, who could hold a rock or a bone in her hand and tell whence it came and what had befallen its owner. Here is the account of a sitting she gave while in Québec." So wrote the scholar Joscelyn Godwin in *Arktos: The Polar Myth in Science, Symbolism, and Nazi Survival* (Rapid City, Michigan.: Phanes Press, 1993). Godwin then noted, "While explorers of several nations spent the latter part of the nineteenth century crossing Greenland and northern Canada, the Boston family of William Denton was making its own investigations." It is not surprising that the psychometrists of the day and its clairvoyants found evidence of a warm Arctic sea encompassing a temperate polar climate. The passage is reproduced by Godwin from Volume I of William Denton and Elizabeth M.F. Denton's *The Soul of Things; or, Psychometric Researches and Discoveries* (1863). The account hardly marks "a new beginning in

Arctic exploration," but it is an item for any study of "psychic archaeology" as well as the enduring legend of the existence of a remote tropical valley along the banks of the Nahanni River of the Yukon Territory.

One evening in December, 1862, when trying a crystal of amethystine quartz from St. Catherine's Bay, on the Saguenay, a tributary of the St. Lawrence, Mrs. Denton seemed to obtain, very readily, comprehensive views of the country to the north of there, and eventually appeared to pass into the polar regions, though nothing of the kind was anticipated when the experiment commenced.

"The Hudson's Bay region is a great deal warmer than I supposed. I see lakes and streams over such a wide surface that they seem like pictures. I had no idea that these extreme northern regions had as temperate a climate as they seem to me now to possess.... It really seems warmer than it does here. It is so strange, it appears like another world. It seems a long way beyond the boundary of this continent. I fancy that must be the very pole itself. There is water between me and it. It does not seem as cold as I should have expected to find it, and I see neither snow nor ice. The heat seems to come from the interior, and yet I cannot think it possible. There seems to be boiling springs there."

SINGULAR PHENOMENA

A Girl Becomes Blind, But Can Tell the Time and See Colours

Winnipeg Free Press, November 16, 1882

A girl who has been lying sick in Peterborough for some time is commanding a fair share of public attention there through phenomenal circumstances connected with her illness. Miss Minnie Tracey was employed in the dining room of the Oriental Hotel, and on October 28, she was attacked by some previous sickness, by convulsions and lockjaw. Her sufferings continued till Tuesday, October 31, when she almost recovered.

During the interval Miss Tracey exhibited some very curious phenomena. The patient was unable to see, but surprised the doctor and those present at a particular time by saying that it was 10 minutes to 1:00. No clock was in the room and the time was correct to a minute. Not only was she blind, but even if she were not so, there was no clock for her to see from where she lay. Moreover she was blindfolded and told the time with accuracy. While blindfolded she felt and designated the colour of gloves, distinguished the colour of two sides of a paper, one of which was white, the other red. In fact the parties about her bed were astonished at the marvellous way in which she distinguished colours which she by no possibility could see. The girl even could tell on what part of a paper there was printed matter if there happened to be any.

More than this, she recognized her friends by touching their hands, and if the person presented to her was a stranger she readily recognized the fact. A reporter of the *Peterborough Review* visited the girl and he was astonished. Below is an extract from his remarks on the occasion of his visit:

"Was it this angel that told you the colours and the time and other things you told us yesterday?" asked the reporter.

"Yes, it was the same angel," she replied; "when I touched a colour it would tell me what it was, and it would tell me the time. When Dr. O'Shea brought in his cousin I could not see him and never knew him, but the angel told me who he was."

Again was her statement confirmed by Mrs. McIntyre and the doctor, in so far as they said Dr. O'Shea's cousin did call to see her, and although his name was not mentioned, she told at once that he was a cousin of the doctor. "On Monday evening," she said in answer to a question, "I could not see any one, and it was then the angels first came to me, and they stayed with me until I could see last evening, and then they said 'goodbye' three times, and have not returned. I cannot tell anything now, only by my ordinary sight."

DEATH WARNINGS

"Death Warnings" appeared in the *Montreal Star* (Montreal, Quebec), October 16, 1883. It was signed "D.E." The original text suffers from poor printing. The key line ("I is dead") may be read in another way ("'Tis dead").

A correspondent writes from Cornwall as follows: —

In reading in your issue of the 11st inst., about the death warnings, it brings to my recollection an incident which happened with my own knowledge, and in my own family, which has left a deep impression on my mind.

My youngest child, a daughter of six years, was suffering from the after symptoms of a severe attack of measles. Her illness continued for upwards of several months before she died. My eldest son, who was then pursuing his studies in University College, Toronto, was greatly attached to his little sister, and hardly a day passed during her illness without an inquiry being made about her, and a message being sent to her.

On the morning of her death a message was received from my son, and giving it in his own words a few days later, "I was awakened out of my sleep by something I cannot intelligently describe, saying in a sharp clear voice, 'I is dead.'" He at this moment awakened his college mate who roomed with him, and who is now one of the leading members of the Ontario Bar in Toronto, and who lives to confirm the circumstances, related to him, the occurrence, and the time was noted. It was on the 27th day of January, 1859, at 20 minutes to five o'clock, a.m. A few years after my son passed over to the silent land, and we often discussed before his death, which was a happy death, these mysterious warnings.

Hush, tiding, at last she is gone before,
A whispering has caught mine ear,
She is waiting for me on the spirit above,
While I linger idly here.
— D.E.

SAW THE FIGHT

In Her Dream

Newfoundland Evening Telegram, St. John's, Newfoundland, March 5, 1900

Toronto, Feb. 23. — Miss Vanderwater, the sister of Morris Vanderwater, of 120 Sorauren avenue, one of the wounded Toronto volunteers, relates a strange incident of second sight, and is confident, although she has not yet received a cablegram from Africa detailing her brother's wound or telling of the encounter in which he was injured, that she is in possession of the circumstances under which her brother was disabled.

Miss Vanderwater, who is a trained nurse and a most matter-of-fact young woman, had a vision of Sunday afternoon's fight on Sunday night and saw her brother fall, struck by a Boer bullet.

"I am not at all superstitious," said Miss Vanderwater, "but the vision I had was as realistic as if I had spent the day on the battlefield in South Africa. I was right in the midst of the struggle, and, though close to my brother, could not reach him. The Canadians were charging over the red veldt sand. The Boers were in small kopjes all along their front, and were keeping up a tremendous fire. The smoke seemed to partially obscure the rest of the Toronto boys that I knew, but I could see Morris clearly in the line as they rushed forward. Then I saw a bullet strike him just below the shoulder and I was released from whatever force kept me from him, and I ran forward.

"The bullet has glanced off his ribs," I said to myself as I ran. He staggered and fell into my arms, and we both went down into the sand.

"I tore off the clothes and had just stanched the flow of blood, when I awoke. Next morning I was unable to eat my breakfast, but said nothing to my parents of the wounding of Morris, though I mentioned dreaming that I had been in Africa. When the message came that Morris was wounded, I told my mother Sunday night's dream in its entirety."

Miss Vanderwater is confident that her brother is only slightly wounded, and, though perturbed by the direct news of his injury, is not worried as much as she otherwise would.

She says she is sorry she did not go with the contingent as a nurse.

I HAVE BEEN MORE OR LESS CLAIRVOYANT

Mrs. John Henderson is identified as a "Trance Medium, Toronto" in B.F. Austin's collection *What Converted Me to Spiritualism: One Hundred Testimonies* (1901). The photographic portrait of Mrs. Henderson shows her to be a stolid-looking, grandmotherly person. In the account which follows, she sounds like she knows what she is thinking and doing.

I was born April 16th, 1824, and am, therefore, in my 78th year. Since childhood I have been more or less clairvoyant, clairaudient and deeply impressional. I have lived in Toronto since I was eight years old, and have had the great joy of giving my services as Trance Medium to our own house circle of friends and enquirers — generally several times per week — for over 40 years. During that time hundreds of teachers, clergymen, professional and business men, have visited our home and professed to find instruction, encouragement, inspiration, in the messages that came through my lips, from unseen friends. A large number have thus become firm believers in spirit return. Latterly my life has been lived seemingly in two realms, and rather more in the spiritual than in the earth realm. My friends in spirit life come to me at all hours of the day and night. I meet them in my house as I pass from one room to another, up and down the stairs, hear their voices and often sense their presence when I do not see or hear them. Frequently when unaware of their presence they join in conversation by answering some remark I have made.

When one's life is so constantly in touch with spirit realms, it seems difficult to select any particular experience for recital. I will, however, at Dr. Austin's request, mention a few of my experiences which will serve as fair samples of the rest.

About 1850, my husband, who has always been in deepest sympathy and kindest co-operation with my spiritual development and mediumship, was in London, Eng. One evening I was sitting on our verandah in presence of Mr. Boswick, his business partner, when I saw an immense glass-covered building and crowds of people thronging the avenues. I mentioned this to Mr. B. and he asked me if I recognized anyone. Almost instantly, upon looking down the aisle I recognized my husband, and he was walking up the aisle with a lady on his arm. We took note of the day and hour and allowing for the difference in time, found my vision was absolutely correct. I also saw him at the day and hour his ship arrived in port. This was also verified.

About 21 years ago my eldest daughter lived in Port Arthur, Ont. I had visited her, but afterwards she had moved to a new house. One bitter, winter night I had a desire to visit her, and did so in spirit as I have frequently done in "soul flight" as it is called. I had a sensation of travelling, and at last arrived at her dwelling — all the surroundings being entirely new to me. I remember the sensation of extreme cold which I felt, and how I suffered from it. I did not enter the dwelling, but seemed to stand outside the window looking in. I saw her reading by the table — her husband lying on the sofa. Basil, the boy, was playing with his dog in the corner. He made the dog stand up, and placed his cap upon his head. Everything was so real and life-like, we took a note of time, and on corresponding with our daughter found we were able to verify all the chief features of the vision.

On another occasion when my husband was on the sea, coming in with my wraps on I lay down on the bed and was soon lost to all around me. The doctor was called in next morning and I was restored to consciousness. Meanwhile I had followed my husband was with him on the ship, and distinctly saw him by my side as we walked the deck. So real was it all to me I grew sea-sick. I appeared to myself, I remember, not larger than a child by his side.

At another time when my son Tom was in England, I distinctly heard him call me "Mother," three times, and I realized he was very ill at the time specified, and still unwell, and, as a consequence, Tom came home while my husband remained in his place.

While walking down a street in this city one day, I felt an instinctive desire to go over to James St. — a street I had seldom walked on. While walking down James St., I began to perceive a peculiar atmosphere about me. It was full of the smell of woods and flowers. Suddenly something grey passed over my shoulder and with it such a thrill of emotion and deep impression that I said, "I have met with death." On entering the store shortly afterwards, my husband and his partner both asked me what ailed me, as I looked so ill. I said, "I have met with death." It was 12 o'clock, and at that hour, my husband's brother, as we afterwards learned by letter, died in the west.

In my teens I was engaged to a young man, but felt and told him I should marry another. He was leaving for England and required a certain paper. I told him to go to a certain store and a young man, John Henderson, would give him the paper, and I remarked casually, "I shall be married to him before you get back from England." I was then but slightly acquainted with Mr.

Henderson, but had on another occasion pointed him out to my uncle through the window of the store we were passing, with the remark — "I shall marry that young man some day."

I have witnessed under circumstances precluding the possibility of fraud on the part of the medium, the phenomena of materialization and held delightful intercourse with my friends and loved ones. To me spirit intercourse is as real as the communion we hold with friends in the body.

I have also had many deep impressions, seemingly unaccountable at the time, which have proved prophetic.

JENNIE BRAMWELL

Canada's equivalent of Carrie White, Stephen King's "fire starter," is the real-life adolescent girl named Jennie Bramwell. The fires that she set are legendary in Maritime life and lore. In an earlier age, the secular and religious authorities would have dealt with her as a witch. Today she would be placed in custody or considered a candidate for Prozac. Hers is a classic case of what is called "fire-setting" poltergeistery.

Two accounts of her doings were published in the *Toronto World*. The first account appeared in the issue of November 1891. Beaverton is located in Thorah Township on the east coast of Lake Simcoe, northeast of Sutton, Ontario.

Spooks, or What Mysterious Doings in a Torah Farmer's House — An Incorporeal Firebug Cats Take Fire, Towels Burn up and Wood Disappears — Queer Pranks in Broad Daylight — A Young Girl's Name Connected with the Mystery — Over Fifty Years in the House in One Day — The Ghost's Queer Pranks Astonishing All the Neighbors, — Who Are Visiting the Scene by Hundreds What the Inmates Say — These Strange Phenomena Have Now Been Going on for Over a Week

Beaverton, Ont., Nov. 6. — The residents of the sleepy township of Thorah have been for the past week considerably excited by the reports of curious antics rumored to be performed by supernatural means, in a house owned and occupied by Robert Dawson, a reputable farmer on the first concession of Thorah, about three miles from this village. The story, told by neighbors arriving here, was that an adopted daughter of Mr. and Mrs. Dawson had been seriously ill with brain fever; that about a week ago she went into a trance and on awakening suddenly jumped up, exclaiming, "Look at that!" and pointing with her finger towards the ceiling of the house. The rest of the members on looking towards the point indicated by the girl were surprised to see the ceiling on fire. They immediately extinguished the fire and nothing more was thought of the matter until the following day, when the girl again startled the family with the same exclamation and the interior of the house broke out in flames. This performance, according to the rumor, was continued every day thereafter.

From an investigation by *The World's* Ghost Exterminator, it is evident that the ghost sleeps just at present, but for a time it was fully as persistent as the one detailed for Banquo's special benefit.

The house is situated about one hundred yards from the road on lot 17, con. 1, Thorah — about seven miles from Cannington and three from Beaverton. It is a small and rather an ancient structure and is built of logs. There is a window in the front of the house, but no door; entrance to it being by a door in the rear through an old summer kitchen.

On arriving at the house Mrs. Dawson, the wife of the farmer, introduced the girl, whose name had been mentioned in connection with these mysteries. She was engaged in washing dishes. The girl was adopted by Mr. and Mrs. Dawson from an immigrant home in Belleville some time ago. She was originally from England, where she was known as Jennie B. Bramwell, but since coming to her present home she has adopted the name of Jennie

B. Dawson. Miss Bramwell, or Miss Dawson, is a bright intelligent girl of about fourteen years of age. She is well educated and an excellent conversationalist.

After being shown over the premises, both up stairs and down, Mrs. Dawson tells this story of the girl's illness and the mysterious fires: On Monday afternoon, Oct. 25, she and her husband went to a neighbor's to spend a few hours, and on returning home in the evening Jennie informed them that the house had been on fire and pointed out the place — near the chimney. Mr. Dawson, thinking that there might still be some fire around the chimney, remained up all night to watch it, but nothing occurred during the night. After breakfast on Tuesday morning Mr. Dawson went out to the barn to load some grain to take to market, and Mrs. Dawson also went out into the yard. They had scarcely left the house when the girl, Jennie, came out shouting the house was again on fire. On entering the house they found that the west gable end was on fire. With the aid of water the fire upstairs was extinguished, but no sooner had that been accomplished than the fire broke out in several places on the wall in the room in the lower flat, and while extinguishing it there it again broke out on the wall in another room in the east end — there being no visible connection between any of the fires. They finally succeeded, with the assistance of some neighbors, in getting the fire extinguished. The next day the fire again broke out, and as on the former day, when it was extinguished in one place it would suddenly break out in some other place, several feet away.

On one occasion, while the fire was burning at the extreme west end of the house, a picture hanging on the wall at the opposite end of the house suddenly took fire and was consumed before their eyes. On examination it was found there was no fire near it. The family had now become thoroughly aroused, and after succeeding in extinguishing the fire, they removed the stove from the house as they had an idea that the fire was caused by it. But the removal of the stove had no effect, as on the following day — Thursday — the fire again broke out. While sitting looking at the wall fire would suddenly break out on it; a stick of wood lying in the old summer kitchen suddenly took fire and was partly consumed; a piece of paper pulled from the wall and thrown on the floor would immediately take fire and burn up. A towel which Mrs. Dawson had been using to wipe a table with on being thrown onto another table suddenly took fire and would have been consumed had not water been thrown over it, and a basket hanging in the woodshed also took fire.

The dress of the girl Jennie took fire and she narrowly escaped being burned to death. Mrs. Dawson also had her right hand burned while helping to extinguish the fire. Wherever the fire appeared it would char into the wood over half an inch in a second, and the other side of the board or log would instantly become so hot that a person could not place their hand on it. A peculiar thing connected with these fires was that as soon as any of the burning lumber, paper, cloth or wood (no matter how furiously they were burning in the house) was thrown outside the fire would immediately die out. After all the fires had been extinguished Mrs. Dawson pulled a piece of paper from the wall and rolled it up in a piece of old muslin dress and roped it on the center of the floor and, accompanied by Mr. Dawson and the rest of the family, stepped outside to see the result. No sooner had they stepped out of the door than the muslin and the paper became ignited and burned furiously. Friday was no exception — in fact the fire was ten times as bad, there being nearly fifty fires in different parts of the house that day. But the climax was reached on Saturday when a kitten, which was lying in the center of the floor of one of the rooms, became enwrapped in flames and rushed out into the orchard, where the flames, like that on the wood, paper, et cetera, immediately died out. On the kitten being examined it was found that the hair on its back was badly singed. The fires in the house also broke out twice that day.

Mrs. Dawson, to prove what she said, showed the towel, basket, kitten, et cetera, which had so mysteriously taken fire, and everything was as she had stated. The kitten, which was examined closely, was badly singed. Mr. John Shier, brother of Mrs. Dawson, was also present and corroborated what his sister had told, as did also the girl Jennie. Mr. Shier also added, "That when he was first told of the fires he just laughed, and so lightly did he treat it that he did not visit the place until Wednesday and saw the mysterious fires himself." He was there when the cat took fire and when the linen and towel were burned, but neither he nor Mrs. Dawson or any other of the members of the family could in any way account for the origin of these fires. Neither can any of the neighbors who were at the fires.

On asking if it was true that the girl Jennie was ill or subject to fits, Mrs. Dawson said: "The girl was taken ill some weeks ago with whooping cough, but when she was recovering from that she was taken down with brain fever, but was now all right again. During the girl's illness the doctor in attendance injected into her arm morphine, and immediately after the girl went into convulsions and for some time after was subject to them. However, she could in no wise connect the girl's illness with the fires."

The house is still standing, but all the partitions have been removed from the top story, and the furniture has been taken to a neighbor's. A peculiar feature was that no fires occurred at night — it being in daylight, and they appeared to be more numerous during the two days when the stove was outside.

Chemist Smith Thompson and Editor Robinson of *The Cannington Gleaner* have visited the scene and are unable to explain the phenomena. Everything has been suggested that reasoning minds could imagine as a natural cause for the phenomena, but they have in turn been rejected. Human agency and electricity have been mentioned, but at every fresh suggestion of cause the apparently angry author of the mysterious fires repelled the insinuation by blazing out in a new place and destroying all topographical calculations. If it be human agency the one who constructed the machinery must be an expert and a model of ingenuity. If it be electricity the house must be charged more powerfully than any building yet tested.

There is a great stir in the neighborhood and the house is daily visited by scores. All are politely received and given every facility for inspecting the rooms, charred articles, et cetera. Both the girl and Mrs. Dawson tell their story in a plain, unvarnished manner, devoid of exaggeration and seemingly with a firm faith in the supernatural character of the manifestations. Mr. and Mrs. Dawson have lived on the place for a number of years and are well-to-do, kind and highly respected people. The neighbors speak in the highest terms of them and also of the girl Jennie. The neighbors are all deeply impressed with both what they saw and what they were told.

The second account of Jennie Bramwell's fiery work appeared in the same newspaper on November 12, 1891. At the time, newspaper reporters were often careless or took liberties with the spellings of personal names. The reporter who wrote up this account is no exception. Here Jennie's surname is mistakenly spelled "Bromwell" rather than "Bramwell." I have left it as it appeared in print.

That Ghostly Firebrand — An Investigator Who Failed to Investigate — The Case Still a Mystery

Brockville, Nov. 11. — The young girl Lillie Bromwell, whose name was mentioned in connection with the mysterious fires in the house of Farmer Dawson near Beaverton, has been returned to Fairknowe Home here. Mr. Burges told a *Recorder* reporter very emphatically that the statement made by *The Globe* that the girl has a knowledge of chemistry is all nonsense, that she possesses no such knowledge, and with this emphatic statement *The Globe* reporter's theory falls to the ground and he will have to begin over again. Mr. Burges states that the Dawsons had got the girl from the orphans' home when she was about five years of age, some nine years ago, and so far as he is concerned he is not inclined to believe that the girl had anything to do with the manifestations.

The Globe reporter after fully questioning the girl's adopted parents admits that the fire could not have been started with matches, and then proceeds to show that the girl had a knowledge of the rudiments of chemistry, and that she procured phosphorus and thus the mysterious fires are accounted for. No one is forthcoming who sold the girl phosphorus, so the reporter concludes that she must have stolen it from a neighboring drug store, and then admits that "it is difficult to see how she applied it." We should think it is. If the reporter knows anything about phosphorus he must know that no mere novice in chemistry could have produced the effects, or could have handled it without danger of burning themselves, so that theory is untenable.

FORETOLD MAN'S DROWNING

Predicting the future, locating missing people, finding lost treasure, chasing away ghosts ... and debunking all of the above activities, including exposing a fake medium ... this article is all about such things!

"Foretold Man's Drowning" is reprinted from the columns of *The Toronto Daily Star*, April 6, 1932. The article was drawn to my attention by fellow researcher Ed Butts, whose hobby is scanning newspapers, looking for oddities like this one. I was intrigued when I read the byline: Archibald Lampman. That is a name that is familiar to readers of Canadian poetry, but the sonnet-writing Lampman died in 1899, so he is not responsible for the article that appears here.

The article covers a lot of ground, but it does so in a sarcastic fashion. The writer is such a smart aleck that the reader does not know what to make of his account, if anything at all. "Professor" Gladstone is not to be confused with Harry Blackstone, the stage magician. References to the disappearance of Ambrose Small, the murder of Rocco

Perri, and the kidnapping of the Lindbergh shed no useful light on those murder mysteries. We know one thing: Archibald Lampman is not taken in by any of this. One wonders why he even bothered to write this report.

Foretold Man's Drowning Three Years in Advance — *Showed the Searchers where to Locate the Baby in River* — *Is a Ghost Finder*

By Archibald Lampman

Claiming he has no cult, mysticism, or supernatural powers, a man in St. Catharines foretells the future, finds murder victims, chases ghosts, locates oil, reads messages from the beyond and spots buried treasure. Not so bad for just six easy lessons, eh?

How come? — or is he a brush salesman? This isn't our party, but pipe this:

Three years ago "Prof." Harry Gladstone, while doing a spot of "message reading" at the Listowel theatre, told Mrs. Orlando Pike death by drowning would come to her husband within three years.

A few days ago Pike was thrown from his buggy into the river near his farm and drowned. Questioned, Gladstone denies the power of suggestion could have caused the man's death. The "professor" also told Mrs. Pike her husband would be feeling a lot better in January, 1932. Just think of that!

"I'm just a freak of nature," the "professor" has said. He senses things. He was born with something or other over his head, which was removed backwards. He has poor eyesight, which peps up under certain phases of the moon.

As a child, he says, he used to give the neighbours a thrill by handing them a line of snappy chatter. And finally took to the road doing a "message act" and bringing sunshine into the show business.

Led to the Body

Finally — we believe you! Now, what about the buried treasure and runs [*sic*] of oil and battalions of ghosts? Or was that just your story? Just a second [*sic*] to this first?

When Pike was drowned, Gladstone was notified by the widow. He started out with only a chauffeur, a motor car and a blizzard. He found quite a crowd on the bank. He made a drag. Told the farmers they would find the body around the corner in a nook down river. Then the big act. He got the seekers to bare their heads and pray.

Yeah — what then? He went home. Did they find the body? Don't you read the papers?

Gladstone first rushed out into the spotlight in the McDonald and McLaughlin cases out west some time ago. It just shows what you can do in a small way — without any supernatural powers, either.

McDonald had been missing for months. "A friend asked me where he was and I told him he had fallen off the bridge into the Red Deer river," says Gladstone. "We all removed our hats and prayed." And, sure enough, he had. He even made it easy by pointing out the spot. Then he called it a day.

A man in the audience of the Beechy, Sask., theatre asked him where McLaughlin, a ranch hand, was. "I told him he had been murdered." And would you believe it — so he had! He saved police unnecessary carfare by taking them to the scene. Oh, yes — they found the body, caught the murderer and let it go at that.

Says Lindy's Baby on Boat

A few days after the Lindbergh baby was kidnapped, he stated, according to a report, it was held at Chester, near Philadelphia, and would be taken on a boat. So that's what happened to the Lindbergh baby?

He says Ambrose Small was murdered in his theatre

and his body burned by criminals in the furnace, who wished to rob him. Also, he could solve the Bessie Perri murder but he'd been bumped off. Jot this down in your helpful hints. There's always a catch.

"I'm just an entertainer," says Gladstone. And how! "I do not prophesy the future. People ask me questions and I tell them what I know." And if it happens to be up your alley — it's just too bad.

He stresses faith in prayer. He adheres to the Church of England. He offers an explanation. Results of the chase, he states, have netted him 200 old dead bodies, flocks of stolen property and the solution to several murders. Figure it out for yourself.

"Do you profess to click every time?" he was asked. "No — I am not infallible." And that goes for a lot of others, too.

Gold and a Ghost

Say, do we hear about this buried treasure and ghosts — or do we get our money back? Coming up.

Recently the "professor" was visited by a farmer from East Flamboro township. "Gold — buried gold," was brought up in the general chit-chat. Gladstone will pay a personal visit to the farm, where legend will have it a hoard has been sunk for centuries. And everybody too sappy to do anything about it.

The wizard pulls an act. He describes an abandoned well and two trees. "The gold is between those trees," he tells the agriculturalist. "$8,000 in gold," puts in the farmer. He has it all figured up.

"And there is a ghost," adds the message reader. "A real ghost."

"I'll say there is," pipes the farmer. "I chased it three miles one night. I thought I'd get him on the curve — but he got away. A neighbour claims he saw him hanging from a rafter of my barn one night — but I could never see him." Tough!

"That's the ghost of the man who buried the gold," says the "professor." "I will come and show you where it is." And another profession adopts the service plus slogan.

Popular belief handles the cheery yarn that a prior owner of the farm buried all his money and then swung off from a barn rafter without even leaving a map.

This same farmer has a fortune in natural gas (so it wasn't oil after all!) 1,200 feet below a mineral spring, on his property, according to Gladstone. That was two days ago.

In the meantime farming's picking up.

MADAME CURRY'S PROPHECY

The author of this remarkable account of a family's story of prophecy is John E. Wall, an editor and writer who lives in Altona, Manitoba. He has a special interest in *anomalous phenomena*, especially events of a Fortean nature, particularly in cryptozoology (the study of fabulous creatures) and pre-Columbian history. He has contributed articles to *Cryptozoology* and *The ISC Newsletter*. The account here comes from a letter written by Mr. Wall in the early 1990s.

> When my mother was a girl — she may have been a young teenager at the time — she and her mother travelled by train from their home in Glenboro, Man., to Winnipeg, for a day's shopping.
>
> The exact day or even time of year this occurred, I do not know. I do remember, however, my mother telling me that the war was on at the time. Therefore, it could not have been earlier than 1939; it may have been as late as 1941. My mother could have been as young as eleven or as old as thirteen. Whatever her age, the incident I am about to relate impressed my mother so much that she never forgot it.
>
> After spending some time shopping, my mother and her mother decided to rest and have a meal in a Chinese café at or near Winnipeg's famous Portage Ave. and Main

St. intersection. It was here that they met a tea-leaf reader who called herself Madame Curry. That was not her real name. Possibly she named herself after the Curry Building, in or near which the restaurant was situated. This building still stands and houses a number of stores.

After their meal my grandmother and her daughter decided to have their tea-leaves read. To do this, one downed one's cup of brew to the last drop and inverted the cup over a saucer; a sharp bang of the cup against the saucer and the tea-leaves would come tumbling down. This was done, and Madame Curry proceeded to tell her customers' fortunes by studying the patterns that the leaves made on their saucers.

My mother did not remember the prophecy uttered by Madame Curry for her mother, but she clearly remembered her own. She would one day, predicted the tea-leaf reader, meet a tall, dark-haired man having the initials J.W. She would marry this man and they would have three children, all boys. Their family would move frequently, and after being married to this man for thirty-five years and some days, her husband would die.

In 1951, my father met my mother in a café in Glenboro, where my mother was working as a waitress. A year later they married. He was tall (six feet or over) with dark brown hair; his name was John Wall. As a requirement of my father's employment with the Interprovincial Pipeline Company, my parents and their children — three boys — moved frequently in Manitoba and Saskatchewan, finally settling in Outlook, Sask., where my father became ill with cancer. He died in a Saskatoon hospital one day short of his sixty-sixth birthday. Thus my parents' marriage ended after thirty-five years and five days. Everything that the tea-leaf reader had predicted, possibly forty-five years earlier, had come to pass.

But the irony was not complete. I happened to mention this prophecy to my aunt, who lives in Altona, one evening as I paid her a social call. She asked me what Madame Curry looked like. I described her to my aunt the way my mother had described her to me — a large, loud, buxom woman with white hair. "That sounds like Harry Smith's wife," said my aunt. "She used to live in Plum Coulee."

Mrs. Harry Smith, my aunt related, had the gift of second sight, prophecy, or so she claimed. Every so often she would go to Winnipeg to read people's fortunes. She lived in the village of Plum Coulee, where my father, his two sisters, and their mother also lived. Mrs. Smith had a loud voice that she used to good effect when calling her children in for supper — one could hear her all over the block. Mrs. Smith was Madame Curry.

I later had independent corroboration of Mrs. Smith's powers from the widowed manager of the Co-op store in Glenboro. She had also had her tea-leaves read by Madame Curry, who had accurately predicted her husband's death as well.

Whether or not the foregoing constitutes the entirety of the tea-leaf reader's prophecy, I do not know. In any event, it is now too late to make further enquiries. My mother died suddenly and without warning of a pulmonary embolism two and a half years after my father's death. Yet she was able to see the fulfillment of Madame Curry's prophecy, uttered half a century or more ago.

THE CAR STARTED TO RISE UP

The following letter was sent to me by Glenn Therens, who lives and works as a cook in Moose Jaw, Saskatchewan. He wrote the letter on June 14, 1990 in response to my request for ghost stories which appeared in *The Moose Jaw Times*.

I wish I could deserve Mr. Therens's thanks. I have no idea what caused his moving automobile to tip to one side while he was speeding along a highway. The experience was a profoundly moving one, one that has been recalled in detail more than one-quarter century after it happened.

There is nothing "ghostly" about what I'm going to write about, but it sure is mysterious.

It happened on July 6, 1964, at about 2:00 p.m., about four or five miles southeast of Weyburn, Sask., on Highway 39. It was very hot, 90 to 95 °F. and there was absolutely no wind. I was with my wife and our two sons, five years and three years. At the time I was thirty years old and my wife twenty-eight. I was driving. My wife was beside me. The three-year-old was standing on the front seat between us. The five-year-old was in the back seat of our car.

Our car was a 1953 Pontiac in mint condition. It was kept in top-notch condition by my father who was a garage operator. We were going home to Moose Jaw, after visiting my sister and her husband at Carlyle, Sask. I was driving approximately 60 mph, about four or five miles southeast of Weyburn, with no traffic ahead or behind me. I slowed down to about 25 or 30 mph. Why? I don't know.

All of a sudden, very, very slowly, the right side (the passenger side) of the car started to rise up, and we were driving on the two left tires. The car continued its rise up until, even with my left arm bent at the elbow, I could have extended the palm of my hand and it would have rubbed against the pavement. The highway was in very good, very smooth condition.

The first person to speak was our older son who was in the back seat. He asked, "Hey, what's going on?"

I spoke second, and yelled to my wife, "Grab hold of the kid," referring to the one standing between us, "he's gonna fall out of the window!"

I had my hands on the steering wheel all the time, but I was definitely not in control of the car. We travelled approximately one hundred yards in the proper lane, then the car started to right itself again, very, very slowly. Then we were driving on four wheels again.

I came to a stop and got out of the car. Still there was no traffic on the highway. I got back into the car and proceeded again. I was about to speak when my wife actually put into words what I was going to say, which was, "I don't think we should tell anyone about this. They'll think we're both crackin' up."

At the time neither of us drank alcohol — we couldn't afford it!

Some years later, on radio station CKRM in Regina, there was a man on a talk show who explained, or tried to explain, unexplained happenings. I tried to phone in, but the lines were busy.

I hope this will be of some use to you for your book. If you could enlighten me as to what may have caused this situation, I thank you.

All of this that I write is true with God as my witness.

THE SPECTRE OF THE BROCKEN

The Spectre of the Brocken is a reference to one of the marvels of nineteenth-century Europe. Tourists and natural scientists would travel great distances to Germany to climb the Brocken, the highest mountain of the Harz chain. From its peak, at dawn or dusk, they would behold the setting or the rising sun as it projected their immensely magnified shadows onto the low-lying clouds. When they witnessed this effect, they were in good company. The poet Heinrich Heine described *der Brokenspeckt*. Sigmund Freud and Adolf Hitler are known to have travelled to the Brocken to behold this wonder of optics and atmospherics.

A letter to the editor published in *The Globe and Mail*, November 25, 1993, brought the effect to mind. The letter was written by Joseph Caplan of Willowdale, Ontario. Here is his account of a latter-day Spectre of the Brocken.

I had a terrifying experience with this phenomenon more than thirty years ago. I was a young RCAF [Royal Canadian Air Force] officer, stationed south of Montreal, with a fiancée in New York. I would drive there Friday and return Sunday night.

My route, which I knew well, was the old Highway

9N, a switchback road that climbs up the hills above the Hudson Valley — the I-87 north from Albany was not yet built.

I was travelling north one night with mist in the road-dips and a truck about half a mile behind me when, to my horror, I saw a car on my side of the road, headlights blazing, coming straight at me through the mist. I frantically pulled for the right gravel shoulder, knowing there was a 1,000-foot drop about ten feet away, and slithered to a stop close to the wire fence. The truck roared by and all was quiet and dark.

After a few moments I wondered what had become of the oncoming car. I cautiously got out and peered over the edge of the hillside. Nothing, no flames or sounds. At this point another car came along, and I saw a figure in the mist ahead. I waved, he waved back. The car passed, and again all was silent.

And then it struck me — I had nearly plunged to my death taking evasive action from the onrushing shadow of my own car created by the truck's headlights on the mist bank. The same effect had produced the waving figure. This was my Brocken Spectre.

I sometimes read of drivers, going to work, inexplicably veering off a clear dry road at dawn. I wonder if the police ever note the exact road direction relative to the low rising sun behind, which could have produced a similar, but fatal, illusion on morning mist.

5

MYSTERIES OF THE SEA

There are mysteries of the land, mysteries of the air, and mysteries of the sea. A ghost will haunt a long-abandoned cabin or house. A spirit may linger at a crossroads or along a seldom-used road or lane. But the sea ... the sea is a place for ships of sail, and the maritime regions of Canada and its commercial waterways are replete with phantom ships and fire ships.

Phantom ships are vessels which are not — or should not — be there! Or, if they are there, they suddenly disappear! Fire ships, or flaming ships, are vessels that old salts spot on the horizon at sundown: their sails are alive with flames, their decks are scenes of bedlam, as captain and crew are discernible scrambling for safety. Then there are tales of sunken treasure, guarded by the spirits of the "vasty deep." Here, for landlubbers, are three tales that evoke such mysteries of the seas as these.

THE SPECTRE BRIG

The most famous brigantine of all time was the *Mary Celeste*, a twin-masted ship of sail with a terrible reputation, the type of vessel avoided whenever possible by experienced sailors. This Nova Scotia-built "hoo-doo ship" was encountered crewless and drifting in the Atlantic Ocean near the Azores on June 10, 1861. To this day no one knows why it was abandoned in mid-Atlantic by its crew, its cargo intact, during calm weather. This unsolved mystery of the sea attracted the attention of Sir Arthur Conan Doyle, who wrote a lively short story about its fate, and Bela Lugosi, who starred in a Hollywood movie based on the treachery behind the ship's abandonment on the high seas.

Here is a somewhat similar, first-person account of life aboard a cursed brigantine. The account appeared as "The Spectre Brig" in *The Examiner* (Charlottetown, Prince Edward Island), January 26, 1863. Its authorship is attributed to a journalist named Frank R. Ross.

The Spectre Brig. — The fall of 1853 saw me on board the bark *Swordfish*, bound from New York to Yarmouth, Nova Scotia, thence to Liverpool and a market. I cannot imagine what odd freak decided the owners of the bark to give her a name so inappropriate, for the swordfish is known to be of uncommon symmetry, and moves with the quickness of light, while its ungainly namesake was tub-built, blunt-bowed, short-sparred, requiring four men at the wheel in a gale of wind to keep her within six points of the compass, and then she would make more lee-way than a Dutch galliot.

However, she proved to be a tolerable sailor, despite her unpromising appearance, and the fifth day out, we made the Seal Islands, in the Bay of Fundy, and a few hours later were moored alongside the wharf at Yarmouth.

Here we were informed that our cargo would not be in readiness for several days, and as but little remained to be attended to aboard the vessel, I concluded to take a cruise over the city and surrounding country.

The city has a gloomy and antique appearance, looking as though the blight of ages had fallen upon her buildings in a night. The houses are of a style and architecture in vogue half a century ago, being built still earlier by Tory refugees, who fled from the Colonies during the Revolutionary war.

Many of these were offshoots of noble families in England, and clinging to their sovereign with fanatical blindness, they fled to this and adjacent provinces, where their descendants have managed to keep up a dingy show of gentility in their old tumble-down tenements.

Their hatred of republicanism, a hatred gathered and intensified through many generations, until it has become almost a passion, is only equalled by their love and veneration for their sovereign. The poorer class, mostly Irish and Scotch, are ardent admirers of republican institutions, and are outspoken in their sentiments.

Between them and their more aristocratic neighbours exists a bitter feeling partizan hostility which increases in intensity with each succeeding year, and must, ere long, break forth in a rougher shape than a mere war of words.

The Home Government is fully alive to this and accordingly grants every indulgence consistent with its dignity. But still the people are dissatisfied. They feel that there is a lack, a moral blight that deadens their enemies and clouds their prospects.

They know their country to be rich in mineral wealth, yet it remains undeveloped. Rich in its fisheries, yet they are unprofitable.

One day, while taking a stroll on the high ground bordering the bay, and watching the tide as it came in from the sea, rolling in the solid wall thirty feet in height that reared and rumbled like distant thunder, I chanced to hear some remarks made by a group of persons near me, that drew my attention. Not wishing to play the part of listener, I was turning from the spot when the foremost speaker of the party exclaimed:

"I tell you, gentlemen, it is no illusion! There is not a person for miles around who has not heard or seen the 'Spectre Brig.' Furthermore, if you will remain a few days longer, you can satisfy yourselves of the truth of my statement, as it is nearly time for her annual visitation."

Being interested by these strange remarks, I turned and joined them. During the conversation that followed, I referred to the above and requested to be enlightened as to its meaning, addressing myself to the person who had attracted my attention. He looked at me as though surprised at the request, but seeing I was a stranger, he replied:

"Certainly, sir; with pleasure if it will be of any interest to you."

Seating ourselves, he then proceeded to relate the story, as nearly as I can recollect as follows:

"Fifty years ago, the brig *Yarmouth*, commanded by Capt. Bruce, and manned by a crew from this neighbourhood, sailed from this port to the West Indies. Days and weeks went by, and the time for her return came and passed. Apprehensions began to be felt for her safety as the days went by, and daily an anxious crowd of women and children might have been seen gathered on the headlands that overlooked the bay, straining their eyes seaward in the faint hope of catching a glimpse of the missing vessel that had borne away a husband, a brother, a father, or son. Each night only witnessed a deeper disappointment, and at last apprehension had become almost certainty, and people began to speak of her as a thing of the past.

"A year had just passed away, when one night as the watchman was going his rounds among the wharves, he chanced to look seaward, and was surprised to see a vessel covered with canvass from truck to kelson, standing boldly into the harbour, although it was blowing a living gale sufficient to swamp the strongest craft with half the amount of sail. On she came, plowing before the blast like a thing of life until she had reached within a cable's length of the shore; when suddenly her main topsail was backed, her anchor dropped into the water with a splash, followed by the rattling of the chains as it ran out through the hawsehole. At the same instant her tacks and sheets were let go, her sails clowed up and furled, and in less time than it takes me to narrate it she had swung round with the current and was riding quietly at a single anchor.

"As she swung broadside to the wharf the astonished watchman recognized her, and started up town with a tearing rate. 'The *Yarmouth* has come.' The glad cry ran from house to house and street to street, and in a few minutes a crowd of people had gathered upon the wharf making the air ring with their cheers, while wives, mothers and sisters were kneeling and with streaming eyes returned thanks for the wanderer's return.

"As yet not a sound had been heard or an object seen aboard the brig to denote that a soul was near her. Every one recognized her as she lay silent and dark, rising and settling with every wave.

"Finding their efforts to arouse the crew to be of no avail, they procured boats, and in spite of the violence of the wind, put out to board her. Bending stoutly to the oars with a hearty good will they soon found themselves within a few yards of her, when they were surprised to hear a hoarse voice exclaim, 'Keep off! Keep off!' Hardly believing their senses, they returned to the shore, which they had scarcely reached before a thick black fog, peculiar in that land of fogs, swept in from the sea and enveloped everything in an impenetrable veil. Surprised and terrified at what they had seen, the people returned to await the morning, hoping, yet scarcely daring to believe that with daylight everything would be explained. The gale still continued, and as morning broke, the vapour raised for a few moments, but not a vestige of the vessel of the preceding night was to be seen.

"Another year went by and the phantom vessel again appeared under nearly the same circumstances, and all attempts to board her resulted as before.

"'Thus,' continued my narrator, 'nearly fifty years have gone by, and still she makes her annual visit at just such a period of each succeeding year. Of late no attention is paid to her whatever, her arrival being hardly noticed, as she comes in invariably at midnight, and disappears within an hour.'"

Here the story concluded, and thanking my informant for his kindness, I arose, bid the party good-bye, and returned to my vessel and retired to my berth, as it was getting late.

I felt feverish and restless, and lay tossing about for several hours. Not being able to rest, I got up, dressed myself and went on deck, where the night air soon cooled my heated blood, and I was about to go to my state-room again, when my attention was arrested by hearing a loud splash in the water, followed by the rattle of a chain as it was rapidly paid out. Looking out into the harbor, I saw to my astonishment, a large, old-fashioned full-rigged brig laying quietly at anchor, with sails snugly furled and everything in ship-shape style. I was at first considerably startled, as I knew it would be impossible for any sailing vessel to come in and anchor when not a breath of wind was stirring. Not believing in anything of a supernatural character, whether it be ghost or ghoul, hobgoblin or witch, I resolved to pay the strange craft a visit, feeling confident it was the "Spectre Brig," whose history I had heard a few hours before.

Going to the forecastle, I turned out two of the men, and ordered them to lower away the boat, throw out a pair of oars, and jump in, which they promptly did. I followed them over the side, and taking the tiller, sat down to wait the result.

In a few minutes we were within a dozen yards of the stranger, and rising in the boat I hailed:

"Brig, ahoy!"

No answer.

"Brig, ahoy!" I again shouted, with all the force of my lungs, but still no answer.

The third hail resulted as before.

There she lay, grim and dark, her sides covered with barnacles and clothed with seaweed. Not a sound could be heard, not even the creaking of a block, or the rattling of a rope.

Determined to board her at all hazards, I directed the men to pull with all their strength, and lay the boat alongside, while I grappled the rigging.

Bending themselves to the oars they sent the light boat seething through the water like a dart; but when, apparently with an oar's length of her side, the stranger craft began to grow indistinct, like a vapour. A moment her outline could be plainly seen, stamped against the sky, and the next she had vanished wholly, without a sound, without a sigh.

A thick fog soon set in from the bay, and we were compelled to grope our way to the shore as best we could, feeling awed and perplexed at what we had seen.

In vain I have tried to explain this phenomenon, but without success, and at last I am forced to the conclusion that it must remain one of those secrets that must continue until the Last Great Day, when the "heavens shall roll away like a scroll, and the mysteries of the universe stand revealed!"

THE MONSTER OF LAKE UTOPIA

The lakes and rivers of the Maritimes are the domain of innumerable "monsters." Of these the Lake Utopia Monster is probably the best known, if only because it bears the best and most memorable name! Who would not wish to boast that he had seen the Lake Utopia Monster?

"The Monster of Lake Utopia" appeared in the *Summerside Progress* of Sunnyside, Prince Edward Island, August 19, 1867. It was contributed by the correspondent of the *St. John Globe* of Saint John, New Brunswick.

A correspondent of the St. John, N.B., *Globe*, writing from "St. George, Aug. 6," gives the following account of a monster in Utopia Lake, in addition to that which he contributed some time ago to the same paper, and which we then transferred to our columns:

Agreeably to my promise that should any further be developed respecting the strange monster in Lake Utopia, I would write you, I now beg to say that it has been seen by a number of persons since, in different parts of the lake, and on Wednesday, July 24th, by thirteen persons, some of whom are of the most reliable character. I would have written you sooner, but being rather sceptical about it myself, I waited to get the correct accounts from the lips of the individuals themselves; and I now have no hesitation in saying that some huge animal of fearful aspect exists in the waters of Utopia. To the north and east of Lake Utopia, there is a small lake well known to the sporting fraternity, which connects with the larger waters by a stream, perhaps 400 yards in length. About midway on this stream, between the two lakes, Messrs. H. & J. Ludgate have a saw mill in operation. The deals when sawn are floated down the stream to the deep water in Utopia, where they are made into rafts to float down to St. George. On the day before alluded to, a number of men engaged in rafting, had their attention drawn to a violent agitation of the water, about 100 yards distant out in the lake, which continued for a time, and then, there appeared distinctly above the water a huge bulky object, variously estimated from 20 to 40 feet in length, and from 4 to 10 feet across the widest part. The men describe the skin as presenting a shaggy appearance, not unlike a buffalo robe, and of a reddish brown color. It created a great quantity of foam which drifted up to the shore in huge flakes. At no time could they see the head of it; but at a distance of 20 or 25 feet in rear of the large mass, could be seen what they supposed to be a tail from the movements. The man called H. Ludgate, Esq., who was at the mill, and he and his son, together with others, ran down and witnessed the evolutions of this strange creature. Mr. Ludgate told me himself that it agitated the water to a perfect boiling, seething state, and threw up in its course edgings and mud from the bottom, occasionally rising itself to the top; a dark cumbrous body — not unlike a large stick of timber — disappearing again almost instantly. It finally moved off, and they could trace its course down the lake by the foam it created long after it went below the surface. Later in the day Mr. Thomas White, his two sons, and a hired man haying in the field, saw it *seven different times,* and Mr. White says it came up at the outer end of the raft, quite close to it; the men at work at the inner end being turned away did not observe their acquaintance of the morning.

Mr. White's description of it is about the same. He being farther off could not describe the skin of the animal, but says that when most exposed it resembled a large rock left bare of the tide, 10 feet across; and he further states that he can safely swear he saw 30 feet in length of it. His statement is corroborated by his sons, and by all of the thirteen persons who saw it the same day. Now,

Mr. Editor, heretofore I could scarcely believe in the existence of such an animal and unprecedented inhabitant of our lake; but when I heard men of the character of H. Ludgate, Esq., Charles Ludgate, Charles Mealy, Thomas White, Robert White and many others say *positively* that they saw it as described, and when I take into consideration the destruction of fish which must take place in Utopia every year — otherwise it would teem with splendid trout, perch, cusk and smelt, and together with these the tradition of forty years, — I must say that in common with the majority of our citizens, I firmly believe that a monster of vast dimensions and formidable appearance is located in the lake. Two of our most enterprising citizens, Mr. H.A. Smith, and W.W. Shaw, have had hooks made and attached to lines buoyed in the lake for some time, but so far without any satisfactory result. It is the opinion of many that a large net will be required to capture the creature, and I understand that a movement is on foot quietly, to make the attempt, which I hope will succeed. The people living in the vicinity of the lake are really afraid to cross it in boats; and if you could only hear some of the oldest settlers who saw this "thing" tell the story with fear and trembling, you would be fully impressed with the truth of their assertions, and consider them justified in their fears.

PHANTOM SHIP

Mysterious Light on Lake Erie — A Curious Phenomenon — [Correspondent of the Erie Despatch]

The Journal (St. Catharines, Ontario), November 20, 1867

I notice in the *Despatch* of the 11th inst. the following paragraph: —

"The statement that a vessel was seen burning off Erie on Tuesday night is corroborated by several persons living on the high lands south of the city, who say they saw it."

On the Tuesday evening mentioned, October 29th, at about seven o'clock my attention was called by one of my family to a bright light on the lake, having much the appearance of a vessel on fire. Bringing several objects into range, I watched the light for some time to ascertain whether there was any perceptible motion. The wind was blowing hard at the time down the lake and a vessel would naturally drift rapidly to leeward, at all events as soon as the propelling power should be interfered with by the fire. No motion, however, in any direction was to be discovered, and I at once concluded that it was nothing more than the "mysterious light," which, for many years past, at longer or shorter intervals, has been seen by the inhabitants at this point on the lake shore. The light has made its appearance generally, if not always, in the fall of the year, and usually in the month of November, and almost always during or immediately after a heavy blow from the southwest. The most brilliant exhibition of the light I have ever seen was during the night of the 24th or 25th, as nearly as I recollect, of November, 1852. It had been my fortune to witness the burning of the steamer *Erie*, near Silver Creek, several years before and the resemblance which this light bore to that of the burning of the steamer was so strong that I confidently expected the arrival of boats from the wreck during the night. Others with myself watched the light for perhaps two hours, and with the aid of the night glass obtained what seemed to be a very distinct view of the burning vessel.

The object appeared to be some 200 or more feet in length upon the water, and about as high above the water as an upper cabin steamer such as was in use upon the lake twenty years ago. At times the flame would start up in spires or sheets of light, then away from side to side, and then die away, precisely as would be the case with a large fire exposed to a strong wind; and two or three times there was the appearance of a cloud of sparks, as if some portion of the upper works had fallen into the burning mass below. The sky and water were beautifully irradiated by the light during its greatest brilliancy. The light gradually subsided, with occasional flashes, until it disappeared altogether.

The light of Tuesday evening, although very bright for a time, was not nearly so brilliant nor of so long duration as that of 1862.

I am told that this light was seen by mariners on the lake as long as fifty years ago, but I am not aware that it has ever been made the subject of philosophical speculation or investigation, or, in fact, has ever obtained the notoriety of a newspaper paragraph before.

The only theory approaching plausibility I have heard is that the shifting of the sands caused by the continued and heavy winds of the autumn has opened some crevices or seams in the rock of the lake bottom through which a gas escapes, and that this gas, owing to some peculiar condition of the atmosphere with which it comes in contact, becomes luminous, or, perhaps, ignited and burning with a positive flame. That there are what are called "gas spring" in the water all along this portion of the lake shore is a well-known fact, and that a highly inflammable gas in large quantities exist at a comparatively shallow depth on the shore, has been sufficiently proved by the boring of wells at different points, as at Erie, Walnut Creek and Lock Haven, and by the natural springs at Westfield and Fredonia.

But whatever the cause, the light is a curious fact, and well worthy the attention of those interested in the investigation of the phenomena of nature.

AN APPARITION

What an Old Sailor Saw Some Years Ago on Lake Ontario

Winnipeg Free Press, December 14, 1882

"Talking about ghosts," said old Captain Jones last evening, as he cast a wary eye over the dark and stormy bosom of Lake Erie, while making a header against the storm down Bank street, "I hain't exactly superstitious, you know, but the dismal roar of that treacherous water and the sullen gloom of those storm clouds hanging over it remind me of a similar night long since past, when I was knocking about in an old-fashioned schooner on Lake Ontario. You see I have been a sailor man pretty much all my life," said he, as he tenderly shifted a very large chew of navy plug into the other cheek, "and I have had some mighty tough times of it, you may calculate. Well, as I was going to say:

"One Fall I shipped on board an old schooner from a port on Lake Ontario. We were engaged in the lumber trade. I had heard from some of the older sailors about the port that the vessel was haunted, but I was young, and not being a believer in ghosts paid but very little attention to the rumor. We made two or three trips and everything went smoothly, but one afternoon, while pounding down the north shore of the lake, we detected signs of a storm coming up from the nor'west. We made all preparation for a night of it, and if ever a crew underwent a tough one we did. The wind rose as the night came on, and the old lake was lashed into a perfect fury, while the darkness was fairly suffocating in its intensity. Of course all hands were on deck and each man had plenty to do. Suddenly the man at the wheel started from his post, and with a wild and terrified exclamation said:

"'Look up there!' All eyes were instantly turned aloft, and the sight which met my gaze was seared and burned into my memory for all time. Standing erect in the cross tree of the old hulk was one of the most frightful apparitions ever seen by mortal. It was the figure of a man posing as silently as the rock of Gibraltar. A dim, unearthly light surrounded the motionless form and shed a pallor of death over it. Its right arm was raised and the fingers pointed steadily into the very teeth of the storm. The face was white as marble, and a look, half terror, half madness, gave it an expression of indescribable horror. Its hair was long and wild, and the furious winds that shrieked through the rigging tossed it in confusion around the head and shoulders. We were fairly benumbed with fright as you can imagine, and every man aboard the vessels stood looking spellbound at the awful visitor. I can't say how long it remained there, but after what seemed an age, the light surrounding it grew fainter, and finally the ghastly specter melted into storm and clouds and was lost to sight. After the first sense of terror had left us, a grizzled old sailor remarked to me that the ship was doomed as sure as fate, and he was right, for we went ashore that night, and all but two of us were swallowed up in the frenzied lake. The schooner was battered all to pieces, and with her cargo proved a total wreck.

"I learned afterward that a sailor had lost his life by falling overboard from the vessel some years previous to her destruction.

"Do I think it was his ghost? Well, if it wasn't no man ever saw one."

THEY CALL IT A PHANTOM SHIP

The Yarn of Sailors on a Vessel Lying at Pictou — Who Say the Craft is Haunted Men Feared to Go Aloft — In Fact They Would Do Nothing — Without Trembling and Left as Soon as Possible

Daily News, St. John's, Newfoundland, November 15, 1898

Joseph Fraser and eight companions tell an interesting story of a vessel lying at Pictou.

The nine men together with the captain, steward and mate, formed the crew of the vessel. She is an old boat, one of the phantom ship character, and the men say she is haunted. All tell the same story regarding certain funny happenings on board and when she reached port, they left her in a hurry. The captain, who seemed to take the matter more coolly than the rest of his crew, endeavoured to induce the men to change their minds, but they turned a deaf ear to all his offers.

The story of the ghost dates back to a former voyage of the vessel. The captain is the only man aboard who knows the history of the tragedy in its fullness, and he is loath to tell all he does know. Half of the yarn is known to the men. It appears that a former sailmaker was sent aloft one stormy night to repair a sail and, when the vessel lurched in a heavy sea, he was thrown to the deck and striking on his head broke his neck. Since then the vessel has been haunted.

The last trip seems to have been worse than any previous one, and the crew solemnly affirm that they were afraid to venture on deck after dark. None would go aloft to trim sail and the men were thoroughly terrified by the strange happenings. Fraser and his companion named Williams state that on several occasions when aloft at their work a headless man stood beside them sewing at the sails. It is unnecessary to say that the sailors lost no time in reaching deck by the shortest route. They fairly tumbled down and refused to go aloft again. The captain was asked to explain but simply contented himself with laughing the matter off.

On another occasion the man at the wheel went asleep at his post and was awakened by a strange noise. His cries attracted his comrades, who, rushing from the forecastle, saw the same headless man standing nearby. The second mate made a run for the stranger, but it disappeared like a flash. After that the men refused to go to the wheel unless in pairs and the watches were looked upon with dread.

But the climax was capped when one night the compass turned about. The captain then became excited and for over an hour it was impossible to tell which way the vessel was heading. In about an hour the instrument resumed its normal condition, but the men became so restless that they almost mutinied. When the vessel left Pictou they

refused to go any further in her and have been shipped at
this port. — Ex.

FIRE OR PHANTOM SHIP

A native of the Maritimes, W.F. Ganong (1864–1941) was a noted botanist and a local historian of distinction. He spent his most productive years
teaching botany at Smith College, Northampton, Massachusetts. But he
returned to Nova Scotia and New Brunswick to holiday and to conduct
research into the geology and the folklore of the region. He made signal
contributions to natural science and the social customs of the region in
the form of scholarly papers delivered before learned societies.

Ganong was drawn to the phenomena of phantom ships and the fire
ships, the sight of which was frequently reported in Maritime waters, particularly in the Gulf of St. Lawrence, and notably in Bay Chaleur and the
Northumberland Strait. Ganong himself was not destined to witness the
apparition or the effect itself, but he interviewed many men and women
who did. He reported his findings in one of his academic papers, "The
Fact Basis of the Fire (or Phantom) Ship of Bay Chaleur." It was published
in the *Bulletins of the Natural History Society of New Brunswick*, Volume V:
Bulletins XXI to XXV, 1903–1907 (Saint John, New Brunswick, 1907).
This paper, read before the Natural History Society on April 4, 1905, was
revised, according to the author's note, in January 1906.

Here in its entirety is that important paper on a natural phenomenon that has swirling around it the mists of myth and legend. Ganong's
account may not be a *memorate* — that is, an eyewitness's account — but,
as a description of the phenomenon of the flaming ship, it is dramatic,
analytic, sympathetic, and definitive. The reader appreciates in every sentence Ganong's objectivity as well as the subjectivity of his informants.

The Fire or Phantom Ship of the Bay of Chaleur

One cannot be long in the Bay Chaleur country, especially its eastern part, without hearing of the fire (or phantom) ship, said often to be seen on the bay. Until a short
time ago I regarded the fire-ship as pure fiction, with no

basis other than the proneness of humanity to see wonders where they are expected, or where others say they exist. But as a result of two visits to that country, during which I questioned many residents on the subject, I have had to change my opinion; and I now believe there is really some natural phenomenon in that region which manifests itself in such a way as to be imaginable as a vessel on fire.

First we note the literature of the subject. Naturally the imaginative writers who have visited Bay Chaleur have seized upon the story of the fire-ship as a rare treasure, and, adding to the wildest local tales sundry fanciful imaginings of their own, with embellishments of banshees, pirates or picturesque historical personages, have produced weird fantasies such as are preferred to truth even by grown-up persons. A type of such stories is found in Miss E.B. Chase's *Quest of the Quaint* (Philadelphia, 1902), which connects the ship with the voyages of the Cortereals, making it a vessel set on fire by one of them when attacked by the Indians. From such a treatment there is every gradation, through many newspaper, guide-book and other accounts up to serious descriptions of the phenomenon as something with probable fact basis. The best account of the latter type that I have seen, written apparently by Mr. A.M. Belding, appeared some years ago in the St. John *Sun*. It reads in part as follows: —

> The extent to which a visitor may be impressed by the story of the phantom ship depends a good deal on the source of the information. Hon. Robert Young [of Caraquet] will tell you, for example, that frequently at night before a storm a large light may be seen on the surface of the bay. It may be seen in winter, when the ice has formed, as well as in summer, and it is not confined to any one portion of the bay. Sometimes it is much brighter than at other times and appears to dance along the

surface. Joseph Poirier said he had seen it so bright that the reflection would appear on the houses at Grande Anse. Rev. Father Allard said he had seen it several times this season. In fact it appears to be quite a common phenomenon, though nobody is able to explain its cause.... Those who decline to place full reliance in this interesting story [viz. the fanciful legend] nevertheless admit that sometimes the mysterious light emits rays that shoot into and athwart the gloom, and might by a particularly well nourished imagination be likened to the flame-lit rigging of a ship.

The information I have myself been able to collect from those who have seen the light is as follows. Of course I have sifted all testimony to the best of my ability, eliminating all exaggerations, whether these be due to the habit of a humanity to make a story as big and good as possible, or to the common tendency to gull an impressionable stranger, or to mere ignorance, superstition or mendacity.

Four years ago Captain Turner of Riverside, Albert County, a clear-headed sea captain, told me, in answer to my mention of the fire-ship as a freak of the imagination, that he had himself seen it and hence knew it to exist. Later, on my first visit to Caraquet, I was told by a lady, in whose word I have absolute confidence, that her attention was attracted one night by a light off Caraquet, which looked so much like a vessel afire that she supposed it to be one of her husband's schooners, and called him in alarm, only to find that it was the fire-ship. A prominent resident of Miscou, Mr. James Harper, told me he has seen it but once, in the winter on the ice off Clifton. It was seemingly some ten miles away and kept rising and falling, dying down to a very small scarcely visible flame, then rising slowly into a column "looking thirty feet high." It was not in the form of a ship, but a column, but people told him it was the fire-ship. He was told it preceded a storm, but he took notice and no storm followed. Mr. Robert Wilson of Miscou, who sails much on Bay Chaleur, tells me he has seen the fire-ship (or as he calls it, the "burning ship") several times. The time he was nearest it was about eleven years ago off Caraquet on a very dark night. The light appeared ahead, and finally he came near and passed within 100 yards to windward of it, so that he saw it with perfect clearness. It was somewhat the shape of a half-moon resting on the water, flat side down, or like a vessel on the water with a bowsprit but no masts et cetera, and "all glowing like a hot coal." He dared not run nearer and passed it, keeping his eyes upon it until far beyond. On other occasions he has seen it, at various distances, and has come to pay little attention to it. Sometimes it looked somewhat like a ship, sometimes not, and sometimes it vanished while he was watching it. Usually it is dancing or vibrating. Again he has seen it as one tall light which would settle down and rise again as three, which would again settle, and so on. Recently I have been told by Dr. J. Orne Green of Boston, whose connection with Miscou is mentioned below, that Mr. Wilson reports seeing the light this (1905) autumn; it appeared ahead of his boat as he sailed up the bay, vanished as he neared it, and in a few minutes re-appeared astern. Mr. Andrew Wilson, the other leading resident of Miscou, has also seen it, when it resembled a whaleboat, not a ship, in form. Mr. McConnell, keeper of the light at Miscou Gulley, tells me that he has seen the fire-ship, about two miles away, but it did not look to him like a ship, but more like a big bonfire. Several others have told me that they have seen it (the great majority of the residents in the region averring that they have seen it at one time or another), most of them agreeing that at times it looks like a ship on fire, but that at others more like a round light. All agree that it usually precedes a storm, and is seen over the ice in winter as well as over the water in summer. On the other hand, other trustworthy residents of Miscou, notably Mr. Jas. Bruno and Mr. Ed.

Vibert, both of whom sail much on the bay, tell me they have never seen it, and do not believe in its existence.

So much for local testimony. But it receives confirmation from another source. For many years past Dr. J. Orne Green of Boston, a Professor in the Harvard Medical School, has spent several weeks on Miscou and has taken a great interest in all that relates to the region. He tells me that he has himself seen a light which he was told was the fire-ship. Many years ago when running at night towards Caraquet he saw a fire off in the bay and called the attention of his companions to it, but finally thought it must be a woods fire on the north side of the bay. Reaching Caraquet, however, he found the people excited, because they said the fire-ship was out in the bay. He told them of his belief that it was a woods fire, but they declared this could not be, because it had moved. The wind at the time was gentle, from the southwest, but it was followed the next day by a great northwester. His interest being thus aroused, Dr. Green, in later years, attempted to investigate the phenomenon. He found that it was reported not only in Bay Chaleur but also in the Gulf of St. Lawrence as far south as Northumberland Straits. He came to the conclusion that while the stories were mostly exaggerated and distorted there was nevertheless some basis for them in fact and that there does occur in this region some natural light of the general nature of *St. Elmo's Fire*. This was exactly the conclusion to which I had come independently, as stated in this note when originally read before this Society.

Grouping together all the evidence it seems plain, — *first*, that a physical light is frequently seen over the waters of Bay Chaleur and vicinity; *second*, that it occurs at all seasons, or at least in winter as well as in summer; *third*, that it usually precedes a storm; *fourth*, that its usual form is roughly hemispherical with the flat side to the water, and that at times it simply glows without much change of form, but that at other times it rises into slender moving columns, giving rise to an appearance capable of interpretation as the flaming rigging of a ship, its vibrating and dancing movements increasing the illusion; *fifth*, its origin is probably electrical, and it is very likely a phase of the phenomenon known to sailors as *St. Elmo's Fire*.

I have, of course, made efforts to ascertain if any such phenomenon is known elsewhere in the world. Professor R. De C. Ward, Assistant Professor of Climatology in Harvard University, writes me that he knows of no record of a similar phenomenon, and no development of *St. Elmo's Fire* so great that it could be mistaken for a burning ship. Professor A.H. Pierce, my companion in my visit to this region last summer, has, however, called my attention to references to an allied subject in the *Journal of the Society for Psychical Research*, XXII, 1905, 108, and again in the Proceedings of the same Society, XIX, 1905, 80, where an account is given of lights claimed to have been seen around Tremadoc Bay in Wales; but the conclusion is reached that in all probability they have only a subjective basis, though the statement is also made that lights of unexplained origin were reported as common on the Welsh Coast over two hundred years ago. It is also of interest to note that Schmitt's newly-published *Monographie de l'Isle d'Anticosti* mentions manifestations of *St. Elmo's Fire* observed at that Island.

It is plain that in this phenomenon we have a subject which invites accurate investigation. It can best be studied by a scientifically-trained person, a physician or other student accustomed to scientific evidence, resident at Caraquet or Grande Anse.

PHANTOM SHIP OF THE BAY OF CHALEUR

The Phantom Ship of the Bay of Chaleur exists in story and song if not on the high seas. Catherine Jolicoeur began to collect ghost-ship legends in 1960 and she eventually compiled over one thousand sightings from all over the world. "People who see the Phantom Ship are not just imagining things," she explained. "They certainly see something. One theory is that it's a kind of mirage; others think it's a marine phosphorescent manifestation."

She found a great many tales of a phantom ship that haunts the Bay of Chaleur, the turbulent body of water that lies between Quebec and New Brunswick. One of the most interesting features of some of the tales of phantom ships is the death motif: to behold it is to have a foretaste of death. Soon someone will die. That belief was sometimes attached to the privateer ship the *Teazer*; Helen Creighton heard one person say: "If you see the *Teazer* you will die before the year is out."

The following account was related by Mrs. Joseph Comeau of Carleton, Gaspé, Quebec. It comes from unpublished research compiled by Edith Fowke which first appeared in my book *Ghost Stories of Canada* (2000).

> In June 1912, when I was twelve years old, after three or four rainy days … one foggy morning near a sandy shoal called Larocque Shoal I had the sudden impression of seeing an enormous ship coming between two rocky capes and moving. I cried, "Papa, look at the ship run aground there near the shore, scarcely three hundred feet from us."
>
> My father said to me after a long silence, "That, my child, is the fire-ship, look at it well." It was indeed the shape of an enormous vessel with dark grey sails flecked with white. You could distinguish the masts, the sails, large and small. I saw no rudder or bow, it was all a big mass. I didn't see any people but instead some black shadows overlapped each other; they resembled bodies or barrels. I was thrown into confusion. It passed very quickly. After a good ten or fifteen minutes the famous ship advanced into the Bay of Chaleur with bigger waves, broke up, disintegrated, as though the hull, the sides, were eaten; finally it all disappeared from our sight, carried away by an enormous wave. My father seemed frightened by the apparition of the phantom ship.
>
> We spoke of it at dinner. I recall that Papa spoke like this: "The first time that I saw it was the year that my father died; and another time, my brother died in

the Klondike. This time I don't know what will happen within the year." In the month of October the same year, a little sister died....

July 1914, after a stormy night ... my brother and I saw a mass of black smoke, which seemed to have a long broad opening surface plunging into the most extensive of the two springs whose surface resembled a layer of water fifteen to thirty feet around. The rest of this mass was high, resembling a little mountain, taking different forms, swelling like sails. One would have said an animal whose sides moved in breathing. We were like jellyfish through fright, holding our breath. After quite a long time, at least half an hour, the black mass, as though satisfied, began to move, rocking, doubtless drawn by the sea, took the form of a great ship, releasing the sails, which we believed to be of smoke, and quietly launched itself into the sea between the two rocky capes.... Concerning this sight of the phantom ship we weren't allowed to tell these stories of the abnormal sights we'd seen; we had to keep the secret lest we be taken for superstitious people.

THE PHANTOM SHIP OF ETOBICOKE

As a young sailor in 1910, Rowley W. Murphy experienced one of "the mysteries of the sea" and he never forgot it. Fifty years later, the veteran seaman and marine historian still cherished the memory of the sight of the strange steamer in Lake Ontario off Etobicoke in the West End of Toronto.

Was it a vision? A sighting? A spectre? According to his own account, written half a century after the initial encounter, Murphy remained of two minds about the nature of the "ghostly lake steamer." Murphy's account is reprinted from "Ghosts of the Great Lakes," *Inland Seas*, summer 1961.

My father, a cousin, and I were on a holiday cruise around the west end of Lake Ontario, and as we were late getting underway from Toronto Island, and were running before a light easterly, decided to spend the night in the quiet, sheltered and beautiful basin at the mouth of the creek, spelled "Etobicoke" — but always pronounced "Tobyco" by old timers. (This seems hard for present residents of that area to tolerate, as they insist on trying to pronounce each syllable.)

In 1910, the Tobyco Creek was really a small river which made an abrupt turn westward and widened into a small lake, with a good beach held by poplar trees, between this harbour and the Lake. There was perfect shelter in this excellent harbour from wind from any direction, though in a hard easterly, it was not easy to reach Lake Ontario through the narrow harbour entrance.

At the date of this cruise, there was one brick farm house to westward of the harbour entrance and no buildings at all among the walnuts and oaks on the lovely grassy banks of the creek, except one ancient landmark, known as "The Old House," from the veranda of which Lieutenant Governor Simcoe is said to have shot a deer in 1794. This house was in good condition, when a few years ago it was torn down to increase parking space for a supermarket! The whole area is now completely built up, but in 1910 the beautiful grassy plains contained no buildings from Lake Ontario to the Lakeshore Road, except the landmark mentioned.

Our cruising yawl, with a larger sister of the same rig and a still larger Mackinaw (one of several "fish boats" converted to cruising yachts with great success), were the only occupants of the harbour this perfect night. The crews of the three yachts numbered eleven in all, and as is generally the case, after dinner was over and dishes done, gathered on deck in the moonlight to engage in the best conversation known to man.

All hands turned in earlier than usual, there being no distractions ashore, and by midnight were deep in happy dreams, helped by the quiet ripple alongside. At what was about 1:30 a.m., the writer was wakened by four blasts on a steamer's whistle. After waiting for a repetition — to be sure it was not part of a dream — he put his head out of the companionway.

There, flooded by moonlight, was a steamer heading about WSW — at about half speed, and approximately half a mile off shore. She had a good chime whistle but not much steam — like *Noronic* on that awful night of September 17, 1949, who also repeated her four blasts many times.

But who was she? On this amazingly beautiful night, with memory strained to the utmost, it was difficult to do more than think of who she was not! She was considerably smaller than the three famous Upper Lakers, *China*, *India*, and *Japan* (about this date under Canadian registry, known as *City of Montreal*, *City of Ottawa*, and *City of Hamilton*). She was not as small as *Lake Michigan*, but like her, did not appear to be of all wooden construction. However, there were many in the past, of quite related design and size. The vessel seen had white topsides and deckhouses, and appeared to be grey below her main deck, like the Welland Canal-sized freighters (at this date, the big wooden steamers of the Ogdensburg Line of the Rutland Transportation Company). *Persia* and *Ocean* were like her in size and arrangement, but were all white and came to known ends, and of course *Arabiana* was of iron, and was black.

In this appearance off "Toby Coke" (a variant of spelling), the starboard light, deck lights and some seen through cabin windows, had the quality of oil lamps; and her tall mast, with fitted topmast, carried gaff and brailed up hain-sail. Her smokestack was all black, and she had no hog beams — but appeared to have four white boats. Her chime whistle was a good one, but was reduced in volume as previously mentioned, and was sounded continuously for perhaps ten minutes. Very soon all hands now watching on the beach decided that something would be done. So a dinghy was quickly hauled over from the basin, and, with a crew of four made up from some of those aboard the three yachts, started to row out with all speed to the vessel in distress, to give her what assistance might be possible.

As the boys in the dinghy reached the area where something definite should have been seen, there was nothing there beyond clear and powerful moonlight, a few gulls wakened from sleep — but something else, impossible to ignore. This was a succession of long curving ripples in a more or less circular pattern, which just might have been the last appearance of those caused by the foundering of a steamer many years before on a night of similar beauty. In any case, the four in the dinghy returned in about an hour, reporting also small scraps of wreckage which were probably just old driftwood, seldom seen with any fresh breezes blowing.

But something more there was. This was the appearance to the visual and audible memory, which those on the beach and those afloat had seen and heard, of something which had occurred in the more or less distant past, and which had returned to the consciousness of living men after a long absence.

Whatever the cause, the experienced crews of the three yachts mentioned were of one mind as to what had been seen and heard. At least eleven lake sailors would be unlikely to agree on the character of this reappearance without good reason! And the reason was certainly not firewater working on the mass imagination, as no one of the three yachts had any aboard. So, reader, what is the answer?

6

SUMMONING THE SPIRITS

There are two ways, experts assure us, of "summoning the spirits." There is the traditional and tried way and then there is the modern and untried way.

The traditional way is through the use of conjuring, prayers, invocations, evocations, spells, charms, enchantments, trances, witchery ... in other words, time-honoured shamanistic practices. In Native lore there was one sure-fire way of conjuring and that was the use of the so-called Shaking Tent. I have recorded descriptions of these practices taking place among the Algonkian-speaking Natives over a period of four hundred years across much of northeastern and central Canada. This way the shaman could supplicate and importune Mikinac, the prophetic Spirit of the Turtle.

The modern way depends on just how modern you want to be. If by modern you mean the nineteenth century, then the way to approach the spirits of the dead — or disembodied spirits, as they were called at the time — is through the seance and psychical research. The great mediums of the past were spiritualists who worked in parlours and sometimes in theatres. It is interesting to recall that the founders of the Modern Spiritualism Movement were two farm girls from Consecon, Upper Canada. The Fox sisters, Katie and Maggie, claimed to have established "two-way" communication with the spirits of the dead at their family cottage at Hydesville, near Palmyra, Upstate New York. Two knocks for no, one knock for yes.

If by modern you mean the twentieth and twenty-first centuries, then the way to do it is through the parapsychological experiments that take place in psychology departments or physical science laboratories of colleges and universities. J.B. Rhine spent much of his professional life as a psychologist who attempted at his Parapsychology Laboratory to prove the existence of "extrasensory perception" (clairvoyance, clairaudience, psychokinesis, telepathy, remote viewing, psi factors, enhanced abilities, psionic abilities, et cetera). His work was continued by a professor of engineering, Robert G. Jahn, at his Engineering Anomalies Research Lab at Princeton University. The jury is still out on the usefulness of Rhine and Jahn's work, though its value in moving the study of spirit-possession, spirit-mediumship, and action-at-a-distance out of the parlour and into the scientific laboratory is laudable.

In the meantime, men and women continue to beckon spirits to leave their other-worldly sanctuary and converse with mere mortals!

WONDERFUL MANIFESTATIONS BY A PIANO

Toronto, October 14, 1856
Messrs. Partridge and Britten:

Dear Friends — For the benefit of your many readers, I give you an account of one of the numerous demonstrations that we occasionally receive through the mediumship of Mrs. Swain, a lady of this city, who, for the different phases of that wonderful power of spirit influence, is rarely equalled.

Happening in her house a few weeks since, four persons beside the medium and myself took our seat around a piano that was in the room — myself locking it and placing the key in my pocket — with the usual lights burning in the room. Shortly after the company had taken their seats, the keys of the instrument were sounded, and answers given in that manner to questions asked. Among many inquiries made was the question, "who it was that was communicating with us," when the name was spelled — by striking a key as the letter of the alphabet was pointed to — of an old friend of my own, one who had been many years at sea, and master of several ships. To prove his identity he, at my request, did several things, such as making the noise of a gale of wind rushing through the rigging and blocks of a vessel; the plash of the water along the side; breaking of the heavy seas on deck; creaking of the guards and blocks; and rolling the heavy instrument, just like a vessel tossed about on a heavy sea. At the time I, and most of the other persons present were leaning all our weight on the instrument, it raised up and down, rolled about as if it were possessed with life, and became light as a feather, instead of weighing several hundred pounds! To make assurance doubly sure, I put the following questions, knowing that no other person present beside myself knew the meaning of what I asked: "Now, friend," said I, "we will call the end of the instrument toward my left the stern of your ship, and the opposite one the bow." I was sitting at the front with my arms leaning on it. "Now, I want you to give your ship, as you call it, a list to port"; when immediately over it went to the opposite side to the one I was leaning on, and perfectly correct in seaman's language. It rested in that position for some time, nor could all our bearing down bring it back. I then asked the spirit to give "lurch to starboard," when over came the piano to the same inclination on the opposite side. I then asked him to give me a sample of a ship riding at anchor in a heavy head sea. Immediately, up raised the instrument at the bow, and then the end representing the stern, and so on, first one and then the other, with an occasional roll to each side. After that was over, one of the party was influenced to sing a sea song, when a beautiful accompaniment was played on the strings to the tune; and one wonder is, that the person who sang, in his normal state could not sing at all, but at this time those who heard him said that he sang beautifully. Now all this was done in a lighted room, with the instrument locked and the key in my own pocket; and I know that one or more of the parties present never had their hands or arms from off the front board all the time....

Yours sincerely, for the truth,
"R."

A SPIRITUALIST IN MONTREAL

Popularity as distinct from genuine fame is so fleeting that the description of someone as "well known" is certain to be self-defeating. For instance, who today has ever heard of Dr. Orton, the author of the next contribution? "The following was communicated by Dr. Orton, a well-known New York physician, to the *Spiritual Telegraph* of March, 1858." These are the words of Emma Hardinge, British spiritualist, also known as Mrs. Emma Hardinge-Britten. In her day she was widely respected as one of the editors of the London publication *Spiritual Telegraph* and is recalled today as the author of a number of books including *Modern American Spiritualism: A Twenty Years' Record of the Communion Between Earth and the World of Spirits* (1869). Mrs. Emma Hardinge-Britten travelled throughout the English-speaking world and promoted the spiritualist cause. According to the contemporary newspaper reports of her public appearances in Montreal, she completely confounded the critics in that city, a city noted for its hostility to spiritualism. (A half-century later, Sir Arthur Conan Doyle, a famous rather than "well-known" advocate of the spiritualists' cause, would declare that the city was hostile to the message of "spirit-return" because of its population which was predominantly Roman Catholic. Both Doyle and Hardinge-Britten were well aware of the Church's traditional stand on mediums and psychics.) The account in Hardinge-Britten's book concludes with these words: "The 'important results' prophesied by Dr. Orton, in additional remarks omitted in this place, have indeed been accomplished. From Montreal to Prince Edward's Island [*sic*], Mrs. Hardinge extended her visits until the largest cities and villages of that section of the province became alive to the truths of Spiritualism, and earnest in evoking the abundant medium-power with which the Canadians seem to be endowed."

Dr. Orton's Tour — Mrs. Hardinge at Montreal — Waterford, February 18, 1858

I have just had the satisfaction of meeting Mrs. Hardinge here, at the house of General Bullard, on her return from Montreal, and of learning, from the Canada papers she has brought along, the results of her Northern mission, which have been, and promise still to be, of a most interesting character. It seems that before leaving the States, at Rutland, Vermont, she was informed that her presence at Montreal as a public speaker, but on account of her sex and the doctrine she advocated, was likely to produce some disturbance; and that certain persons were threatening to procure her arrest, should she undertake to lecture, as a disturber of the public peace; hence, she was advised not to proceed.

On her arrival at Montreal all this proved true. Nevertheless, she proceeded to the fulfillment of her engagement. On entering the hall where she was to speak, on the first evening, she was met by sneers and audibly discourteous remarks, on the part of some of the audience. This, however, ceased when she had spoken a few words, and all remained quiet and attentive to the close of the lecture.

The audience on this first occasion was not large; but amongst it was a strong array of learning, — of priests, lawyers, doctors of various orders, and reporters. The time having arrived for questioning the speaker, a Jewish rabbi, of great scholarship and intelligence, was placed in the van as chief spokesman. A period of profound and exciting interest succeeded. The questions, at least some of them, according to the journals of that city, were put with the obvious purpose of confounding the speaker; but, according to the same authority, each successive attempt was promptly frustrated, and the tables turned upon the querists. It was declared that the speaker must have devoted her life to study, in order to be able to exhibit the learning she displayed. The rabbi announced that it was plain that she was acquainted with the Hebrew language, and interrogated her on that point. She replied that she had never studied the Hebrew. But very shortly after, she tripped him on a point relating to that language, and reasoned him down until he acknowledged his error. At the close of the session, the victory remained triumphantly with the speaker.

On the second evening the hall was crowded, but with the lecture, the exercises terminated. No one, according to the journals referred to, seemed willing to enter the list and oppose himself to the ready with an acknowledgement of the speaker.

Two more evenings of crowded audiences, at an admission fee of twenty-five cents, succeeded with like results. The questions were again resumed, but with no better success on the part of the querists. On all points raised, the lady speaker remained confessedly master of the field; and with a fifth and free lecture on the Sabbath, on which occasion, she was tendered, and occupied the Unitarian Church, Mrs. Hardinge closed her labours at Montreal, where Spiritualism seems, previously, only to have been known in name.

THE HARMONY "RAPPINGS"

The Harmony "Rappings"

(From the Ontario Reporter)

Well, we have been on a visit to hear the mysterious sounds that are at present creating so much sensation in Whitby. A part of our curiosity in this respect, has been gratified; but not the whole. — The real solution of the mystery we leave to those more profound in the philosophy of natural magic, or cause and effect, than ourselves. The matter is beyond our ken. On Tuesday evening, last, we drove to the house of Mr. A.M. Farewell, Jun., one of the first families, in which the "spirits," as they are called, were discovered. After being sufficiently warmed in the comfortable sitting room in which the family were gathered, a chair was placed at the table, and on being seated, a young lad, apparently abut nine or ten years of age, the son of Mr. Farewell, also took his seat and invited the presence of the "spirits" by placing his hands on the table. This lad is not the "cunning looking youth" represented, but the reverse — rather sleepy looking, and certainly incapable of carrying on so successful a deceit, if it be one. On asking, "Are the spirits here?" a volley of faint rappings were heard under the table. None were touching the table except the boy, whose hands were laid flat on it with no perceptible movement. On asking if it would communicate with the person present, it answered by three distinctive raps, which are said to be signs of the affirmative. After a thorough examination to see that there was nothing in connection with the table but the boy's hands, and to detect, if possible, any collusion between parties, we proceeded to ask various questions, touching matters on which the family must be totally ignorant, and received affirmative or negative raps, some as distinct as if striking the end of a pen holder, or a knife handle gently under the table. We are aware that it is fashionable among many to set down everything approaching the marvellous as a humbug, and all that; but it must certainly be a very humiliating satisfaction for such to adopt the proposition without being at all able to enlighten the less discerning wherein it lies. We cannot.

After remaining about an hour in Mr. Farewell's family, our next visit was to that of Mr. Terwilligar's, accompanied by Mr. Farewell, where we were informed the rappings were occasionally more distinct. Here we were shown in to the family room, in the centre of which stood a large dining table, around which Mr. Terwilligar and a young man of the family, who is the "medium," sat. There were none in the room but the two mentioned, together with Mr. Farewell and the writer. The young man placed his hands on the table and asked, "Are the spirits here?" Three loud raps were heard on the table. The young man sat back, after asking the usual question if "they would communicate with the stranger present?" for we were here informed the sounds are frequently heard as well when the hands are off, as on the table; and we proceeded with the scrutiny as before. The raps came loud and distinct at our call — none were touching the table but the writer, nor to the best of one's knowledge, within a foot or sixteen inches of it. Every question was answered by more or less raps, which, if they were produced by any human agency, was more than we could discover. We were informed by Mr. T., that the day before, the "spirits" had moved the large family bible around the table, in the presence of several whom he named, but upon being asked if they would do the same for us they answered in the negative. This was a sore disappointment; nevertheless, we had to submit to their coquetry in that matter. This feat, of shoving things in the room, is apparently incredible; but we have Mr. Terwilligar's word for it. We vouch only for what we have seen and heard. That it requires the force of matter to remove matter is unquestionable; but, again, does it not require the same physical power to produce the raps on the table? The one is no less incomprehensible than the other, and both are at present, to say the very least, really astonishing. The noises, we were informed, frequently occur on the wall, in the windows, on the floor, and other parts of the house. At one time the raps came on the floor while we were present at the home of Mr. Terwilligar, but only once.

Men may call these mysterious phenomena by what name they will, but they are unquestionably worthy of enquiry.

Spirit Poetry

The Globe, Toronto, February 28, 1852

The spirits of the Poets are manifesting themselves through their mediums, if we can place any faith in one or two productions which have recently appeared, purporting to emanate from Edgar A. Poe, Samuel Taylor Coleridge, and others, and given to the public by those who are, from some unknown cause, in communication with the departed. In the late number of the Spirit Messenger there is the following poem, dictated, it is said, by the Spirit of Edgar A. Poe: —

"Listen to me and I will tell you of beautiful things — of thoughts both wild and tender, both soothing and tumultuous, which dwelt in a human heart. A question which has moved the minds of millions is — What is the end and aim of imagination? — for what was it implanted in the human organization? What was my own? but a vortex rushing within itself, upon whose brink I could seem to stand and see what was being swallowed and reproduced — thorns, jagged rocks, beautiful flowers — all in the whirl of this ceaseless current emerged."

O, in the dark, the awful chaunt;
O, the fearful spirit-spasm,
Wrought by unresisted passion,
In my heart.

Fancies hideous, but alluring,
Love pure, but unenduring,
From time to time securing
Each's past.

Then embraced by seraph bands —
Drawn by tender, loving hands —
From those treacherous, hateful sands
Of despair.

How any soul was waked in gladness,
And cast off the deadening sadness,
And the soul-devouring madness
Writhing there

Then came dreams so soft and holy,
Over roses wandering slowly,
With sweet music, stealing lovely
To my ear.

Hark! I hear — I hear her calling.
In tones no more of waiting,
But a dewy sweetness falling —
"Here — up here!"

Thanks, Great Heaven, I am stronger —
Slave to earthly lust no longer,
I am free

O, this lightness! O, this brightness!
O, this pure and heavenly wholeness,
Marking thee!

Freed from earth and sin forever,
Death can us no more dissever.
Humbly thank Great god together,
Thou and me.

The *Springfield Republican* alluding to the above, truly remarks: — "The poem and the prose message introducing it, challenge attention, at once, by their intrinsic literary merit, and by a marvellously close alliance to the style of versification, thought, and genius of the author, from whose spirit they are alleged to have emanated. They were communicated through the 'writing medium,' Lydia Tenny. We ask for these productions a close examination, by all who have studied the erratic genius of Poe, who, whether good, bad, or indifferent as a writer never had a parallel. We may overrate these productions, yet while we are aware of certain limpings in the measure, they appear too steeped in the very spirit of Poe, whether they emanated from his spirit or not. The allusion to the 'spirit spasm' a phrase most felicitous in describing Poe's life of darkness; the "hideous but alluring fancies" in which he groaned and on which he gloated, the incidental, hardly perceptible, allusion to that one soul! that haunted all his poems — the 'Lost Lenore' — all tend to show that it is the work of a rare master of deception, a most thorough adept in art, or that it is precisely what it claims to be.

"We must confess that the above poem defies disbelief almost, and if it is a cheat or a piece of deception it far exceeds any attempt ever made by Chatterton, who was eminently successful in literary deception. We have also seen another poem, dictated as it is said by the spirit of Samuel Taylor Coleridge, which could only have been written by a master spirit, one who if living need not have recourse to any humbug to obtain the laureal wealth. It is ten stanzas in length. Here are three verses which strike us as the most meritorous:

> "Oh, Man! the soul within thee cries,
> Against the Pantheist's creed of lies,
> And stricken conscience from the cloud
> Of inward evil groans aloud;
> Fears through thy mind's dim zodiac fly,
> Like ravens calling from the sky,
> 'The spirit lives when breath is fled,
> And judgment waiteth for the dead.'
> The drops of life-like sands depart,
> From the vein'd hour glass of the heart,
> And mournful whisper as they fall,
> 'Death came by sin, death comes for all.'"

[Note: The original publication includes more verses than the ones that are reproduced here. A little goes a long way.]

THE KEYS OF THE INSTRUMENT WERE SOUNDED

The identity of "R.," the writer of the letter that follows, is not recorded and will probably never be determined. The letter, on the occasion of its original appearance in the London journal *Spiritual Telegraph*, bore the intriguing title "Wonderful Manifestations by a Piano."

The editor of that journal and the leading British spiritualist of her day was none other than Emma Hardinge, who was also known as Mrs. Emma Hardinge-Britten. She published R.'s letter in the journal and reprinted it in her travel memoirs *Modern American Spiritualism: A Twenty Years'*

Record of the Communion Between Earth and the World of Spirits (1869). In this volume she went on to make some general points about the Canadian cities she visited:

> Spiritualism has taken a firm and deep hold upon the inhabitants of this country, and in some parts exhibits a condition of progress little behind that of the States.
>
> In Toronto, Mrs. Swain, one of the most powerful physical mediums of the day, has for years been producing irresistible conviction of spirit communion upon the minds of hundreds who have attended her séances.
>
> In London, Canada West, a number of true-hearted believers have rallied round the lead of Mr. John Spetigue, who, himself a devoted Spiritualist, has for years laboured in the cause, engaging speakers and aiding in the development of media, until his efforts have resulted in procuring a respectful hearing for the one, and a very general growth for the other.
>
> In Ottawa may be found a brave and devoted little band of Spiritualists, who depend chiefly on the abundant medium power existing amongst their own ranks, the place being too remote to secure the services of travelling lecturers and media.
>
> At St. Catherine's [*sic*] there are a large number of Spiritualists, including several very excellent and successful healing mediums.

In the letter reproduced below, R. comments on the remarkable abilities of Toronto's leading physical medium at the time, Mrs. Swain.

The account concluded with the following note: "The author of the above communication sends his full name, in attestation of the facts stated. — Ed., *Telegraph*."

A POWER OVER WHICH
WE HAVE NO CONTROL

All that is known of Alfred H. Smith, aside from the fact that he was an enthusiastic spiritualist, is that in the 1850s he was a resident of the small community of Laprairie in Canada East. (No longer an isolated community on the south shore of the St. Lawrence River, La Prairie is today a suburb of teeming Metropolitan Montreal.) Smith was anxious to publicize the cause of spiritualism, but when the local newspaper editors derided the notion of spirit-communication, he took the bold step of writing to Emma Hardinge-Britten. He addressed her in her capacity as a leading editor of the influential *Spiritual Telegraph*. Mrs. Hardinge-Britten travelled around the world in the cause of spiritualism. When it came time to prepare an account of her travels in America, she reproduced Smith's commentary which describes some of his strange experiences. The following account of the death of a friend and its aftermath is taken from Emma Hardinge's *Modern American Spiritualism: A Twenty Years' Record of the Communion Between Earth and the World of Spirits* (1869).

Editor of the *Spiritual Telegraph*:

Sir, — The newspaper editors of Montreal having unanimously refused to insert a single word in favour of Spiritualism, while they open their columns to every idiot who may find anything to say against that doctrine, the friends of the cause have determined to apply to you, as your journal is devoted to the spread of Spiritualism, and if necessary to pay for the insertion of each communication.

It may be asked, why are we so anxious to publish our communications with spirits? Our answer is, we cannot tell. We are forced to it by a power over which we have no control, and in consequence we ask you, in the name of God and of truth, to give publicity to the following:

It is about three years since I heard the phenomenon of Spiritualism first spoken of in Canada. I then, as well as at several periods since, looked upon the thing as a monstrous imposition. I however continued at the request of several friends to attend "circles" of the believers in this new doctrine, but to no other effect than to confirm me in my scepticism; and all the arguments of my friends and all the alleged manifestations were insufficient to convince me. But Providence chooses its own time.

In July, 1853, I left Canada, in company with an estimable friend, W.F. Hawley, Esq., of the Ordnance Department, C.E., on a tour through the Middle and Western States; and on Saturday, the 27th of August, we arrived in Louisville, Kentucky, where my friend was seized with yellow fever, and after an illness of nine days he expired.

It has never been my fortune to be acquainted with a more honest, upright, or learned man than Mr. Hawley. He, as well as myself, had investigated the subject of Spiritualism, but with a contrary result. He was a believer, while I, until the moment of his death, remained incredulous.

As I seldom left the bedside of my friend during his illness, I took frequent occasion to talk to him of the new faith, when he invariably expressed his entire belief in it; and in a few days I had the inexpressible delight of witnessing the reward of his faith and the realization of all his hopes. Oh, sir! I cannot find words to express the transporting emotions which filled my mind at the moment of his death. Although I was the only living being present, yet I distinctly saw hundreds of moving forms around his bed, and in every part of the chamber, but of such dazzling splendour that I could not distinguish their features; the room was filled with superhuman sounds, which appeared to come from the ceiling; and involuntarily looking up I distinctly saw the spirit hover over the body which it had just left, as if uncertain whither to direct its course. It remained thus during the space of a minute, then moving gently to one side it entered a body whose transcendent splendour the tongue of man cannot express.

At that moment I felt my mind, as it were, regenerated.

I shall now give a few out of the many manifestations which have been witnessed, and can be attested, by the most respectable citizens of this village.

On Saturday, the 27th of August, 1853, my friend, Mr.

William Fox, invited me to meet a circle of friends at his house; accordingly I repaired thither at eight o'clock that evening, and met a highly respectable company, among them a clergyman who came to investigate the subject for his own satisfaction. We had not sat more than twenty minutes when Mrs. Fox became greatly agitated; she was lifted forcibly from her chair, and suspended about a foot from the earth for a minute and a half; she was then placed in her chair again, but still agitated and unable to speak. It was evident the spirit had not sufficient influence over her. After some moments Mr. James Macdonald approached, and made a few passes over her, when she immediately spoke as follows:

> Friends, it is now five weeks since I left your society on earth, and when I tell you my name, you will not be surprised that I desire to return amongst you in spirit, confirming the glad anticipations of a bright existence in the spheres which I cherished on earth, desirous to instruct you in the glorious realities of my present exalted condition, and give you a foretaste of joys which await the good and true in these blissful regions. But as there is another spirit who wishes to communicate, I shall withdraw until to-morrow night.
>
> Farewell; your friend,
> "W.F. Hawley."

To me that communication was most convincing. The style, language, and certain words of the phraseology, were essentially that of my friend. The influence then changed, when the medium said, addressing Mr. Macdonald, —

> Friend Macdonald, I know the thoughts that now occupy your mind, and I come to

tell you about your son, whom it was your earnest desire to hear of when you came to this circle. I have just left him where in spirit, I visited him, in a very bad condition both of body and mind, lying in a hospital in New Orleans, suffering from a severe attack of scrofula; but you need not feel uneasy; he is surrounded by the spirits of his friends, and your father, who occupies a higher sphere than that which I inhabit, tells me that your son, although obstinate, is a chosen vessel, destined to do incalculable good among the faithful....

Mr. Macdonald then asked: "How am I to know that you are speaking the truth? What proofs can you give me? What is your name? It was written: 'Your father, who is present, will answer these questions to your satisfaction.'"

At this moment the husband of the medium came into the room, and, from some cause, the communication ceased; however, after a conversation of about twenty minutes on general topics, it was written:

My Dear Son, — Your questions to the spirit who has just left, I shall answer to your satisfaction. As a proof that what he told you is true, you shall receive a letter from New Orleans on Thursday next, corroborating the statement of your son's illness, and on Friday, the 28th of October, you shall receive a letter from himself requesting to be again admitted to your friendship. The name of the spirit is Thomas Henry Caldwell, your son-in-law, and the favour which he requests you to do him is to pay an account which he owed Mr. John Charlton at the time of his death. You can pay this account, as the whole of

Caroline's fortune is still in your hands,
and Caldwell has left no issue.

Good-night,
"William Macdonald"

Of the numerous family circumstances contained in these communications, not a soul present but Mr. Macdonald himself had the least knowledge. Although the communications were of so delicate and personal a nature, however, he candidly informed the medium as well as all present, in a few weeks subsequent, that the letters promised from his son had arrived. Every statement of the spirit was fully corroborated. "In a word," added Mr. Macdonald, "unless it was spirits, no power under heaven could have made those disclosures to me...."

I am, yours, faithfully,
"Alfred H. Smith"

SPIRITUALISM AT MAPLE BAY

"Spiritualism at Maple Bay" appeared in the *Victoria Daily Colonist* (Victoria, British Columbia), January 1, 1876. Mr. Beaumont seems to be the newspaper's stringer as well as a local hotelier. Too bad he gave his readers no particulars about "Mrs. —"

We have received two interesting letters from Mr. Beaumont at Maple Bay concerning recent manifestations at that place. Amongst other appearances were those of a Mr. Simpson, who was murdered in his cabin at the bay four years ago and a lady who gave her name as Mrs. —, who was lost in the Pacific. The spirit of Mr. Crate, who died just after he had completed his grist mill at Cowichan, appeared at the seance and sent a message to his son to stop the millwheel, as it was wearing away the joints. But the most remarkable circumstance was the appearance of a spirit who had died from the effects of drink; and a description of the torturing thirst which assailed the poor wraith has so affected Mr. Beaumont that he has determined to discontinue the sale of intoxicating liquors in his hotel.

"SAILING 'ROUND THE STARS"

A Trip to the Planets — Fortune-Telling by Consultation with the Heavenly Bodies

Victoria Daily Colonist, September 24, 1886

There is a rare pathos and beauty in the mythological stories of the planets, although it is a branch of literature overlooked by a vast majority of people. The attraction has not been wanting, however, to many superstitious persons both in the United States and England who are to-day turning their limited knowledge to good account pecuniarily. It is estimated that there are a thousand fortune-tellers who use the planets as a means of plying their calling. From a source so exalted the subjects expect to hear marvellous things about themselves, and despite the seeming absurdity of it, hundreds of people seek these supposed planetary agents for advice and a peep into the future. Hearing that a fortune-teller received visitors here in Victoria a gentleman lately from the east called to test her powers, and, according to his own story, the experience was a novel one. Being ushered into a cozy sitting room he met a pleasant lady, who hearing his errand became enthusiastic on the subject at once. Producing a pencil and a slip of paper she said:

"Write your name, date of birth, and the hour, if you are positive of it, on this slip of paper. That will do. So you were born on the 3rd of January at 2 o'clock in the afternoon. I don't believe you are right about being born in the afternoon, it was in the morning about the time

Jupiter first appeared above the horizon."

"Why? Were you present when I made my bow to the world, madam!"

"No, I was not."

"Well, I was, and ought to know when I first wrestled with life."

The planet reader paused, then continued: "It may be so, yet your planet is Jupiter, if my calculations are correct."

"Hardly Jupiter, madam, for had I been descendant from the ancient God of war Zeus my natural instinct would have guided me to a more heroic life than that of a plumber, which I don't mind telling you is my occupation."

"A plumber!" and with such soft hands, she exclaimed: "I saw I was cornered."

"Madam!" I replied quickly, "I am a boss plumber; I plan the work, my men execute it."

"Ah! yes, I see; I thought you might be one of those abominable newspaper reporters. Well, Mr. —"

"Smooth is my name, Eph. Smooth," I interrupted.

"Well, Mr. Smooth," she continued, "you are born under a lucky planet. According to the belief of the Romans, Jupiter determined the course of all earthly affairs, and revealed the future through signs in the heavens and the flight of birds. I refer to Jupiter Capitolinus, the mythological God known as Optimus Maximus."

"Excuse me, Madam, but the God Jupiter of mythology has very little connection with the planet Jupiter."

"Yes, he has, but antiquity is not to be viewed and explained according to the ideas and customs of modern times. Has it never occurred to you that from the first matter containing the seeds of all future being a race was created through God able to comprehend the source from which the various forms of the material world were produced; and in contemplating these forms as they were distributed into abiding places they perceived that the same energy of emanation gave existence to living beings as well as the God who inhabit the heavenly bodies and various other parts. These first people looked upon every planet and star as a living, breathing thing. To them the vast space in which they floated was not too great for comprehension, and they moved about in familiar contact with the inhabitants of these various parts thrown off from the same matter and distributed throughout the universe. Would it be reasonable to believe that of all the bodies formed from chaos, that the earth, the smallest should be the only one inhabited by human beings? Would it bespeak the infinite wisdom of the creature to suppose that from his effort only the minor part of matter was turned to account, and the major part left a worthless mass? If he had desired to produce the earth, from chaos, without creating other worlds, could he not have done so, without forming six other bodies of twice the magnitude and importance in the planetary world? Therefore I contend that as every planet emanated from the same matter, was formed by the same creator, they are all inhabited by a race of living rational beings."

"That is all very well, madam; but how could a race of beings exist on Mercury, or even Jupiter with their proximity to the sun?"

"I do not say people of the earth temperament could exist on these planets, — they are endowed with temperaments suited to the planet upon which they live. I believe there is a constant interchange of souls or life sparks between the planets. To die is but to live again. Death is a change necessary to fit a soul for the climate of another planet. It is the reformation of matter and conducted by the same agency that first produced the planetary bodies and then caused them to be inhabited. Can you reasonably say that Jupiter, revolving around the sun at a mean distance of 475,000,000 miles is uninhabitable? Here we have a planet 88,000 miles in diameter, or one-tenth of the sun, its volume 1400 times that of the earth, revolving at the rate of 500 miles per minute, to the earth's 17 miles per minute. Was all this created for naught? I tell you there are living beings on that planet, and, young man, they are souls from this world prepared for existence there. They are transformed by death into beings who can live in a ten hour day and years that are equal to travel of ours, — comprising nearly 10,000 of our days."

"Then you believe in the immortality of the soul, madam?"

"Most assuredly I do; it seems to me any one of ordinary sense ought to be convinced on this point. As birds migrate from one zone to another, so I believe human souls migrate, through intervention of the supreme power that rules the universe, from one planet to another. Nothing dies but life is formed from that death, and the great work of progression goes steadily on. A horse dies, soon worms are created, they in turn are transformed into moths and thence into beautiful butterflies. Every tree and plant of nature is reproductive in this manner. Could a power so infinite that it watches these minute details to perfection, create all the great planets and only perform these things on the smallest and most unimportant of them? I am as positive that the planets are inhabited as I am that the earth holds me, and young man when your work is finished on earth you will undergo the change that fits you for an existence on your proper planet, Jupiter. After that in time I believe you will undergo another change and be transmitted to some other planet, for life is eternal in some shape or another."

"Tell me, madam, will I be a plumber on Jupiter, or is the climate so warm that there are no frozen water pipes?"

"What!" she exclaimed, and springing from her chair she grasped my wrist, and gazing into my eyes as if my whole soul was there laid bare for inspection, continued in a sort of Hamlet soliloquy whisper, "would you like to go there now?" There was a bright glitter in her eye, she was inspired, the lines about the corners of her mouth twitched perceptibly with emotion. There was a dangerous vehemence in her manner. Instinctively I looked around for my hat and shifted uneasily on my chair. I thought over all the mean things I ever did, and wiped the perspiration from my brow with my coat sleeve.

Opening my hand she furtively traced the lines along the palm, and then in a sad voice said, "You have not long to stay on this earth; your hours are numbered."

I began to feel that something terrible was about to happen and involuntarily shuddered as I thought of my prospective migration.

At last in sheer desperation I drew my hand away and jumped to the door. It was locked.

"Wait," she said. "I am permitted through the influence of your planet to reveal much of your future. Listen! You are already under the spell of Proserpina who presides over the death of mankind, and if you remain silent I will unveil to you the scenes through which you will pass in the transmission of your soul from earth to your planet, Jupiter.

Closing her eyes she was silent for a moment, and then in a low, plaintive voice began: "You will first perceive a number of terrible forms, disease, old age, terror, hunger, death, the avengers of guilt. On you go to the resort for departed spirits. Among them you mingle. There are those who suicided, victims of love and despair, and hundreds of the sad experiences known to life. Then you will pass into fields adorned with all the beauties of nature — a most delightful recreation to your mind. There are hills covered with fragrant shrubs, grand valleys, flowery plains, shady groves, lucid streams, gentle and unclouded sunshine. Being freed from the passions and prejudices of mortality, you enjoy the pleasures of contemplation, until at the command of Zeno you drink the fatal waters and the oblivious draught causes you to lose all remembrance of the past, so when again you assume the cares and sorrows of humanity on Jupiter elysium is forgotten, the past is obliterated, and amid the new scenes you find nothing strange, for that other life has faded forever from your memory."

"That's very smooth, madam," I managed to say.

"Very smooth, indeed; that's about the appreciation I might expect from a plumber. You have no more sentiment or imagination in your soul than a stick. However, I have told you all I can, and in closing my seance I conjure you by all means to be ready at any moment to die, for your life is short. One dollar and twenty-five cents please. Thanks! Good night."

I WOULD HAVE STRANGE EXPERIENCES

The photographic portrait of J.K. Cranston which appears in *What Converted Me to Spiritualism: One Hundred Testimonies* (1901), edited by B.F. Austin, shows Cranston to be a forceful-looking man, with a full moustache and a determined look in his eyes. He describes his spiritual experiences in a forthright manner in this account. Some of his spiritual experiences are spiritualistic in nature.

I was born near Galt, Aug. 14, 1856. My parents were Scotch and were of the sturdy, intelligent type that characterized many Scotch people.

As a child I had several peculiar experiences and was thought strange and imaginative. I grew very sensitive and felt the edge of criticism so keenly that I often wished myself out of existence. I grew reticent and kept my thoughts and experiences to myself or would go to the woods to ponder and commune with nature.

When 15 I left home to make my way in the world, going to Port Hope to learn the book and stationery business. I joined the Presbyterian church there and endeavored to live a consistent life, but found the good I would do was often left undone and the evil yielded to. My cry would go forth, "Oh, wretched man that I am. Who shall deliver me?" Returning to Galt some years afterwards I engaged in the book and stationery business. Then I attended Knox church and entered heartily into the work connected therewith; but still life to me was very unsatisfactory, and I felt within me a call to a higher and better life. In my search after truth I learned of a people now called the Burnsites, who taught and claimed to be able to live continuously a victorious life. I sought them out and found to my own satisfaction that the truth they preached was of God and became one with them. Life had now new pleasures. I carried the good news to my Knox church friends, and to my surprise got snubbed for my pains and was finally tried for heresy by the church courts, and I with six others was expelled — for what? Because we believed and taught that it was possible for the child of God in this world to live a continuously obedient life and for professing this as our personal experience. We did not claim infallibility or absolute perfection, but that holiness and progress co-existed, knowledge increased and would do so unto all eternity. We claimed that God was guide absolute unto all truth. We continued enjoying life as never before and our labors bore fruit and others learned a like experience. Still, ever and anon I would have strange experiences and felt strong forces at work within me that mystified me. I told friends of my feelings and I both felt and was thought odd. I could see, hear and understand what was thought by unseen intelligences. I did not believe in spirit return and was not aware that spirit friends were working with me to develop my forces so as to bless my life and others.

On Aug. 4, 1899, at Niagara Falls, I was awakened by a hand being placed on my shoulder, and looking up I saw a hand above my bed holding the Scripture motto, "In quietness and confidence shall your strength be." To make sure that I was neither asleep or dreaming I got up and washed my head and body with cold water and then lay down again, and almost at once my mother's (who is in the spirit world) face appeared and smiled upon me. She called me by name and talked to me about what I was passing through for about eight minutes and then disappeared. At a meeting that day I told of what I had seen and heard, and of course I was thought queer. Since then I decided to let the occult in my nature have full swing, as that was what mother seemed to say was necessary for comfort and development. I became clairvoyant and clairaudient. I saw and described distant scenes and what was going on in Canada, England, South Africa, and took pains to have what I described verified, accounts of which were published in the Sermon in Nov. and Dec., 1900, and in May, 1901. I found also that I had magnetic healing power, and have since been using that power for the good healing both of myself and others. I have on different occasions diagnosed and located diseases and pains which had baffled physicians. I have read and studied and attended lectures and seances and have become thoroughly convinced that our "so-called dead" still live, and can and do communicate with us by numerous methods, namely, by table rapping, slate writing, through trumpets, trance mediumship. I now frequently converse with my spirit friends in my own home and on the street and am able to recognize their voices and have seen them and felt their kiss on my cheek. My daughter Helen, who died when three weeks old, is often with me and has told me time and again that she was my reminder. She often reminds me of things I am forgetting to do. In Toronto last December I lost an important order for books which could not be duplicated, and after I had looked in vain for it I asked the Lord to give me guidance. Almost at once I heard Helen's voice saluting me with, "Hello, pap. God sent me to tell you that your list of books which you lost is at Mr. B —, Yonge st." I went at once and found it there as directed. I thanked God for help received so promptly.

I find my own safety and the development of my psychic forces, character and happiness is dependent on my absolute obedience to the Guide Divine. I find, also, that judgment, reason and good common sense are not outraged but harmonized with. It has proved to me that death hath no terror. Friends who are gone still live and communicate. There are natural or psychic laws which, if harmonized with, make it possible to both receive and transmit messages. The utilization of these laws is not necessarily confined to a so-called religion any more than the use of electricity is to a restricted class. The law is universal.

Let us not, whoever, be carried away by the mere "phenomenal side" of modern Spiritualism. Let us seek to develop the mental, spiritual and higher possibilities of the life that is bestowed upon us.

> Living for those that love us,
> For those that know us true,
> For the God who gave us being,
> For the good that we can do.

RESIST NOT THE SPIRIT

B.F. Austin included the testimony of C.F. Broadhurst, a resident of Arnprior, Ontario, in his collection *What Converted Me to Spiritualism: One Hundred Testimonies* (1901). His photograph shows Broadhurst to be a burly individual, conservatively dressed, with a full handlebar moustache and a receding hairline. It is easy to see him as the son of a farmer from the north of England. Broadhurst's testimony covers a lot of ground, including a premonition, divine inspiration, a crisis apparition, the operation of a medium, and astral travel.

> At the age of 22 I was engaged in Christian work in Hereford, Eng. I left there and went to my home, my father being a farmer living near a village called Mamble in Worcestershire. I had been at home two weeks and each Sunday had attended the church at Clowstop, one mile away. The third Sunday morning when I came down I told my father that I had to take the service at Clowstop. He asked me how I knew. I told him I had seen myself three times in the night standing in the pulpit preaching to the people, and every time preaching from the same text. He said, "Go, my boy, and the Lord be with you, but if you are going to preach at Clowstop to-night you ought to prepare yourself." I asked him what preparation I needed, as the one who gave me the vision would speak through

me. That night was stormy, but I started off by myself and sat by the door. The chapel was well filled. Each time the door opened people would look around for the minister, but none came. After waiting twenty minutes I walked up into the pulpit and began the service. All went well until I gave out the same text I had used in my dream (the conversion of St. Paul). That was all I remembered. I felt as though I was floating. When I came to myself I saw by my watch I had been speaking three quarters of an hour, but knew nothing that was said. I went home greatly mystified. I have had the same experience many times since.

I came to Canada in '93. I had heard a great deal about Spiritualism in England, but it was supposed to be of the devil, so I steered clear of it.

On the night of Feb. 3rd, 1900, we had retired for the night. I was awake, thinking, when I felt a strange feeling and heard a report as if a revolver had been fired. I looked, and standing at the foot of my bed was a man in shining light. The hair was dark, his eyes blue, and he was standing like a statue. He had purple pants, but the rest of the body was nude. I did not speak — I could not. He gradually passed away. I told my wife what I had seen and got up, lit the lamp, looked at the clock and found it was 12:30. We retired about 12:00. I met a friend, Mr. M ---, a miner, who is a medium. I asked him to come up in the evening. He took up a slate and pencil. I then asked who it was I saw the night before. His hand began to move and wrote "Theodore Brown, West Bromwich, England." He then spoke through the medium and said, "Mr. Broadhurst, you have seen me." I said I did not remember him and had only been through West Bromwich once, and then on my wheel. He then asked, "How would you like to see my astral body?" I said I would like to see one. "What did you think of me last night when I came?" I asked him what he was in England. He said he was a minister of the Gospel. He also gave me good advice respecting my health and said he would come again. I asked my wife if she knew him. She said she was once introduced to a young lady who was to be married to him, but had not seen him. He came again the night of the 3rd. I have not seen him since, but others have, and given his name in full. At a sitting with Mrs. Etta Wreidt, the trumpet medium, I had a long talk with Theodore Brown.

My first "soul flight" was early last winter, while staying in Victoria, B.C. We retired about 9:30. I felt a great power pass over me. I wondered what it meant. The thought came to me: Resist not the spirit. I kept passive and felt a sensation of floating away. My eyes were open to a glorious sight, which I have longed many times to behold again. Under our feet were lovely flowers, on each side beautiful trees. I was in company with one whom I knew. We were floating over the country at a rapid rate. I could see myself. I looked the same as in my body. I said to my companion, "This is grand; let's keep on going." I was travelling on the right hand side of him. At last we came to some great mountains. We seemed to be going at lightning speed. I heard the roar of rushing water, and in an instant I seemed crowded, and struck the great volume. I had the sensation of spitting it out of my mouth. I was afraid. My companion took my hand and said, "Be not afraid, though you pass through deep waters I will uphold you." We went on over a great lake. I could see for miles the sparkling water on my left and the great waterfall on my right, which must have been hundreds of feet high. In front was an opening between two mountains, where we tarried, standing upon flat rock. Behind us was the lake. Here we talked together. Every word of the conversation I can remember and never could forget. At last we started to go. The lovely sights passed from view. I lost consciousness and could feel I was gradually coming to myself. My wife asked me what was the matter, as she had been trying to make me hear her but could not, as I was like one dead. I have been away several times since.

THE SPIRIT OF THE HANGING JUDGE

The Hanging Judge is the moniker by which the public recalls Sir Matthew Begbie (1819–1894), the pioneer law-giver of the Cariboo, who was known far and wide for his harsh but generally fair judicial decisions. It is said that Sir Matthew knew more about human nature than he did the law.

I first learned that the spirit of British Columbia's Hanging Judge may still dwell among us from Robin Skelton. A widely admired poet, an industrious scholar, Robin was also a practicing witch. In the latter years of his life he formed an alliance with Jean Kozocari, a well-respected medium and practitioner of wicca. Robin and Jean would visit haunted sites, and if requested to do so by their owners or occupants would exorcise them.

In response to my query about Sir Matthew, Jean sent me an audio cassette in which she recounted the details of her encounter with the spirit of the Hanging Judge. Here is the text of that cassette.

In 1980 we were invited to investigate a haunted house. We found the house to be a fifties bungalow built on the side of a hill in Saanich, which is just outside Victoria, B.C. It was a comfortable house, a very beautiful one. The people as newlyweds had drawn up a plan for their dream house, and this house fit every criterion they had. Years later they found and bought it. They owned it for more than three years. And although they were paying two mortgages, they were never able to live there in comfort.

Strange things happened. Workmen made commitments and never showed up. There were floods although the house was built on top of a hill. There were plagues of rats, and when the rats died in the building, there were plagues of flies. No matter what they did, always something came up to make the house unliveable. The woman suffered severe personality changes there. The man found that an incredible lethargy came over him whenever he tried to do work on the hill.

We arrived on Father's Day, and on the way out, the two mediums whom I took with me, although best of friends and always pleasant and congenial, fought constantly all the way out. When we arrived at the house, we went in, walked through it, and investigated it. There were several places that were very uncomfortable, including one room in the basement that had been built over a large protruding rock so that the rock became part of the room. Over the three years that we investigated the house, this rock frequently oozed a very strange, oily substance that had the consistency of thick motor oil that was shiny and aluminum looking. We would find it on clothing, on dowsing instruments, all over us, all over the people who came in and out of the house.

The haunting resisted exorcism. We had all sorts of meetings. We had dowsers come in to see if there were water deposits under the earth. One afternoon my eight-year-old son was having tea with us in the living room of the house. As he was sitting there, drinking tea, a beautiful glass picture frame lifted up off the bookshelf, did a complete somersault in the air, and landed in his lap! There was absolutely no way that it could have fallen — four feet high! — into the air, and in a complete circle, before it landed into his sister's lap. He's now twenty, and we were talking about it last night. It is one of the lasting memories of his childhood, much outweighing Christmas and Halloween.

One of the unexplained phenomena was that the owners of the house had fastened glass mirrors to the wall and then built bookshelves in front of them. Slowly over the weeks the letter *M* appeared. It was scratched into the silvering on the back of the mirror in a place where no one could have got at it. At the time we didn't see any great significance to the letter *M*.

All our efforts failed in the house. All we were able to do was clean it up temporarily, then something else would happen. We began a research on the property. The house was reasonably modern, but in researching it back to its first owner, we found that the property had been the property of Sir Matthew Begbie, the Hanging Judge. We found that, although he had never lived there, built a shed, built a building, or did anything else on the land, he used to ride out on his horse, taking his lunch with him. He was seen from the distance sitting on the large rock (the one that now protruded through the basement) and meditating. He would spend hours just staring off into space.

This made a lot of sense to us because for some reason or other ropes accumulated in the basement of the house. The lean-to shed where they put their car had the modified shape of a gallows. But of course until we had the clue that this was Sir Matthew Begbie's property, we were never able to contact Sir Matthew Begbie.

At this time the owners were offered an enormous sum of money for the house. They sold it and threatened me: "Please, don't tell anyone that the house is haunted!" They were terrified that the deal would not go through.

On the last day they were in the house, I went there with a photographer who sometimes has the ability to photograph "extras" — shapes, sizes, or ghosts. We use an old-fashioned Polaroid camera, the kind with the pictures that separate. You have a negative and a positive with a gummy substance on it. She put the film pack into the camera and walked around, taking pictures of the house. However, we were unable to get a photograph of the corner of the house that extends over the rock. That corresponded to the dining room. It was always missing from the picture. If we took it in the middle of the pictures, the rest of the picture would be fine, but there would be a white column down the middle. If we took it from the side, that part of the house never photographed. We went to two drugstores and got two different packs of film, thinking that perhaps there was a problem with the film. The packs were not labelled consecutively, so we knew they were from different batches. However, we were unable to take pictures of the dining room. Everything else — the front of the house, the back of the house, the trees, the rock garden, the pond — were fine. It was only the one part of the house that refused to be photographed.

As we were driving away, the owners were standing, waving to us, and the photographer had one more negative. So she put the camera out the window and took a quick picture. As we drove down the driveway, she pulled out the film and held it for the proper time, then pulled it apart. The image turned out to be badly under-exposed. We placed the negative, which was sticky, on the dashboard of the car and promptly forgot about it. (That sounds awful, but I am a slob about my car!)

One evening several weeks later we were sitting talk-ing, and someone said, "Well, the negative is out in the car." So someone went out and got it and placed it on the table. On the negative was a picture of Sir Matthew Begbie. All of us had seen the photographs of him that appear in books and articles. In these he wears a broad-brimmed, cowboyish hat, he has a dark beard, and looks very elegant. So we were able to recognize him immedi-ately, despite the fact that in our picture he had no hat on and his beard and hair were white and curly. It was not until three years later that I found a picture of him in his older years. Indeed, his beard and hair were white and curly. The Polaroid photograph is very old now. I put a strip of plastic across it to preserve it as much as I could. But for anyone who has ever seen a picture of Sir Matthew Begbie, it is quite obvious that Sir Matthew was there with the owners of the house saying goodbye to us — obviously quite relieved that we were leaving him and his property in peace.

One of the awkward things about investigating ghosts and haunted houses is that you can't, really, ten years later, go back and knock on the door and say, "Hello, I was here ten years ago, and this house was haunted. Do you still have a ghost?" Somehow, if I were a little bit pushier, maybe I could do that. But, at present, it's just not part of my reality.

That is Sir Matthew's story. While he is certainly not the offending ghost, it is obvious that his very strong presence at the house made it possible for other and later things to manifest. And we did find out in researching that practically everybody who had lived in the house had

had problems with it. The previous owners had been a Navy gentleman and his wife. He had retired early and decided to become a minister. He studied there, rehearsing and memorizing passages from the Bible and hymns and prayers and so on. His wife, on the other hand, was totally devoted to the Maharishi Mahesh Yogi. She was deeply into meditation and her mantras. So perhaps all this mental, spiritual activity added to the already overpowering presence of Sir Matthew Begbie, made this haunting indeed most violent.

II
HAUNTINGS OF THE PRESENT

1

AT HOME ... ALONE?

I have always felt that there is something a little odd about being at home alone. I would not call it a creepy feeling, precisely, but there is something peculiar about it. The house is suddenly empty of people, but is it empty of spirits? By "spirits" in this instance I mean the sense that the rooms of the house are occupied by other occupants, in my case by my wife, Ruth, who walks along the hall from room to room turning lights off and on and making an agreeable amount of noise. When I am alone, those sounds are absent. Instead of them, what I hear are creaks and groans, noises that filter in from outside (in winter) or waft in the window screens (in summer). I find I mumble to myself, clear my throat, tap my toes ... if only to assure myself that the house is not a vacuum chamber, or an anechoic chamber like the one you can enter at the Ontario Science Centre, where "the silence is deafening."

If you have not entered one of these chambers, you should do so. You walk into a hall-like room that has baffles on its walls, floor, and ceiling. As you enter, the outside sounds — the ambient sounds — begin to decrease. Then you hear ... silence ... and your heart beating ... and the sounds of your own movements ... and (I sometimes think) the sounds of your own thoughts!

Houses held to be haunted resemble anechoic chambers. Sounds are magnified rather than diminished; the same holds for the absence of sounds. Sensibility and imagination are suddenly set to work!

It is one step from audible distortions to visual distortions and after a while you begin to "see things." Was that a shadow in the corner? Was there movement in the next room?

Haunted houses may be more than that. There may be a legacy of reports of ghosts or spirits that haunt the place. There may be a story about a previous occupant who killed someone (according to one account) or was killed by someone (according to another account). The stories are regularly gruesome and seem to lack a genuine resolution, a final chapter. Here is where you come in. You are now the witness to the spirit's confession or to the re-enactment of the event itself. My advice to you: take notes!

The stories in this section have some of these characteristics in common. But generally the narrators, the witnesses, are taken by surprise. Though, when they come to think of it, they are surprised to discover that the place really is ... creepy!

GHOST OF A GIRL IN CORNWALL

Don Bellamy lives in Bradford, Ontario. He heard me chatting with Bill Carroll on AM 640's *Toronto Talks* and was inspired to send me the following hand-written letter dated February 9, 1994.

Dear Mr. Colombo:

Heard you on the radio this morning. In the summer of 1964, my family and I were staying in an old farmhouse near Newquay, Cornwall, England. The family that owned the farm told us the building was over 300 years old. My wife and I and our 18-month-old son were in one room, my two daughters in another room across the landing, my mother in a room next to them.

At around 1:00 a.m., I came awake and realized that a girl was standing at the side of my son's cot. She had on a cotton bonnet and was wearing a long cotton dress, very plain, and was looking into the cot with a smile on her face. I thought my eyes were playing tricks on me, but she was right there, the room being lit by the moonlight from the windows. I had a torch under my pillow and switched it on. There was a grey blur and the window curtains were agitated though there was no wind. As well, the window was closed. I woke up my wife, and then we did a tour of the other rooms. Everyone was asleep.

The farm was at Degenbris Minor and the family that owned it at the time was called Carhart. They would not admit to any previous knowledge of ghostly appearances in that room.

Since my wife passed over, I have had other experiences occur with witnesses present. But have never written them down.

D.R. Bellamy

IT CIRCLED BEHIND ME

Here is a mood piece that by focusing on the writer's reactions requires the reader to imagine the worst.

"It Circled Behind Me" was awarded first prize in *Toronto Voice's* annual Halloween true ghost-story contest. It was published in the October, 1995 issue. Its author, Helen Healy, won a dinner for two at an Italian restaurant ... compensation, but not enough to offset the horror and fright she experienced that night in the early spring of 1990.

It was early spring of 1990 when I walked out the door of that house for the last time. I sensed the dark force that had tormented me was watching me from the blackened windows, smirking, self-satisfied in its success to drive me away. I hurried on, believing that I would never return.

I first saw the house a month earlier in daylight when I jumped off the streetcar still holding the address of my new job in my hand. The old two-storey row-house looked ordinary enough, though a little out of place in this dreary, desolate industrial area of King Street East. It had been renovated and converted to offices, flanked on one side by an overpass and on the other by buildings inhabited only by day.

The main floor was office space for another company. The office I was shown to was on the second floor at the top of a steep staircase, off the middle of a long, narrow hallway.

The door to the attic and a room with a kitchen and bathroom was at the back end overlooking the parking lot. An empty room, looking over the street, was at the front. The attic, I was told, was rented by a woman living in Barrie who was going to use it when in town on business.

Within minutes the day shift left and I was alone. A strange feeling of uneasiness came over me that I shrugged off as being the unfamiliar surroundings. I began processing the paper work when I heard movement in the hallway right outside the door. I got up from my desk and looked up and down the hall, seeing nothing. I checked the other two rooms. My stomach was tightening as the first queasiness of fear rose in me. It had gotten dark suddenly so I switched on lights, moving faster and faster to reach every light I could find.

The shadows took on elusive forms that I couldn't quite identify. My scalp was warm and prickly as the hairs rose on the back of my neck. I knew I wasn't alone. Every step I took felt like something was right behind me, breathing, staring, gliding malevolently with hands groping for me but just out of reach.

Evil images popped rapidly into my mind like subliminal messages. I was panicking with my imagination, I told myself, and needed to get back to the safety of the office to calm down. My heart was hot and thumping wildly by the time I reached my desk. The sounds continued as I forced myself to work. I didn't dare to go to the bathroom down the hall. When my shift was over I ran from the house to the relative safety of the deserted, dark street to wait for the streetcar, not daring to look back at the house.

I needed the job so I went back every night, but each time with increasing dread. It was always the same unexpected thumps and bumps and sliding, slithering sounds along the wall, each night gaining intensity — until the last night. It was the worst.

It began with sounds of footsteps and furniture being moved and objects dropped in the attic apartment above me. Thank God, she's here, I thought, relieved that the woman from Barrie had finally moved in. I was comforted knowing another human being was near by.

Until I felt the unknown evil force coming closer and closer up the hallway. I clutched the desk as I sat frozen, facing the open doorway. I never closed the door, out of fear of seeing the horrible thing lunging at me when I opened it. My finger nails gouged into the wood. I talked out loud and sang distractedly. My entire body was tingling and buzzing like I'd stuck my finger in a light socket. My desk began vibrating and shifting. Even if I'd wanted to jump up and run, I couldn't. I was pinned in my chair by a powerful force. At the doorway I could see energy forming, whirling molecules coming together. A figure, barely perceptible, glided towards me. My eyes froze wide and I was close to passing out. I couldn't yell for help. I was paralyzed.

It circled behind me, swarming over me and I felt fingers of electricity combing through my hair. I went blank. The next thing I remember was lunging through the door onto the street right into the woman from Barrie who was just arriving.

I never went back. I don't know how long the woman stayed, but I know that the company moved out shortly after. Someone had discovered concealed in a boarded-up hole in the wall in the basement, a painted pentagram and a wilted rose.

I WAS NOT REALLY HOME ALONE

Beverley Ann Akers lives in Midland, Ontario. She did not hear me when I talked about ghosts with Bill Carroll on his program on radio station AM 640, but a friend of hers did. The friend apparently relayed to her the fact that I was a sympathetic soul. Whether or not this is true, Beverley contacted me and told me that her house is haunted by "man's best friend." Pony, her ghost dog, is apparently her best friend! I convinced Beverley she should write up — and then type up — her story. She did so. Here it is in the form of her letter to me, dated March 1, 1994, with all the "atrocious" spelling corrected! (It wasn't all that atrocious after all!)

Dear John:

I'm sorry that I haven't gotten this letter off to you sooner. Usually when I procrastinate there is a reason, as you will see when you read the ending to this story. At any rate, here is the "spirit" story you asked me to send along.

I bought the house in which I am now living on Fitton Street in Midland, Ont., mainly because I had a good feeling about it. After settling in, I found that if I looked back at the front window, as I drove away from the house, I would have the sense that someone was looking out the window. There was no one I could really see, just a sense that someone was there, looking out.

In Jan. 1993, I was sitting, late at night, at the dining-room table, talking to one of my boarders. I looked into the kitchen and saw a brown mist cross in front of the fridge. I decided I was tired, and so I went to bed without giving it another thought.

It was at about this time that my Burmese cat, Psycho, began to act strangely. He would suddenly wake up from his sleep, put his ears back, and in a round-about way make his way to the basement. He would often stay there for two to three hours. This is totally out of character for him.

One evening I happened to be home alone, watching a good movie on TV. I made a quick dash to the washroom and left the door open. What can I say? It was a good movie, and I didn't want to miss any of the dialogue! I looked out the door and down the hallway in time to see a brown mist come up the basement stairs, turn right, and go into the kitchen.

While I was trying to shove my heart back down my throat, I noticed Psycho making his dash downstairs. My initial thought was that I was not really home alone.

My son Adam came to visit over the Easter weekend. One night he stayed up to watch a movie. When I got up in the morning, the coat closet and front doors were wide open. Since no one else was home, I did the motherly thing and scolded him for leaving the doors open. He explained that, at approximately 3:00 a.m., the closet opened, as if someone were standing there. I suggested that the cat might have been in the closet, but Adam said that the cat had been in the basement when he came in from the garage after having a cigarette. (No one smokes in the house.) Who or what had opened the closet door?

Friends suggested that I use a pendulum and ask questions that could be answered yes or no. Imagine me, a sceptic about pendulums, actually using one. The pendulum answered the questions I put to it: No, whatever it was wasn't here to scare me; no, it didn't come with the house; yes, it did follow me here; yes, it did open the closet door....

Well, that did it for me! I put the pendulum away.

A month after this, I learned that the boarders in the house would be leaving. The idea of being all alone in the house, especially at night, with a cowardly cat and an unnamed spirit, was too much for me. I decided to address the spirit.

I explained to it that I knew it meant well and that it hadn't hurt me. But I asked it if it could leave me alone for a while, at least until I got used to being alone in the house.

Well, it left, and I immediately felt guilty. Nothing strange has happened since then.

John, this is a follow up, as a result of my procrastination. So help me, it's true.

On Feb. 27, I went to a health-awareness day held in Barrie. There were various displays for alternative therapies. At the suggestion of friends and because I am fascinated with UFOs and such things, I approached a gentleman from Toronto who was there who specializes in crystal and sound therapy. (Sound therapy is really something new; I guess I'm getting better at not bursting out in laughter at some of the New Age things I see.)

At any rate, I explained to the gentleman what I hoped he could help me accomplish in the fifteen minutes he allotted to me for a reading. When he finished, he very quietly asked me if, as a child, I had ever had a large dog, and if I had, what its colour was. He sensed that this dog was around me. You could have knocked me off the chair with a feather. He repeated three or four times that the dog didn't know it was dead.

Pony was the name of the Great Dane I had had as a small child. Pony was brindle in colour and bigger than I was. He was my protector and no stranger could come near me when Pony was around. My parents gave him to friends who owned a farm. Not long afterwards, he ran out onto the road and was killed.

When I got home on Sunday, I went through the house, calling him, apologizing for not understanding the situation. I told him that he could stay if he wished, but not to scare the other animals. At the risk of becoming certifiable, I again resorted to the pendulum. If animal spirits can make pendulums move, then Pony is here in the house, has been here, and doesn't want to leave.

When I went to bed, I settled down to read. I had to fight with the cat for my spot on the bed. The cat was sleeping when he suddenly sat up, walked to the edge of the bed, and stood there for about three minutes, staring down at the floor. Then he resettled and went back to sleep. My only assumption is that the cat sensed that the spirit is back and was lying beside my bed.

I know this sounds unbelievable and I sometimes wonder why these things happen to me, but I do swear it's all true. I am sorry that I am so long-winded, but that's the way I am — ask my friends.

I also apologize for the atrocious typing (this is my second corrected version). Use what you need out of all this and good luck!

One thing I do know is that I have my hands full

with the complete food chain I have residing in my house: lizard / turtle / canary / cockatiel / cat / one live dog / and one dead dog's spirit.

Lord, help the next teen who thinks he wants to bring home another part of the food chain!

Sincerely yours,
Beverley Ann Akers

A HAUNTED HOUSE IN PRESCOTT

Readers who are familiar with the Internet and with email will know that it is possible to join a newsgroup and be sent letters or postings about subjects of interest. Each day, at no cost, a kind-hearted person who calls himself Khalloween selects and sends a new true-life ghost story to me and to other like-minded newsgroup subscribers. Here is one such message from James F. Robinson. It has been nominally edited but is otherwise complete with transmission information. It was received on June 15, 1995.

I think it is about time that I contributed a story. This is it!

I grew up in a haunted house in Prescott, Ontario. My father had bought an old carriage barn that had been behind a funeral parlour. A great aunt of ours had died in it of a heart attack when the coffin of her late husband fell off the wagon, broke open, and his body sat up in reflex. They say that a deranged man hanged himself in the rafters of the same barn.

My father moved the barn to a triple lot down the street and placed it on a foundation. He stripped the planks off and built a spacious, three-bedroom home around the shell of the squared timbers and what ever else lived there. After we moved in, we began to experience some strange happenings. There was a closet in the east bedroom that would not stay locked. Back then we had the old latch-key locks. We would lock the closet door in the evening and then sit back and watch. At about midnight, the key would turn by itself, unlocking the door. Then the door would swing open. It got to the point where we simply left the door unlocked and open. My sister, who slept in the room for a while, would wake up screaming, claiming to see a man hovering over her, showing only from the waist up and having a hangman's noose around his neck. The apparition appeared to be trying to choke her. Dad moved us boys in. We never saw the ghost, but both of us would occasionally wake up with constricted throats.

My sister, who appeared to be psychic, also saw our dead great-aunt, who would rush down the hall. If you were in the hall, you would feel a cold rush of wind. Auntie would then pass through the bedroom door and scare off the ghost with the noose.

Response

Stories on the Internet often generate responses. "A Haunted House in Prescott" did just that. Here is that response, shorn of the transmittal information. I do not know the identity of Angie, but I assume that she is a happy soul, because she signs her name like this:

Angie :)

and that, for readers who are not computer literate, is known as an emoticon. The emoticon, in this instance, is a happy face. (To see the happy face, turn the page ninety degrees clockwise.)

Great story, Jim.

Good thing the great-aunt kept an eye out for the family.

The story regarding the circumstances of her death reminds me of a story my dad told me. Mind you he told us this story when we were kids.

This story will throw everyone for a loop....

I don't remember if he witnessed it or a relative of his did, but nonetheless, he and mom are visiting me this weekend, and I'll find a way to pop his question "out of the blue."

Anyway, apparently my family was tending to my granddad's funeral, mind you, this is Mexico a long, long time ago. The family was poor and usually the funerals were held at the home. Well, it seems that this granddad was laid out on the table. (He died due to heart problems.) Just envision all these people praying, crying, etc., at the house when ... BE WARNED THE NEXT PARAGRAPH YOU READ WILL BE GRAPHIC AND VERY GROSS: Apparently, the late granddad sits up (in reflex?), looks around (while people are screaming in panic and just being scared witless), vomits, and collapses on the table again, "dead." =:-O!

Long time after everyone calmed down, ol' granddad was promptly buried. And to the best of my guess, last rites administered, again.

Angie :)

FOOTSTEPS IN THE ATTIC

Pat Watson is the author of this ghost story, courtesy Obiwan's Ghost Stories Mailing List. I first read it on my monitor on May 28, 1996. It tells the story of a haunted house on the shore of the Powell River, British Columbia.

I, and a couple of my cousins, along with an uncle who is close to our age, camp out in some remote areas as often as we can. This particular incident happened about eleven years ago on one of our trips.

My great-grandfather had a somewhat large farm on a ridge top overlooking the Powell River. When he passed on, he of course divided up the land and buildings between his children, one of these being my maternal grandmother. She had told us of a small cabin deep in the middle of her father's farm, which had stood empty for many years. We decided to plan a trip to it one weekend.

After bouncing down the rough, unused road to the cabin, we parked in the front yard and began unloading gear. It was during the first of spring, so we decided not to pitch tents, but retire to the cabin to sleep, it being much warmer inside. Sometime before midnight we were sitting around the fire, when we heard a noise coming from the direction of the cabin. It sounded like footsteps in the attic. We gathered weapons and lights and went to investigate. Nothing was disturbed. This sound was repeated several times during the course of the night. Later, as we were getting ready to retire, one of my cousins came back from nature's call and said he heard something that sounded like a baby crying. We'd all felt that funny feeling you get when you think you're being watched, but had tried to ignore it.

We returned to my grandmother's place the next day around noon. My uncle and I ate lunch with her, and she asked where we'd been. We told her, and asked if she knew anything about the cabin or that area. She said that, around the turn of the century, a couple with their small child lived there. The man was a woodcutter and was gone from home quite a bit. She said that one day the mother went into the baby's room (since turned into a kitchen) and found the baby dead. She supposedly went insane with grief, and paced the floor of the attic day and night until her husband had her committed.

Kind of boring maybe, but what struck me was the fact that we'd heard nothing at all about this place prior to our first trip there, and then had the story told to us after our experiencing the strange things there.

WE FIGURED IT WAS A FEMALE SPIRIT

"Ghost Stories" was the title of a feature article on hauntings, the work of veteran journalist John Mentek published in *The Hamilton Spectator* on July 29, 1995. It included the following account of a haunting contributed by a witness named Andrée. It is an exceptionally interesting account because the experience is so meaningful to Andrée and her husband.

This happened in an apartment in Hamilton about five years ago.

Not long after we'd moved in, I started hearing strange noises. It began to feel like somebody was walking right behind me as I walked down the hallway. The presence was so strong, I'd say aloud, "What do you want? What are you doing here?"

My husband and I both felt the presence for about four or five months before we told each other about it. He didn't want to bother me with it, and I didn't want to bother him, because I knew he was really not into this kind of thing.

One night I was doing dishes and I heard this noise again. I started to tell my husband how I'd not only heard strange noises in the apartment, but also felt someone's presence behind me. I would even walk into a smell of perfume, which disappeared in the time it would take me to take a breath.

He turned to me and said, "I can't believe you're telling me this. There are nights when I can't even stay in the room, because I know somebody's there with me."

We'd smell perfume and figure there's got to be a vent somewhere, but there wasn't. The smell would be in the middle of a room and then it would be gone. It wasn't like it was trailing in from somewhere. It was a very flowery strong perfume.

We also found cold spots in the apartment. You'd just be sitting there watching TV, and suddenly you'd be freezing. Then you'd get up and move, and you'd feel the difference in the room immediately. When you went back to where you'd been sitting, it was gone.

We figured from the presence of the perfume that it was a female spirit. I didn't really get the feeling it was malicious or anything. Then my husband had the idea that it was the spirit of my grandmother because when she died, my aunt had given me the cross from off her coffin. My grandmother always had this saying, "You have a cross to bear in life." For some reason, my husband thought of this cross that I had tucked away in a chest somewhere, and he said, "She wants it back."

So I took the cross from the chest and we went to my grandmother's grave. We got some very strange looks when we walked into the cemetery with a shovel. We dug a foot or two down, wrapped the cross in a clean white hanky and buried it beside her.

Then we said a little prayer for her. And then everything stopped as suddenly as it had started. It just went away.

It was very, very strange.

I WAIT FOR HIM

Lillian I. is the contributor of this memoir to the article "Ghost Stories" written and compiled by the journalist John Mentek for *The Hamilton Spectator*, July 29, 1995. I am grateful to him and to the witness for permission to reprint it here.

A lot of people laugh when you tell them things like this. But nothing like this ever happened to me before.

Jimmy was my eldest boy. He used to come to my house in the morning after work. I'd hear him and from the kitchen he'd yell upstairs, "Come on, Momma, come on. I've got some breakfast ready for you."

We were very, very close. I had four children, but he was the only one who would ever really sit and really, really talk to me.

He'd been gone nine years, but I never stop thinking about him. He dropped dead right at his desk — he told them he was tired, and then he just dropped dead. He was thirty-six. It was a great loss. I've still got his pictures all over the place, and I talk to his pictures.

It was maybe a month ago I saw him. I never even told my husband. I don't know why it happened when it did, nine years after he died. Maybe it was because I've been so down lately. You see, that's when he was always helping me a lot when he was living. He would come and talk to me about anything or everything.

This happened at night. It seemed to me I'd fallen asleep, and all of a sudden, I woke up. I thought I heard my door open. When I looked up, I saw Jimmy standing by my window, inside my bedroom. He was himself, as he was before he died. I wasn't frightened. He was there, and he was my boy. I wasn't afraid.

I said, "Jimmy, where'd you come from? What are you doing?"

And he said, "Mama, I come to tell you to cheer up and don't let things bother you so much. Don't be so down. Take it in stride and keep going." He told me that things would get better.

I looked at him and laughed. When he was little, I used to say, "Get over here and cuddle up with me." And so I said to him, "Behave yourself, now get over here and cuddle up with me."

And he did. It was so real. Just like when he was a little boy, he climbed on the bed and cuddled right up close to me.

I dropped off to sleep, with him in my arms.

Now when I'm like that, I watch the window to see if he's standing there.

He left me a beautiful daughter-in-law and two nice boys. But now I'm waiting and waiting for him to come back. I have a feeling he's going to come back to me, and talk to me. I really do.

I wait for him to come.

STRANGE HAPPENINGS

I received this email from a woman who signed her name as "Kelly" on February 16, 1996. I was fascinated, so I corresponded with her. It emerged that the correspondent's full name is Kelly Kirkland and that she is a resident of Chatham, Ontario. She has had a number of extraordinary experiences and eventually she sent me a total of three ghost stories. Here they are. The second one arrived on February 17 and the third on March 13, with some follow-up remarks on June 10. The correspondent finds that odd occurrences turn up wherever she happens to be. It seems people may be haunted as well as places.

1.

This is a true story that happened to me. I'm not sure what it was but it was really weird!

One day just before New Year's 1996, I was going to see my Dad by train to Toronto. My train was scheduled to leave by 3:27 p.m., and my boyfriend Jon was supposed to drive me to the station. He had gone to the store to pick something up and he was not home yet when I was supposed to be on my way to the station. I was looking out the front door to watch for him and I was very upset that I was going to miss my train (I did!) and I finally saw him coming up the street. I turned around to get my suitcase and when I turned back around I expected him to be in the driveway but he wasn't.

By then I was furious and I started to flip out and wonder where the hell he went to. Did he drive by the house and keep going? Did he forget something at the store he went to? Anyway, he finally showed up about fifteen minutes after I saw him and I confronted him as he walked in the door. I asked him why he hadn't pulled in the driveway and he told me that he hadn't even been on the street! I said that I had seen him fifteen minutes ago and he still insisted that he hadn't been anywhere near the house!

I still can't figure out what happened that day. I swear up and down that I saw his car coming up the street with him driving it! His car is hard to mistake because it has white spots on the roof where the paint peeled off. It was a very strange experience and I won't forget it any time soon.

2.

My Grandmother's house has been haunted for years. I definitely won't stay overnight there!

When I was a kid, I used to sleep over at her house. The address is King St. in Chatham. I won't give the exact address for obvious reasons. It is a one and a half storey house with white siding. The house is approximately one hundred years old, and I've heard various stories over the years about people who have died there.

There are three rooms on the main floor. As you walk in the front door, you are in the front hall. To the left there is the dining-room; to the right are the stairs to go up. If you walk straight from the front door, you will end up in the living-room. If you keep going straight, you will find yourself in the kitchen. In the back of the small kitchen, there are the back steps to go outside. Just before you get to the outside door, there are a few more steps to go to the basement. In the basement there is my uncle's barber shop. Behind the shop is the back room of the basement where the washer and dryer are.

Now to the second floor. At the top of the stairs, there is a small hallway with the main bedroom on the left, a small bedroom on the right, and farther down another small bedroom on the right with a bathroom at the end. In the first small bedroom on the right, there is a dark stain under the carpet. No matter how hard you scrub it, it won't come out. I was told that it only gets brighter.

I was also told that a child suffocated to death in the main bedroom upstairs. The spirit of that child is supposedly what is haunting the house. The entity likes to take things, break things, and play with the lights.

One day I was teasing my little brother who was three years old at the time. I took his yo-yo and was running around the house with it and he was chasing me. I had just bought a pair of sunglasses and had them with me while I was running around. I had them hooked in the top of my shorts. I noticed later that I no longer had the glasses. I looked in every last nook and cranny of that house. I looked everywhere I had been and even in places I hadn't been! I couldn't find them anywhere.

That was about nine years ago and I still haven't found those sunglasses. Our joke is that the ghost is walking around wearing them.

My Grandma told me about a ghost that they used to see on the second step from the top of the stairs. The ghost was that of a woman who was sitting there, rocking back and forth. My Mom used to jump over that step every time.

Another story is one that only happened a couple of years ago. My older brother was living at my Grandma's for a summer and he thought he saw a shadow at the top of the stairs. When he told my Grandma about it, she believed him, but when my step-Grandfather came home and was told about the incident, he said, "Ah, I don't believe in ghosts!" And at that moment the lights went out!

I hope you like these. I still have more!

3.

Hello again, I just thought I'd drop you a line to tell you about my "new" apartment. A few strange things have been happening since I moved in on July first.

It was about the third night in the new place and I went to bed with all the lights OFF ... when I woke up the next morning the ceiling light was ON. I know I didn't turn it on in the night and I know that the cats couldn't have turned it on by accident because the switch is up over the stove and they never go up there.

The second thing that happened could probably be explained but it was still strange to me. I fell asleep with the TV on one night and when I woke up in the morning it was off. I might have turned it off in the night and just don't remember. The radio turned on during another night but that could have been the cat.

The day before yesterday, my older cat, Sneaker, was staring at the window and was spooked by something. My bed is situated under the window and to see what she was afraid of, I picked her up and took her over to the bed and she struggled to get out of my arms and ran off in the opposite direction. She was like that for about an hour ... I couldn't get her to stay on the bed for anything. She always ran back to the same spot and stared. Sneaker always comes to you when you call her, but this time I couldn't get her to come to me. It was pretty strange.

The house that my apartment is in is a Chatham Heritage House. It is a Victorian house that was recently renovated and restored. The people who originally lived in the house were the Greys (or Grays) of Chatham. The maker of the Grey-Dort car, William Grey (Gray?).

I haven't talked to the owners about any strange happenings yet. I'm waiting for other things to happen. I don't want to look foolish.... I could just be letting my imagination run away with me.

Email me back and let me know what you think.

Thank You,
Kelly Kirkland

2

SOME PSYCHICAL EXPERIENCES

Before I began to collect real-life ghost stories, I simply assumed like most people that some places are haunted and some places are hallowed, just as cemeteries seem to be haunted and churches seem to be hallowed. When I began to collect them, I began to think about my assumption, and it slowly sank in that, historically, churches adjoined cemeteries, or cemeteries adjoined churches, so that the transition from the quick to the dead was if not painless then at least speedy! There were no detours! I still think that some places have an aura of some sort that is perceptible to sensitive people, imperceptible to insensitive ones. There is nothing mystical here: the aura may be an expression or effulgence of beauty or symmetry. Masters of the ancient Chinese discipline of feng shui feel they are able to detect such influences or forces of the landscapes, negative or positive, both natural and human. I regard feng shui as a discipline rather than as a science, but one that when it is practised diligently is successful to the degree that the practitioner is an artist or craftsperson in his own right. It takes training and sensitivity to be meaningful.

All of the above is a round-about way to suggest that while places may or may not be haunted, it is really people who are haunted, in the sense that they are sensitive to forces or influences that are not readily acknowledged by the rest of us. Such "sensitivities" run in families. Traditionally, witches and warlocks breed witches and warlocks down to the seventh generation. The Celts — the Irish, the Scots, the Welsh — revel in anecdotes about "the seventh son of the seventh son" having the curse or the blessing, being bent or inclined. Among the folk of Europe, both Eastern and Western, the Old Ones had great powers, which they passed on from generation to generation. But they are now mainly, but not entirely, lost. These traditions are not limited to Europe but are found throughout the rest of the world: Middle East, Africa, the Far East, where they coexist with modernism with its secularism and materialism. Such traditions are also found throughout the Americas, both North and South, and among the aboriginal or indigenous peoples, especially in the Arctic Regions. Popular paganism and neo-shamanism are very much the vogue, as are traditional instructors who carry the knowledge of healing and even weather forecasting from father to son, from mother to daughter.

Here are stories that turn on people who are best described as "sensitives." For them, ghostly experiences are not extraordinary experiences but, because of their frequency, rather ordinary ones ... not to be counted upon, perhaps, but not to be counted out, either. The sensitivities seem to run in families, though I am unaware that there are families of ghosts!

MORE A "SENSITIVE" THAN A PSYCHIC

"As you suggested a couple of weeks ago, I have written the story of my unusual experiences, and it is enclosed." So wrote Doug Turner in a personal letter dated June 10, 1994. After reading one of my collections of unusual experiences, he wrote to me and offered to send to me an account of some of his own experiences. I wrote back and encouraged him to do so. The following text comes from one of his letters, the last dated June 7, 1995.

Doug Turner was born in 1935 in the farming village of Henfryn, Huron County, Ontario. His ancestry is English with a little admixture of Scottish and German. He grew up on a farm and loves farming life but has worked in a bank, as a bookkeeper, and with a luggage manufacturer. He lives with his wife, Carol, in Stratford, Ontario, and they have four adult children. "I have always had an interest in the unexplained, and I think that the fact that I am a Pisces may have some bearing on that," he explained.

His account is interesting for a number of reasons. I like the distinction between being "sensitive" and being "psychic," and the way that odd events and peculiar experiences are part of the wharf and woof of his life. The reader has the opportunity to make of them what they will. For Doug Turner, they enrich one's life and broaden one's outlook.

My first experience of a psychic nature took place when I was six to eight years old, during the early 1940s. At that time I slept upstairs in my own room, and alone. On a number of occasions, while I was going to sleep, I would "float" up out of my body, so that I was just above it, and about eight to twelve inches above the bed. When I wakened enough to realize that I was "floating," I would "fall" back on to the bed, with the definite feeling of falling and a distinct shock when I hit the bed. At the time I did not realize what was taking place, nor was I concerned about supernatural matters. I realized years later that these "floating" experiences had been out-of-the-body experiences, even though I had not gone as far out as many others.

At that time I also had many floating dreams, or at least I have considered them dreams for most of my life. The stairway that led downstairs when I was young had a door at the bottom which was usually latched. I often dreamed that I was floating down the stairs towards the door, and I recall that I always felt that I was going to hit the door and suffer physical injury. Yet that never happened. I always floated right through the door. On reflection I suppose that these may also have been out-of-the-body experiences.

Unfortunately such interesting adventures did not last. During my high school years, from 1948 to 1952, my experiences were limited to several incidents of *déjà vu*. In those cases, I would realize, during an incident in the classroom, that I had experienced these exact words and actions during a dream I had had during the past few days.

There were no more such incidents until almost twenty years later, in 1967. In June of that year my father took his own life for reasons unknown, though I think that depression caused by feelings of failure and alienation may have been the cause. For about three months prior to his death, I dreamed almost every night of fire, although it was not until after the event that I realized the significance of the dreams. After Dad's death my wife Ann and I stayed overnight with my mother at their home. After we had gone to bed we both felt the strong presence of my father's spirit. I did not find the experience at all frightening. Since my wife had mentioned this feeling first, I have often wondered if it was a real feeling on my part, or something I imagined because of her suggestion. In 1993, it was confirmed in dramatic fashion that the feeling had been real — but that comes later in the story.

Both I and my wife have considerable interest in the supernatural. In my case I have inherited a love of Scotland, as well as an interest in the unexplained, from my Scottish great-grandmother. My wife is even more Scottish than I and has a great psychic ability. Cecily, a friend in New Zealand, has suggested that I am more a "sensitive" than a psychic, and I am inclined to agree with her. My wife has her own story to tell, but she has been involved in some of my experiences, as indicated elsewhere.

In 1967, there were two deaths in my family in addition to that of my father. The first was the death of a nephew of mine less than a month after he was born. We did not experience anything unusual in that case. Prior to the death of my father, the second death in the year, as well as my own dreams, my wife had a dream which indicated that my father might die. She was with him in a church facing a large, round, stained-glass window. A bat was trying to break through the window and my wife said to my father, "If that bat gets in one of us will die!" The bat did break part of the window and enter the church. My wife woke up then, and it was the next day that my father took his life. A couple of months later my wife and I came home to our apartment and found a bat in the hallway. She insisted that I get the bat out, which I was able to do after several minutes, but she said then, "That means someone is going to die!" It was only about an hour later that my sister phoned to say that my niece had died.

It was after these events of 1967 that I decided to learn all I could about supernatural events, and over the years I have read every book I could find about everything from UFOs to the near-death experience. That, along with my personal experiences, has convinced me that there is much more to life than the physical existence we lead every day. I feel certain that some form of reincarnation exists, though I'm not sure how it works. I also feel that I have what is usually called a Guardian Angel, though in my case I have not seen or felt anything directly. The feeling is based on a series of extraordinarily fortunate events throughout my life. For instance, while I have driven many thousands of miles during my life, I have only twice had a car quit on the road, and on those occasions I was close to home and help was at hand.

I have also had good fortune financially in cases where things could easily have turned out badly instead. I have not been given any lucky lottery numbers though! Guardian Angels don't seem to operate that way.

After the 1984 federal election, I had a strangely queasy feeling in my stomach, a feeling that the next few years would not be good. In retrospect, that seems to have been an accurate feeling. I do not intend that as political criticism because I have had similar feelings at other times. It was at about that time that I began to realize that my feelings were becoming predominant.

In 1985, I had an experience which demonstrated that even more. When I was young, we lived on a farm outside a small village in Southwestern Ontario, and in the mid-1950s had moved into the village. In 1985, I went for a drive past that farm, something I had not done for many years. As I did so, I was overcome by an intense feeling of sadness and nostalgia. That feeling was so unusual and so strong that I made note of it in my diary, though I couldn't forget it in any case.

My next unusual experience was in 1989. I have for years enjoyed corresponding with people around the world. Of those, the friend I have known longest is Gwen, from Australia, whom I have been writing to for about forty years. In 1960–61, she and a friend travelled around the world and stayed six weeks with my family and me. She married in 1963 and after raising a family she and her husband Leon have visited us, and many other friends in various places, several times since 1986. As they were leaving after their visit in 1989, I hugged Gwen and gave her a goodbye kiss. A moment or two later, as they were driving away, I suddenly felt a tremendous sense of loss, and then a real, physical heartache! I had always thought "heartache" was a figure of speech, yet here I was experiencing the real thing. The ache continued for a couple of hours until I eventually fell asleep. I have never been able to explain that in physical terms, and I should point out, too, that I have never had a physical attraction to Gwen, even though she was beautiful when she was younger, and is still a lovely woman. I have had a feeling for years that Gwen is someone I knew in a previous life. That might explain the love I have for her, and also the appropriate circumstances would explain my lack of physical interest.

I have a similar love for my wife's sister-in-law, Marlene, and I feel that it is also because she is someone I knew in a previous life. In her case, there is a definite physical attraction, which would indicate to me that she is perhaps someone I was married to at one time. I should point out that I do not feel this attraction to everyone, and so far it has been limited to Gwen, Marlene and two other ladies, to whom I also felt a strong physical attraction. I feel that four is a number that I could easily have known. I'm not sure how to explain the attraction except to say that it is a strong feeling of attraction inside me which can at times leave me feeling weak.

In September of 1990, I had another very interesting experience. I had in the preceding years acquired an interest in my family tree. On this occasion I had driven to a rural area a few miles from my home in search of a cemetery where my mother's ancestors are buried. The cemetery is small and no longer used. I did not know the area, never having been there before, although I had general directions. I found the general area with no trouble, but came to a crossroads, and from there did not know which way to go. I could see no sign of any cemetery, and I was momentarily confused, with the question in my mind being, "Where is it?" I looked around, then saw a

Canadian flag on a pole beside one of the roads about three-quarters of a mile away. The instant I saw that flag my question was answered. I knew that the cemetery was there near the flag, even though I could see nothing. When I drove down the road the cemetery was, of course, there, almost directly across the road from the flag and pole. I had never experienced anything like that before and I still wonder where the information came from. From my deceased ancestors, perhaps?

It was later in 1990, near the end of November, that another event occurred which I find almost miraculous. I was then part of a group which gathered in the cafeteria at my place of employment for a meeting which turned out to be fairly long. I sat near a lady with whom I was friendly, but she is not a special friend. Near the conclusion of the meeting, I felt a special kind of love for this lady. It was not similar to the love I have described which I have for Gwen and Marlene, and I have never had any "special" feeling for the lady. This love was like a "cloud of love" enveloping both of us, and the only appropriate description I can think of is the Biblical "love that passeth all understanding." The feeling only lasted for a few seconds, and I'm sure was only my own, but it was something I will never forget. I feel very privileged to have had such an experience, and to know, at least to some extent, the meaning of the phrase from the Bible. I also know now what people who have had a near-death experience mean when they refer to such love.

The most interesting event of 1991 happened in May when I read in our newspaper that a horse called Strike the Gold was going to run in the Kentucky Derby. I felt that he would win, and I found out a couple of hours later that he had in fact won. Since I didn't read the paper until late in the day, it is possible that the race may have actually been run before I read about it. If that was the case, as seems likely, it would seem to be a case of clairvoyance rather than a psychic prediction.

In late 1992, I experienced a strong feeling of

depression at work. The reason became apparent next day when I learned that twelve people had been laid off effective just before Christmas. While I was not affected myself, I did "pick up" apprehension and anger, which is, I'm sure, what those laid off felt.

In February of 1993, I saw, on TV, a video of a UFO at Carp, Ont. Several days later I read an item in the paper in which someone claimed that this had been only a balloon. I felt then that I needed to see the video again, and that same film was shown on another program a few days later. I don't think it was shown because I wanted to see it, but I do feel that I was perhaps able to sense in some manner that it would be shown again.

My final experience is also one of the most interesting and happened in April of 1993. I have always enjoyed correspondence with people around the world and in 1986 I was writing to a lady in London, England, called Grace. My wife wanted at that time to find some pen friends in Scotland, and, since Grace was the friend of a newspaper editor in Glasgow, she volunteered to help. My wife wrote a short letter which was published in the Glasgow paper, and she received about half-a-dozen replies. One of those was from a lady named Evelyn. It turned out that Evelyn, her husband Walter, and their family had lived in Stratford, where we also live, for a number of years. Evelyn had worked at the hospital and knew the city well. She and her family had also lived directly across the road from where we lived at that time. Evelyn and her family had returned to Scotland before we moved there, so we had never met, but this geographical closeness was the main reason for her writing in the first place. She and my wife became very good friends, and we had also talked on the phone several times.

In the fall of 1992, Evelyn suffered stomach pains and was hospitalized for tests. These revealed stomach cancer, and she had an operation to remove half of her stomach, along with her spleen and gall bladder. She continued to suffer stomach pains, and in late March was back in hospital for another operation. When doctors opened her stomach they found widespread cancer, and all they could do was close her up again. On April 8, Evelyn died.

We did not learn of her death until April 19, when we received a letter from Walter. That evening I retired about 11:30 p.m., as usual, and my wife came to bed at about 2:00 a.m. I had been asleep, but woke when my wife came to bed, and I recall that I had been dreaming about souls, which is unusual in itself. My wife says that she said something to me but I don't recall that. I felt then the presence of a spirit and I knew that it was Evelyn. The presence was very strong. Then I felt the spirit move through me, moving from my waist up through my chest and head, in a wave effect. The feeling was akin to what you get when your hair stands on end, but much stronger. There was also a very definite cold feeling. The spiritual wave happened a total of three times, taking a total of about twenty to thirty seconds. I was not afraid and in fact, knowing that it was Evelyn's spirit, I found the experience rather pleasant. The whole thing was very real, and there is no possibility that it was only my imagination. The only other time I have felt anything similar was after my father died.

The next day I learned from my wife that she had been with Evelyn's spirit in our living-room, and that Evelyn had come to the bedroom with her. Because of Evelyn's strong connection with Stratford, as well as with my wife and me, it makes perfect sense that she would visit here before going on. It is also worth noting that she did not visit us until we knew of her death. That would also mean that she was aware of when we did know. If she had come before we were aware of her death, we would not have realized the significance.

Almost exactly two years later, in April of 1995, I had an experience very similar to the one that had happened after Evelyn died. In this case the person who died, also a lady, was Janny. She had been born in Holland before World War II and had spent the war years there where her family had helped the Underground and sheltered some people. Jan is the Dutch equivalent of John, and it was because her father wanted boys that both Janny and a sister were given boys' names. We often called her Jenny, but her real name was Janny, and her family lived in the very same house where Evelyn and Walter had lived some years before. They were the across-the-street neighbours of ours for many years.

Early in 1994, after both of our families had moved to different locations, Janny was diagnosed as having cancer of a type that turned out to be incurable. She spent long hours taking treatments that proved to be of no value, and shortly before Easter of 1995 she ended up in hospital on a permanent basis. Both my wife and I had always liked Janny, and I talked to her from time to time during her illness, so that I had perhaps a special feeling of closeness to her. We visited her in the hospital and had hoped to see her again, but it was not to be.

On the night of April 19, I had a dream. Not just an ordinary dream, but a dream of fire, something I had not had since 1967, when three of my family died. I dreamed that I was in a large building, like a hospital or library. There was a fire in the upper part of the building, somewhere above me, but lots of smoke was coming down, rather than going up, for some reason. I went back into the building several times, but eventually got out. Many of my dreams are like will-o'-the-wisps and fade away when I wake up, but not this one. I woke up after the dream at about 4:00 a.m., but it stayed with me in a very clear way. I went to the bathroom then, and it was there that I continued to think of the dream, and got a very strong feeling of impending death. It was so strong that I wondered who was going to die. I thought of my own family, even myself, but at the time I didn't think of Janny. While I knew that she was seriously ill, there was no real indication that she wasn't going to live for some time, though I suppose I should have thought of the possibility of her imminent death. Even her husband was caught by surprise when she died. She was all right when he saw her about 8:00 a.m. At about 10:15 a.m., she was suddenly gone, only six hours after my dream.

Five days later, after her funeral had taken place, my wife stayed up later than I, as is her custom. She had a visit from Janny's spirit, very similar to the visit from Evelyn two years earlier. When she came to bed, Janny came with her. I partially wakened, and it was then that I had a definite spiritual contact with Janny. In fact, earlier I had asked her, silently in my mind, to visit us, and I was pleased when she did. The contact was not as long or as pronounced as the one with Evelyn, but it was contact nevertheless, and I have no doubt at all that it was Janny.

I look upon this dream and contact by Janny, as I do Evelyn's contact, as evidence of the reality of life after death. I feel that these experiences show that there is more to life than we normally think, and that there is a spiritual life after this one.

GHOSTS IN MY LIFE

I have always invited the readers of my books to contact me and share with me some of their own experiences of ghosts and related matters. I issued just such an invitation in my book *Ghost Stories of Ontario* (1995). It caught the eye of the following contributor. Margaret J. Young of Barrie, Ontario took the invitation seriously and phoned me. She mentioned that she was the mother of Jim Young, who had contributed a ghost story to my earlier book. She then began to relate some of the odd and eerie experiences that had happened to other members of her family. I urged her to write them out for me. She said that her son had a computer, so I encouraged her to write out her experiences as a narrative and ask the son to keyboard them and send them to me on computer disk (in ASCII). This she and he did. When I receive an account like this one, I read it through, copy-edit it, and print it out. Then I send the copy to the contributor for fact-checking. When both of us are satisfied that everything is as it should be, I add the account to the other accounts I had amassed for use in the next book of extraordinary experiences. What I did not expect is that Mrs. Young would send me so long an account, one that involved so many people and so many incidents. I am not quite sure what to make of it. Not that I doubt Mrs. Young's word. I accept the reality of what she says as she describes it. I am simply amazed at the "coincidences" and all the suffering (especially around Easter).

In her letter to me on June 4, 1997, Mrs. Young asked a question. "I would be interested to know if you have had any experiences in your life, John. You write of other people's stories, but not of your own. As you are a relatively new author in my collection, perhaps you have written some that I have yet to discover. Understandably, I enjoy your writing, and the subject is definitely a fascinating one ... one that is much more acceptable now than it was a few years ago."

Mrs. Young is not the first contributor or reader of my books to ask me if I have ever had experiences like the ones described here. Let me answer that question. I have not had any experiences of ghosts or poltergeists, forerunners or premonitions. I am what Colin Wilson called himself: "ESP-dead." There is no tradition of Extra Sensory Perception in my family. (Nor is there any Celtic blood flowing through my veins!) Indeed, although I respect people who have such experiences and have the courage to share them with others, I am not sure that I would want to be "ESP-alive."

Dear John:

Your invitation to share unusual experiences noted at the conclusion of Acknowledgments in your book *Ghost Stories of Ontario* was all I required to put my grey cells to work, pen to paper, and contact you. Boy, does my brain need exercise! Already I am at a loss as to how to proceed. Hopefully my son will compute this and by the time it is ready to mail, it will be in order enough to understand.

First I feel some family background information may be of some interest. My parents are of Scottish background. Their parents (except my maternal grandfather who was killed in World War I in France) were immigrants from Scotland. To my knowledge, Dad's ancestors were Scottish but Mom's maternal grandparents were Irish. That is quite a combination for the supernatural!

I didn't see as much of my father's family, so have no recollection of any "happenings" on that side. Any mention of grandmother or aunt will be to my mother's family of five children, the two youngest daughters being the only ones to emigrate to Canada with grandmother.

I was born in Toronto in 1928 and lived there until 1948, when I married George and moved to Stroud (just south of Barrie). By 1954 we had four children, Kathie, Leah, Jimmie, and Lennie (Lenore). In 1960 we built a home in Painswick, now a suburb of Barrie, where I still live. In 1963 and 1964 we had two more daughters, Gina and Lori. I now have eleven grandchildren. You are already acquainted with my son Jim Young, as you used a story of his and his wife Shirley, "A Ghost Named Matthew," in your *Ontario* book.

I believe my grandmother was very psychic. As a hobby she would read fortunes with cards and with tea leaves. She would also read fortunes in a way I have never seen before or since. She would break an egg white in a clear glass of water, leave it overnight, and "read" it the next day. Unique, huh? She would predict deaths, sickness, and accidents, and she had many visits from her dead husband and other relatives.

If *inherited* is the proper term, she passed this gift on to my mother and me. My mother has a unique type of prediction as well. If she dreams of seeing someone through a window, she will hear of that person's death within a short period of time. I have partially experienced this same thing. In the 1970s I dreamed of looking out of my window and seeing a large plane losing altitude. (I didn't see it crash because at the time there was a row of trees on the horizon; there is a subdivision there now.) Due to time change and the fact that Mom was away for a month visiting in Scotland, I lost track of the date of her flight home. During my first contact with her after her return, she told me that her plane ran into difficulty just off the coast of Ireland. The pilot had to dump their fuel and return to Ireland for repairs. On checking times and dates, we found this happened the night I had experienced my dream. I have often wondered if my mother would still be with us at age ninety if "my plane" had crashed.

That was only one of my experiences. I could write a complete book of them!

The paranormal does not normally frighten me. But on three occasions that I recall, and on one occasion when I was too young to recall, it did frighten me.

My mom and grandmother related this experience to me. It occurred when I was less than two years old. Mom, my baby sister, and I were visiting my grandmother. Mom sent me into the living-room to get my coat as we were leaving. The lights were out but I had been in the room in the dark before, even earlier that evening. They heard me scream and run out of the room. Our dog, a huge Airedale, also ran out of the room, his hair raised, growling. They said I was trembling and badly frightened. It took them some time to get me to return to the room that night, but our dog would never set foot in it. What I saw I'll never know, as I stubbornly refused to talk about it at the time. Today I cannot recall the experience at all.

My second scare happened when I was about ten years old. We lived in North York on Cedric Avenue. I was in bed in my bedroom. One night I abruptly woke up to see a small lady (approximately two and one-half feet tall) coming towards me. She approached from the outside wall right up to the foot of my bed. She was in full view about half-way between the floor and the ceiling. She had long hair that was a light brown colour and coned in ringlets. She wore a pink dress with a tight bodice and a very full hooped skirt. Her dress and hair style were in the fashion of the Seventeenth Century.

I can still see her clearly, even after all these years. Her face was perfectly shaped with fine features, and she was very beautiful. But she should not have been in my bedroom in the middle of the night! I screamed and Dad came in to comfort me, but she didn't go away. She would glide backwards and then come towards the bed again. I couldn't believe Dad didn't see her. Even with the light on she didn't disappear. I was pointing to her to indicate to Dad where she was, but to no avail. I also found it hard to believe that my sister, in bed beside me, could sleep through it all. Dad stayed with me until I fell asleep. When he left, he left the light on. I don't know who the small lady was or what she wanted. I never saw her again. On looking back, I believe she was a benign presence. If I saw her now, I think I would welcome her.

I had no more visions until I moved to Stroud in the mid-1950s. There we lived in an apartment above a store. I awakened one night to see five or six angels outside our bedroom window. They were perched in the branches of a tree, but there was no tree there! My first thought was, "Where do they come from?" and my second thought was, "What the heck do they want?" The angels looked exactly like those seen in Christmas illustrations. They had wings, heads with long wavy hair, and long flowing gowns.

I wakened my husband George so he could see the sight. Of course, my macho man laughed and turned on the light to prove to me there was nothing out there. The funny side of this story is that I had to go to the bathroom and was afraid to do so. George said he would not accompany me. Suffering some discomfort I finally got up enough courage for what seemed to be a long trek. Actually, the bathroom was located immediately across the hall from our bedroom. As I flipped the switch, the bulb blew. George said I raced back to bed without my feet touching the floor! The angels? They were gone, no doubt laughing as hard as we were. The purpose of their visit? Once again, I don't know. Did I go to the bathroom that night? No, and I didn't wet the bed either!

The 1960s and 1970s, once we moved to our present house, turned out to be busy years for company, human and otherwise. Our home was a gathering place for our children and their friends. Many nights I would awaken and feel a presence in the room. I don't recall that I saw anyone or anything, but I just sensed someone there and I always had the feeling of serenity and peace. I never told the kids about these "visitors." There was no particular reason why I refrained from mentioning the "visitors" but it never happened. "The unexplained" was a topic that was not talked about in our home.

As our first four children grew into mature teenagers, we often left them home to be with their friends, while George, Gina, Lori and I went to our cottage in Muskoka. In 1966 or 1967, when we came home Leah, who had slept in our bed, asked if I knew there was a ghost in our room. She had seen one. I told her yes and asked if she had been frightened. She assured me that she wasn't, and felt it was her paternal grandmother (who had died in 1962) who was watching over us. Leah and I were the only ones who felt or saw this "spirit." It was felt only in our bedroom.

Leah and I were also the only ones in our immediate family ever to experience a premonition when a bird hits our window. My premonition occurred at the cottage in 1968. A sparrow flew into my closed bedroom window and was killed. Two days later I heard of the death of an uncle. (Leah's incident will come later, as I am trying to keep these events in order by date.)

One night in 1969, I was lying awake and saw two clouds form on the wall. The top cloud was white and it had "A29" imprinted in it. The bottom cloud was red and slightly smaller. There was a word in it, but I was only able to determine the initial *B* before it faded away. I felt that this was an omen or a message about something that would happen. I'm afraid I drove my family mad with my warnings about the dangers of April 29th and August 29th! Nothing related to the initial *B* was allowed — boats, bikes, balconies, barbecues, etc. — and no associations with people whose names began with this letter. After a few years, when nothing untoward happened, my warnings were totally ignored. But I keep these warnings in mind for future use!

In 1979, two things happened that no one will ever convince me were not premonitions. Leah's husband Wayne was a constant visitor to our house for a few years previous to their marriage in 1971. So we were very close to him. One day I was working at the kitchen sink and saw a movement in the hall. When I looked up, I saw Wayne's image walk from our bedroom into the bathroom, not through the doorway but through the wall! Strange to say, due to the presence of a closet in the hall, the bathroom is not visible from the kitchen.

The 1980 Thanksgiving weekend brought the entire family together at the cottage for our traditional dinner. When Wayne, Leah, Greg, aged six, and Brad, aged three, came in, Wayne, who was not a physically demonstrative or emotionally expressive person, gave me an extra long, tight hug. I was a little surprised and thought it was because two days earlier we had been told Leah had a malignant growth in one breast. That weekend was the last time I saw Wayne. Three weeks later he was rushed to the Toronto General Hospital and the diagnosis was acute haemolytic anemia. Three weeks after being admitted, he died.

Leah literally moved into the hospital ward and was allowed the use of an adjacent room. I moved into their home to look after their boys. They lived in Ivy, an agricultural area near Barrie, quite isolated, with one house next door and one across the road. The night Wayne died I was sleeping on the couch in the family room off the kitchen. Beyond the couch there were patio doors, which I was facing, and their drapes were closed. I could see lights passing below the drapes. I got up and looked out the window. There were no cars passing, no one with a flashlight, and both neighbours' houses were in darkness. I went back to bed and soon after heard someone trying frantically to open the garage door, which led into the kitchen. I thought someone was trying to get in and was angry at finding it locked. Later, when I discussed this with my children, I told them I thought it was Wayne, and Lennie suggested that it was not anger he felt but frustration. This made sense to me, as I realized that six weeks earlier he had been a healthy, happy young man at home with his family.

He had been given no time to say good-bye or to prepare for his death.

Leah had her operation shortly thereafter. I stayed on with her a few more weeks. One evening the boys and I were in the recreation room in the basement. I walked to the other end of the basement to get some firewood. When I reached the centre of the room to turn on the light, I broke into a cold sweat, and my hair stood on end. I backed out of the room and closed the door.

The other experience of 1979 was Leah's bird premonition, mentioned earlier. For that entire summer they were plagued by the presence of a crow or starling that persisted in pecking at their basement windows all day and well into the evening. Other than the annoyance, the bird didn't really upset or worry them, but they couldn't chase it away.

By 1984, Leah's cancer required her admission to Princess Margaret Hospital in Toronto. She was determined to spend Easter of that year at home with Greg and Brad, now nine and six respectively. We got a weekend pass and an ambulance brought her home. However, she was only home a few hours before she had to be transferred to the Royal Victorian Hospital in Barrie because of a pathological broken hip. Leah died in Barrie on April 29. It was Gina who reminded me of my omen in 1969. Did Wayne's appearance in my hall and the blackbird in 1979 foreshadow the deaths of two health conscious, physically fit young people? Both died in their thirty-fourth years. I know what I think.

In August of 1991, my husband George died. Approximately six months later, two things happened. Gina's youngest son, Jesse, had turned two in January and had recently learned to talk. One night he told his mother that he had seen Gramps and Gramps was on a star. The second incident concerned Lori's son, Zach, who had celebrated his third birthday in February of 1992. One night he insisted his mother close the drapes in his bedroom because he had seen Grampa's face looking through the window the night before. Lori explained that Gramps was only watching over us to make sure that we were safe and happy. Although Zach seemed to accept this explanation, he still wanted his drapes closed. The thing that has made me often wonder about these two happenings was the young age of our grandsons and the fact that the two incidents occurred on the same night in different parts of the town.

In the summer of 1992, Lennie and I were relaxing on the deck of our cottage. A favourite pastime of mine is enjoying the beauty of the clouds on a quiet day. As I lay back gazing at the sky, one cloud passed over the cottage and it had George's face clearly inset in it. The face was looking down. By the time Lennie looked up, the cloud was out of sight. We decided that her dad was saying good-bye; that he was moving on. I guess he must have done so, for as far as I am aware no one has seen him since.

Many times have I experienced the beginnings of what I call "astral flights." They always take place when I am asleep. I fight to rise over telephone wires and over the tops of buildings. I feel I am holding myself back, afraid to completely leave my body. Two years ago I had a totally different astral flight. I was in a strange house and I could hear a family talking and laughing. I entered a room to encounter a family of ghosts; mother, father, young daughter, son. I visited with them until they left, drifting up through the ceiling. They were very happy and they always welcomed me. I had this dream three or four times before there was any change. The last time I visited the house, I entered the room they were always in but they weren't there. I could hear them beyond the ceiling. When I called out to them, they would stop talking and laughing, and when I waited for a reply, they would start conversing again. I finally called out to them that if they wouldn't join me I would join them. There was silence, as if they anticipated my arrival. I started rising from the floor, but when my hair lightly brushed the ceiling, I told them I was sorry but I was not ready to do this yet. Then I slowly descended to the floor.

That was the last experience I have had. Since then I have had no more ghosts, omens, premonitions, astral flights. I honestly miss them.

A couple of experiences follow. They are not mine, but they were related to me and are worth mentioning. A friend of Leah's, who was also a nurse in Toronto, called when Leah was in the Princess Margaret Hospital to say that I should go down because Leah was very upset. When I got there, Leah told me she had seen herself die the night before. We never discussed the incident at the time because there were friends visiting her and they got terribly upset and joked about it. The subject never came up between us again, but I wish now that I had insisted that she tell me about it.

Mom's sister was also "one of us." One day she, a friend of mine, and I visited Lennie. When we left, my aunt told me that she was worried about my friend, as she had seen a black cloud hovering over her. Less than a month later, on Easter weekend, my friend's nineteen-year-old son was drowned. Easter seems to be a bad date for our family.

I realize this is a very lengthy account. If you are inclined to use it in the future, you have my permission to omit and edit to suit your needs. I hope that you find at least some of it interesting. I am sure everyone feels his or her own tales are unique. I did, until I read your book.

Most sincerely,
Margaret J. Young

THE BOYD GANG AND SOME GHOSTS

Imagine my surprise and delight when I checked my email the morning of March 17, 1998 and found on my screen not one ghost story but three ghostly stories! The stories were contributed by Bob Murdoch. They were four months old, having been originally filed over a period of three days, the 17th, 19th, and 20th of November 1997. Then they were collected by Khalloween, the moderator of the mailing list *Khalloween@aol.com*. The account began in a friendly manner: "Hi all. I thought I had already posted this story to this list before but I had reason to check my past posting and found it was sent to some one else instead. I've been advised to forward it on to you all to be followed by a couple of others. I hope you like it. We bought this house in 1986 and have been living here since then. It's been an interesting place to live." It then refers to the bank robber Edwin Alonzo Boyd who with members of his gang made a daring escape from Toronto's Don Jail on September 8, 1952.

> This old house of ours was built in about 1886 or 1890 by a man named Andrew C. Boyd, a lumberjack who worked for the Young Timber Track Company. He kept the house until he died in about 1953. In about 1940–1945, a gang of bank robbers who robbed banks all over Ontario were captured and sentenced to die for killing a police officer. The gang leader was named Alonzo Boyd, the nephew of Andrew, and the gang was known as the Boyd Gang.
>
> Apparently they would hide out here from time to time and some say bury things in the backyard. I was afraid to ask what they buried, maybe treasure, maybe bodies. I didn't know, but when we were building the house, we had to dig a septic bed in the backyard. While we were digging we found bones, human bones, the bones of two children.
>
> The police said the bones were older than fifty years, so they didn't care about them. But somebody cared because sometimes at night we could hear children's voices, as if playing. I could never make out what they were saying, but I knew they were voices because I could hear the pitch rise and fall, and the sounds of laughter coming from what we called the haunted room. Whenever I got up to go and see, the sounds would stop. The lady who lived there before us also heard the children, although she thought she heard the sounds coming from outside.
>
> The haunted room was my daughter's bedroom, and she always loved sleeping there because she always had nice dreams in vivid colour. We never really paid too much

attention to this room until she moved out. After she moved out, we found we couldn't keep the door of the room closed. If I closed and latched the door, it would be open again in the morning, or the following morning for sure. My wife chose not to believe it could be the voices that opened the door. Maybe she was afraid to admit it, or maybe she thought if she did admit it, the ghosts would come for her. I don't know, but we talked about it one night just before she was going out. We almost argued about it, our voices getting higher and higher. I was saying that there was definitely something in that room, and she was saying, "No there isn't. There's nothing there, and I don't want to hear any more about it," and she left.

She came back home late that night, about two in the morning. She walked up the stairs to come to bed, and as she walked past the haunted room, as though the occupant of the room was trying to convince her there was more to it than she was willing to believe, the latch moved! She looked — then saw the latch lift and the door open. She stopped, reached for the door, and heard an ominous shuffle of feet on the other side of the door. She shut the door and ran into the bedroom to join me. We were the only ones home at the time.

This is another story. It sort of ties in with the first. Sorry but the stories are not going to come chronologically. I'm simply sending them as I write them at the moment. There are many others, if anyone would like to read them. The person I was corresponding with about this thread suggested the children wanted to play and this experience rather supported that thought on her part. This is cut and paste from another letter.

As to the question of the ghostly children being playful, I think they proved this on my son's sixteenth birthday, five years ago.

For his birthday we went to a restaurant that is very loud and boisterous. We had balloons and cake and a wonderful time. We took the balloons home and turned them loose. They were filled with helium and floated up to the ceiling. The one aluminium balloon stayed up, while the other ones dropped down after losing some helium. The next night the aluminium balloon was still flying high up to the ceiling in the living-room.

By the time everyone was ready for bed, the balloon had drifted over to the staircase and then up the stairs. It was resting against the ceiling right above the staircase when I went up to bed. I pushed the long colourful ribbons that trailed down from the balloon out of my way as I went by them.

My wife was in the upstairs washroom, and I went into our bedroom across from where the balloon was resting. While I was standing there, the balloon drifted across the hall to our bedroom. It dipped down to get under the door header, then continued past me, so close that my breath would have moved it had I breathed on it. It stopped at the little church window that looks out on the front lawn.

While I was standing there, my wife came out of the bathroom and entered the bedroom. The balloon drifted back across the room under the door header, down the hall, past the bathroom to my son's room. It went under the door header across his room and stopped at a small window that looks out on to the backyard.

I said to my wife, "Did you see that?"

She said, "It's just the wind."

It could have been because the windows were opened, but I said, "I don't think so. There's something about the way it moves."

While we were standing there watching it and discussing the way it moved, it came back out of the bedroom, went under the door header and back down the hall, past the bathroom heading right at us.

My wife said, "It's just the wind."

The balloon moved diagonally across the hall in front of us. I said, "It's not the wind. Look at the ribbons."

The balloon continued past us under the haunted room's door header and stopped at a small window looking out to the side yard.

Let me explain what we both saw.

If it was the wind blowing the balloon along, the balloon would go first and the ribbons would follow; instead, the ribbons were going first, pulling the balloon along by an unseen hand. This haunted room is where we sometimes heard the children's voices.

The next day the balloon came down stairs. I found it floating in the living-room where I was working. As the day progressed, I caught the balloon at one point near the front porch and at another almost out the back door. I moved it back into the living-room. When my son came home from school, he burst into the house and demanded to know why I had turned his balloon loose. He said he saw it floating up into the sky as he got off the school bus.

I explained that I found it drifting in the living-room and I then caught it near the porch before it went out the door and I brought it back into the living-room. I didn't know that it made it out the door.

My son pointed out quite rightly that for the balloon to go from the living-room out to the back door, it would have to travel under the header from the living-room into the kitchen, then under the header from the kitchen into the porch, then under the header from the porch out the back door. He also very astutely pointed out that a gentle but persistent breeze was coming in the back door. I assured him, that I had nothing to do with it going out the door.

This is a cut and paste from a letter I sent to someone a week or so ago. It fills in some gaps in the others, I think.

When we first bought this place, I was drawn to it like a magnet. For some reason, I was meant to buy this old place. When I first saw it I was compelled to own it.

I would buy houses for people at the time and hold the mortgages on them. When I investigated this house, a real-estate agent friend of mine checked it out and found out the owner didn't want to sell. I dropped the project and went about my business.

Three years later, because of my mortgage interests, a young man I knew asked me if I would back him on a house. I said I would if it was right. The house he described was this very same house. I told him that I would not back him on the house because I wanted the house myself, but that I would give him a week to arrange another way of buying it before I moved on it.

He called me back about two days later and said he wasn't interested in it because it had no water, no electricity, no insulation, and only wood heat. Plus it was a complete wreck and he and his wife had just had a baby.

I moved on the place and bought it, without seeing it inside. There were a couple of very belligerent tenants living in it at the time, so I just bought it on the basis that the vendor would get them out of there. He did, so I did.

The place was a mess, all right. I have pictures, if you're interested. From the first minute I walked into the place, it was familiar to me. With the exception of an upstairs window, I felt very comfortable in it. Whenever I came near the window, I got the feeling that I was standing in someone else's space.

During the rebuilding, I experienced my first encounter. I lay down for a small power nap in the mid-afternoon. When I woke up there was an old woman standing at the end of my little day bed. She was a large-boned woman with her hair done up in a bun on the back and top of her head. She wore a common full-length dress with a full-length apron, frills on the shoulders, nothing fancy, very practical. She had her fists planted firmly on her hips. She was studying the large barn beams I had just put up, as if she was trying to make up her mind if she approved. She was enveloped in a purple haze that moved like smoke but instead of moving it stayed around her.

She looked me in the eye, seemed to approve, then drifted away up the stairs. From that day to this day, we have experienced some interesting occurrences. The people who lived here before us apparently heard children's voices, as we have heard them, but they never saw anything. There seems to be more activity at times when my personal energy levels are high, when my son is around, or when children or young people are present.

Somebody asked me if I have ever noticed that my "friend" is more active under certain conditions more so than others. The answer is I don't think so.

I have many more things written up, but there are lots if you are interested.

Bye for now,
Bob

SOMETHING EVIL ABROAD

Was the long-time residence of Healey Willan haunted by two spirits whose footsteps were heard time and time again? His daughter thinks so....

The one-time home of Healey Willan and family on Inglewood Drive in Toronto was believed to be haunted from 1920 to 1968. Mary Mason, actress and writer, who described her experiences on June 24, 1999, is the daughter of the late Healey Willan, composer and choirmaster of St. Mary Magdalene Church. From her birth in 1921 to her marriage in 1943 she lived in the Willan Residence at 139 Inglewood Drive. The family sold the three-storey house following Dr. Willan's death in 1968. In an interview in 1994, Mary Mason recalled how the spirits of the house affected her and the rest of the family.

So often people feel they're in control of their lives, but it seems as though there is something evil abroad that we cannot control because of our reliance on something called "science," which is really another name for knowledge, and nothing else seems to count. There is a loss of spiritual cognizance. It is a tremendous loss.

I first realized there was a "presence" in the house

when I was five. It happened one day in 1926. I had had scarlet fever and was in isolation in my bedroom on the second floor. I was awfully bored. The window of my room was closed so the door of my room was open all night. I distinctly heard footsteps descending the stairs from the third floor. I sat up in bed. I had a narrow view of the hall but I could see nothing there. I thought it's my youngest brother who was then in the cadet band at Upper Canada College. He was coming to visit me before early practice and I would have someone to talk to. The footsteps continued coming down the stairs and along the hall and approached my room where they stopped. That was it. There was no one there. It was very odd. This happened a number of times. The door was no barrier. There was a nasty feeling. I felt awful and frightened.

My mother and father had both heard the phantom footsteps on other occasions. "Don't tell anyone," mother cautioned me, "we may want to sell the house!" Sometimes I woke rigid with fear; I felt a disembodied presence beside me. I couldn't see anyone in the room with me, yet there was someone there. Mother spoke to Father Hiscocks, the rector of St. Mary Magdalene, because she knew I was disturbed. He came and had tea with us and then spoke to me privately. "Let me tell you about the time I was the vicar of the little Anglican church at Cannes. It had been part of a Catholic monastery years before. Every Sunday evening the people came for vespers and sometimes we saw a little monk coming up the centre aisle. He floated up the aisle and seemed to be searching for something. He disturbed the service and I had to do something. So I addressed the congregation. 'We all know someone else is here, a little monk looking for something. Let's all pray that he finds whatever it is he seeks.' So we bowed our heads and prayed in silence. We didn't see him again. So try to pray for this soul who is troubling you." What Father Hiscocks said helped a lot.

One time my eldest brother had a party and one of the entertainers was a psychic. When it came time to have supper, everyone went downstairs to the dining room. So I asked her if she had been offered anything to eat. When she said no, I took her a tray of food. We began to chat and she said, "I see you lying flat on your back in bed and you are frightened. You know someone is in the bedroom with you. That someone is troubling your brother too. Don't worry. Your grandfather is looking out for him. Grandmother is looking out for you. They are guarding you. Don't worry." I found what she said comforting. Both my grandparents had died before I was born.

It was not limited to family members. The cleaning woman once told me, "Mary, someone is walking about in the house upstairs when nobody else is here." I suggested it might be the dog but she would have none of it.

Once, when I was fourteen or fifteen, everyone went to a concert and I was left alone in the house with our dog, Nicky, a collie. I heard footsteps descending from the second to the first floor. The footsteps were heavy, as if someone were carrying something. Our dog leapt up on the sofa beside me, every hair on his body sticking straight out. He stared at something, eyes wide, watching something coming down the stairs. It was horrifying.

One Sunday afternoon I was in one of the third-floor rooms studying for exams. Downstairs, afternoon tea was being served. The door of the room was closed. I heard footsteps coming right up to the closed door. They were light-footed steps. I thought it was my young nephew. There was nobody there.

They surprised you when you had no thought of them in your head. I felt they were mean-spirited. Our house was the original house in the area. It had been a farming area. Perhaps one or more of the early occupants of the house had committed a crime. Maybe the heavy-footed one and the soft-footed one were compelled to repeat their actions. It might be what purgatory or hell or damnation is. I think there's a retribution there somewhere.

I left the house when I married in 1943. I have three brothers. After the Second World War, my middle brother returned from England with his war bride. Sheila is Irish and she sensed there were spirits in the house. Mother called Father Brain, the rector of St. Mary Magdalene. He exorcised the house, going in a procession around the outside, praying. What the neighbours thought of the "bell, book, and candle" routine I do not know! The rite helped but did not put the spirits to rest completely.

Basically the family ignored the disturbances. We never gave the spirits names. You don't want to assign them personalities.

After my father died in 1968, the house was sold. The new owners gutted and renovated it. I wonder what happened to the spirits. If people want to say I'm crazy, that's their privilege. Mother and dad and my brothers were well aware of the haunting but we were all philosophical about it. If anybody tries to tell me that once the body stops breathing the spirit dies, I disagree. It is obvious to me that such a person has not had these experiences. For those of us who have, it is not a laughing matter.

THE GREY LADY

When I was researching the book that appeared as *Haunted Toronto*, I realized I needed some photographs of the interior and exterior of the Church of St. Mary Magdalene. This church, which is located near the intersection of Harbord and Bathurst Streets in Toronto, has a notable musical tradition as well as a notable ghostly tradition, and both of these involve one man: Healey Willan.

Members of the congregation cherish the memory of Dr. Willan, who was for much of his professional life the resident organist and choral conductor. Lovers of serious music across Canada respect his work and legacy as a leading composer and musician. It is no secret that Dr. Willan said that on a number of occasions he was astonished to behold "the grey lady" in the church when he knew no one was there!

My need for photographs led me to Tom Hyland, a long-time member of the gallery choir of the church and a close friend of Dr. Willan. Tom is a character in his own right. Until his retirement he was employed in the photography department at Eaton's downtown store. A skilled photographer, he showed me his sensitive black-and-white portraits of Dr. Willan and also a number of fine atmospheric shots of the church's interior. He allowed me to reproduce a group of these in the entries on the church and its organist in *Haunted Toronto*. We established rapport and Tom shared with me the suspicion that he too had seen the ghost. At my request he prepared a narrative account of his experiences and sent it to me on November 13, 1997. I am very happy to be able to include that account here in Tom's inimitable style.

Tom has now passed away, but he took immense efforts to write and correct the printout of "A Fable Turned Fact." He regarded it as very important. I do too. Thank you, Tom.

A Fable Turned Fact

At this time of writing, I've lived almost seven years beyond my allotted three-score-and-ten. My rather mature age, combined with the problem that I write of an incident close to fifty years old, makes this narrative exercise a most taxing effort. But yet it affords me the nostalgic pleasure of reliving some precious moments of the past.

There seems to be an indignant consensus among young people — especially hard-rock enthusiasts, aspiring computer analysts, and other adolescent ignoramuses — that older persons lose their memories. Or, as they playfully put it, "marbles." This, of course, is completely false! After all, we've lived longer, have a great deal more to remember and, if we didn't discard the trivia, we'd burst our memory banks! Therefore we are inclined to remember the importance of the personal; treat the impersonal as excess; embrace the fact, but dismiss the inexplicable as coincidence. Thus, in order to put to rest any concern as to my mental stability, and to bolster your belief in the validity of this tale, I must meander through some of my personal history that has a direct bearing on your assessment of myself and my sanity.

I began singing, as a boy soprano, in the Anglican choir of Christ Church, Belleville, before my eleventh birthday. I soon became lead boy and soprano soloist. Then, with the onset of manhood, successively graduated through the choral ranks of alto, tenor, to bass. Also, for several years, I served as choir librarian for that parish choir. (You might say — with all that training and responsibility — I knew every piece of music from the top to the bottom and the correct alphabetical sequence of our complete repertoire!) The duties of that post gave me free access to the church, day and night. Quite often, I laid out Sunday morning's music in the choir stalls the Saturday night before, and became accustomed to being mortally alone in the building. The loneliness of those occasions gave birth to my lifelong addiction to test the acoustics of the empty church by the sound of my own voice.

In September, 1945 (my wife and I having moved to Toronto from our native Belleville in the summer of '44), I had the extremely good fortune to be accepted as a bass member in the gallery choir of the Church of St. Mary Magdalene by its eminent director and precentor, the late Dr. Healey Willan. The gallery choir consisted of sixteen voices in those golden days of liturgical music, and Willan left no stone unturned to achieve choral perfection. Time seemed to be expendable. Within ten days, preceding and including Easter Sunday, we sang two full-length rehearsals, several short rehearsals, attended and sang eight services! *Nothing* was left to chance — not even the simplest of hymns — and, from our busy schedule of rehearsals, services, recitals, it was easily imagined the average choir becoming so totally exhausted they'd "throw-in-the-towel" and *quit!*

At the beginning of my lengthy tenure of service in the choir, I was a fledgling photographer. When I became familiar with Anglo-Catholic rites, the fluent beauty of properly sung plainsong, and the precision with which all rites, rituals, masses, motets, processions, etc., were performed, I fell madly in love with the music and the uniqueness of the church: The austere solemnity of its architecture; the inviting refuge of its colourful appointments.

There was a mystical aura about the place that defies adequate description. I can only suppose it was generated by the dramatic differences in its contrasts. The entire interior of the nave was bare and grey — walls; pillars; arches ... cold as death! Whereas the chancel and side chapels were *alive* with warmth. In the Chapel of St. Joseph, a children's altar: pink in motif; portrait of child in field of wildflowers, butterflies, and birds. In the Chapel of Our Lady: heavenly serenity; blue, vaulted ceiling; Virgin Mother and Child looking down lovingly, forgivingly on all who came and all who passed by. In the chancel, sanctuary: aptly named high altar; massive canopy, seasonal trappings; candles; ever-present Host, and magnificent gold cross — resplendent — infinite — commanding reverence in the brilliance of its shining. And the huge rood suspended high above the entrance from the main, broad arch with its Christ seemingly saying, "This is the House of God." "Here is the Gate of Heaven." They all gave one a strange sense of feeling a part of antiquity, without being old, and a part of the present, without being blatantly modern.

Here, indeed, was ample opportunity for me to pursue the art, capture the mood, and make memorable photographs with permanent appeal. There were *so* many things and atmospheres in that building crying out to be recorded on film that I started toting my camera along with me.

Eventually, by trial and error, by investment in equipment and the sacrifice of persistence, my skill became quite effectual. The results of my painstaking efforts were soon rewarded by the friendship and confidence of the clergy, and I found myself in the enviable position of coming and going as I pleased at any reasonable hour of the day or night to photograph whatever I wished. Thereafter, I spent innumerable hours by daylight or incandescent light (and, sometimes, the near lack of either!) to satisfy my desire that the church, in its varied aspects of sanctity, should be visually preserved as a special environment for Christian worship. And I'm forever grateful that some of those prints have found their places in books, on record jackets and music covers, and in the homes of many individuals whose love of that church and its music was equal to mine.

The gallery choir never donned the conventional choir robes. To some, that may seem sacrilegious. But, if anything, it was the opposite, as well as unnecessary. Being seated high above the back of the nave, we were out of sight and hidden from the view of the congregation. The absence of those robes had three distinct advantages. First, it was economical, saving us the expense of upkeep and the wasted time of dressing and undressing before and after each service. Second, it was convenient, should we have to silently slip down the gallery stairs during the sermon and rush, via an exterior route, to the basement lavatory. Third — and perhaps *most* important — it saved us the emotional distress of feeling "holier than thou" along with the damnations of women's mortarboards and makeup!

Healey was kind and considerate to all people of good intent — especially the members of his choirs (there were two). But that did not deter his stern demand for their sincere devotion to *both* the music *and* the words. I can still hear his most oft-uttered critical precaution: "*Any* fool can sing *notes!*"

Our weekly rehearsals were held Friday nights between the hours of eight and ten, *precisely*, with a ten-minute "smoke and gossip" break approximately halfway through. The ritual choir (the other choir and an exceptionally capable group of men and cantor who sang [traditionally robed] in the chancel and responsible for all plainchant) held their rehearsal the same night, prior to ours, from seven to eight, and *again*, precisely. When we arrived, the two choirs joined forces to practise all music in which we had mutual or overlapping parts (hymns, responses, canticles, etc.) that was required for the following Sunday's services. They then departed and we continued with our rehearsal.

The rehearsal room was in the basement of the church, directly below the chancel and sanctuary. It was adequately large but had the advantage of "flat" acoustics which prevented echoes from masking errors. The outside entrance to that room and the basement was through a street-level doorway on the southeast side of the church and a landing for stairs that went up to the vestry, chancel, and nave, and down to our rehearsal room. When the members of the ritual choir made their exit, the last one out tripped the latch on that door, and any gallery member who dared to arrive later — without Healey's permission — would have to knock; be let in; come down those stairs and ... face the music!

There were two petty annoyances that plagued the choirs, clergy, and congregation in those days, even though they were confined to frigid temperatures. That door to the basement, when opened, ushered in an arctic blast of air that came rushing down the stairs, flooding our rehearsal room with chilly discomfort. The other annoyance was caused by the heating system in the church. There were radiators spaced along the perimeter walls at floor level that made their presence known by their noisy expansions and contractions. One of those convenience eyesores, in particular, had the habit of infusing its off-key harmony right smack-in-the-middle of our motet, or punctuating a solemn, sermon sentence with a loud "ssss" and a "bang"! Also, the supply pipes for those radiators ran beneath the floorboards of the chancel and chapels, leaving those boards *so* dry they "squeaked" at the least of foot pressures. In short, we were *all* thankful for warmer weather!

But I remember it *was* in the cold of winter when this disturbing incident occurred, for there were overcoats, hats, and parkas hanging along the walls on hooks and hangers — one of the few necessities in our rehearsal room. The others being a piano, a music cupboard, an assortment of wooden chairs; a washbasin, one-seater toilet, and a table on which Healey placed his music; sat upon with one leg up and one leg down to conduct, or lecture us for our (thankfully few!) *faux-pas* and occasionally emphasize, by illustration, the proper pronunciation of ecclesiastical Latin ... usually followed by a relevant witticism quoted from one source or another.

One Friday night, during our break, Healey called me aside: "Tommy, old man, be a good chap; run up to the gallery and fetch me my copy of ... You'll find it...." (I honestly can't remember the title of the organ score, nor where I should find it.) Giving me his key for the gallery door, he explained his need of it the following day and expressed his frustration for not having had time to go get it himself. So off I went.

There were two flights of stairs from the basement to the main body of the church. The one on the south side, which I've already described, and another on the north with a passageway at its top, running parallel with the chancel to a doorway for entry to the nave. I opted to take those stairs for they were nearer to the gallery stairway in the northwest corner of the church. In the passageway, there was a single light bulb in a pull-chain socket hanging from the ceiling. This I pulled on, opened the door, propped it open, and made my way to the opposite end of the church.

Healey and I had become close friends. So much so that I welcomed the opportunity, and pleasure, to stay behind after mass or evensong, lock up the gallery, and accompany him down to the basement where a large pot of hot tea was waiting to lubricate the vocal chords of choir members ... courtesy of a very kindly lady and parishioner, Mrs. Bailey. (I do hope I've spelled "Bailey" correctly. She justly deserves proper recognition.) On those journeys he might ask, "What did you think of the Kyrie this morning, old man?" or discuss a problem with the tempo in a certain hymn. (And you have *no* idea how vainly proud *I* felt at being asked for *my* personal opinion — sometimes advice! — from such a renowned musician as Healey.)

The path we travelled on those intimate occasions was

the same as I followed in this instance, and so familiar I probably could have traversed it fully with my eyes closed, as in the unconscious sight of sleep. But the dim light from the open doorway partially lifted the eerie shroud of darkness from the unlit aisle and prevented me from bumping into a pew or two.

There was a high, spacious vestibule the full length of the west wall of the church for coats and hats and more silent and draft-free entry to the nave. It had three sets of double doors with the gallery stairway in the north corner. I opened one of the nearest set, switched on the vestibule light, and mounted the gallery stairs. At the top, I switched on the two lights in the gallery, unlocked the door, and went in. Unfortunately, the empty church proved too tempting for me to resist my youthful addiction, and I started humming, quite loudly, with a few bass "booms" thrown in to more enjoy the echo. Having found the requested score, I was about to leave the gallery when I noticed the effect of those gallery lights fading into the darkness of the sanctuary.

Always on the lookout for a different angle, different highlight, different shadow, I paused to analyze the photographic possibilities. I was standing near the back wall, and from that position could barely see the front row of pews in the nave as the gallery railing was table-top high and heavily draped to block the view of any obnoxious gawker from below. So I moved closer until I could scan the entire nave. Still humming, I looked down and caught sight of something so *totally* unexpected that I nearly fell over the railing in cardiac arrest!

There, below me, kneeling in a pew part way up the south side of the nave, was a woman on whom I'd never laid eyes before! I was *so* startled that my lungs forgot to breathe — my vocal chords ceased to function — and my eyes became fixed like a lifeless statue's! Her faded, grey apparel appeared to be more suitable for warm weather than for the frigid temperature outside, and, oddly enough, no protective outerwear was anywhere visible. I was so *petrified* by surprise and so mortified with embarrassment, my wits became *so* befuddled that I *could* not *think* straight, and could *not* determine whether to attempt a pleading apology for intruding on the privacy of prayer, or to vacate the premises as quickly and quietly as possible. But as she was an absolute stranger to me, and I, probably to her, I thought I'd better *leave* it that way and chose the latter option.

As I locked the door, switched off the gallery lights, descended the stairs, switched off the vestibule light, and retraced my steps to the passageway door, I kept thinking it also *very* odd that my considerable vocalizing seemed not to have disturbed her! I did not look back. There was little point to staring at the blackness of the nave. But as I closed that door, pulled off the light, and descended the stairs to our rehearsal room, I felt an immense sense of relief at leaving her and the church to the darkness in which I'd found them.

When I entered the room, Healey was poised to conduct the second half of our practice. So I took my seat, after laying the copy on his table, and my common sense suggested that I shouldn't report the unbelievable lest I be deemed a loony — if not *called* one! But through the remainder of that rehearsal, I kept one ear cocked for the sound of a squeaky board overhead, and one foot firmly on the floor for the feel of a cold draft ... but I neither heard nor felt, either.

(There was a *third* oddity about that woman's appearance — a haunting enigma that's eluded my comprehension ever since that night. But now, in the poignant remembering of so *many* personal and related truths of the past, I've finally solved the mystery of her presence. *And* the motivation that's prompted my telling of this tale.)

I write this on the 10th day of November, 1997. Comes the 27th day of this month, my wife and I will celebrate our fifty-fourth wedding anniversary — God willing. On that Saturday date, 1943, we came to Toronto for our honeymoon. The following day, Sunday, the 28th, we attended High Mass at St. Mary Magdalene. The music of the mass and motet that morning was exquisitely beautiful, and sung so clearly and devoutly by the gallery choir that I actually wept. (That, I think, is the greatest compliment that can be paid for a sterling, sincere performance.)

Shortly after I'd joined the choir, I learned of a particular area in the nave where the gallery choir could best be heard. A place almost in isolation with angels. It so happened, on that glorious Sunday morning of our honeymoon, my wife and I — by accident and because of its availability — sat, knelt, and prayed in that same area — perhaps in the very same pew where this grey-clad lady knelt!

The vivid recollection of that most precious time; that special place — that *separate* beatitude of beauty — had finally solved the riddle of the third oddity: It was her location!... As if in anticipation, she occupied the exact spot, chosen by many an astute listener as the ideal ambience to fully experience the ecstasy of sound floating from that loft in an *a cappella* halo of faultless harmony — veritably enveloping *all* within our resonant House of God in a polyphonous paradise of immaculate adoration!

Healey used to tell of a ghost, dubbed "the grey lady," who interrupted his private organ practice in the church by her visual presence. Frankly, I never knew whether to doubt his sober sincerity or marvel at his clairvoyant sensitivity ... whether we had a female phantom in our midst, or a figure evolved in a spasm of indigestion! But, after putting all the facts of two and two (or twenty and twenty) together: the dark, unlit church; the late hour; the long-locked doors; the squeaky boards; the frigid temperature; the cold draft; her lack of outer clothing; her undisturbed composure, and the pew she occupied, I'm thoroughly convinced there really *was* a "grey lady," and I — most surely — had seen her!

Now this anecdote would still be a latent episode, locked for life in my own mind — straddling the fence of indecision with its facts, doubts, and possibilities — had it not been for a request from our local author, John Colombo, to supply prints of the church and Healey. These were gladly given and faithfully reproduced in two articles of his excellent book *Haunted Toronto* published last year (1996) by Dundurn Press. Obviously, I've read those entries *and* the book itself, and would urge all those interested in the subject of "ghosts" — however remotely — to do also.

Colombo's request and that reading had revived my lazy memory, and my ostentatious ego suggested *I* could write of "ghosts" as well as *he*! And since I had witnessed a *bona-fide* visit of an apparition, I've given it a shot. And there it is ... faults and all ... and *that's that!*

Tom Hyland
The [yet] City of Scarborough
November 10, 1997

A VERY STRANGE EXPERIENCE

From time to time, for some people, the sense of the reality of the world seems to wax and wane. It recedes from their senses and memories. It does not always return. Familiar things take on a curiously unfamiliar aspect; unfamiliar things assume a surprisingly familiar form. Such experiences are quite striking and unsettling and make a strong impression.

Psychiatrists, observing elements of dissociation, speak of the condition they call *derealization* (and of its companion *depersonalization*). Psychologists, noting the ability of memory to knit the factual and the fictitious into a seamless whole, refer to *confabulation*. Parapsychologists are free to talk about altered states of consciousness (ASCs) and other dimensions of reality.

Here is one account of the familiar becoming the unfamiliar — or the unfamiliar becoming the familiar. It was prepared for me by "Margaret Fyfe" and when it was originally published in one of my earlier books of mysteries, it appeared as by "Margaret Fyfe." I am now able to identify the writer. This pen name was assumed by the well-known folklorist, the late Edith Fowke, a good friend, fellow researcher, and companion on the pathways of folklore. Her reminiscence was written in October 1989 and it refers to an event that she had experienced that had taken place in England two months earlier, in August of that year. She could never explain it and was deeply puzzled by it.

Last summer I had a very strange experience. I was going to a festival in England, and needed to reserve a room before I left Canada. The festival was being held in the seaside town of Sidmouth which is quite small and very popular so hotels tend to fill up early.

I phoned the festival office and asked them to see if they could find a room for me, saying I would phone again the next day. When I called the second time I was told that the Devoran Hotel had a cancellation and that I should phone Mrs. Clifford at Sidmouth 3151. I said that was fine because I'd stayed at the Devoran the year before and had liked it. Accordingly I phoned the number and booked for the week. When I mentioned that I had stayed there for a few days the previous summer, Mrs. Clifford said I hadn't, because she booked only by the week.

When I got to London I took a train from Paddington to Honiton, the railway station closest to Sidmouth, and got a taxi there, telling the driver to take me to the Devoran Hotel. When we reached Sidmouth I remembered the hotel's location and directed the driver to it. When we got there, it looked just as I remembered it. However, when I went in I didn't recognize Mrs. Clifford. Thinking that the hotel might have changed hands, I asked how long she had been there and she told me fifteen years. I then noticed some differences to what I remembered. The desk was placed at right angles to the front door while I remembered it as being parallel last year. The dining room was on the opposite side of the front hall to what I remembered. However, the location was just as I remembered, and when I started going to the various festival programs I knew exactly how to reach them from the Devoran. The whole block was familiar to me, and there was no other hotel in it that looked enough like the Devoran for me to think that that was where I had stayed.

Another strange point was that the previous year the festival office had given me a phone number to book a room, saying it was for the Elizabeth Hotel. I had called and made my booking, but when, on reaching the town, I went to the Elizabeth Hotel, which was at the corner of a block, they had no record of my booking. I showed the clerk the phone number I had been given and he said it might be for the Devoran, which was right next door. I went into the Devoran, and they had my reservation. The confusion over the phone number and hotel name apparently resulted from the fact that the Devoran and the Elizabeth were together on the festival office's alphabetical listing. If my memory was wrong on this point, it might have been the Elizabeth Hotel I stayed at the previous year. However, it was considerably larger than the Devoran: I remembered it, but it didn't seem to me that I had stayed there.

This confusion naturally puzzled me, and during the week I was there I tried to think of some explanation. I looked at all the hotels in the block where I knew I had stayed, and none except the Devoran looked familiar. When I came home I looked to see if I had kept my receipt from the previous year, but I hadn't. Thus this experience remains a mystery to me.

SOME FRIGHTENED ME
MORE THAN OTHERS

I received this email on September 24, 2007, from a reader who lives on the West Coast who has a whole series of eerie experiences to relate, beginning with those in childhood and advancing into those of early adulthood.

Victoria Hood, the sender, writes with great ease and fluency about her unusual experiences. They seem to me to lie on the "no man's land" between consciousness and unconsciousness. It is hard to know what to make of them, and that is Ms. Hood's point. The episodes do not horrify her, although they could, because she finds something that might be affirming about them. Where they are concerned, she emerges as neither a believer nor a doubter, neither a spiritualist nor a sceptic. She seems to me to be entirely level-headed about these experiences. She also strikes me as being entirely sincere and not interested in exaggerating her sensations, feelings, and thoughts. A psychologist might describe her as a person who is "fantasy prone" — that is, predisposed to confuse "marginal" encounters, but that psychological category fits so much of the adult population that it is probably meaningless.

Ms. Hood is a young woman with at least a half-century of life ahead of her. I wonder if she will find that the years to come will be made memorable by yet more appearances of these shadowy figures, forerunners or spirit guides.

Dear Mr. Colombo:

I recently purchased *True Canadian Haunting Stories*, I very much enjoyed reading it and will be sure to check out your other publications! I thought you may be interested in hearing my experiences. Please feel free to contact me if you have any questions, comments, or would like further details. If you choose to include my account in one of your collections, please edit as you see fit. I know I tend to ramble!

I was always what one might call an imaginative child. Born the second of four children in the small town of 100 Mile House, B.C., I was the only one in my family to have an imaginary friend (although as an adult I tend to believe "imaginary friends" are something more like ghostly visitors, but that's another topic altogether). I was plagued by nightmares almost every night from a young age, something that has continued into my adulthood. (I also sleepwalk!) I remember many of my dreams as clearly as my actual life-experiences, and due to my acquaintance with vivid dreams, I am very comfortable with my ability to distinguish dreams from reality. However, such things make it easy for my family and friends to dismiss my experiences as the work of an over-active imagination, while I can assure you they are not.

When I was about three years old, I had a recurring

nightmare that particularly terrified me. I guess I could hear my pulse while I slept, because I would dream there was a pack of men in white clothes with dark hair marching down the street in front of our house to the beat of my pulse. I would hear or see them coming and somehow knew I had to get in bed and pretend to be asleep before they found me or something awful would happen. I never found out what that something was but I was very frightened every time I had this dream.

This particular nightmare is relevant because of something that happened when I was a teenager. One night I was getting in the shower, fiddling with the taps to achieve the perfect water temperature. In the reflection in the faucet suddenly one of the men who had marched down the street in my dreams appeared behind me! I let out a shriek and turned around quickly, but of course there was nobody there. I looked back at the faucet but the reflection was gone, and there was nothing in the shower that could have created this type of reflection. I saw the same man's reflection once again about two years later while getting something out of the freezer in our basement and I think that was the fastest I ever ran up the stairs!

Despite these experiences, if someone had asked if I had ever seen a ghost, I would have said no; that all changed when I was nineteen. I was renting a basement suite in Coquitlam while attending Simon Fraser University and my grandfather was very ill. I was taking it very hard because I hadn't seen him for two years and he was at the point where he didn't recognize the family members who visited him. I was carrying a lot of grief because of a lot of things I'd always wanted to tell him but never would get the chance. He passed away on March 3, 2001.

At some point during the days before his funeral, I was roused from sleep by a bright light shining in the corner of my bedroom. I stared at it, squinting and blinking, trying to figure out what was causing it. Slowly a figure emerged from it and started walking towards my bed. Despite the fact that the figure was unmistakably my grandfather, I screamed like I have never screamed before, terrified at what was happening since I had never seen a spirit before. Both my granddad and the light disappeared in an instant while I was screaming and I have regretted my fear and the scream ever since. I sincerely believe my granddad was coming to visit me because once on the other side he knew how much I had wanted to talk to him, but I don't think he will ever come back again because of how scared I was.

After that, my suite became a hotbed for ghostly visitors. I suspect that in his haste to leave because of my fright, my grandfather somehow didn't close the door to the spirit world properly, leaving a portal open to any spirit who wanted to use it. On a regular basis I would be awakened by the light in the corner of my bedroom, and various shadowy figures would appear from it and roam my room. At first I was terrified at such occurrences but then I got used to it and even had a little fun with it.

I went online to see if there was a way to summon specific ghosts; I found a set of instructions but was unable to inspire my granddad to return. However, one of my favourite musicians, Bradley Nowell (from the band Sublime), had passed away several years earlier, so for fun I thought I'd see if I could get him to come visit me. To my surprise, he came! He emerged out of the light one night and began talking to me. I eagerly and fearlessly sat up at the end of my bed to see and hear him better. This was the only time I've heard a spirit talk and it was very distorted and hard to understand. I was straining to hear what he was saying — it sounded like he was giving me instructions to do something. He then began to fade back into the light, and I cried out, "Wait! I have so many questions to ask you!" He responded by saying, "First, get the —," but because I couldn't understand what he was saying, of course I could not follow his instructions and have not seen him since.

I should also mention that of the ghostly visitors I had in that suite, some frightened me more than others. I remember one that crawled up my wall and across the ceiling over my bed (*à la* Spiderman), then paused and stared down at me for a moment — he scared me out of my wits. Also, during the day my cat would often seem to be watching something that I could not see. Furthermore, the family that lived in the house above me had a little boy who slept in the room above mine; I would often hear him start crying and screaming in the night so I've wondered if these visitors were showing up in his room as well.

I moved around a lot during my early twenties, and after leaving the basement suite in Coquitlam did not have any more paranormal experiences until I was twenty-four. I moved into an apartment building in New Westminster, where I continue to live now at the age of twenty-six. The first few months living here were uneventful. I always sleep with my bedroom door open so my cats are able to wander freely through the apartment during the night; where my bed was positioned at the time I could see straight down the hallway to the entrance door of my suite.

At some point I began to wake up and see a tall, shadowy man (somehow I know he's a man) standing by the entrance door. At first I was scared, thinking someone had broken into my apartment, but then as I stared at him he would vanish. It was startling to wake up and see him but due to my experiences in the Coquitlam basement suite I quickly came to the understanding that he meant me no harm and therefore I was not frightened. However, that did not stop me from becoming annoyed that he kept interrupting my sleep! One night I woke up to see him standing there, and in frustration I charged down the hallway at him; he sort of wisped away into the living room. I ran after him and flicked on the light, only to find myself standing in the middle of the room, alone. After that he did not return for about two months, but then continued his habit of visiting regularly.

Several months ago my boyfriend moved in with me, and as a result the furniture in the bedroom has been rearranged so I cannot see the entrance door from the bed. It was quite some time after my boyfriend moved in before I saw The Man (as I call him); I actually had somewhat hoped he would no longer visit due to my boyfriend's presence, or that I just wouldn't see him because I couldn't see down the hallway anymore. However, now The Man stands at the bedroom door, just watching me as I sleep. (My boyfriend has not seen him, but he is a very sound sleeper, so even if The Man started jumping up and down on the bed, I don't think he'd notice!)

It is still a little startling to wake up and see him there, but I have grown accustomed to him and am not bothered by his presence. I comfort myself by telling myself he's my Guardian Angel or Spirit Guide, or, although I do not recognize him, perhaps he is a deceased loved one checking in on me and reassuring me that life does in fact continue after physical death.

With utmost sincerity,
Victoria Hood

3

VERY INTERESTING CASES

In this section you will find some very interesting cases that are favourites of mine. They are favourites because they are detailed and lead the reader down untrodden paths.

Let me draw your attention to the spooky aspects of William Lyon Mackenzie and William Lyon Mackenzie King. Both the grandfather (the rebel of 1837) and the grandson (the prime minister who "never let his one hand know what his on the other was doing") have stories and legends told about them. Here you will enter the grandfather's haunted house in Toronto and also behold the ghost of the grandson at his estate at Kingsmere (also known as Moorside) in the Gatineau Hills outside Ottawa.

Let me also draw your attention to one of the most curiously haunting cases that I have encountered. It is called "The 'Twilight Zone' Truck Stop." I find this haunting to be vivid and quite perplexing — and imaginatively appealing. Rod Serling could well have adapted it for his *Twilight Zone* television series.

Let me finally draw your attention to a series of articles that relate true crime and psychic detection. It has become customary to maintain that "psychics help the police to solve their crimes," and while there are instances of this happening, or seeming to happen, these are few and far between. So in lieu of much evidence for psychics witnessing criminal activity or locating the bodies of victims, we have the exploits of Dr. A.M. Langsner, who is himself something of a mystery.

A few words of preamble. If psychics are able to read minds, they should be able to read the minds of perpetrators of crimes. If clairvoyants are able to see actions that are taking place at a distance, they should be able to witness the commission of crimes as they occur. If fortune tellers are able to predict the course of human events, they may be able to stop crimes from occurring and thereby deny the truth of their own predictions. If psychometrists are able to read objects or places, no doubt they can describe what happened in the recent or distant past.

Proof is lacking that psychics, clairvoyants, fortune tellers, or psychometrists have ever helped the police in their work. But legion are the stories of "the blue sense," the powers that gifted people are said to have in order to practise "psychic detection." Yuri Geller and Peter Hurkos are the names of two psychics who are said to have assisted the police in their inquiries.

The name A.M. Langsner is hardly on anyone's lips. The incredible exploits of this self-styled psychic are described below. Readers have to take Dr. Langsner's word for just how remarkable his acts of detection actually were. Judging by what he says, he was quite a character. So too was R.E. Knowles, the chronicler of Langsner's achievements. For most of what we know about Lagnsner we are indebted to the interviews conducted in a number of cities over a period of time by Knowles.

If the readers are able to accept as the gospel truth what Knowles has written in these articles, Adolph Maximilian Langsner was a well-known, Viennese-born stage performer, magician, and mentalist who had earned his spurs as a psychic detective. If readers have doubts about Langsner, who had a gift for self-promotion, as Knowles had an interest in entertaining his readers in a lively but uncritical manner, they have to decide whether Langsner was suffering self-delusions or was a sophisticated fraudster.

By all accounts, Langsner was a man of impressive appearance and imposing demeanour. Whatever the nature of his talents or gifts, one ability he possessed in abundance was the power to attract publicity. He was a magnet for it. He toured widely, and arriving at a new city, he sought out the gentlemen of the press and the chief of police. By offering to make his powers of telepathy and clairvoyance available to the police to close current criminal cases, for a fee or some other consideration, he acquired the reputation across Canada of a "crime solver" and (in the words of Knowles) a "craftsman of the unknown."

It is a curious fact that Langsner is "world-famous in Canada" (to borrow a phrase popularized by Mordecai Richler); he is not at all "the toast of Europe." There are no known references to Langsner in the foreign press of the day or since. I checked with Marcello Truzzi, who has written extensively on psychic detection, which he refers to as "the blue sense," and he said he has encountered no other references to Langsner besides these, which appeared in Canadian newspapers following in the wake of this series of stories in the *Toronto Daily Star*.

Yet a reference to Langsner does make its appearance in Leo Talamonti's book *Forbidden Universe: Mysteries of the Psychic World* (London: Garnstone Press, 1974) translated from the Italian by Paul Stevenson. Here is the reference: "Dr. Maximilian Langsner, an indefatigable traveller who died in Alaska, rendered aid of this description to the police of various countries, but only when he felt a certain specific impulse: on one occasion he detected a murderer at Edmonton (Canada), who had left no clues." However, Talamonti continues to make another unsubstantiated claim: "The Canadian police also received valuable help from the clairvoyant Cayce.... Another sensitive, Peter Hurkos, aided the Virginia police to detect a fourfold murderer. However, clairvoyance cannot be relied upon as a regular adjunct to criminal investigations."

Yet for all the press coverage that Langsner and his activities received, the Viennese gentleman is hard to pin down. In no single place did he remain for any extended period of time. He put the local newspapermen through the hoops of his own devising. He appealed to the local police to support him and his wife for the duration of his local sleuthing. He was the dream of every interviewer — "good copy."

The newspaperman who rose to Langsner's bait was Robert E. Knowles, Special Writer for *The Toronto Star*. A Presbyterian clergyman and a Christian novelist before he became a journalist and an interviewer, Knowles thought of himself in grandiose terms. He liked to think that he brought to the celebrities whom he interviewed his own interest in matters of the spirit as well as a developed sense of high drama. Knowles encouraged his readers to think that he himself was at least as fascinating as the subjects who "sat" for him. Indeed, Jean O'Grady compiled Knowles's celebrity interviews and published them under a revealing title: *Famous People Who Have Known Me* (1999). That was Knowles's view of himself. For his part, Knowles was pleased to add Langsner's name to the ever-growing list of celebrities and "nine-day wonders" he profiled in Canada's leading newspaper. When he prepared for the *Star* a year's end review of his activities on December 15, 1928, he wrote, tantalizingly, "Langsner too, Dr., or Mr., or Prof., as you please, to interview whom is like interviewing a combination of Mephistopheles and the Sphynx."

Knowles was mainly concerned to have Langsner's views on the Small case. For nine years the mysterious disappearance of millionaire theatre-owner Ambrose Small in downtown Toronto in 1919 continued to confound the police and puzzle the public. Knowles was anxious to have Langsner's views on the case which still filled columns of newspapers with speculation and suggestion. What did Langsner add to the ongoing investigation of the case? Nothing — except that his "thought waves" told him that Small's body was burning, or burnt, in a house in Montreal.

Yet Langsner does have some accomplishments in the field of psychic detection. He apparently performed the feat of deducing the identity of a murderer and bringing about his confession. He identified the culprit in the Booher multiple-murder case, which occurred in 1928 outside Mannville, east of Edmonton; he broke the stalemate by "psyching out" the murderer and directing him to confess.

The English writer Colin Wilson, in *The Psychic Detectives* (1987), described this incident as "one of the most puzzling murder cases in Canadian history." Wilson wrote, "With the single exception of Langsner's intervention in the Booher case, I can think of no murder case — or, for that matter, any other criminal case — that was actually solved by a clairvoyant." There is a synopsis of the case in my book *Mysterious Canada* (1987) and it establishes the fact that Langsner's contribution to the case is not as clear-cut as Wilson seems to believe it was. (The incident has yet to be examined from a contemporary, critical perspective, so the reader has to take Langsner's word for the case's successful resolution and the decisive part he played in it.) Still, it was the Booher case that brought Langsner to national attention.

These interviews with Langsner may be dated, but they remain "good copy." As interviewer, Knowles strikes poses. As a crowd-pleaser, he poses only those questions his readers would ask. Langsner, for his part, supplies only those answers that he wants his readers to know. Throughout he skillfully evades pointed questions; he equivocates about his "work"; he generates a swirl of mystery around himself and his activities. In the process he charms the interviewer and no doubt the newspaper's readers — his intention all along.

It is interesting to speculate about the nature of the information that Knowles had to convey to Langsner. What was the "matter" that was so "urgent"? Was it *The Toronto Star*'s offer to commission Langsner to travel to Toronto to study and perhaps solve the Small case? Did Langsner offer to come to Toronto, or was the newspaper, known for its journalistic scoops at the time, making an offer to Langsner to come to Toronto? And what role did Langsner's charming and seemingly innocent young wife play in the proceedings? It seems there is a mystery here after all!

Here, in their entirety, are Knowles's known interviews with Langsner (plus one uncredited news story).

PSYCHIC DETECTION

LANGSNER A MYSTERY — USES LATENT POWERS — SOJOURNED IN TORONTO — Discovered Peculiar Gift as Boy at School Years Ago — A STRANGE STRANGER — Says Nobody Will Know About It When He Comes to Toronto

Calgary, Sept. 28. — Col. O'Brien told me that Adolph Maximilian Langsner solved the Edmonton Booher murder. He expressed his entire confidence in the genuineness of the aforesaid criminologist.

Col. O'Brien, whom I resolved to interview before I should interview Langsner, is the commissioner of police for Alberta. The trade commissioner for the same province, Howard Stutchbury, sent me to see O'Brien. "If O'Brien says Langsner is worth while," said he, "then Langsner is worth while."

So I pilgrimaged to Edmonton and had a long talk with the astute and soldierly O'Brien.

From Edmonton, an 11-hour trip, I travelled to Calgary. I wanted to see Calgary, anyhow, due to a painful perplexity as to whether Edmonton or Calgary is the finer city. I was so confused. For, whenever I talked to an Edmontonian I was told that Edmonton is to Calgary as Paris is to Pittsburgh; and whenever I met a Calgarian I am assured that Calgary is to Edmonton as the New Jerusalem is to Newcastle. I therefore scrutinized both, asking many questions, especially about the climate from November to

April and came to the conclusion that I would sooner live in vain than in either of them.

I found Dr. Langsner at the Palliser hotel, the pride of that so pride-ful city. The office clerk informed me that the "Professor" was at breakfast. "Then he evidently sleeps long, perhaps loud," I said to myself as I made my way to the dining-room. Of the head waiter, I inquired for Mr. Langsner, wishing only to have him pointed out. But — and I believe this to be due to the remarkable personality of this man — the whole staff seemed to be thrown into a state of excitement at once. Every under-waiter seemed to know of it in a minute, and all seemed interested, even agitated. I learned afterwards that Langsner was living almost in a stage of siege, so beset was the place with spies and reporters and other birds of prey. Langsner told me himself that the Hearst papers had been represented there weeks, and that, so closely was everything watched, he had been compelled to have some men, whom he wanted to see, come to the hotel disguised as decrepit old parties, cripples, etc.

But at length the famous psychopathic artist was pointed out to me. I watched him. He seemed a cheerful feeder, his wife opposite him following afar off with dainty step.

Mrs. Langsner — and I speak with the diffidence becoming one who knows little of such matters — is a lady of almost unequalled charm. She is only 26 — her husband is nine years older — a native of Germany, educated in Italy and France. She is beautiful, of the Spanish or Italian type, with jet-black hair, a complexion of ivory and pink, eyes whose beauty and light cannot be forgotten. Her English, while brittle in construction, is almost uniformly correct, and her whole personality as fragrant as the rose.

I intercepted the pair as they came out of the dining-room.

As Langsner greeted me with great gravity, bowing low, and presented me to his wife. When I told him my mission, he bowed again, and said: "I did know that you were coming." Of this, I sought some explanation. But in vain, he would say no more. I found later that Langsner was quite familiar with the *Daily Star*. It may as well be told now as later on, what Langsner himself told me, that he has been in Toronto. This amazed me, for his first contact with this continent came three or four months ago when he landed at Vancouver. So far as anybody knows, all the intervening time was spent in British Columbia, in Edmonton and Calgary.

But I had no sooner, later on in the morning, referred to the Ambrose Small case than this strange stranger disclosed that he knew far more about the case than I did. And, after a little questioning, and with a quiet smile, he informed me that, unknown to a single soul, he had visited Toronto, made a substantial stay there, and found out how much or how little, must be a matter of conjecture.

Mr. Langsner, for some cause delayed, dismissed me, his wife my guide, in his parlor on the fourth floor of the hotel. Mrs. Langsner started off with conversation of almost faultless English. Inquiry revealed that she has never been in either England or America.

"You are a miracle," I said, amazed.

"Of own family," she replied with a little curtsy, "my husband is the miracle one."

"How long have you known Mr. Langsner," I asked as we were crossing the rotunda.

"He did see me first when I was a little girl in Germany. But he did not look at me then," as if she were speaking of the sun and a rush-light. "May I tell you my age?" The first time, I fancy, these words ever fell from a woman's lips. I consented, and she disclosed as already revealed. "No, not yet," was her calm-eyed reply to a question as to children. She is a wife, she told me, of fourteen months.

"Does Mr. Langsner ever exercise his psychic powers on you?" I ventured.

"No — except when I try a little lie. You see, he will not ever want to make me nervous. But when I tired am, my husband, he will then, sometimes then, say, 'My dear, you will take a little rest,' and so easy that I rest he will make it for me."

After we reached the "study," a room rich in thoughtful books in diverse tongues — Langsner speaks readily in twelve languages — we chatted merrily away for a while. Then Mrs. Langsner suddenly arose and came over to where I too had risen to my feet. "Excuse me," she said, her eyes downward, as she ran her fingers deftly over the buttons on my coat and vest, "you must not mind, but the photograph, you see — once it was this way concealed — and my husband will not ever picture-taken — and will you please your watch show to me," which I produced, duly returned as innocent. Later conversation with the "Professor" confirmed this caution; for he extracted my word of honour that even a pen picture of himself should be sternly foregone.

Mrs. Langsner withdrew as soon as her husband arrived, upon which he and I settled down to talk, but not before an incident of some interest occurred. I had seated myself with my back to a window through which the bright Alberta sun was pouring. My pencil and pad were in my hand.

"Please sit here," said Mr. Langsner, pointing to a desk at which I would have had to face the window. "You can write better here."

I demurred — could write quite well on my knee.

"That I wish to sit there," urged this man of such fearsome eyes.

"But I wish to sit there," urged this man of such fearsome eyes.

We parlayed — till finally I said, "Mr. Langsner, I wouldn't take everything in this room, in this hotel, and sit facing you with my face in the light and yours in the shadow."

He laughed, consenting — but the clash was pronounced, and significant.

"It must be strange, is it not, to land in a new world and find yourself so suddenly in the public eye?" I began.

"I do not like the public eye at all," he rejoined. "There is so much jealousy — it hurts."

"How did you discover, Mr. Langsner, that you possess your peculiar gift?"

"When a boy at school. But I did not discover it. It came. When I was a little boy, I did not study and I did not play. But my parents and my teachers knew about my gift — about what you call my gift."

"How long have you been exercising it?"

"You mean my service for humanity? About 16 years. But my vanity, as a boy, was great. When a lad, I thought, "I knew as much as Jesus Christ." (This, which threw me into consternation, left my colloquist as calm as a day in June.) "I say so myself every day: 'I know lots' — but my father made me immediately quiet. He tell me that one gold coin in a glass makes plenty noise, but fill it full and no noise at all. Then I find that I know nothing, and I grow very calm. But others, they try to spoil me, always. All my life I have to fight. Official science, it fight me. And also all charlatans, they fight me. I mean, they fight our side — I myself am nothing. But those that understand, they help me. Like your Col. O'Brien — send you from Edmonton to me. I do not blame the skeptics. I am myself a skeptic. I believe with difficulty what I do. It baffle me." (Interviewer's note: This is no shallow stuff.) "I, too, think what I do impossible. But what can one say? One does it — one proves it — and then one makes friends of skeptics, of honest skeptics."

"Mr. Langsner, do you have any assistance? For instance, what assistance would you need in the Ambrose Small case, in Toronto, if you took that up?"

The reply came with dignity, almost majesty. "My allies are invisible, strong forces, all silent. I do not see them, do not know them. They know me, I think. All I can do is to keep myself right — and ready. Like the harp, what is it you call it — the aeolian harp? I must not worry — I must keep my nerves open — I must be ready that my invisible allies may use me. When I am more quiet, then progress is more fast. Life is latent all."

"When did you first hear of the case of Ambrose Small?"

"It will not be necessary that I tell you. When I shall hear the last of it — that, is it not, is the matter of more greatness? It is a great bid, a challenge of greatness, to me. But it did hurt my feelings."

"In what way, Mr. Langsner?"

"There came in Edmonton to me a paper, a newspaper, to say that Mr. Langsner offered his services to solve the Small mystery. Offer, I did not. And Mayor McBride, he was right, not wrong, when he said the city, not Mr. Langsner, should offer. The family of Mr. Small, or the chief of police, or the attorney-general, or the government, or somebody, not me, should offer, should, you understand, approach me. But nobody, nobody, approach me. All everybody does is talk, talk, about the 'so mysterious' of the case."

At which juncture I volunteered to enlarge upon the case, only to find, as aforestated, that neither I nor any other living man except one — could tell this strange Viennese anything about it that he did not know. It was at this point, and after a fashion I do not think it wise or fair to disclose, that Mr. Langsner let me know of his clandestine visit to Toronto.

I resume. "Do you consider the case so mysterious, Mr. Langsner?"

"I do not find it so," was the low reply. "I have studied it, for weeks, on the ground, and have worked on it with fascination. I will say this, not more than this, that I hope to be not wrong. My expenses I myself did pay," was the naive remark with which he closed.

But I sought for more. "Then you think, do you, that you can solve the Ambrose Small case?"

"I am a chess player," was his cryptic reply. "It is my habit, mostly in my bed, to solve them all. My sense, not my common sense, tells me it is full of hopefulness. When it is done, then thousands will say — but never mind what they will say; you remember Columbus and his egg?"

"By what means did you solve the Booher murder in Edmonton? What faculty did you employ to find that gun?"

"It was an easy job," was the only and but slightly illuminating answer I could get. But he went on: "Col. O'Brien telegraphed me at Vancouver, and I came. The police were so good, so co-operative. It was like a dinner all ready for me to sit down and eat. Only 36 hours altogether did I think, and walk, and talk, and work. If all officials were Col. O'Briens, I could clean up Chicago."

"Even if Toronto should not co-operate with you in the Ambrose Small case, would you still work on it?"

"When I start, I finish."

"When will you come to Toronto again?"

"Nobody will know when I come to Toronto. Nobody will know when I am in Toronto."

"Do you think it would interfere?"

"I do not say. But for one thing, you understand this, my little wife — I do not want her to be a quick widow. She greatly helps me, too — did you know she is a novelist and writes novels in French and Italian?"

This struck me as wandering a little from the point, so I recalled my friend with: "Do you study the miracles of the New Testament?"

"I know all the religious books of the world," he answered, "and the greatest is the Talmud. It has everything — all else are translations."

"Do you believe in Conan Doyle and his spiritualism?"

"He has no proofs — he has delivered no goods."

"Have you, Mr. Langsner, any religion of your own?"

"I surely have — but I have no church. I am a freemason. The only true religion is the Religion of Help."

Thus concluded my interview with this famous and remarkable man, recently emerged from seven years spent in the jungles of the occult mentality and psychopathy of the Orient. I should call him a child of Nature and the East. I felt that a strange atmosphere surrounds and issues from him.

And, to close, I shall tell a bit of uncanny experience I had with him. I shall claim no significance for it. My readers may make of it what they will.

On the close of the day I interviewed Mr. Langsner. Communications between us, of character not to be disclosed, rendered it necessary that I should telegraph Toronto. I did so, a reply reaching me about an hour before I was imperatively impelled to take the train for Saskatoon.

This telegram received by me contained material which it was urgent that I should lay before this criminologist. I went, therefore, immediately to his rooms. His wife, who was there, informed me that her husband, in company with the Calgary chief of police, had left for a game of golf at a course some miles from the city. "He cannot be back in time," she said, "for I did hear him say that the whole eighteen holes he would play altogether." She then suggested our taking a taxi and seeking him on the links, but this, owing to time limit, was not feasible.

Disappointed, I rose to go. "Shall telegraph later," or something to that effect, I said. But at that very moment, overhearing something I had not heard, Mrs. Langsner gave a little cry and sprang toward the outer hall of their suite. She flung the door open — and there, calmly removing his overcoat, stood the always grave and self-possessed craftsman of the unknown.

I followed quickly, expressed my delight at this surprise, and could not forbear to add: "But how did you happen to come back so soon?" To which, with only the trace of a smile in the far-seeing eyes, he replied: "It was I who did know that you wanted me all the time."

Of this, as I said, those who read may make what they will — and may think what they like of this silent and stealthy man who, for anything I know, may even now be here in Toronto.

I venture to close with saying that, if great is the mystery of Ambrose Small, great also is the mystery of Maxmilian Langsner.

HAS "GONE FAR" IN SMALL CASE — Langsner Determined to Fathom — Nine-Year-Old Enigma — "Mystery Man" Declares — Viennese Criminologist — Abandons Alias of "Mr. Larete" — After Seeing Attorney-Gen. — Lauds the Latter — Fears Press More Than Police — Confident He Will Solve Theatre Magnate's Fate — Langsner Shares — View of Police — In Small Case?

Dr. Maximilian Langsner has already formed a definite opinion on the Small case, it is reported today.

It is understood that he has decided in his own mind who Small's slayer was and is now attempting to accumulate proof. His decision is said to be identical with that of the police department. Six years ago the police are said to have been satisfied as to the identity of the murderer of Small.

No charge can be laid, however, without production of the missing man's body, or a portion of it, as proof that he is dead.

It is more than likely that some of the half million readers of *The Daily Star* will recall my report of a lengthy interview, some time last month, and in Calgary, with the Viennese criminologist, Prof. Adolph Maximilian Langsner, the most discussed man in Toronto today.

On that occasion Mr. Langsner informed me that, although he had only just landed a few months before on this western world, and although he had been much engrossed in an Alberta murder, to help solve which he was called in for by the Alberta government; he had yet found time, and money, and inclination, to cross the continent to Toronto and spend some weeks in a study, off his own boat, and at his own expense, of the mystery of Ambrose Small, a maze of hazy darkness, whose story has filled the world.

Mr. Langsner further informed me, in reply to my question as to whether or not he would again visit Toronto, and if so probably when, that all that was wrapped in mystery:

"You will not know," he said, "and it will not to anybody be known whatever, when I shall appear in Toronto."

He kept his word. Out of a blue sky has come the tidings that this famous sleuth (in whom, let me say, I for one do at least not disbelieve) began to be felt in Toronto, 600,000 population of a city though it is.

Three or four times, the while I was sojourning about, sixty miles away from the madding crowd's ignoble strife, I was inquired for by phone at *The Daily Star* by a mysterious "Fred Smith," who gave some hint that he was acting for Mr. Langsner, but whom, as afterwards proved, I suspected, when told of it, was none other than Mr. Langsner himself or his immediate representative.

In consequence of which, having the kindliest memories of this quite attractive deep-sea pilot, I repaired to the Westminster hotel, having learned that such was the probable headquarters of this denizen of earth and sky and sea and air, of the upper world and the under, of the visible and invisible, the tangible and intangible, the hidden and revealed.

After much spade work of an intermediary kind, during which I spoke with a Scotchman (Mr. Devine, the secretary) and during which the soft and sweet tones of a woman came like music amid discord, I found myself speaking to Langsner himself.

The interview began sternly. I declared my identity, addressed the invisible as "Mr. Larete," and required audience with Mr. Langsner himself.

"Do you know Mr. Langsner?" came the voice like one from the tombs.

"Sure thing — I talked two hours with you in Calgary."

"With me!" surprise and horror registered, "you mean Mr. Langsner."

"I mean both — I talked to you, and I want to talk to you again."

"Can you describe Mr. Langsner?"

"Assuredly I can."

"Which way do you describe him?"

"This way: he is short and square, with a rather pale face, with an eye of intelligence and penetration, with a look of ability —"

"That will nicely do," interrupted the psychic man-hunter, "you may upstairs come and my secretary will meet you at the alleviator."

Which the secretary did, ushering me along the hall of the third floor to the door of 302; upon which he knocked after a fashion that would make a Masonic tyler green with despair, the knock answered by a sepulchral monosyllable which was followed by cautious opening and our immediate entrance.

Mrs. Langsner, a 27-year-old woman of exceptional beauty and charm, was the first to welcome me. I should say that she too has something of psychic power and truth seems to lie in her dark eyes like water in a well. We chatted a little along reminiscent lines, just as if the occult and crime, and commerce with the unseen, and pursuit of murderers by the air route had never disturbed the peace of the world.

Then, Mr. Langsner, the hall door of the elaborate suite audibly knocked, took me into his sitting-room and closed the door.

The secretary, who evidently attends all audiences (for I have been in "the presence" more than once on Jarvis St.), sat down to a typewriter, his hands busy, his ears extended.

We talked long. The professor, first, wanted to know why I had not answered either one of two telegrams he had sent me since our Calgary interview. I could not just explain — but he was quite patient and reasonable.

I asked him as to how things were going in the Ambrose Small case.

"I have gone far," he said, this followed up by one or two facts of detail, communications which I cannot, in honour, disclose here or elsewhere. He responded but scantily to my inquiry as to the methods, the mental methods, he called to his aid.

"Have you read Free-oyd's (Freud's) Psychoanalysis?" he asked me, filling afresh one of the most ornate and elaborately carved pipes I have ever envied.

"Not in any exhaustive way," was my reply, resorting to the usual way of saying we have never looked at a book.

"You much have missed," was the sad reply.

I then asked Mr. Langsner if he had any opinion as to who murdered Small.

His answer was as positive and cryptic. "We all know that — everybody knows that — it is known to everybody, even if not to prove," was the rather repetitive reply.

"Will you get the skeleton?"

"I believe the skeleton, it will be got" — and I here affirm, with the disdainful smile, that Mr. Langsner believes that he believes that it will be found. "You see the papers to-day, and they say that the police say that, of course, naturally perhaps, that much can be done, but who will tell whose skeleton it is? You see, the police, the first they laugh altogether — now they admit one little bit — by and by they admit more — do you see?"

I said I saw. "Do you think, Mr. Langsner, it is likely that you yourself are being watched?"

Langsner shrugged his broad shoulders. "They can not watch me."

"Not a private detective?"

The seer laughed scornfully. "I am not afraid of the private detective. I more afraid of the newspaper reporters; they do our lives harm miserable make. My little wife is kept on the defensive, with the telephone, night and day."

"Do you think you can maintain your incognito and your 'Mr. Latele' disguise here in Toronto, in any permanent way?"

The reply was one of great confidence that he could. "It is necessary for my work. I have been working night and day. I go through the hotel entrance, full of people who want to see Langsner and they not one know me at all. It is in earnest I am. Why else I come here, all the way, at expense so great, if not? Me, who can so much money make in other ways — why, my dear Mr. Knowles, I have contract to lecture to great money advantage, which I so soon must take up. I come here, money out of my own pocket" (at which the richly carved pipe developed the faculty of a smoke-stack) "because I know I yet shall clear the darn thing up. I come first to the King Edward hotel, then we go to a boarding house" (whereat intervened a vivid paragraph of deep disgust) "then some place other, there, here. Why all of these thing, if not believe Langsner do what he start to do? You know," with a swift turn of his handsome head to the statuesque secretary, "what Langsner can do," the silent Scotchman in the corner replying with a swift concurrence and a psychical obeisance which suggested that his chief's expenses were by no means confined to railways and hotels.

"Has the government helped you?"

"I tell you gladly everything — Mr. Price, the general attorney, he nice, and splendid to me. He not promise anythings, but he treat me like a gentleman — I tell you I thank him much."

And as I went on my way I reflected that Col. Price was right. Langsner, of course, has credentials by the sheaf. Whatever they may or may not amount to, those who know most about Maximilian Langsner will at least contend that he is not to be dismissed with a wave of the hand.

Dr. Langsner has made no arrangements to see Deputy Attorney-General E.W. Bayly or Deputy Commissioner of Provincial Police Cuddy, it was stated at Queen's Park to-day. Attorney-General Price has asked the criminologist to lay any information he has before these men, and has promised that the government will take the necessary action.

If Langsner divulges new information, it is unlikely that it will be made public until it is acted upon and arrests made, if such appear to be warranted.

DR. LANGSNER GOES TO LECTURE TOUR
— Province Has Offered — To Cover the Expenses — Incurred by Langsner — Prefers $2,000-a-Week Platform — Engagement to Government's Terms — Stays on Case — Will Leave City Only Temporarily to make Money — With Which to Finance Inquiries

Attorney-General Price to-day denied the report that the government had offered Dr. Langsner $1,000 per month to work on.

Dr. Langsner was asked to submit a report of the expenses that will be incurred in his investigation regarding the Small case. No estimate of the cost has yet been received by the government and no definite action has been decided upon.

It is possible that the government will give some assistance to Dr. Langsner. "They discussed this angle of the matter yesterday when Dr. Langsner met Mr. Bayly and Deputy Commissioner of Provincial Police Cuddy," Col. Price stated. "Dr. Langsner was asked approximately what his expenses would amount to, and it was suggested that he submit an account or report to the attorney-general's department. This will be attended to then and will likely come before me."

"Did the government offer him a thousand dollars per month to carry on his investigations?" he was asked. "No," the Col. stated, "no amount was mentioned and we did not make any definite offer."

Though the matter has not yet been fully verified, *The Star* learns to-day that a report was received this morning at provincial police headquarters, presumably from Dr. Langsner or one of his agents, that one of the parties who figured prominently in the news at the time when Ambrose Small vanished has left the city since yesterday. If this news be correct, it may be of significance and on the other hand, it may have no importance other than that it demonstrates the close watch which is being kept by Dr. Langsner on everyone, even though only remotely connected to-day with the problem he is endeavouring to solve.

By mid-day this morning *The Star* called at Dr. Langsner's palatial suite at the Westminster hotel and met him as he was making his way, hatted and coated, down the stairway to the main hall of the building.

"I am going out," said Dr. Langsner, "I have calls to make."

The Star offered to convey him to his destination and Dr. Langsner consented on condition that no photographs were taken. Entering the taxi he suddenly sprang up with the remark, "There are photographers behind me. I must vanish." Quickly leaving the taxi, he returned to his apartment in the hotel, waving his hand en route to two reporters in another automobile who were apparently anxious to obtain a photograph.

Prior to leaving the hotel, Dr. Langsner was handed his mail by the clerk in the hotel office. One letter which had found its way into his box by mistake was presumably for a lady.

"That letter is for a good looking young lady with brown eyes and about your own height," he remarked to the lady clerk, as he returned the envelope. "When you locate her see whether or no I am correct."

When queried by *The Star*, the doctor acknowledged that he was going to lecture in Edmonton next week.

"It is necessary for me," he said, "to make money in order that I may properly continue my investigations here."

Asked whether he intended to call upon Chief of Police Draper since the latter had expressed, through the columns of the press, a willingness to receive him, Dr. Langsner stated: "I shall of course pay my respects to General Draper. That is a matter of simple politeness."

Asked if he intended to discuss the Small case with General Draper, he replied: "That is as General Draper wishes."

Dr. Langsner is to deliver his lectures in western Canada, the first to be in Edmonton on October 29, and inasmuch as he has indicated that a sensational statement may be forthcoming soon from another city observers suggest that it may be from a city in the west, although New York and other United States cities are also mentioned. Bearing on the possibility that revelations may be expected from the west is a letter from W.W. Babience, chiropractor-naturopath, of 185 Carlton St., Toronto, who asks *The Star* to convey certain information he volunteers to Dr. Langsner.

W.W. Babience writes: "I was practicing with Madame D.F. Lublinska when Ambrose Small disappeared. At first I did not pay much attention to the case, but when the photograph of Mr. Small appeared in a Winnipeg paper I read the news to my sister, Madame Lublinska, and showed her the picture.

"Madame Lublinska at once recognized the picture as that of a gentleman who a few days before had applied to her for treatment. She described him as quite nervous and in haste. He was well dressed, and his companion was young. He received treatment and made arrangements to come the next day. He and his companion then departed, but they did not return to keep their appointment.

"The gentleman told my sister that he was about to leave for Austria, and when we came to Toronto on September 2, 1920, I wrote a letter to some trust company that professed to be interested in Mr. Small's whereabouts. I was asked by letter to come to their office and lay the information before the manager, but I had not time to go.

"Madame Lublinska told me that she could not mistake the man who had called on her, and is certain that the picture of Mr. Small as published is that of her visitor. She has said that she could also recognize the man who accompanied him, and I believe it is my duty to lay the information before the investigator who is now engaged in solving the mystery."

Dr. Langsner's forthcoming appearance on the lecture platform in Edmonton is being widely advertised. In the advertisements he is referred to as "the world's greatest telepathist," and as "the man of the hour, demonstrating hypnotic control of birds and animals, criminology, will-power — in fact, the same entertaining features which astounded police chiefs of the world." His press agent adds this paragraph in a full page advertisement.

"And what of this Dr. Adolph Langsner, a man who has startled the people of three continents by his uncanny powers, and has materially assisted police of a score of countries in solving the tangled skeins left by desperate criminals? He is truly a man of mystery, a man who has reduced mental telepathy to such a science that it is an open book to him. But Dr. Langsner, while secretive to almost a fault when working on a case, is always willing to lift the veil of secrecy once the criminal has been brought to justice, and it will be of decided interest to Edmontonians to learn that the criminologist, in the east at present on an important mission, will return to this city incognito, and fearing that some of the threatening letters he has received may be more than idle threats, he has required police protection during his Edmonton stay."

Langsner will leave Toronto tomorrow night for the west to commence his lectures. His departure will not be a permanent one and behind him he will leave certain agents who will continue to work under his direction. It is expected that the doctor will return in the course of a week or so.

His decision to leave the city was revealed to *The Star* in the course of an interview which followed a conference between himself, Deputy Commissioner Alfred Cuddy of the provincial police, and Deputy Attorney-General Bayly in the police commissioner's office. In describing the results of this interview to *The Star* the doctor expressed confidence in Mr. Cuddy, Col. W.H. Price and officials of the department and indicated that a definite offer of financial assistance had been made to him.

Dr. Langsner acknowledged that the offer might be sufficient to satisfy an ordinary investigator, and that $1,000 a month and expenses constitutes good pay.

"But my methods are not ordinary," said Dr. Langsner. "It is because they are not ordinary that I often succeed where others fail. At present I am only here by permission of certain parties with whom I have signed a contract to lecture. My contract brings me $2,000 a week in addition to all expenses and this is the sum I am losing while I remain here, not to mention my outlay on the upkeep of myself and staff. This delay in obtaining the adequate support embarrasses me. I am, however, determined not yet to withdraw from this case. I will yet astonish the world. It may be necessary for me to be absent for short periods in order that I may earn the money necessary to proceed. But I am even prepared to do this so convinced am I that this problem can be solved.

"The men I will leave here will [be] in constant touch with me. As I have already said an important announcement concerning the case may be forthcoming shortly from another city."

On the occasion of his next return to Toronto the doctor intimated that he will not be so easily located. The enthralling question of the disappearance of Ambrose Small has gripped his imagination, he said, just as firmly as it has that of the general public. Delays may be wearing on public curiosity, he pointed out, but such suspense is equally wearing on the mentality of those who have guilty knowledge.

The guilty are weakening, he declared again to-day. "A just retribution has overtaken them in the agony of mind which they suffer and strange though it may seem peace can only come to them when they have disclosed to the world the knowledge which is theirs," he added.

Dr. Langsner has several interviews arranged in connection with the case to-day. His departure from Toronto will be as unobtrusive as his arrival in the city.

That Ambrose Small was not murdered but is living in seclusion is the firm conviction of Mrs. E. Simmons, a former employee of the Small family.

"I knew Mr. Small well by sight," she told *The Star*. "Even after I left there, I was often in the Small home in the capacity of waitress. I worked for the Smalls and their friends, the Jacobis, for many years and should know him if anybody should, and I saw him just four years ago this October."

Mrs. Simmons stated that one afternoon she got on a Bay Street car at Breadalbane St. and a few minutes later a couple who had walked behind her from St. Michael's College also got on the car and sat down beside her.

"I was so surprised I suppose I must have stared at him because the woman suddenly got up and put some tickets in the conductor's box and motioned to Mr. Small to follow her."

She is also firmly convinced that Ambrose Small was in hiding at St. Michael's College for several years after his disappearance. "Why, they even had a notice put up in St. Basil's church, asking for prayers for Mr. Small, as he was very sick. This was four years ago and the sisters raised an awful fuss trying to find out who put it up."

MADAME LANGSNER LEARNS — ENGLISH IN DODGING PRESS — *Wife of Criminologist Has Full — Confidence in His Ability to Solve Small Case — Tells of Career — Was Wedded by Dutch Magistrate — on 8,000-Foot Java Mountain*

Yesterday, at high noon plus one hour, Mrs. Maximilian Langsner, celebrity by marriage, invited me to luncheon at the Jarvis St. hotel which has of late had more inexpensive advertising than any other since an Egyptian princess did for her spouse at the Savoy in old London.

I was on time, but not for luncheon. Conversation began with the taking off of an overcoat, ran on for an hour in the parlor, and ended with the post-prandial coffee. At which time the criminological husband got back from a parliament building conference, the conversation then ear-marked for his own.

By the kind consent of Mrs. Langsner, when I frankly avowed my journalistic intentions, I was permitted to take nourishment and "notes" at one and the same time — all that was not to "go in" was inhibited by my lovely hostess as our talk went on.

I began with the highest of all topics, my first question being: "Mrs. Langsner, may I ask what is your religious affiliation?"

So soon as the last two words had been reduced to English, Mrs. Langsner replied: "I am a Roman Catholic — or, perhaps I should say, I passed from being a Catholic to being a human being. It is lovely to be both — will you be kindly enough to tell me what you are, is it not so, please?"

I yielded, not without many an unseemly smile, to the fascinating inquisition.

"What is your husband's religion?" I followed up with, getting back on the rail.

"Mr. Langsner is of the religion of being kindly good — that is his God, you see, please? And will be always so the same."

"Please, my friend, give me a short sketch of your life."

"Well, then so, I was born — the same way as all peoples else — in Germany, in Cologne. And it was 26 year since before I was born. You say it was yesterday, in *The Star*, that I was 27 years of old — but it is not even so, it was 26 only, my so dear friend, and all the womans want it not to be more than when they were born."

"Did you live in Cologne?" I interposed, seeking cover.

"Oh, yes, till I was bigger. I was christened of the church in the grand Cologne cathedral — and my first communion, it was taken of me there. My father and mother do live there yet always."

"Where were you and Mr. Langsner married? At Cologne?"

"Oh, no, please — we made our marriage at Java — and not in church at all — it was a, a, what you call a magisteer."

"A magistrate?" I assisted.

"Yes, I thank you, yes, a magistrate. And it was such a funny marriage we make. Nobody did be there except the magistrate — it was at Mr. Langsner's home, 8,000 feet high — and a German painter and a doctor and his wife. Well, the magistrate, he speak only Dutch — which Mr. Langsner know not a bit. So all the things, the — the vows — I did have to translate to my husband, and I wish me some time I put in for him to obey — you see, please? — and the magistrate (the Dutch, they do this) at the end give three strokes with a hammer. But I not know this mean married — the only way I know all done and over, the doctor's wife, she start to cry — the elderly ladies always cry when that part come — what for they cry you suppose, please? — and so then I know Mr. Langsner and myself all married. It was so funny, was it not? I believe — don't you, please? — in the laugh, not the cry."

"Mrs. Langsner, does your husband have any secrets from you?"

"His work you mean? I know not anything — except by the telephone, which never stops. I never ask. I am not strong enough. What I know, I know when it is done, solved, you see, please."

"Then you believe implicitly in him?"

"Oh, yes, I believe him all ways, all times. I was a skeptic once — but he convinced me — his work, I am — he do so much things and so big. But I pity with my husband very much — so much work — so much questions — so much telephone — we never once before have so much telephone as in Toronto."

"Who is your favourite author?"

"When I was young," and the lonely face was as grave and sad as any girl's in her 20's can be, "I read much Schiller and much Goethe — but I have seen of life so much, it is hard to keep young and read love stories nothing else — so I just try to be young yet."

"How does one be young?"

"Just to be happy, and to throw away the things not nice, and to keep the nicest things, and to look in front not back, and to be like any Gretchen sister in Germany — I am the Italian one — but she is the German one, long fair curls and blue eyes and so nice and comfortable and so much to sing and laugh, that is how to keep young always — is it not so, please?

At this juncture I ventured: "Mrs. Langsner, although you tell me you have never lived among English-speaking people, yet your English is remarkable. How do you account for it?"

"You are so kindly to speak — and I am glad because I read your much writing, and your — your style it is so personality and it makes you see when you read. So you to be so kindly makes me glad. Well, I will tell you how I learn my English — it is from the reporters on the telephone — that is my school, and you understand me, please? We do have most funny time here with the newspaper telephone — and only one woman I hear altogether: she invite me to the Press club, the ladies' press, but I could not once go, so I have so careful always to be."

This conversation, luncheon past and gone and taken into memory's imperishable keeping, was now coming to a close in the suite drawing rooms whither we had returned. A few minutes later the professor returned also — and he did the rest.

He (Mr. Langsner) was at higher tension than I had ever before seen him reach. What had happened at Queen's Park was not disclosed, save for various references to the need for mutual confidence and for co-operation.

The unweariable professor paced up and down the lengthy parlor, engrossed in thought and speech that ran together. I finally ventured to say that I had not seen such a moving spectacle since I had watched other lions in the London Zoo. The learned pedestrian smiled economically and explained: "I think best when I walk alway. When I play against four tables of chess — you that remember, my dear? — I will all the time walk up and down."

Shortly after which, and immediately precedent to my departure, came a lovely scene. Mrs. Langsner, beginning with the statement that her husband had had no breakfast, ascertained that he had gone lunch-less as well. Whereupon, in the depth of insistent assurances from her husband to the effect "I have no appetite," "I cannot anything eat at all," this beautiful and gracious and most womanly woman calmly plied her way via the pestiferous telephone, utterly ignoring the abstemious protests as she ordered this little dainty thing and that — and "be so kindly to send some coffee, too." Whereat, all of a sudden, and I could have embraced this other-worldy craftsman for his humanness, her husband suddenly right about faced and, with the eagerness of a child, drew close and began a series of supplementary suggestions: "And a little roast beef, my dear ... and a salad perhaps ... and whatever it is you think, my dear."

SMALL MYSTERY IS SOLVED — ACCORDING TO DR. LANGSNER — Promises to Reveal Detail After Expiration of Theatrical Contract — "I Have Nothing to Fear," He Adds — Has Been in Toronto Several Times Incognito

Debonair, detached, distinguished looking of his kind, the fur-clad Dr. Langsner, deep-sea pilot and sleuth by scientific means, looked glad to be back in Toronto.

"Isn't it nice," I began, "to come up to breathe?"

"What is that — if you will so kindly be?" was the retort.

"Isn't it nice to throw aside the mask?"

"It is no longer a thing I must do. The public is now so sympathetic to me. They are on my side with me and I have nothing to fear."

"Is the Small case solved yet?"

"Me, I am through — the case is solved — I do not need more to bother."

"Have you been working on it since you left?"

Dr. Langsner smiled the smile that is childlike and bland: "My headquarters in Montreal I did make — but my work, I worked in Toronto."

"You have been in Toronto since you left us?"

"Several, several times. Oh, yes. I came here to work. I live in Montreal to get away from — I must say — from newspaper men, they persecute me," the Oriental smile quite out of turn with the language.

"What is your solution to the Small case?"

"I cannot now say. I am under contract with Pantages — when that finished is, more will I tell you then."

"Has your Pantages appearance any bearing on your Small labors?"

"Oh, no. It bears not upon anything except I would make a little money — to carry on the Small case, if you like. Why should I not make money? My work is honest work. I am a sellsman, a salesman — but my goods are mental goods. You will yet see. You will for yourself judge. The world will see, the world will judge. Then everything, with me, with any man, is not what people say I am — but what I, Langsner, know I am myself."

"Dr. Langsner, a Toronto paper reported you as saying that you had been disappointed in a certain source that promised you financial assistance but had not kept its promise. Is that true?"

"Yes, that is true."

"And that same Toronto paper reported you as saying that *The Daily Star* had, before you first came to Toronto, promised to help you financially. What about that?"

"It is not true," was the emphatic reply. "I did not ever say that about *The Star*. I tell you now I am promised from private sources. And will at length yet come. And then you will see, all will see."

Before leaving, Dr. Langsner spoke of the Hon. Mackenzie King's visit to Toronto. There is not much overlooked by this astute Viennese. "I would much like his Excellent, the prime minister, to meet personally beside," he said earnestly. "His Excellent is the man of the big brain," and Dr. Langsner herewith raised finger to his own, by way of illustration. To me, he is a Napoleon, yes, a Napoleon he is to me. And Europe, in my country, in Europe I say his Excellent, the Premier Mr. King is high, very high," as the eulogist stretched his own frame to its full but not impressive height, the rest left to the imagination.

SOME FAMOUS HAUNTS OF MODERN TIMES

You have the right to be amazed when you read the experiences described in this section of the book. They are pretty amazing, and we do not expect amazing things to happen to our public figures. We are inclined to think of our politicians and especially our prime ministers as a pretty rum lot, men (mainly) who have a lot of determination but not much in the way of imagination, certainly not people concerned with psychical research and the paranormal experiences. Yet that is the case with Mackenzie and King.

I am referring to William Lyon Mackenzie (1795–1861) and his grandson William Lyon Mackenzie King (1874–1950). Mackenzie was known as "the firebrand" for his fiery red hair, his fiery temper, and his fiery leadership of the Rebellion of 1837. The handsome residence in downtown Toronto, where he spent the last years of his life, has a long tradition of being a haunt.

King was proud of his grandfather but he was quite unlike him, being a cautious career politician. King served as prime minister for a total of twenty-one years, between 1921 and 1948, when he retired from public life. It was only following his death that the general public learned that he was a convinced spiritualist, that he attended seances throughout his career, and that he believed he was in communication with the spirits of his predecessors, notably Prime Minister Sir Wilfrid Laurier who blessed his efforts to bring unity to Canadian public life.

In this section you will find a noted newspaperman's account of how, relaxing in Kingsmere, King's estate in the Gatineau Hills outside Ottawa, he communed with King's spirit, two years following the latter's death. It seems King's ghost was alive — or is alive — in Kingsmere. In a separate article, the journalist, Percy J. Philip, describes the public reaction to his spirited encounter.

Mackenzie House is often described as "the most haunted house in Canada." Certainly it is the country's most handsome house that is reputed to be haunted by the ghost of Mackenzie. It is one of a number of haunted sites managed by the Toronto Historical Board — Old Fort York is another — and it is open to the public. When touring the historic residence, be sure to ask the guides about the parts of the place that are haunted: the second-story bedroom, the hallway, the parlour, and the basement.

King died a decade before the first hauntings of Mackenzie House were reported. If only he had lived to learn that the spirit of his ancestor lives on!

MACKENZIE KING'S GHOST

It might seem strange to regard the ghost of Mackenzie King as a "monster." Yet it would be monstrous indeed if the spirits of the deceased prime ministers of Canada returned from the dead and entered into colloquies with their successors, their friends, and their colleagues. I am aware that two prime ministers are said to have returned from the dead to address the living (and they are Sir John A. Macdonald and W.L. Mackenzie King).

The witness for the return of Mackenzie King is Percy J. Philip (1880–1956), former war correspondent and Ottawa correspondent for *The New York Times*, who created quite a commotion when he broadcast a talk on CBC Radio about his conversation with the late prime minister, and subsequently wrote up an account of his experiences and then an article of the reception of his revelation. The latter contribution gives the reader some sense of the reaction of the public and even of friends when witnesses "come out of the closet."

The account itself appeared as "I Talked with Mackenzie King's Ghost," *Fate Magazine*, December 1955. It is followed by Philip's article on the subject, which appeared as "My Conversation with Mackenzie King's Ghost," *Liberty*, January 1955.

I Talked with Mackenzie King's Ghost
By Percy J. Philip

On a June evening in 1954 I had a long conversation with the former Canadian Prime Minister William L. Mackenzie King as we sat on a bench in the grounds of his old summer home at Kingsmere, 12 miles from Ottawa. It seemed to me an entirely normal thing although I knew perfectly well that Mr. King had been dead for four years.

Of course, when I returned to Ottawa and told my story nobody quite believed me. I myself became just the least bit uncertain as to whether it really had happened, or at least as to how it had happened. Did I fall asleep and dream? Was this due to paranormal circumstances which cannot be explained?

Of one thing I am sure. Mr. King himself would believe

me. He once held similar conversations — almost daily in some cases — with persons who had left this world. He talked with his father and mother regularly and with great men and women of the past. His diary, in which he recorded his spiritual experiences, as well as his political activities and contacts, gives detailed accounts of these conversations. Unfortunately it is not likely to be published in full because his will provided that certain parts should be destroyed. His literary executors feel bound to carry out these instructions.

It was not until after his death that the Canadian people learned that their bachelor, liberal Prime Minister communed with the dead both directly and, occasionally, through mediums. When it did become known — in a rather sensational way — it shocked many.

Yet the Prime Minister made no secret of his beliefs and practices. To friends who had lost dear ones he wrote in this manner: "I know how you feel. It seems as though you cannot bear to go on without that wonderful companionship and affection. But let me assure you that love still exists. A bond as strong as that is not broken by death or anything else. Your father is still near you. If you can be still and listen and feel, you will realize he is close to you all your life. I know that because it is so with my mother and me."

That quotation is from one of the many hundreds of letters of condolence which Mr. King wrote with his own hand for he was punctilious in such matters. At funerals he always spoke similar words of comfort to those bereaved. Otherwise, although he made no secret of his beliefs, he did not parade them.

Once, at Government House, about Christmas time in 1945, he told the Governor General, the Earl of Athlone, that he had spoken with President Roosevelt the previous night. "President Truman, you mean," said the Governor. The Earl saw that some of his staff were making signs from behind Mr. King's back, evidently trying to convey some message. He was puzzled but, being a good constitutional

Governor General, he kept quiet and did not again correct the Prime Minister when he repeated, "Oh, no, I mean the late President Roosevelt."

The occasion of the incident was the showing of the Noel Coward film, *Blythe Spirit*, which Mr. King found "most interesting."

"It is difficult to imagine the life after death," he said, chatting gaily. "Probably the best thing to do is to regard it as a continuation of the one we know with the same processes of growth and change until, eventually, we forget our life and associations on this earth, just as old people tend to forget their childhood experiences."

His Excellency who was a brother of the late Queen Mary and a soldier by profession muttered, "Yes, yes, probably." He obviously was shaken. He had been chosen by Mr. King to be Governor General of Canada and it made him nervous to learn that his Prime Minister was receiving advice from extra-mundane sources.

"Good God," he exclaimed when his staff explained why they had tried to shush him, "is that where the man gets his policies?"

Having an open mind about the occult and being inquisitive by nature, I later managed to turn several conversations with Mr. King to this subject. Once, especially, when we were crossing the Atlantic to Europe, he talked freely about his beliefs and experiences as we walked the deck.

"If one believes in God and a life after death," he said, "it is inevitable that one must believe that the spirits of those who have gone take an interest in the people and places they loved during their lives on earth. It is the matter of communication that is difficult. For myself I have found that the method of solitary, direct, communion is best. After my father and mother died I felt terribly alone. But I also felt that they were near me. Almost accidentally I established contact by talking to them as if they were present and soon I began to get replies."

These and other things that the Prime Minister said to

me at different times came back to my mind as, on that June evening, I drove up the Kingsmere road and was reminded by a sign that the estate of Moorside, which Mr. King had left to the Canadian people in his will, lay just ahead.

It is a beautiful place. There are 550 acres of woodland and clearings, through most of which everyone is free to wander at will. A little stream with a waterfall flows through it down to the valley below. Mr. King accumulated it almost acre by acre, adding steadily in his methodical way, to the original lot he had bought when he first came to Ottawa at the beginning of the century. His quick temper seldom flashed more hotly than when he discovered that some neighbor had sold a parcel of land without giving him a chance to buy. Adding to his estate became a passion with the future Prime Minister. There he loved to receive visitors and also to be alone.

In buying the land Mr. King showed his Scottish shrewdness. But the building of the "ruins" was a perfect example of that romantic daftness that sometimes bewitches the supposedly hard-headed Scot. The direction sign now set up for tourists calls them "ruins" but the uninformed must wonder what they once were. There were doorways and windows, a fireplace, a row of columns, which Mr. King called the cloisters, coats of arms carved in stone, bits and pieces of the old Parliament Buildings, the mint, banks and private houses all built into an artistic enough a wholly whimsical suggestion of a ruined castle. Somehow, perhaps because the surroundings with outcrop rock and pine are so fitting, they escape being silly.

On that evening there were no other visitors. The air was clear and cool. I sat down on a bench beside the ruins and thought about the strange little man who loved his hill-top home so dearly. I suppose I was in what I called a receptive mood. Although I had not then read it I was following the instructions in that letter from which I already have quoted, to "be still and listen and feel."

I became conscious that I was not alone. Someone sat

on the park bench beside me.

There were no sighs, groans and lightning flashes such as mark a spirit's arrival on the Shakespearian stage. There was, if anything, a deeper peace. Through a fold in the hills I could see stretch of the broad Ottawa Valley. I tried to concentrate on it and keep contact with the normal but the presence on the bench would not be denied.

Without turning my head, for somehow I feared to look, I said as naturally as I could, "Good evening, Mr. King."

In that warm tone which always marked his conversation the voice of Mr. King replied, "Good evening, Philip. I am so glad you spoke to me."

That surprised me. "I was thinking of you," I muttered.

"Oh, yes," he replied. "I knew that. But one of the rules which govern our conduct on this side is that we are like the children and must not speak unless we are spoken to. I suppose it is a good rule because it would be very disturbing if we went around talking to people. The sad thing is that so few of them ever talk to us."

Here I think I should say that the reader must decide for himself whether or not he believes this story. It puzzles me greatly.

"I suppose," I said, or I think I said, resuming the conversation, "that we are just a bit scared. You know how hard it is to speak into a dark, empty room."

"That certainly is a difficulty for many people," Mr. King said. "But the room is never really empty. It is often filled with lonely ones who would like to be spoken to. They must, however, be called by name, confidently, affectionately, now challenged to declare themselves."

"Your name," I said, "must often be so mentioned in this lovely place you bequeathed to the Canadian people."

"Oh, yes, mentioned," he said. I glanced at him and seemed to see his eyes sparkle as they did in life, for he had a great deal of puckish humor. "But between being mentioned and being addressed by name, as you addressed me, there is a great deal of difference. I have heard things about my character, motives, political actions and even my personal appearance and habits that have made me laugh so loudly I thought I must break the sound barrier. And I have heard things about myself, too, that have made me shrink."

In the evening silence I had the sensation of being suspended in time and space as the quiet voice went on. "There are things that I said and did that I could regret but, on this side, we soon learn to have no regrets. Life would be meaningless if we did not all make mistakes, and eternity intolerable if we spent it regretting them."

He paused and I thought he looked at me quizzically. "By the way," he said, "Do you still write for the *New York Times?*"

When I said that I had retired he chuckled. "But still," he said, "I think I had better not give indiscreet answers to your questions."

I asked several but he answered with the same skill as marked his replies to questions in the House of Commons and at meetings with the press, divulging nothing. It was I who was the interviewed. He was eager for news and it surprised me then, as it does now, that he seemed not to know fully what was happening in the world. The dead, I discovered, are not omniscient. Or perhaps what we think important is not important to them.

We talked of the development of Canada, of housing and new enterprises like the St. Lawrence Seaway. "My successor has been lucky," Mr. King said. That was as far as he went in any personal reference. "Canada has been very prosperous. I hope it will continue to be so. But you cannot expect good times always. It is adversity that proves the real value of men and nations."

The conversation drifted to the international scene, to philosophic discussion of forms of government, of the balance between Liberty and Authority, the growth and decay of nations and of systems. I cannot tell how long it lasted but I noticed that the sickle moon was getting brighter. I mentioned the time, fumbling for my watch.

"Time," said Mr. King, "I had almost forgotten about time. I suppose I spend a great deal of time up here. There is so much beauty and peace. I gave it to the Canadian people but in a way I have preserved it for myself. It is good to have some familiar, well-loved place to spend 'time' in, until one gets used to eternity."

We both rose from the bench — or at least I did. When I looked at him, as I then did for the first time directly, he seemed just as I had known him in life, just as when I had talked with him once at this very spot.

"I think you told me once that you are Scottish born and a wee bit 'fey,'" he said. "It's a good thing to be. We have two worlds. Those people who think their world is the only one, and who take it and themselves too seriously, have a very dull time. Do come back and talk with me again."

I muttered words of thanks and then, following the habit of a lifetime, stretched out my hand to bid goodbye. He was not there.

My Conversation with Mackenzie King's Ghost
By Percy J. Philip

So many people have asked me to tell them "the real truth" about my recent "interview" with the late Prime Minister Mackenzie King on the park bench at Kingsmere, Que., that I am glad to have the opportunity offered me by *Liberty*, to fill in the background and correct some misunderstandings, of the "ghost story" which I told over the CBC network last September 24.

Perhaps I should begin by saying that in Scotland, where I was born, we believe in ghosts. My father, who was a minister of the Church of Scotland, told me how his father had come to him in dreams, and on the edge of sleep, so vividly he could not afterwards believe that it was not real. Even more oddly, though he died at the age of eighty-six when I was three years old, my gaunt old grandfather, wrapped in his homespun plaid, has paid me several visits. Afterwards, I could not say definitely whether I had been asleep or awake. But the whole conversation, even to the old man's slight Aberdeenshire accent, was so vivid that I was positive it had actually taken place.

And that is how it was in my conversation with Mr. King on the park bench among the ruins at Kingsmere last June.

What the explanation may be of such phenomena I do not claim to understand. They may be due to psychic influence, to a stimulated imagination, or to that subconscious working of the mind which happens in dreams.

Yet there is no incompatibility between being a Christian and church-goer, as Mr. King was, and being a searcher into the mystery of the hereafter. During his life, we had several discussions on the fascinating subject, and it came to me as a surprise when, after his death, it was "revealed" in a magazine article that he had been a practising spiritualist. I thought everybody knew about it.

Like many others of his friends, I resented this, perhaps unintentional, exposure of Mr. King to ridicule. Perhaps I should have been warned not to touch such a sensitive subject. There may be no witches in Canada, but there are witch-hunters.

Still I have been a reporter all my life, and I could not resist trying to write an account of that strange experience at Kingsmere. I did it with the greatest care.

I offered what I had written to a national Canadian magazine — not *Liberty* — but it was courteously rejected. I was told later it had gone to the fiction department and had not been regarded as very good fiction.

So I redrafted it for broadcasting. I thought that my Scottish voice might convey my meaning with more subtlety than the cold printed word. I stress its unusual character, I called the talk *Fantasia*. As I would have a much wider audience on the air, I strengthened the warnings that it should not be taken too literally, writing that I was not sure that I believed my story myself, and prefacing my account of the "facts" with the conditional phrase — "If in the mystery of life and the hereafter, there are such things as facts."

That, it seemed to me, provided the key to the story. It was a mystery, and a pleasant one.

The CBC editors, to whom the script was submitted, read it understandingly, and accepted it for broadcasting.

Listeners from one end of the country to another seem also to have understood. Two of Mr. King's literary executors, who have had access to all his private papers, and a former member of his cabinet, were enthusiastic about the portrait I had drawn of their old leader.

But when we come to the treatment of the story by the press, that is another matter.

It perhaps ill becomes one who has been a newspaper reporter all his life, and has undoubtedly made his full measure of mistakes of interpretation and even of fact, to be critical of his colleagues who may fall into error.

I find, however, that some account of how my broadcast was handled by the press is necessary for the proper understanding of the Legend of the Bench at Kingsmere.

That legend has already travelled far beyond Canada. It has brought more than 200 letters, from every province and from many states of the American Union. Every weekend, and even during the week, hundreds of visitors have been flocking up to Moorside and arguing hotly whether or not the "ghost" really appeared. The delegates of the Colombo Plan conference in Ottawa have carried the story to the ends of the earth. Political commentators have seized on it as a peg on which to hang pontifical articles. Collins, in the Montreal *Gazette*, lifted it to a high point of humor with his cartoon of Prime Minister St. Laurent sitting on the bench among the ruins, looking pensively upward and asking: "Have you anything to say to *me*?"

But the condensed version of the talk circulated by The Canadian Press was not so well inspired. Probably it was the first time that that news agency had ever put a ghost story on its wires. Certainly it was the fist time a CP staff member, in the Ottawa bureau, had ever been asked to provide one.

It was no excuse that the poor fellow had not heard the

broadcast. The first thing to do, of course, was to secure the text. There was none available at the CBC studios, as the broadcast had been recorded. I live at Aylmer, Ont., 10 miles from Ottawa, and apparently the CP Ottawa bureau is not equipped to send an intelligent reporter so far to get a story.

I soon found it was impossible to get the facts, nuances, qualifications, suggestions, anecdotes and imponderables into position by telephone. After a struggle, I consented to drive in myself with the text. I might, I thought, be able to keep the story from running wild.

My efforts were wasted. The CP had asked for a ghost story, and the more I insisted that the subject was delicate and the treatment whimsical, the more certain I became that the ghost story I had told over the CBC network, and the one that would be printed, would have little resemblance.

What a fool I had been. I had thought that my broadcast might stir some interest, but I had definitely underestimated its impact on the ghost-hungry newspaper mind. It made the front pages all across Canada, pushing aside the argument then in progress between Mr. St. Laurent and Quebec Premier Maurice Duplessis.

There were odd little changes. Whereas I had said Mr. King talked to me, the headlines ran that I had talked with Mr. King. The title word, *Fantasia*, became "Fantastic," which is quite different. Sentences were transposed and others, which had seemed so important to me, were entirely omitted.

Not a single newspaper published the text of the talk. Even those, to which a copy had been sent in advance, preferred to publish the CBC version, rather than go to the trouble of writing their own.

The telephone began ringing. Was it true? Argument was warm.

Editors began telegraphing their Ottawa correspondents: Had Philip gone "crackers"? One wit, of sorts, telephoned to ask what brand of whisky I drank.

At 8:30 a.m., on the following Sunday, one of the most enterprising and joyous of my colleagues burst into my cottage, shouting gaily: "The question is — is it true, or is it not true?"

There were others who did not bother even to telephone but began writing freely, interviewing parsons, chauffeurs, CBC officials and residents of Kingsmere.

In the press, the skeptics certainly outnumbered the believers, but the latter were much more industrious in writing private letters. Two spiritualists told of recent conversations with Mr. King who, they said, had confirmed my story. I shall not call them witnesses.

THE HAUNTING OF MACKENZIE HOUSE

Mackenzie House is one of the most historic homes in Toronto. Since 1960 it has been maintained as a museum by the Toronto Historical Board. Despite the fact that Mackenzie House has been called the most haunted house in Toronto — and perhaps the most haunted house in all of Canada — it was the policy of the Board to maintain that Mackenzie House is not haunted. Guides dressed in period costume who escort visitors through its halls and rooms, which are furnished to recall the period of the 1860s, make no mention of reports of ghosts or poltergeists or mysterious happenings.

The residence bears the proud name of William Lyon Mackenzie (1795–1861). Mackenzie was the energetic publisher of the *Colonial Advocate*, first Mayor of the City of Toronto in 1834, the promoter of responsible government, and the leader of the Rebellion of 1837 in Upper Canada. When the rebellions were suppressed, Mackenzie fled (dressed as a woman) and found refuge in New York State. There he continued his agitation. With the amnesty he returned to Toronto in triumph. He is known to this day as "the firebrand."

The three-storey brick residence at 82 Bond Street, erected in the 1850s, was acquired and presented to him by grateful friends in recognition of his public service. He lived in the house from 1859 until his death in the second-floor bedroom on August 28. 1861. Isabel Grace King, his youngest daughter, also lived and died in the residence. She was the wife of the lawyer John King and the mother of William Lyon Mackenzie King.

William Lyon Mackenzie King (1874–1950), the grandson of William Lyon Mackenzie, was born at "Woodside" in Berlin (now Kitchener), Ontario. The grandson took great pride in the grandfather's commitment to responsible government. He studied law and went on to become Canada's tenth prime minister and the country's most curious and long-lasting leader. It is now known that throughout his life Mackenzie King was fascinated with spiritualism and with the question of human survival after death. Indeed, one of his friends, the correspondent Percy J. Philip, claimed that in 1954 the ghost of Mackenzie King joined him and conversed with him for some time on a park bench at Kingsmere, Mackenzie King's country estate in the Gatineau region of Quebec. While Mackenzie King's spiritualistic beliefs and practices are well documented, the views of his grandfather, William Lyon Mackenzie, go unrecorded. Yet it is hard to believe that the grandfather, who was Scottish-born, was unfamiliar with the subject.

There are no reports of any psychical occurrences in Mackenzie House prior to 1956; there is none of substance later than 1966. The earliest accounts come from a responsible couple, Mr. and Mrs. Charles Edmunds. They were the house's first live-in, caretaking couple. They occupied Mackenzie House from August 13, 1956 to April 1960 and only left because of the disturbances. They were followed by Mr. and Mrs. Alex Dobban who arrived in April 1960. The Dobbans, complaining of the same disturbances as the Edmunds, left that June. Archdeacon John Frank of Holy Trinity Anglican Church was called to conduct an exorcism in the parlour, which he did in the presence of reporters on July 2, 1960. Since that time the house's caretakers have lived off the premises, but workmen on the premises and visitors have intermittently complained of disturbances.

The most intelligent discussion — and debunking — of the ghostly happenings at Mackenzie House was conducted by investigator Joe Nickell in his book *Secrets of the Supernatural: Investigating the World's Occult Mysteries* (1988). Nickell is both a professional stage magician and a licensed private investigator. He has both prosaic and highly imaginative explanations for all the disturbances. Although he writes well, the story he has to tell is simply not as gripping as the stories that were told by members of the Edmunds family!

Mr. and Mrs. Charles Edmunds, the first caretaking couple, lived in the house for four years. Their reports are included here, as are the shorter reports of their son Robert and his wife, Minnie, who were guests in the house. The four reports first appeared in the *Toronto Telegram* on June 28, 1960, as part of a series of articles titled "The Ghosts that Live in Toronto" written by the paper's enterprising reporter Andrew MacFarlane. The series appeared following the refusal of the Dobbans to remain in the house. MacFarlane secured sworn affidavits from all four members of the Edmunds family. They are reproduced here, along with an interview with Roger Chicoine, a non-resident custodian in 1962 and 1963, in a slightly edited form.

1. Mrs. Charles Edmunds

From the first day my husband and I went to stay at the Mackenzie Homestead, we could hear footsteps on the stairs when there was nobody in the house but us.

The first day, when I was alone in the house, I could hear someone clearly, walking up the stairs from the second floor to the top. Nearly every day there were footsteps at times when there was no one there to make them.

One night I woke up at midnight. I couldn't sleep, although I am normally a good sleeper. I saw a Lady standing over my bed. She wasn't at the side, but at the head of the bed, leaning over me. There is no room for anyone to stand where she was. The bed is pushed up against the wall.

She was hanging down, like a shadow, but I could see her clearly. Something seemed to touch me on the shoulder to wake me up. She had long hair hanging down in front of her shoulders, not black or gray or white, but dark brown, I think. She had a long narrow face. Then it was gone.

Two years ago, early in March, I saw the Lady again. It was the same — except this time she reached out and hit me. When I woke up, my left eye was purple and bloodshot.

I also saw the man at night, a little bald man in a frock coat. I would just see him for a few seconds, and then he would vanish.

I often saw one or the other standing in the room — at least eight or nine times.

A year ago last April, I told my husband: "I have to get out of here." I had to get out of that house. If I didn't get out, I knew I'd be carried out in a box.

I think it was the strain all the time that made me feel this way. I went from 130 pounds to 90½ pounds. I wasn't frightened, but it was getting my nerves down.

It was just like knowing there was someone watching you from behind all the time, from just over your shoulder.

Sometimes we'd sit watching the television. My husband might look up all of a sudden at the doorway. I knew what it was. You felt that someone had just come in.

My son and his wife heard the piano playing at night when they were staying with us. When my husband and my son went to look — it stopped.

We could feel the homestead shaking with a rumbling noise some nights. It must have been the press in the basement. We thought at first it might be the subway. But we were too far from the subway....

I did not believe in ghosts when I went to stay at the Mackenzie Homestead. But I do now. It's the only explanation I can think of.

I wish to say that I would not say anything against the Mackenzies. They were hard-working people and so are we. They were not hard on us ... it's just that the house was a strain on the nerves.

2. Mr. Charles Edmunds

Certain happenings during the three years and eight months my wife and I served as caretakers of the Mackenzie Homestead have convinced me that there is something peculiar about the place.

On one occasion my wife and I were sleeping in the upstairs bedroom. She woke me up in the middle of the night and said that she had seen a man standing beside her bed.

My wife, to my certain knowledge, knew nothing of Mackenzie or his history. All of the pictures in the homestead show Mackenzie as a man with hair on his head. The man my wife saw and described to me was completely bald with side whiskers. I had read about Mackenzie. And I know that the man she described to me was Mackenzie. He wore a wig to cover his baldness. But she did not know this.

On another occasion, just after we moved in, my two grandchildren, Susan (then aged 4) and Ronnie (then aged 3) went from the upstairs bedroom down to the second-floor bathroom at night.

A few minutes later there were terrific screams. I went down and they were both huddled in the bathroom, terrified. They said there was a Lady in the bathroom. I asked where she was now and they said she just disappeared.

On another night my wife woke up screaming. She said: "There was a small man standing over my bed." She described Mackenzie.

Another night, a woman came up to the bed and looked at my missus. She was a little woman, about my wife's height. My wife said: "Dad — there was a woman here." I told her she was dreaming.

Another night my wife woke up and woke me. She was upset. She said the Lady had hit her. There were three red welts on the left side of her face. They were like finger marks. The next day her eye was bloodshot. Then it turned black and blue. Something hit her. It wasn't me. And I don't think she could have done it herself. And there wasn't anyone else in the house.

On another occasion something peculiar happened with some flowers we had in pots on a window ledge inside the house. This was in winter and we had the geraniums inside. We watered the plants twice a week on Sundays and Wednesdays.

On a Saturday morning we found that they had all

been watered, although we hadn't done it. There was water spilled all over the plants and the saucers they were standing in were full. There was mud on the curtains, and holes in the earth as someone had poked their fingers in the earth. There was water on the dressing table. Neither of us had watered the plants, and neither had anyone else.

We often heard footsteps on the stairs. Thumping footsteps like someone with heavy boots on. This happened frequently when there was no one in the house but us, when we were sitting together upstairs.

The whole house used to shake with a rumbling sound sometimes. My wife is convinced that this was Mackenzie's press.

I am not an imaginative man, and I do not believe in ghosts. But the fact is that the house was strange enough so that we had to leave.

We would have stayed if it had not been for these happenings. But my wife could not stand it any longer.

3. Robert Edmunds

One night my wife woke me up. She said she heard the piano playing downstairs. I heard it, too. I cannot remember what the music was like, but it was the piano downstairs playing.

Dad and I went downstairs. When we got to the last landing before the bottom, the piano stopped.

It was similar with the printing press in the basement. My wife heard it first and wakened me. I heard it, too. I identified the sound because it was the same as old presses I'd seen in movies and on television. A rumbling, clanking noise — not like modern presses. When Dad and I went downstairs to see about it, it stopped when we reached the same landing.

We heard the piano three or four times, the press just once.

I was not walking in my sleep. I heard them. I don't

know what the explanation is. I am not prepared to say I saw any ghosts or apparitions. But I can say that I dreamt more in that house than I ever have before or since.

I do not believe in ghosts. But I find it hard to explain what we heard.

4. Mrs. Minnie Edmunds

When my husband and I were staying at Mackenzie Homestead I heard the piano playing downstairs at night three or four times.

We discovered that there was no one downstairs to play it these times, and yet I heard it distinctly. Each time, I woke my husband, and when he and his father went downstairs to investigate it, it stopped.

On one other occasion I heard the printing press running in the basement. I woke my husband, and he and his father went to investigate it. It stopped.

It is not possible to operate the press, because it is locked, and on the occasions when I heard the piano, there was no one downstairs to play it. I can find no natural explanation for these occurrences.

5. Mr. Alex Dobbin

We couldn't stay any longer because of the effect the lace was having on my wife's nerves. The things she heard were getting her down. We wouldn't have left otherwise; but she couldn't stand to stay overnight....

6. Mrs. Alex Dobbin

We hadn't been here long when I heard footsteps going up the stairs. I called to my husband. But he wasn't there. There was no one else in the house. But I heard feet on the stairs.

One night I woke up. There was a rumbling noise in the basement. At first I took it to be the oil burner. But my husband checked — and the furnace wasn't on.

The noise I heard was the press. It's locked. But I heard it running. I heard it that night, and one or two other nights.

On another night I heard the piano in the front room downstairs playing, after we were in bed. There was no one else in the house, but the piano was playing. It wasn't a tune — just as if someone was hitting the keys with closed fists, or a child playing at the piano.... You see, it's locked. And yet I heard it running. How could you explain that.

There was no one else in the house, just the two of us.... It was coming from the basement. It was the press.... There's something in this house, and I'm not staying with it....

Yes, I do think it was a ghost. I didn't believe in that sort of thing before. But how else can you explain it?

7. Mr. Roger Chicoine

Don't get the idea I see Mrs. Mackenzie every time I sleep here. There's a good chance she doesn't like strangers....

The first time I saw Mrs. Mackenzie was right in that doorway. I awoke just at dawn and looked out the window. I remember thinking how stupid that was because I never wake at this time; about 5:00 or 6:00 a.m. Suddenly it seemed as though I wasn't alone in the room.

A chill went racing up and down my spine. I was lying with my hands under my head and I turned slowly, taking in the whole room. My eyes came to the door and there was a woman. I recognized her from the portrait: it was Mrs. Mackenzie.

She seemed to be leaning around the corner of the door for I could only see the top half of her. I felt the hair on my head start to stand straight up on its end. I blinked, but she didn't move.

She was not transparent. That is, I could not see the

wall through her. She looked fleshy. Alive. Believe me, I thought it was all in my imagination, but she looked so real, this ghost. Finally I moved and she disappeared....

I try to rationalize that I only *thought* I saw her. But it happened four times.

THE "TWILIGHT ZONE" TRUCK STOP

"Visit to the 'Twilight Zone' Truck Stop" is the title of this account of an eerie experience. In this instance the "monster" is the atmosphere and the surroundings, the trip back in time and perhaps also in place, perhaps into another dimension, the truck stop that should not have been there at all. The experience itself evokes a sense of the decade of the 1960s and it does so in such detail that the event might well have been an episode of Rod Serling's long-running *Twilight Zone* television series. The reader visualizes it.

Yet whatever it was that sparked this shared experience, it occurred not in the 1960s but in the year 1978. It happened to Phyllis and Don Griffiths. Mrs. Griffiths sent me this account after she heard me talk about "extraordinary experiences" on CFAX Radio in Victoria, British Columbia.

"I have a story that you may wish to add to your files of strange experiences," she explained in her letter of March 17, 1989. "My husband and I refer to this as our 'twilight zone' visit. If it was a hallucination, then it is one that we both shared. The story is enclosed with this letter."

I first published Mrs. Griffiths' account in my book *Mysterious Encounters* (1990). Here it is again.

Sky Chief indeed!

In March of 1978, we were returning to our home in Lethbridge, Alberta, after spending Easter Week visiting relatives on Vancouver Island. This was a trip that the family had taken many times before, and the route we usually followed was first along Highway 1, the northern route, and then south from Calgary. This time, we decided, just for a change of pace, that we would take Highway 3. We

had not taken this southern highway before when returning from Vancouver Island.

As usual with return trips, this one was to be driven
straight through. But the route was unfamiliar to us, and
the southern route was taking much longer than the familiar, northern route. Our two young sons slept cuddled up
to their dog in the back seat of the family station wagon.
My husband and I drove through the night and into the
early hours of the next day without a rest.

At two-thirty in the morning we drove into the town
of Creston, B.C. The only place open at that early hour
was a tiny service station, where we stopped to refuel the
car. Tired as we were, we had no choice but to drive on.
There was no money for a motel room, nor were there
camp-grounds in the area.

Relief was found about half way between Creston and
Cranbrook. It took the form of an old Texaco Truck Stop
which we were approaching. It was on the north side of
the highway, Highway 3, but it was located in the middle
of nowhere. It was a totally unexpected sight, but a very
welcome one.

The Texaco Truck Stop had an unusual location, but
it also had an unusual appearance. The large old Texaco
sign was a solid sign lit by spotlights mounted on top and
focused on the painted surface. The gas pumps were also
old-fashioned looking, and they dispensed good old Fire
Chief and Sky Chief gasoline. There was a diesel pump at
the side, but no pumps for unleaded gas were in sight.

The station itself looked as if it had not changed one
bit since the year 1960. Even the semi-trailer unit, idling
in the truck lot to one side, was of an early Sixties vintage.
Everything looked strange indeed. Was this a scene from
Rod Serling's *Twilight Zone*?

Nevertheless, my husband and I, tired and thirsty as
we were, drove in, pulled up under the pump lights, got out
of the car, and locked it. We left our two children asleep in
the back seat of the car.

The inside of the restaurant matched the outside to such

a degree that everything felt spooky. The interior was frozen in time in the year 1960, yet the decor showed none of the wear and tear that would be found after nearly twenty years of use. We could see nothing that was out of place. There was nothing new or modern about the appointments or the personnel. The waitress was dressed in period clothes, as was the driver of the semi parked in the yard.

The price of the coffee was all of a dime a cup, and a placard advertised the price of a piece of pie as a quarter. The music blaring from the radio dated from the late Fifties, and the d.j. introduced the songs without once referring to the period or to any item of news. No calendar was in sight. But the coffee was good and was appreciated. We felt uneasy in the place, so we were not unhappy to be out and on the road for home once more.

We had driven this stretch of Highway 3 on previous occasions, but it had always been in daylight and heading in the other direction. We had never taken it at night or while returning from Vancouver Island. We had memorized the location of every truck stop on Highway 3, and we thought we knew the location of all the truck stops that were open twenty-four hours a day on this highway as well. But never before had we seen this one. Nor did we ever see it again.

The visit left us with an eerie feeling. Try as we might, we could not shake it off. We asked those of our friends and relatives who occasionally travelled that stretch of Highway 3 if they were familiar with the old Texaco Truck Stop. No one knew anything about it. Everyone was of the opinion that there was no such establishment between Lethbridge, Alta., and Hope, B.C.

The only thing that we could do was re-drive that stretch of highway in broad daylight and watch out for it to see for ourselves whether or not the place really existed. Some months later we did just that. We re-travelled Highway 3. Mid-way between Cranbrook and Creston, on the north side of the road, we found the place where we had stopped that eerie night.

The building had long been boarded over. The presence of the pumps was marked only by their cement bases. The same was true of the Texaco signpost. The yard where the semi had sat was overgrown with bush and with aspen poplars which were twenty or more feet in height. It had been many years since that particular service station had pumped gas or served coffee at a dime a cup. But my husband and I know that the old Truck Stop had been open for business that lonely March night in 1978, when a weary family had stopped — in need of a cup of coffee and a bit of rest.

4

THE POWER OF FEAR

The sensation that most people have in mind when the word *ghost* or the words *haunted house* are uttered is *fear*. The frisson of fear is characteristic of ghost stories. As listeners or readers of them, we seem to enjoy being scared! Goose pimples, hairs on the head rising, temperatures soaring (or, conversely, temperatures dropping), unable to flex a muscle or utter a word, not being able to scream! A social biologist of the evolutionary persuasion would say that these are coping strategies, useful to our forebears in the forests of our past, largely irrelevant in big cities. Yet, suppose that such symptoms of fear, such manifestations of the power of dread, are useful, even in today's urbanized world. Suppose they keep us from approaching ghosts or spirits; suppose they are protective and require us to keep our distance. Should this be the case, we survive the sightings of ghosts and are able to report what we have seen and felt and sensed, and we have lived to tell of it! Survival tactics!

There is no questioning the power of fear. The events and experiences described in this section took place in recent times, but in duration they hardly lasted more than minutes in time. What I always find remarkable is that a few seconds or a couple of minutes of sheer panic are recalled years if not decades thereafter, with an accompanying sense of awe and wonder. Such is fear's power.

THE GHOST OF MARY MOWAT

On June 7, 1994, the following story was posted to one of the websites on the Internet that is devoted to ghost stories. The title of the website is *alt.folklore.ghost-stories*. The story was subsequently posted on March

22, 1997 to the mailing list established by a person named Obiwan and maintained by another person called Khalloween. The story of Mary Mowat is a good one. It was written and filed by David Sztybel of the Department of Philosophy of the University of Toronto. His address follows: *sztybel@chass.utoronto.ca.*

I would now like to post a ghost story that I was told by a friend who experienced the haunting in question. My friend, like me, is a university student pursuing philosophy. She lives a couple of hours away from me by train. She seemed completely sincere in telling me this, and her account was corroborated by her father, mother, and one of her friends who also encountered an unaccountable presence in the midst of this haunting. The setting is in London, Ontario, a small city in the southern part of the province. Here is the story itself, with my friend's name changed in order to protect the privacy of her and her family.

Cat Robertson is the name of my friend. Her father is a manager of a local grocery store, and came to befriend a client of the store, Mrs. Mowat. As Mr. Robertson was a kindly fellow, he assisted Mary Mowat on occasion when she needed it. The woman was elderly, and was living with a sister who was older. When the sister passed on, Mary came to depend more and more on Mr. Robertson. She felt alone in the world without him, as she was otherwise bereft of family, at least in that part of the world. As time wore on, Mary fell ill. Gravely ill. Mr. Robertson was at her deathbed, and she specifically instructed him that she had left her old house to him and his family in her will, and the Robertson family was to live there after Mary's death. Mr. Robertson agreed.

Mary died, and an inspection of an old grandfather clock in Mary's home revealed that the hand stopped at exactly the time of the woman's death. This was remarked to be odd, but nothing much was made of it at the time.

As things developed, Mary's old home went uninhab- ited. As later events unfolded, however, it became evident that where the Robertson's were living was not to be inhabited by them alone. Several incidents, suggestive of a full-scale haunting, lead me to believe that the Robertsons themselves were haunted by the spirit of Mary Mowat. Haunting of persons is much less common, supposedly, than haunting of dwellings, but this appeared to be just such a rare case.

My friend Cat was almost in her mid-teens at the time, and remembers being terrified of being alone in the house. She would be in her room, and hear footsteps out in the hall, and finally a knocking at her door when she knew that no one was home. She would hide in the closet in terror until her family came back home. Others in the family could hear the sound of voices coming from other rooms, as though a television set were playing on a low volume setting. The words were not quite audible. Whenever a Robertson would go into the room from whence the sound seemed to emanate, however, silence would ensue.

Not all the strange sounds were unaccompanied by other strange phenomena. A heaving and rumbling from the basement prompted one of the braver Robertson's to rush down to the basement, where the sound seemed to come from. Arriving in the laundry area, the Robertson was astonished to see that the washing machine was now in the middle of the laundry room, whereas it had not been before. It would seem that the rumbling sound was the machine being moved, by some unknown entity, across the floor.

And the movement of objects did not end there. Cat's boyfriend at the time, call him Fritz, appeared to be an object of displeasure for the spirit. One time when he was visiting Cat, a nearby chair was seen by many to be flung through the air at him, hitting him. Objects from a basement room were found upstairs, although no one had moved them. Such occurred even when this room was locked. Perhaps the most astonishing transubstantiation was observed when an object, which someone lost while touring Eastern Canada, appeared in the Robertson's midst. They were bewildered. But it did not end there.

Some friends of Cat, against her wishes, conducted

a sitting with a Ouija board, in order to determine what was behind these strange occurrences. The board became active, it seemed, but the message received did not seem to make sense. The participants (Cat was not among them) asked who was present (besides the living). The board said, "MMVMOM."

Only later did Cat and her family realize that this represented the initials of the dead woman's family: Mary Mowat, Violet Mowat, and Oliver Mowat. The last two named were Mary's older sister, and younger brother, who perished in the ditches of World War One.

Many of the ghostly effects that the Robertsons experienced were downright eerie. A statue of a blacksmith, a likeness of a man who inhabited the site of Mary's home early in the century, when that part of London was still young and rural, was among the objects inherited from Mary Mowat. Its eyes once glowed red. Cat's brother claimed he saw slime dripping down a mirror, and then disappear when he did a double-take. The mother of the family recalls napping in her room, lying on the bed, and hearing someone open the door, enter the room, and then lie down beside her. She assumed it was her husband. Mrs. Robertson rolled over and opened her eyes. She screamed. It was a corpse that she saw lying beside her.

One day, Mrs. Robertson, the only one ever to see a spectre, saw an apparition of Mrs. Mowat while in the upstairs hallway. The ghost was standing at the top of the stairs, gazing towards the front door.

Finally, the Robertsons did move into the Mowat residence, and all ghostly phenomena immediately ceased.

THE FUTON GHOST

"The Futon Ghost" was distributed on the mailing list maintained by Obiwan (*obiwan@netcom.com*). It was originally posted by Lisa Anne Ferrari (*lferrari@lynx.dac.neu.edu*) to the newsgroup *alt.folklore.ghost-stories* and then distributed by Khalloween. It bore the date June 16, 1995. The story may be more American than Canadian, but I am including it in this collection because it does have a connection with this country and because it is scary and it makes such good reading!

Well, okay. This didn't happen in my house or apartment, but it was creepy all the same.

Three years ago my then-boyfriend and I went to a small hunting / fishing "resort" in New Hampshire, fourteen miles from the Canadian border. It is a beautiful little place located on the First Connecticut Lake, and is very popular with hunters and fishermen during the respective seasons because of the abundance of deer, moose, fox, etc. My ex and I were/are big wildlife freaks — we love to camp and hike and this was a great place to do so. The three or four times we stayed there, we would leave our cabin at midnight or so and walk up Route 3 towards the Canadian border and just have a look around. This particular night we had walked a few miles up Route 3 and didn't see much in the way of wildlife, so we decided to get in the car and go all the way to the border and back, just to see what we might observe (this stretch of Route 3 is basically deserted). So, off we went.

Roughly five miles from the resort area, we came across a white wooden cross planted in the ground on the side of the road. It was obviously a grave marker and looked as though it had been there for some time, but it had a brass plate nailed to the center. I asked my boyfriend to pull over so that I could shine the flashlight on the marker, and as I leaned out the car window to try to make out what it said, this shudder went through me and my eyes started to water and all the hair on my neck stood on end and I said to him, "Uh, I don't feel so comfortable with this anymore ... can we get out of here?" He admitted that he felt a little strange, too. On the drive back to the resort area, we saw some moose and a bobcat and a coyote, so we soon forgot about the grave thing and chattered about the animals. We got back to our cabin at about 1:00 a.m., I took a shower and got into bed, and he followed suit. During the time that he was in the shower, I kept hearing strange noises, but I didn't think anything of them, really. These cabins are pretty rustic and the hot water heaters are noisy, and I attributed any weird banging to the heater, so I started to drift off to sleep when he got into bed. Some time later, we heard a sound that distinctly sounded like the front door shutting (we had never heard it opening) and my boyfriend was visibly bothered by the noise. Again, I was not as worried — out in the wilderness, everything seems like it makes weird noises — until we heard noises that sounded exactly like heavy work boots tromping up and down the wood floor from the front door to our bedroom door (in this cabin, the walls weren't "finished" per se; they were more like partitions between rooms, rather than full walls). By now, we were sitting bolt upright, hearts pounding. I sat up and turned on the light, and the noise stopped.

Quizzically, we looked at each other, and I shut off the light. Within five minutes, the noise had started again. Again, we turned on the light and the noise stopped. Off went the light again, and again, within five minutes, the same pacing footsteps. I said to my boyfriend that I didn't think whatever it was is going to hurt us, and he agreed but he wasn't comfortable with staying in the cabin and he suggested that maybe we should leave. I turned on the light again and got up and threw open the bedroom door, and of course there was nothing there ... but the room felt weird ... you could tell something wasn't right.

I decided that it was ridiculous for us to leave — it was 2:30 in the morning and there were no other resorts, hotels or motels for a good three-hour drive south into New Hampshire. I figured that unless pots and pans started flying or some other bizarre poltergeisty thing started happening, I wasn't going to get hysterical. So, off went the light. Up started the noises. This time though, the footsteps went all the way to the bedroom door and we sat, saucer eyed in the dark in horror as we listened to the door latch clatter.

Needless to say, we slept with the lights on the whole rest of the night. Greg says he didn't sleep at all — I fell asleep around four-thirty or so. Anyway, the next day we were checking out and we asked the proprietors if they'd ever heard weird noises in their cabins or if anything strange had ever happened on the land. They laughed and said no (of course).

On the way home in the car, I asked if we could go back to the weird grave site — it had occurred to me that maybe that had something to do with the events of the night. Greg was adamant about not going there, so I never found out about the grave or if it had any correlation to the weird events in this cabin.

Two years ago I started dating another man, whom I am still with, and I told him the story. He acted very nonchalant at the time and sort of treated me like I was being ridiculous, but the following summer we went back to that particular resort. He then confided to me that the story had scared him and he was just the tiniest bit freaked out and curious about what might happen. Different mix of psychic energy, I guess — all was quiet, but I was unbelievably uncomfortable.

During the next day, while Michael was taking a shower, I took the car up to the grave. Everything was as it had been the previous year, and I knelt down in front of the marker to read the brass plate. I don't remember the specifics of what it said, but I recall that it marked a spot of an anonymous drifter, assumed to be Canadian, that was found frozen to death on that spot in the late '30s. After reading this, my eyes watered, I got chills and got back in the car and drove back to the resort.

Friends of mine who are highly into the spiritual speculate that I had a brush with an earth-bound spirit ... to this day, I'm still not sure what to make of it.

Any ideas?

THERE WAS A STORY BEHIND IT

I have the following story from Catherine P., a resident of Hamilton, Ontario, courtesy of the journalist John Mentek. He published this account in a spread titled "Ghost Stories" in *The Hamilton Spectator* on July 29, 1995. It is an interesting episode because it shows how a vision that lasts but a few seconds may change a person's life and indeed last a lifetime. At the author's request I have given only the initial of her last name.

I work for the Board of Education. About five years ago, I was a custodian. One summer day I was on the third floor of a school, cleaning the girls' washroom. No one else was there at the time but the caretaker and myself.

I came around the corner and saw a woman washing her hands at the sink. I thought, "The water's not running. Why is she washing her hands when the water's not running?"

I remember exactly what she was like. She had a white blouse, her hair was in a bun, she had a long skirt on. She was bent over and she had both hands underneath the faucet.

It happened in seconds, and then she was gone.

My hands, my forehead, everything just started to sweat. I walked out of the washroom, went downstairs, and said, "I'm not feeling well. I'm going home."

Later, I went and saw somebody about it, because I wasn't sure if I'd seen somebody or not. She said that I actually did see something, because even though it had only lasted for a few seconds, I have remembered what she looked to this day.

Her face was in profile. She was young, about thirty. The dress seemed old-fashioned, like the early 1920s. Her hair was brown.

When I realized that she wasn't really there, and then she was gone, I was startled, but I wasn't scared of her. It was like I wasn't really there at all, like I was looking at a scene far away from me.

There was a story behind it. She was supposed to be somebody who worked in the school and killed herself or died in an unusual way. The story is that she loved working there, and that this was her life, so she stayed.

I couldn't talk to anyone about it for three years. But when I started telling other people, they started talking about things they'd seen or heard too, and I found out that other people had seen her.

Security people say they won't go into some schools late at night. There's one where they hear children laughing in a classroom, doors slamming, and children running in the gym late at night. One man said he'd never tell anybody because they wouldn't believe him.

THE GHOST OF DARCEL AVENUE

Here is a personal account of a site-specific haunt from the typewriter of Lawrence J. Fenwick. The writer is known to ufologists across the country and in many other countries for his work on behalf of CUFORN (Canadian UFO Research Network) and as the editor of its bimonthly newsletter. Fenwick wrote this account of his own and his wife Betty's experiences for his own use in November 1997. But he has kindly agreed to share it with me and with my readers.

The term *pusher* is associated with aggressive people. When my wife Betty and I think of the word now, we can think of its personification. It happened when we moved from Toronto to Mississauga.

On the warm night of August 30, 1997, we moved with the help of a professional mover and my friend Raymond Borg from an apartment in the City of York, which is part of Metropolitan Toronto, to a two-bedroom condominium apartment in the Malton area of Mississauga west of Metro Toronto. Our anxiety to move to the building at 7280 Darcel Avenue meant that we had to take whatever apartment was available at the time. So we moved into apartment No. 131. We were told that we could then move again to the third floor at the end of September. It turned out that we had to wait for the third-floor move until October 10.

I was short of bus fare for the next day, so Raymond gave me a bus ticket, which I put on top of the TV set. Betty and I settled down for the night on the two living-room couches in the same room as the TV set. When we woke the next morning, the ticket had vanished. We searched the entire apartment and never found it. We had no thought of ghosts at that point. Our ideas changed on the morning of September 30.

I had to return to our old neighbourhood to run a few errands. It turned out to be a three-hour trip there and back. I left at 8:30 a.m. As I drove off Highway 401 to turn onto the Allen Road, I felt that there was something wrong at home, but I shrugged it off as my imagination.

When I returned home, Betty was lying on the couch in pain. Her shoes and socks were off and when I touched her toe in jest, she screamed. I asked her what had happened. She said she was carrying some of my sweaters down from the second floor of our two-storey condo. When she reached the third step from the bottom, she felt herself pushed into the air, "like I floated," she said. When she hit the floor, her right foot bent beneath her. She sat on her right foot. I could see right away that her ankle was swollen and her toes black with bruises.

We knew then that this had to be a ghost that pushed her. The apartment was locked up securely. No one could have entered it. When I asked her if she had tripped, she said she had not done so.

I took her to a nearby walk-in emergency clinic but was advised to take her to the Etobicoke General Hospital, where technicians x-rayed her and found out that she had broken her baby toe and badly sprained her ankle. They put on a temporary cast, later to be replaced by a harder cast. The sprain took nearly eight weeks to heal; the toe healed in one month.

A week after the incident, my sister-in-law, my mother-in-law, and Betty's four-year-old nephew visited one evening. We had two light fixtures in the kitchen. One was on and one was off. As my sister-in-law Susan stood talking, I at her side, we faced the kitchen. Suddenly, we saw the fixture that was on start to sway back and forth touching the ceiling. This went on for seven seconds, by my count. Susan was astonished as she is quite sceptical by nature. We told Betty and my mother-in-law Evelyn but, by that time, the movement had stopped. We had said nothing while we watched, so we had no time to alert them to look. The other fixture did not move.

When we moved to the third floor on October 10, Betty had to use crutches. She put them against the dining-room wall, firmly planted in our thick broadloom carpeting. She had difficulty using the crutches which bothered her back. When I returned home from work one day, she told me that the crutches moved over simultaneously onto their sides and hit the floor as she watched.

There was one more incident to come. On November 3, while I was at work, Betty was sitting with her back to the kitchen while our twelve-year-old cat Victor was eating from his dish on the kitchen floor. Betty said she "heard a screech, and when I turned around, Victor was gone. I searched everywhere for at least an hour. Finally, I saw him behind the refrigerator. He was wedged in against the coil that sticks out from the fridge. I had heard nothing from Victor even after calling out to him as I looked. In order to get him out I had to pull the fridge out from the wall a bit, reach in, and pick him up, and push the fridge back against the wall. There was no way in which he could have gotten in there unless something or someone picked him up and put him there. Whatever did it, did so "in the wink of an eye," she said. Betty is partly disabled because of her back as it is, so this did not help. In fact, it was a week before her back stopped aching.

We never saw a ghost, but we sure saw what happens when something "pushy" decides to demonstrate its aggressiveness. I asked the apartment superintendents and building managers, as well as several tenants, but no one knew of any other ghostly incidents in the building. No one had died suddenly in the building, nor was this an ancient Indian burial ground. But then, most people would never mention ghosts for fear of being laughed at. Not only that, it might scare away prospective tenants and cause others to move out. So maybe there were other ghostly events here. There is no way of our knowing about it. The only way in which one might suspect that there was anything wrong in the old apartment No. 131 was, that, during the time we lived there, the entire apartment felt cold and clammy, even when the heat was on. What happened to us was the final proof.

ON OLD ROAD

One of the enthusiastic readers of my book *Mysterious Canada* is a young man who wishes to be identified as "Kheru." About nine months after its appearance, he contacted me and asked me if I wanted to hear his own ghost story, a story set outside a city not far from Toronto. I asked him, politely, not to tell it to me on the phone. I asked him, instead, to write it out. He did that, literally, in a very clear script using a ballpoint pen on lined paper. I received his account on August 20, 1997 and read it with interest. It sounded like fiction to me, so some days later, when he phoned me to ask what I felt about the account, I asked him for further details about himself and his experience. He offered them.

"Kheru" is the pen name of a thirty-year-old male who is a croupier or card dealer. The experience he describes in the account that appears here took place at a farmhouse in Orono, Ontario. "The house is located on Highway 35 / 115, just before the town's main exit. Heading north from Oshawa it is on one's left, past the gas station, and across from the motel."

On Old Road; or, Satan Lives in This House

In June of '94 I first heard the story of the haunted house "on Old Road." During a casual conversation the subject turned to ghosts. One of the other persons then spoke of an old farmhouse which he knew was haunted. He had been there and maintained that it was a place to be avoided. He was quite serious and sincere. I questioned him further and was told the tale of a murdering madman who one day went about slaughtering his wife and children in the house before taking his own life out in the barn. The date of this occurrence is unknown to me but the house is over 100 years old. I inquired as to the present situation and was informed that the aging house and barn still stood and was vacant. The most recent tenants were in some way involved in the occult and they lived there for three months after which they left abruptly. The person who told me all this had grown up in the area and still visited there periodically. I had my informant show me the location on a map. He earnestly warned me not to go there but I was too excited to listen for I had always wanted to go to a "true" haunted house; in fact, I've had vivid and memorable nightmares of doing just that. I called for bus information and found that there was one bus in the early morning going in to the town and one bus to return in the late afternoon. The next morning I caught the bus going in. I brought provisions to stay the night.

The property was about 4 km from the "downtown" area where I was dropped off. I had passed what seemed to be the house on the highway coming in so I had a general idea of the direction to go. Down the quiet street, through some woods and over a creek I went to get back to the highway. I walked along the shoulder. There was trash and broken bottles; it felt like walking on an icy sponge. The sky was grey and overcast. Everything seemed damp. I felt a looming ahead and soon came into view of the ancient two-storey farmhouse. I stopped to look and saw that the side screen-door swung freely open in the slight breeze. Glancing down before continuing, I saw a fat skunk belly up in the gutter. There was no smell. I approached the house and went to the back of its outside. I had brought a disposable camera and there I took the first picture. The foundation was crumbling and it felt as if at any moment the house would topple over onto me. This was an excellent photo op. Unfortunately, when I had the film developed, none of the pictures of the house came back.

I entered through the side screen-door into the enormous kitchen. What a mess! Garbage was everywhere. Empty beer cases and bottles, broken dishes and clothes were on the floor. A huge musty couch sat right in the centre of the room facing the door. There were also many cans of food still in the open cupboards. A vandal had spray-painted "SATAN LIVES IN THIS HOUSE" in big red letters upon the wall. The walls themselves were a gloomy yellow colour. There were drippings of red candle wax on the floor and counters. I went into an uncomfortably small room with a tiny stone fireplace. This was the fireplace the killer had smashed his infant's body to death on, as the story goes. Just then I noticed the sun was coming out as rays brightened up the room.

Suddenly, a small yellow bird began flying into the window over and over. After about six thuds, I made a move to get up out of the chair and it was gone. I went into the front entrance next. The front door was nailed shut. The stairs going up were wide and wonderfully crafted from wood. Next, I went into the front parlour. It was furnished with a couch and a chair. There were boxes of dirty clothes and an old 1940s radio which was vandalized. I sat down on the couch with my back to the window listening to the cars zooming by outside. There was thick, tangled growth obscuring any view out. I was about to lie down for some sleep, when I saw the carcass of a small black bird just inside the door against the wall. There was more red candle wax. It looked ritually prepared. Just as I was falling asleep, I heard a loud bang which woke me. Then I heard voices. Shaken, I stepped out into the hall to see a gang of school kids walking in. We met and I told them I was staying there until I could catch a bus out of town. The one kid who seemed to be the leader of the gang began telling me the story of the house; it was almost exact as to what I'd already been told. I was given a tour. There was a small opening inside the ceiling of the closet which led into the blackness of the attic where "childlike cries" have been heard. All the upstairs rooms were small and cramped. One had a mattress. The other had a chest of drawers and a desk upon which were children's books on astrology. We went back down to the main floor via the back stairway. It was unusually narrow. At the bottom to the left was a small bathroom which was disgustingly filthy. More dead black birds and candle wax was there also. We went into the basement next with its earthen floor. The only light came through small apertures in the floor above. Looking up, I noticed the massive floor-boards, at least four times the width of a railway tie and running the length of the structure. I had heard they were from an old ship. We didn't stay down there too long. It was dark and clammy and just didn't feel right. Soon after, the boys left to go back to school. I went back upstairs to look into the attic with my flashlight which I didn't have on my first trip. Before I could climb up, I heard what sounded like chains softly rattling. I silently crept into the hall to search for the sound. I discovered it was only bare hangers being blown in the increasing wind which came through the broken windows. Then the hairs on the back of my neck stood up.

Next, I went outside to investigate the barn. The place where the murders / suicide ended with the killer's self-termination. I saw a thick, old, greasy rope still hanging high from a rafter. It ended with a well-made noose about twelve feet from the floor.

I then went back into the house and quietly wandered around looking for the secret room I had heard about. I never found it. I felt uneasy about staying the night. The place was depressing enough during the day; I wondered what the night would bring. I wished I had a companion. I left.

The sky was overcast and it seemed too dark for that time of the day. It also seemed too cool for early June. I caught the bus just in time. Passing the house on the highway, I saw the side screen-door swing open in the wind.

STRANGE NOISES IN THE BASEMENT

I have this text from the Ghost Stories Mailing List on the Net. The address is *obiwan@netcom.com*. It arrived on September 11, 1997. It was contributed by Robert G. Files and Valerie A. Chatham.

Hi Folks,

I've lurked, I've discussed, now it's time to share a ghost story with you.

The situation took place in my parent's home, in mid-January 1984. Like a typical mid-January evening in Hamilton, Ontario, Canada, it was bitterly cold outside. I was helping my brother shovel snow off of the backyard patio and walkway. We put the shovels in the garage, and we were just about to open the back door, when I noticed a strange odour. It smelled like something dead somewhere around the porch. The odour was especially strong near the back door. I asked my brother if he could smell something weird. He said that it smelled like an animal (mouse or rat) probably crawled behind something around the porch and died. We checked everywhere, under and around the porch. It was not cluttered, so it was easy to do a thorough check. We found nothing, and we went inside, thinking nothing about it further.

Later that evening, my sister and I were sitting in the kitchen. I was on the phone with a friend, and my sister was sitting in the rocking chair with her cat on her lap. During my phone conversation, I heard the "beep" of the Call Waiting service, so I put my friend on hold and answered the incoming call. It was a friend of my brother's, wondering if he was home. I was positive my brother was home, because I could hear his weight set clanking occasionally (he was into body building). I put the phone down and called my brother's name. My sister then said he wasn't home. I said, "Sure he is ... he's in the basement ..." and I started walking toward the basement door. My sister repeated, "Val, he's not home ... he left a couple hours ago. He's at Mark's." We both went completely silent and still for a few seconds, then we heard one of his weights rolling across the floor! We both became extremely creeped out. I returned to the phone, took a message for my brother, got back to my friend and told him I'd call him back later. My sister and I just sat there listening closely to the noises coming from the basement. We confirmed that nobody else was home, we had no other animals in the house (the cat was with us), and whoever was downstairs could move a minimum 5 lbs. (the lightest unit weight in the set). We then heard what sounded like a very heavy weight roll across the concrete floor of the basement, and we screamed and ran out of the kitchen, and into our parent's bedroom. We sat by the cold air return vent, listening to the clanking and commotion in the basement. Finally, my brother came home, and we told him about everything we'd been hearing. He went down to the basement, and he accused us of messing with his weights. They were scattered all around the basement. He checked the basement for anything or anyone that might be down there, and didn't find anything. No one could figure out what caused this. Actually, my brother thought we were playing a joke on him, so he didn't take us seriously. That really bothered us.

This activity continued for about a week (between dusk and dawn), and would stop if someone entered the basement. It focused on the weights and barbells. They were the steel cast Real McCoy weights, so they made a thundering sound when they rolled across the concrete floor. We heard footsteps creeking up the basement steps, and they would stop at the basement door, which opens to our kitchen.

One evening, we didn't hear any strange noises in the basement. The next day, as I opened the back door and stepped onto the porch, I noticed that the rotting meat smell was gone. The odour had remained on the porch and at the back door for the entire duration of the basement activity. I mentioned this to my brother, and then he looked at me with a confused look on his face. He said,

"You know, it's f***ing cold out here and everything is frozen ... even if something died out hear or was dead, it wouldn't be rotting and smelling like that." Another thing I noticed about the odour, was that it didn't fade at all over the week. It was not overpowering, but it was distinctly pungent, and then suddenly, it was completely gone, within the same time that the activity stopped.

No one else has lived in our house before us (my parents had it custom built). We've thought about it many times, and we've tried to come up with a logical explanation for it, but we can't. We all think it was a ghost, who might have been into working out with weights in his life, and we had the impression it was a guy in his 20's or 30's. It might have been 'passing by' and decided to hang around our basement for a week. Go figure!

I'd love to hear people's thoughts on this one.

Thanks,
Valerie Chatham

A CALL IN THE NIGHT

The following handwritten note is dated January 26, 2007. It was addressed to me care of Key Porter Books, the publisher of *True Canadian Ghost Stories* and its successor, *More True Canadian Ghost Stories*, and was forwarded to me a few days later. Here is the note. It speaks for itself.

Dear John,

I read and enjoyed your book *Ghost Stories*. I am sending my ghost story (or rather my mom's and dad's), hoping you may see fit to include it in a future book.

Sincerely,
Gusty

I am always pleased to receive mails and emails from readers of my books, and I make it a point to respond to all such communications. I certainly have to respond with gusto to a woman who signs herself "Gusty"! (This seems to be the familiar form of my correspondent's first name, Augusta, who is a resident of Regina, Saskatchewan.)

The hearing of voices is a widely reported phenomenon. Explorers in the Arctic have stated that they distinctly heard the sounds of their own names being pronounced in the wilderness — summonses in the solitude, so to speak. It is an oddly disorienting phenomenon. (From time to time I have heard my own name being sounded, when I was alone in a room, sometimes at dusk, sometimes at dawn.) It is rare that two or more people report hearing the same effect but it is not unknown. Folklore holds that such sounds act as "forerunners," vocalizations of preoccupations, concerns, and perhaps future events.

Ms. Chartrand's account is interesting in a number of ways. First, the vocal phenomenon is reportedly heard by two people in the same place at the same time. Second, when the voice is heeded and answered, the phenomenon usually ceases, as it does in this case. Third, in this instance, there is a direct connection between the audible effect and the author of this account. Fourth, the reader is offered a vignette of what pioneer conditions on the prairies were like in the early decades of the twentieth century, a period that is still (but not for long) within living memory.

If you hear a voice calling your name, listen. And then reply. Once.

> In 1921 my pioneer parents, Fred and Rosalie Kurbs, had been married for 14 years and had a family of five children, ages 13, 11, 9, 7, and 5.
>
> Dad had come to Canada in 1902 and his parents followed him three years later. Grandpa helped dad improve the homestead — digging rocks, breaking the land on the quarter-section, and building shelters for the animals. Grandma did the housework and found it very lonesome with no one to talk to during the day. So when dad finally found his wife, grandma was delighted, especially after the children started arriving. Looking after them became her priority.
>
> When the youngest one was 5, grandma thought that must be the last one and the thought saddened her, as babies were so dear to her. (She had raised five of her own

back in her homeland.) So, when in September mom told her there would be a new baby in mid-May 1922, Gram began to happily prepare for the event.

But, tragically, shortly after this announcement, Gram fell and broke her hip and become bedridden. The two oldest girls, 11 and 9, were a big help when they were home from school. The two younger ones also did their share, but mom was kept busy with cooking, housework, and tending to Gram. But Gram was very patient and never called for help unless the pain got too severe. This often happened during the night and mom would get up and turn Gram in her bed, fluff up her pillows, and massage her hip until she felt more comfortable again. This went on for three months. There was no other help. Doctors were 30 or 40 miles away. Mercifully, one night in early December, Gram passed away in her sleep.

For many nights after, mom would waken and get up to tend to Gram before she realized Gram wasn't there any more. After Christmas, mom was able to rest more often during the day and enjoy uninterrupted sleep at night.

Winter passed and spring was in the air. During the night of April 23rd, mom was awakened by Gram's voice calling her name. She was about to get up and go and tend to Gram, but quickly realized Gram was gone. Before mom got back to sleep again, the voice called, "Rosa," again.

Mom turned to dad, who was lying awake beside her, and asked, "Did you hear that?"

Dad replied, "Yes, if she calls again answer her."

Gram called one more time and mom answered, "Yes, what can I do?"

Silence. No more calls.

The next afternoon, April 24, at 4:30, I was born. Three weeks premature!

Go figure.

CHARACTERS AND CREATURES

Over the years I have collected descriptions in newspapers, magazines, books, and correspondence of accounts of encounters with monsters experienced and described by Canadians. I have quite a file of published and unpublished material. The published ones come from newspapers and magazines of the past; the unpublished ones, from correspondence and interviews with contemporary Canadians. In 2004, I made good use of this material by compiling *The Monster Book of Canadian Monsters*. The title is accurate and descriptive because the book is large (folio-format in size; roughly the dimensions of one thousand sheets of typing paper) and each page offers two full columns of type. There are two hundred accounts of "told-as-true" stories and tales. Some of these accounts are more imaginative than others, but all of them are presented as true. For the purposes of that anthology my definition of a monster was a loose one: a monster is a personality or a power that is menacing to mankind. That way I was able to include beings ranging from sea serpents and lake monsters to ghosts from beyond and aliens from outer space. As it happens, this excluded the most powerful monster of all: man!

I presented a copy of this book to Ed Butts, a colleague, researcher, and writer. (His main interest is researching and writing books about Canadian outlaws, if you can imagine.) Ed was born in Toronto but has lived in Cape Breton and various Ontario communities. He has spent the greatest part of his life in Guelph, Ontario, which he considers his hometown. He is now in his fifties and is a talented writer and a generous fellow. He must be because he sat down and having some time to spare between Christmas and New Year's Day, sent me this email reminiscence. It is dated December 28, 2004. To my knowledge Ed has not seen or experienced a ghost or encountered any monsters, but he remembers full well what it was like to be a youngster and to be told about such powers.

Readers of the present book will be able to identify with Ed and with his recollections of the Igor Lady.

Hi, John Robert.

I was reading the introduction to your *Monster* book, and it jarred a few things in my memory. I might have remembered these things earlier, but I thought that by

"monsters," you meant things like Sasquatch and sea serpents. Anyhow, I don't know if any of these would be of
any use to you, but you might find them interesting.

I went to Catholic schools as a kid. I had never heard of
the Devil until I started in the first grade, and the nuns told
us about him. They told us he was everywhere, whispering
in our ears to be bad. If a kid misbehaved in class, he or
she was told to go to the back of the classroom where the
coats were hung, and stand facing the wall — which meant
that the kid's face was stuck in someone's coat. Back there,
said the nuns, was where the Devil lurked. They showed
us pictures of this scary looking creature with horns on
his head, clawed hands and goat's feet. They assured us
that this monster was real, and wanted the souls of little
boys and girls. Those nuns scared the daylights out of me!
I used to lie in my bed at night, awake, but with my eyes
shut tight. I was afraid that if I opened them, I would see
the devil standing at the foot of my bed.

When I was a kid in Guelph, there was a story going
around about a woman known as "The Igor Lady"; at least,
the kids in my school and neighbourhood knew about her.
I guess it was something that would now be called an urban
legend, but as far as we were concerned, the Igor Lady was
really out there. The story went like this. An old man named
Igor had died, and his old wife could not accept that he was
gone. She would wander the streets and parks of Guelph at
night, searching for him. She had a face like a witch, long
grey hair, and wore a long dress that billowed in the wind.
She was, generally, a pretty spooky sight. If she saw you outside at night, she would come up to you and say in a very
scary voice, "Have you seen Igor-r-r?" It was supposed to
be so scary an experience that the kid peed his or her pants.
Now, nobody ever said they actually had seen the Igor Lady.
It was always somebody's best friend's cousin....

I was in Cub Scouts then, and after a Cub meeting in the
security of the basement of the Church of Our Lady, I had
to walk home alone in the dark. I had to go down tree-lined
streets, and was sure that the Igor Lady was behind every

tree, waiting to swoop out at me. It did not help that at the bottom of Dublin Street there was a dark, old, abandoned factory on one side of the road (there is an apartment building there now), and a funeral home (still there) on the other. The last leg of my route home took me along Exhibition Street, which runs along one side of Exhibition Park, one of the favourite "haunts" of the Igor Lady. My house was at the corner of a street that ran onto Exhibition Street, and the side door faced the park directly. After I'd walked that last but most unnerving leg of my journey home, I would pretty well fly up the side steps of my house to get inside, afraid that the Igor Lady might be right behind me.

As a child I was frightened by movie "monsters." The evil witch in Disney's *Sleeping Beauty* scared the socks off me when I was eight, and several years later I had nightmares after watching Christopher Lee's film portrayal of Dracula. But there were adults who reassured me that witches and vampires were not real. The devil and the Igor Lady were even more terrifying to me, because people told me that they actually existed.

Finally, I recall a friend from Parry Sound telling me that up there kids used to talk about a creature called "Little Willie." This was some kind of nasty little beast that lurked in boathouses, waiting to pounce on people. I haven't seen the guy who told me that story in many years, but if you know someone from Parry Sound perhaps they'd know something about it.

Yours,
E

5

MONSTROUS BEINGS

When we think about ghosts, what comes to mind? Do we think of the ghosts of the long-time dead? Or do we think of ghosts of the recently departed? Do we think of people unknown to ourselves? Or do we think of dear friends who have left us? When we think about spirits, do we have in mind energies or powers? Do we have in mind essences or presences? Perhaps we have in mind non-human entities like forces of nature or animals or angels. We might even in our darkest moments envisage beasts and demons and devils!

This section of the book consists of monstrous beings, some more menacing than others. There are a number of descriptions of the Wendigo, or Windigo, or Whetigo; it has many names. It is the Algonkian spirit of cannibalism. The early missionaries were tempted to dismiss it as a bogeyman, good for frightening children, but this cannibalistic spirit is really something else again. It represents the spirit of the untamed wilderness, and it attacks and mercilessly slays the lone hunter in the woods, draining him of his individuality, rendering him one of the "walking dead," a zombie. In its grandest conception it represents the spirit of "me, myself," — that is, unbridled individualism, untamed greed — not merely the individual but the industry, the paper mills that pollute rivers and streams, that visit mercury poisoning on native lands.

MONSTER TURTLE

Monster? Turtle?
Do the two words go together?
Turtle Monster?

Probably not, yet....

The following news item appeared in *The Globe* (Toronto), September 2, 1931. It huffed and it puffed but it was there to surprise the newspaper's readers, for in the same breath as it reported ridiculous claims in an unabashed manner, it related the notion of mammoth turtles to Native belief systems. Indeed, Mikinak, the spirit of the Great Turtle, is the name of the Oracle of the Indians which speaks through the rite of the Shaking Tent. Interestingly, briefly, the writer of this article suggests that the "monster turtle" may comes from distant climes or distant times — faraway places and faraway epochs.

Monster Turtle abroad in North Sea Creature Laughs at Axe Blows and Menaces Canoeists — Age May Be 300 Years — (Canadian Press Despatch.)

Chapleau, Sept. 1. — The sea-serpent, which struck terror into a party of fire rangers in this district a few years ago has now turned out to have been a sea turtle of monster proportions and of great age, possibly 300 years old.

The special Game Committee of the Ontario Government incidentally obtained this information while on a motor trip into the wilds 15 miles east of Chapleau this afternoon. Their informant was Tom Godfrey, who told how his men were scared by this monster, which rose out of the water and almost upset their canoe. It is said to be more than three feet in width, while its head and neck thrust out of the water resembled a large snake. When it swims the commotion in the water is like that made by a motor boat, and its tracks seen on the shore are like those of a tractor, it is affirmed with great earnestness. The Indians have known of the presence of the turtle for many years. One Indian, named Nemegas, aged 95 years, said that he first saw it 50 years ago. He and the Indians have struck the turtle with an axe without penetrating its shell.

Tom Godfrey says he is determined to catch the turtle, which interferes with his men operating in the creek.

There are mud-turtles in these waters, but there is a

theory that this is a genuine sea-turtle, which has either strayed up from the ocean through the Great Lakes, or may be a surviving denizen of prehistoric aeons.

THE SIM-MOQUI

Here is an account of a race of humanoids unknown to modern science but a staple of folklore.

"An Indian Tradition" appeared in the *Daily Colonist* (Victoria, British Columbia), October 6, 1860. The identity of the correspondent, whose initials are J.D., is unknown. The Sim-moquis seem to be "wild men of the woods" but not hairy sasquatches.

An Indian Tradition

Having a little leisure time, one fine evening in the spring of 1853, I started out for a few hours' ramble on the banks of the Camas-sau (the Indian name for the Victoria arm of slough). As I walked along, I met a Cowichan Indian, and understanding the language perfectly, I entered into conversation with him. He commenced telling a heap of stories about hob-goblins, ghosts, etc., and after I had listened some time, he asked if I had ever heard of the Sim-moquis? I replied I never had. "Well," said he, "sit down a bit, and I'll tell you a story about them."

I obeyed and, sitting down, listened to his tale, which ran very much as follows:

"By the side of a lake amongst the highest mountains of this Island, where the crack of a rifle has never yet been heard and the deer and bears roam all unacquainted with the smell of the deadly gunpowder, lives the terrible Sim-moquis. From these mountains the daring hunter, who ventures to pursue the game to their fastnesses, seldom returns to tell the tale of his wanderings. No berries in the whole world are so large, or so sweet, or so nourishing, as the berries in the Sim-moquis country; yet who dare gather them besides their terrible owners?

"The Sim-moquis are a tall, strong, athletic race, with heavy black whiskers and matted hair. They are totally without knee or elbow-joints, and depend upon staffs to assist them in rising from recumbent attitudes, or in sitting down. They never rise but leap with the aid of their staffs to a great distance. Like the deer, whose wide-spread antlers would seem to be a hindrance to its rapid progress through the forests and thickets, the Sim-moqui never miscalculates the distance he has to spring, or the space allowed him in which to leap. His eyes are large and red, and shine like a torch; his teeth are black; his hands and feet are webbed like a water-fowl. They have canoes and hunt with bows and arrows made from the bones of dead Sim-moquis.

"The unfortunates, who chance to visit their country, are immediately seized upon and led into captivity. If they happen to be men, they perform all the drudgery; if women, they take them to wife, to try if they cannot introduce the fashion of knee and elbow-joints into the race."

"Did you ever see any of those strange people?" I asked my companion.

"No," he replied; "but my father did. It was one time when some of the Nanimooch (Nanaimo) Indian women went out berrying, and wandered far up the side of a very high mountain. The farther they went, the larger and the better the berries became, and as they gathered them into their baskets, they wondered at their size and excellence. Higher and higher they went, alternately filling their baskets and pouring them out upon the ground, only to fill them again with still finer *olallies*. At last they reached the top of the mountain, and there their wondering eyes gazed upon a sight which caused them to cry aloud. Berries grew everywhere as large as their baskets; the air was filled with the fragrance from the many-coloured flowers that adorned the green carpet at their feet. The trees, too, were mighty, and their tops were lost to view among a few fleecy clouds that were wafted by a gentle breeze through the air high above them.

"As they stood and wondered at the strange sights above and around them, the sun suddenly sank to rest behind a still higher mountain in the west, and then they felt their danger. The 'Sim-moquis!' burst from their pallid lips, and they seized their baskets and swiftly prepared to descend. But, alas! they had not bent the twigs of the saplings as they came along, and they had no mark by which to guide them back to their homes. They sought for a Sim-moquis trail; but those people leave no trail. As I said before, they leap, by aid of their staffs, over the closest thickets and through the densest forests. After searching for a long, long time in vain for the way down, the poor women threw themselves upon the ground and wept bitterly. Tears dropped like rain, and the ground at their feet was moistened by the crystal drops that fell from their eyes. They thought of their homes and of their little ones, and bemoaned their sad lots in accents of grief and despair.

"Suddenly, while they were seated thus, they saw two lights in the distance, and heard a rushing sound through the air (as of a limb of a tree falling to the ground). The poor creatures started to their feet and essayed to run; but, too late! A Sim-moqui leaped with the swiftness of an arrow shot from a bow into their midst, and motioned them to stay. The affrighted maidens obeyed, and examined the stranger critically. He was tall and straight; his hair was blacker than the features of the blackest raven, and it was neatly combed too. His features were regular and handsome, and half concealed by the flowing whiskers and moustaches that adorned his face; but his colour was much darker than that of any Indian ever before seen. His limbs — who shall describe them? — were straight and appeared strong, but were thin as that sapling (our friend here pointed to a young fir-tree about six inches in circumference). "His arms, too, were straight like sticks, and as he extended his hand as a token of friendship towards the unfortunate girls, they saw that the stories which their grandparents had often told them of the absence of knee and elbow-joints among the Sim-moquis were indeed true. His red eyes glistened and shone in the dark like a lantern, and were the lights which had first attracted the women's attention. After they had sat some little time in silence — for the Sim-moqui language was strange to them — their visitor rose, by means of his staff, and placing his hand to his chin, opened his mouth, and uttered a loud, piercing cry. In an instant a commotion was heard in the bushes, and in a few seconds lights glanced in all directions, and soon huge, unwashed, unjointed Sim-moquis leaped into the open space in which the captives stood. The light from their flaming eyes fell upon the maidens, and objects in the immediate vicinity became as clear as noon-day. No need for torches where the Sim-moquis live," continued the narrator. "Every Sim-moqui is provided with two torches — that is, his eyes. If a fire be needed, dry sticks of matches are not required — his eyes start the wood into a blaze; if his hands be cold, he raises them to a level with his natural torches and warms them.

"The newcomers held a short consultation with the Sim-moqui who had first joined the unhappy women, and then, at the word of command, six stalwart youths approached, and each seizing a woman threw her over his shoulder and commenced leaping through the air, on their way up the mountain. The rest of the party followed, singing a war-song, and so they went on during the night, toiling up the mountainside, until the first dawn of day. Then they sat down by the side of a running brook, prepared a hasty meal of dried venison, and coiling themselves up like hedgehogs, went to sleep, after binding their captives securely. I might here remark that the Sim-moqui never travels in the day-time, as he is as blind as a bat while the sun is shining.

"When the night came, and the women did not return, the lodges of the Nanimooches were in a state of excitement, and a solemn council was held. The unanimous opinion was that the Sim-moquis had carried their females off. For some time, no one ventured to go forth and attempt their rescue, such was the dread in which the mountain savages were held by the coast Indians. At last my father, who was a chief, addressed them in tones of eloquence — pictured the distress which the poor creatures must feel, and the horrible treatment they would receive. At the conclusion of his speech a dozen braves started up, seized their rifles, and prepared to follow my father in search of the lost ones. It was midnight when they commenced to travel up the mountain side, but they walked briskly, and by daylight reached the top of the mountain, the beauties of which had so charmed their countrywomen the evening before. They were so astonished, and wished to remain a short time to feast their eyes upon the wonders of nature. But my father urged them to continue their search, and after a brief rest, they commenced to climb another high mountain — he same over which the Sim-moquis had passed with their captives a few hours before. Night was coming on apace when the pursuers reached the summit, and throwing themselves upon the ground, after a hasty meal, sought repose.

"My father, however, could not sleep, but lay wrapped in his blankets for a short time musing upon the lost ones and the probabilities of rescuing them. At last, he rose from his couch, and was walking up and down in front of the camp, when his eyes suddenly detected the glimmer of a light at some distance to the north. Awakening his companions, they stole, gun in hand, towards the light, and soon came upon the band of Sim-moquis, who had encamped for the night on a grassy knoll. They were all asleep; and to the utter amazement of my father, he discovered that the light he had seen came from the eye of a sentry, perched upon a high rock. Levelling his gun at this sentinel, my father directed his followers each to pick his man. This having been done, a dozen rifles cracked at once, and a dozen Sim-moquis bit the dust. The rest, owing to the absence of joints, were slaughtered before they could rise to their feet. The captives were unloosened, and they threw themselves sobbing upon the breasts of their rescuers. My father, before he left the spot, examined the body of the sentry, and discovered that one of his red eyes was still open; the other was closed tightly. The party, after securing all the valuables they could find, started down the mountain and reached home the next day."

"And are there any Sim-moquis now-a-days?" I asked the narrator, as he turned to leave.

"Oh, yes," said he as he walked away; "lots of them. They live by the side of a lake on a big mountain, and the shores of the lake are covered with gold."

I walked home in the dark, Mr. Editor, musing on what I had heard, and after seven years' lapse have committed it to paper for your especial benefit. If you believe it, publish it; but if you are at all sceptical on the subject, commit the document to the flames.

JACKO

Jacko is the name of a gorilla-like creature and the subject of this correspondent's report which appeared in the *Daily Colonist* (Victoria, British Columbia), July 4, 1884. The account has been widely discussed. Is it the first record of the elusive Bigfoot? Does it constitute the first appearance, in print at least, of the fugitive sasquatch? What should be made of this account of the capture of a "half man and half beast" in the wilds of British Columbia?

Connoisseurs of the weird are inclined to accept the report as a news story, whereas cryptozoologists are happy to dismiss it as a tall tale or a hoax, an entertaining one to be sure, as did researchers Loren Coleman and Jerome Clark, writing in *Cryptozoology A to Z* (1999): "A young Sasquatch? Alas, no. Historically minded Bigfoot researchers have reluctantly concluded that this is just another tall tale cooked up by a local newspaper."

If the account is true, why are there no follow-up stories about Jacko in later issues of the *Daily Colonist* or in the province's other newspapers? Then there is the oddity of the dating of the event. Why was the story two years old upon publication? Finally, there is the curious matter of the correspondent making no attempt to determine whether the smallish creature is a hairy animal or a hirsute human being.

The reader may make up his or her mind about these matters. In the meantime, it makes intriguing reading....

A Strange Capture above Yale — A British Columbia Gorilla (Correspondent of The Colonist) — Yale, B.C., July 3, 1883

In the immediate vicinity of No. 4 tunnel, situated some twenty miles about this village, are bluffs of rock which have hitherto been unsurmountable, but on Monday morning last were successfully scaled by Mr. Onderonk's employees on the regular train from Lytton. Assisted by Mr. Costerton, the British Columbia Express Company's messenger, and a number of gentlemen from Lytton and points east of that place who, after considerable trouble and perilous climbing, succeeded in capturing a creature which may truly be called half man and half beast. "Jacko," as the creature has been called by his capturers, is something of the gorilla type standing about four feet seven inches in height and weighing 127 pounds. He has long, black, strong hair and resembles a human being with one exception, his entire body, excepting his hands, (or paws) and feet are covered with glossy hair about one inch long. His fore arm is much longer than a man's fore arm, and he possesses extraordinary strength, as he will take hold of a stick and break it by wrenching or twisting it, which no man living could break in the same way. Since his capture he is very reticent, only occasionally uttering a noise which is half bark and half growl. He is, however, becoming daily more attached to his keeper, Mr. George Tilbury, of this place, who proposes shortly starting for London, England, to exhibit him. His favourite food so far is berries, and he drinks fresh milk with evident relish. By advice of Dr. Hannington raw meats have been withheld from Jacko, as the doctor thinks it would have a tendency to make him savage. The mode of capture was as follows: Ned Austin, the engineer, on coming in sight of the bluff at the eastern end of No. 4 tunnel, saw what he supposed to be a man lying asleep in close proximity to the track, and as quick as thought blew the signal to apply the brakes. The brakes were instantly applied, and in a few seconds the train was brought to a standstill. At this moment the supposed man sprang up, and uttering a sharp quick bark began to climb the steep bluff. Conductor R.J. Craig and Express Messenger Costerton, followed by the baggageman and brakesman, jumped from the train and knowing they were some twenty minutes ahead of time immediately gave chase. After five minutes of perilous climbing the then supposed demented Indian was corralled on a projecting shelf of rock where he could neither ascend nor descend. The query now was how to capture him alive, which was quickly decided by Mr. Craig, who crawled on his hands and knees until he was about forty feet above the creature. Taking a small piece of loose rock he let it fall and it had the desired effect of rendering poor Jacko incapable of resistance for a time at least. The bell rope was then brought up and Jacko was now lowered to terra firma. After firmly binding him and placing him in the baggage car "off brakes" was sounded and the train started for Yale. At the station a large crowd who had heard of the capture by telephone from Spuzzum Flat were assembled, each one anxious to have the first look at the monstrosity, but they were disappointed, as Jacko had been taken off at the machine shops and placed in charge of his present keeper.

The question naturally arises, how came the creature where it was first seen by Mr. Austin? From bruises about its head and body, and apparent soreness since its capture, it is supposed that Jacko ventured too near the edge of the bluff, slipped, fell and lay where found until the sound of the rushing train aroused him. Mr. Thos. White and Mr. Gouin, C.E., as well as Mr. Major, who kept a small store about half a mile west of the tunnel during the past two years, have mentioned having seen a curious creature at different points between Camps 13 and 17, but no attention was paid to their remarks as people came to the conclusion that they had either seen a bear or stray Indian dog. Who can unravel the mystery that now surrounds Jacko? Does he belong to a species hitherto unknown in this part of the continent, or is he really what the train men first thought he was, a crazy Indian?

IT MAKES ME SHUDDER EVEN NOW

Here is a scary tale about a creature all the more frightening for being unseen. "The Swamp Horror" appeared in the *Calgary Herald* on January 18, 1890. Its editors reprinted it from the *Winnipeg Free Press*. It seems the reminiscence was written by someone named Luke Sharp for the *Free Press* (Detroit, Michigan).

The Swamp Horror

I spoke in the previous article of the dismal swamp that stood on the eastern limits of the village of Bruceville. Some time or other, probably before the village had been settled, there had come through the forest a tornado, and it had lashed the trees down in all sorts of shapes over the partly submerged land. Then at some other period a fire had swept through this, and had left it one of the most desolate, forlorn-looking, tangled mazes of half-burnt wood that could be imagined. Years had passed since that time, and repeated rains had washed most of the black off the wood and left the white, gaunt limbs sticking up in the air, like spectral arms, and made the ghostly place to us boys a region of terror and a first-rate place to avoid. Nobody, as far as I have been able to learn, had penetrated into the innermost recesses of that swamp. No boy that I ever knew dared to enter the swamp even in the brightest sunlight, while the thought of that swamp at night! — whew — it makes me shudder even now.

Nobody was more afraid of that swamp than I was, yet I think I may claim to have been the first boy that ever explored it, and that is the reason that my hair today is gray. I may say that about this time a great mystery shook the village from its circumference to its centre. The mystery was the strange disappearance of three cows that belonged to three of our villagers. Nearly every one of the villagers kept a cow, and these cows grazed on the commons that adjoined the village.

One day three of the most valuable cows were missing, and a search all over the country for them was unsuccessful. This mysterious disappearance caused more talk and gossip in that village than the murder of three men would have done in a larger town. Everybody had a theory as to how the cows had disappeared. I remember that a lot of wandering gypsies came along at that time, and one of the owners of the cows consulted a gypsy as to their whereabouts. After paying the fee the gypsy told him, somewhat vaguely, that he would hear of the cow, but that she feared he would not take as much interest in the animal after she was found as he had done before. This turned out, however, to be strictly accurate.

About this time someone introduced in the village a strange contrivance which was known as a kite. Improbable as it may seem, this invention would sail in the upper skies without the aid of gas, which is used to elevate a balloon. The way it was made was thus:

A hoop of a barrel was taken and was cut so that it made a semi-circle; then a piece of lath was fastened to the centre of that semi-circular hoop, and a piece of string was tied to the end of the hoop and down to the bottom of the lath. A cross piece of lath was also made to strengthen the affair, and then we cut a newspaper into shape and pasted it over the string and lath and hoop ends. A long tail was attached to the end of the lath, made of string, to which was tied little bits of paper, somewhat after the forms of curl papers used by ladies in those days to keep their hair in curl. Then a long string was attached to this kite, and if the breeze was good and you held on one end of the string, the affair rose gracefully in the heavens.

There was great competition among us boys in kite flying, and the wild desire to own the kite that would fly the highest caused bitter rivalry. I succeeded in getting a very good kite, and bankrupted myself in buying a lot of string as an attachment. After purchasing that ball of twine, I was poor in this world's goods, with the exception of that kite, which proudly floated away above its fellows. We used to tie our kite string to the fences, and leave the kites floating up all day, and I have seen as many as ten or fifteen kites hovering away above the village.

One day, when the wind was blowing from the village over the swamp, some envious villain, whose identity I have not been able to discover to this day, cut the string of my kite at the fence. If I had found out who the boy was at the time, I venture to say that there would have been the biggest fight that the village of Bruceville ever saw. I was in another part of the village when the disaster happened, and I saw with horror that my kite, which floated so high above the rest, suddenly began to waver and then floated off towards the east, wobbling to one side and then to the other in a drunken, stupid sort of fashion, and finally fluttered down to the ground somewhere on the other side of the swamp. In doing this it trailed the long line of valuable string clear across the dismal swamp.

It was hard to believe that there could exist in the world such desperate villainy as would prompt a boy to the awful deed. I passed through the village weeping loudly over the disaster, but this attracted very little attention; it was merely thought that I had got one of my usual thrashings, and there seemed to be a belief in the village that whenever that interesting episode occurred, it was richly deserved. I found the end of the string near the edge of the swamp, and I got a stick and began to wind it and save as much as possible of the string. I don't suppose any less consideration would have induced me to brave the terrors of that swamp, but through the wild entanglement I went, winding up the string, which was stretched over bush and bramble, and now and then stuck on the gaunt branches of some of the dead trees.

When I got about half way through the swamp, I began to realize that I was going to present a very picturesque sight when I got to the other side of it. My clothes were all in rags. I had fallen into the mud three or four times and my face and hands were scratched and bleeding with the brambles, but I saw that if I kept on I was going to save all the string and ultimately get the kite.

Just beyond the middle of the swamp there appeared to be an open place, and when I broke through the bushes I found there a little lake and in the center a dry and grassy island. The dead stillness of the spot, although it was so near the village, began to make an impression on my sensitive nerves, and I wondered whether, after all, the string was worth the fearful price I was paying for it. I began to fear ghosts, spooks, bears, lions, tigers and one thing and another, when a sight more horrible than all of those together burst upon me as I cleared the brambles and stood in this green place. There, huddled together, lay the three cows. Their bulging, sightless eyeballs stared at me. Their throats were cut so that their heads were nearly half off. Their bodies were bloated and swollen out of all semblance to the original cows.

Thousands of years of life could not bring to me a moment of greater horror than that was. It would not have been so bad if I had been on the road, where I could have run at the top of my speed for the village. But here I was, hemmed in by an almost impassable swamp, that had taken me already an hour of hard wear and tear to get through. With a yell that pierced the heavens and must have startled the villagers, if any of them had been listening, I dropped the coveted string and dashed madly through the wilderness. How I ever got out to dry land again I never knew. It was a fearful struggle of unprecedented horror. I dared not look around. The hot breath of the cows was on the back of my neck. I felt that their ghosts were following. Those awful eyeballs peered from every dark recess of the swamp.

When I tore through the outer edge of the swamp, I had still strength enough to rush across the commons and dash madly down the main street of the village, all tattered and torn and bleeding, the light of insanity in my eye and the strength of insanity in my limbs, yelling at the top of my voice, calling: "The cows! The cows! They are in the middle of the big swamp with their throats cut!" and when I reached my own door, stumbled and fell into the entrance, to the consternation of my relatives, and, either from the excitement of the fearful episode or the fall, lay there insensible.

A body of men, although they seemed to doubt my story, penetrated in to the green island of the swamp, where they found the cows and buried them, but no one ever knew how the animals got in there or who committed the dastardly deed that led to their death.

WINDAGOOS! CANNIBALS!

The Windigo, the spirit of cannibalism and covetousness among the Algonkian-speaking Indians, is a creature of the woods or a condition of the human spirit, or both or neither. In recent years the Windigo (or Windego or Windagoo) has been compared and confused with a cannibalistic fiend, a sasquatch or a Bigfoot, a mindless malignancy, and even the acquisitiveness of capitalism and corporate concentration. Plainly the Windigo is as free as the wind and not one thing but many things.

Fear is coupled with whimsy in this passage about the beliefs of the Saulteaux (or Ojibwa) at Norway House, north of Lake Winnipeg, in today's Manitoba, between 1868 and 1888. Egerton Ryerson Young (1840–1909) was a Methodist missionary and the author of *Stories from Indian Wigwams and Northern Camp-Fires* (London, 1893) in which this true account first appeared.

Young mentions maps. For an outline of the frightful head of the Windigo, invert the map of James Bay and behold the figure of a hooded terrorist. Terrorist? It is the head and shoulders of the dreaded Windigo; its eye, Akimsk Island, glares through its balaklava-like cape.

[That] these Indians should have in many of the tribes a most remarkable tradition of a great deluge, in which the world was overwhelmed, and the whole human race perished except one family who escaped either in a big canoe or on a great raft, is very suggestive and instructive. Among the many errors and superstitions into which they have fallen is the belief in the existence of windagoos, or gigantic creatures half satanic and half human, whom they represent as being of great size and dwelling in the dark, dreary forests. They describe them as being so powerful that when they march along they can brush aside the great pine-trees as an ordinary man does the grass of the prairies as he strides along through it. We found the Saulteaux Indians especially living in dread of these imaginary monsters. At many a camp-fire they used to tell us with bated breath that these windagoos were terrible cannibals, and that whenever they caught a lonely hunter far away from his home they soon devoured him. When I tried to disabuse their minds of these fears they proceeded to tell me of this one and that one who had been seized and devoured. The instances they brought before me were of hunters who had gone away on long journeys down dangerous rivers and treacherous rapids. On my expressing my opinion that the poor fellows had been drowned or had met with some other accident the Indians refused to be convinced. They will never admit that an accident could happen to any of their great hunters, and so the one theory always before them is that those who mysteriously disappear have been caught and devoured by the windagoos.

Of the power and grip this superstition had on these Saulteaux I had a startling and somewhat amusing illustration shortly after I had gone to their first missionary to live among them. Very cordially were we received, and much encouraged were we by the attention given to our words and the really sincere desire manifested to improve their circumstances socially as well as religiously. As there were many of their countrymen still without missionaries they used to frequently ask why it was that more missionaries with the great book were not sent among them. So one Sunday afternoon I held a kind of a missionary meeting with them. I took into the church my large maps of the world, with a number of pictures of heathens of many lands. I explained the map to them and showed them their own country, and told them that while we had a great land as regards size, yet there were many single cities with more people in them than all the Indians in our land put together. Then I showed them pictures of the cannibals of the isles of the Pacific, and described others of the wild, wicked nations of the earth, and told them that good white people were sending missionaries to a great many of these lands, and they must not expect to have them all come to them. "For," said I, "as bad as you and your forefathers were, some of these other people were much worse." And then I particularized by describing some of the vilest and most degraded of the sinful races. I dwelt on cannibalism especially, and told of the man-eaters of the Pacific islands, who did not even object to a roasted missionary and some of his people cooked up with him. They were intensely interested, and also became very much excited before I finished, especially at what I had said about the cannibals.

The service closed and the people quickly returned to their little houses and wigwams at the Indian village, which was a little distance from the mission-house and church. The next morning, bright and early, I was up, and after breakfast and prayers started off to continue the work in which I had been engaged, namely, acting the part of a surveyor and helping the men run the dividing-lines between their little fields. To my great surprise, when I reached the first home I found that everybody was away, and stick tied across the door was the sign that they did not soon expect to return. On to the next and the next houses I went, and thus on through the whole village, and found, to my amazement, that I was literally a shepherd without a flock, a missionary without his people. Not a man, woman, child, dog, or canoe was to be found. After about an hour of aimless wandering around the wondering what had happened I returned to my home and told my good wife of the loss of our flock. Like myself she was perplexed, and neither of us could make out what it meant.

The Indians had often, in large numbers, gone away on their great hunting excursions, but they never all went at the same time, and never without telling us of their going. So we were indeed perplexed. Toward evening I saw a solitary Indian coming from a distant island in his canoe. I quickly hurried down to the shore, and as he stopped paddling a few hundred feet from the beach I shouted to him to come to land. He immediately came in, and when at the shore I said to him:

"Where are the Indians?"

"Out there far away on that island in Lake Winnipeg," he replied.

"Why are they there?" I asked.

"Very much afraid," he said.

"Very much afraid! Of what are they afraid?" I asked.

"Windagoos! Cannibals!" he answered.

"Did any of you see any windagoos?" I asked.

"No, I don't think we did, but what you said about them in your address in the church made our hearts melt like water, and then the winds began to blow, and there from the dark forests, with the sighing winds we seemed to hear strange sounds, and some said, 'Windagoos! windagoos!' and that was enough, so we all got so alarmed that we launched our canoes, and, taking our families and dogs, away we paddled out to that distant island, and there the people all are now."

I confess I was amused as well as annoyed at the startling effect of my *moving* speech, and picking up a paddle I sprang into the canoe, and telling the Indian to show me what he could do as a canoe-man I struck in with him, and in less than an hour we had traversed the distance of several miles that lay between the mainland and that island. The Indians crowded down to the shore to meet us, and seemed delighted to see me. They wanted to shake hands and make a great fuss over me, but I repelled all their advances and would not shake hands with one of them. At this they were very much crestfallen and surprised.

"Why did you leave us in this way?" I asked the principal ones.

"Windagoos, windagoos!" they fairly shouted. "When you told us about those windagoos who used to eat the missionaries and their people you made us very much afraid, and our hearts got like water, and the more we talked the worse we got, and so we all hurried over here."

"Did I not tell you that those windagoos were more than a hundred days' journey away, even with your best canoes?" I asked.

"O, yes, you did, missionary," they said; "but we did not know but some of them might have started many days ago to come and catch us, and so we hurried out here."

"And you left your missionary and his wife and their little ones, whom you profess so to love, behind to be eaten by the windagoos, did you? And yet you say you so love us and are so thankful we have come to live among you and teach you the good way. Why, I am ashamed of you. Suppose the windagoos had come and no stalwart men had been there to help the missionary fight them off. What would he have thought of your love when he heard you had all, like a lot of old grandmothers, run away?"

Heartily ashamed of themselves, they speedily launched their canoes and returned with me to their village, and very little did we hear after that about the windagoos.

EXORCISM OF A WENDIGO

Wehtiko, Wendigo, Windigo ... the spellings are legion.

"Exorcism Tried in Vain, Axe Supplanted Medicine" appeared in the *Standard* (Regina, Saskatchewan), September 20, 1899. The account seems to be based on one that appeared in the *Post* (Edmonton). The condescension of the editorial writer is lamentable, yet his compassion is considerable.

Exorcism Tried in Vain, Axe Supplantism Medicine, Trial of Indians for Slaying a Whetiko or Wendigo

The Edmonton *Post* contains a report of the trial of the Indians charged with killing a Wendigo or Wehtiko. It is as follows:

The very interesting trial of the Indians charged with killing Louison Moostoos ended on Saturday last by the conviction of Napaysoosis and the acquittal of Payoo. The former, as he had been in prison since March last, was sentenced to only two months' hard labour. Although it was confidently expected both Indians would have been acquitted, this verdict and sentence are satisfactory, inasmuch as they will teach the northern tribes respect for the majesty of the law, and prove a salutary lesson.

The whole story of the killing is an interesting example of one of the deep-rooted beliefs and superstitions of these unfortunate people, and better than a whole volume shows up the devil worship and sorcery of the Wood Crees, to which tribe both the prisoners belong.

The history of the crime, if crime there were, may be best learned from the words of Napaysoosis himself, as taken down from his own lips by Mr. George W. Gairdner, who was retained by the Crown as interpreter for the accused and was in constant attendance at the trial. Mr. Gairdner, having spent many years in the north country as a factor in the Hudson's Bay Company, is proficient in Cree and other Indian dialects, and well versed in Indian lore, and readers of the *Post* may expect from his pen a series of sketches of life in this country in the early days which promise to be most interesting.

Last winter a band of us, thirty-two in number, counting women and children, were living at the Bald Hills, some seventy-five miles west of Lesser Slave Lake. We lived in two shacks and two teepees. Entominahoo, our Chief, along with Kunuksoos and myself and our families, lived in one shack, Moostoos and his family, with some others, lived in the other shack, and the other Indians in the two teepees. We were all on the best of terms with one another and Moostoos was especially well liked by all of us.

Some months before he was killed Moostoos told several of us that he was afraid an evil spirit was getting the better of him and that he would turn Sehtiko (Cannibal), adding, "If I ever go wrong you had better kill me, as I do not wish to destroy my children." The time passed on, however, till about the 23rd of March.

At that time some sickness was affecting the Indians, and two of them — Napaysis and the "little old man" — were being treated by Entominahoo, in his own shack, which might be termed the hospital, as all the sick were taken there to be doctored. Entominahoo was chief medicine man. The third day before he was killed Moostoos also went there to join in the medicine-making and sorceries, which were being practised with a view to curing the sick men.

During the last day and night I saw Moostoos was not looking as usual. His eyes were rolling and glittering, and he seemed afraid to look anyone in the face, and he was all the time muttering to himself. On one occasion he said: "I look on these children as young moose, and long to eat them." I was absent from the shack part of the day, and when I came back towards evening, Moostoos looked wilder and more dangerous than ever, and it was clear to all present that he was becoming a Wehtiko.

Ordinary incantations were tried, but without result, and as a last resort the "medicine lodge" was erected in the shack, and the whole skill and power of all our sorceries was enlisted in the attempt to bring Moostoos back to reason. It was certain from his appearance, words and actions, that he had no bodily complaint, but that he was possessed with a devil. Our usual ceremonies were begun. The singing of medicine songs, drumming and dancing were carried on from sundown till about midnight, and as Moostoos was lying, covered with two blankets, comparatively quiet, the medicine seemed to have a good effect.

There were in the house at that time Entominahoo and his wife, Eliza, the wife of "Redhead," Felix's wife, "Redhead," Kunuksoos and his wife, Napaysis, and "the little old man"; as I said before, these last were lying sick. All but the sick men and Kunuksoos, who was taking care of them, were grouped round Moostoos, striving, by medicine songs and other means at our command, to drive the evil spirit out of him. Entominahoo, our chief "doctor," was inside the "medicine" circle, waving his wand, and using all his science and skill toward the same end.

Suddenly Moostoos called out, "This night you will all die," and commenced twitching his limbs and rolling his eyes. Two of us, Chuckachuck and myself, went and sat on each side of him at his shoulders, prepared to hold him down if he became violent, while the two young women, Eliza and Felix's wife, sat at his feet. At this juncture, "Redhead," sick with fright, left the shack. Moostoos began throwing his arms about, and tried to get up, saying again, "If I get up I will kill you all tonight." The four of us laid hold of his arms and legs and held him down, while Entominahoo continued his "medicine," using the most powerful songs and incantations at his command.

Moostoos now became unmanageable, flung us off, rose to his feet, and sprang into the air, exclaiming, "I will kill you all; I will not leave one alive." Fear, intense, blind fear, took hold of us. We jumped up and, in spite of his gigantic struggles, we managed to pull him down and cover him with blankets. Entominahoo left his medicine lodge and sat down close to Moostoos, saying, "It's no use; I can do no more; do your best to hold him."

Moostoos struggled fearfully, throwing his head about and grinding his teeth, and twice he tried to bite me, tearing my coat. At that time I was holding his right arm, Chuckachuck his left, while the two women held his feet. I covered his face after he tried to bite me. The noise of the drumming and singing had been going on all the time.

By this time we were crazy with fear, and what followed is like a dream. Eliza sprang to her feet holding in her right hand a medicine belt and in her left an axe. Her hair was flying loose, and she was dancing and singing. All of a sudden she ran around and thrashed Moostoos over the face and breast with this medicine help several times.

"Did she strike him with the axe?"

I cannot say as my head was bent low over Moostoos, say, but I saw blood outside the blanket after she thrashed him, and I only knew of two cuts on the head, while the policeman found three. She then handed the axe to Chuckachuck (which I saw) and said, "Here, brother-in-law." Chuckachuck struck him with the axe and split his skull.

That blow killed Moostoos. Chuckachuck then handed me the axe and a knife which I refused at first, till Chuckachuck called me a coward, and said I wanted them all killed. I then drove the knife into his belly, and stuck the axe into his body over the heart, leaving both weapons in the wounds.

"Did Moostoos breath after he got the first blow?"

Yes, a little; but he had stopped breathing before I struck him. At that moment Payoo, the other prisoner, alarmed by the screams of fear from the women and the calls of the men, entered the shack. He was handed an axe, and very reluctantly, and actually without looking where he was striking, struck the corpse on the head with the axe.

"What did we do that night?"

Why, we sat around the body till daylight, by the light of the fire.

"What for?"

We expected him to rise from the dead, and we wanted to kill him again if he tried to get up.

"What do you think was the matter with Moostoos?"

He was a Wehtiko, and I know he had a lump of ice in his body causing the malady. Why, we made strong tea and poured it boiling hot into the axe hole and the breast to thaw that ice, but first Dayoo and I drove a stake into the ground; then we pulled out the stake and poured in the hot tea. After that towards morning, Entominahoo's wife and I tied his legs with chains to two pickets driven into the ground.

"Why did you do this?"

So that if he came to life again he could not get up and run after us. And last of all, next day I cut his head off with an axe.

"What was that for?"

To be sure he was dead, and in order that even if he got up he could not eat us. Then we left him in the shack, tied up the door and left the place.

"What is a Wehtiko?"

A Wehtiko is a person, man or woman, into whose body enters a most malignant evil spirit, which incites him to kill and eat his fellow men. He is possessed of superhuman strength and cunning, and the only thing that saves the Indians is that a Wehtiko generally warns them of his coming state some time beforehand. It has always been our custom to kill these people. It was the only way to protect our lives from their violence.

This story was not taken from the lips of a raving maniac, nor was it copied from some old black-letter history of the ninth or tenth century. The atrocity occurred not five months ago, within three hundred miles of this town, and, above all, the details were sworn to in open court. The pitiful story, shocking in its hideous circumstance, must excite detestation on account of its depravity, but at the same time it must arouse compassion for these debased beings who can be so remorselessly moved by their superstitions.

THE OSHAWA SEA SERPENT

Here is an exceptionally serious news story about a "monster" that was reportedly seen by residents of Oshawa to disport in the waters of Lake Ontario. The report appeared on the front page of *The Globe* (Toronto), Tuesday, July 21, 1931, and the story considers the reports of the eyewitnesses of that sighting and of others in the distant path with a rare degree of objectivity.

Oshawa is known today as Ontario's "motor city" on account of its concentration of automotive manufacturing plants. In the 1930s its residents were claiming "monster" sightings, and these reports amused the editors of *The Globe*. Elsewhere in this issue, the editors threw up their hands in amusement. Witness the following item from the "Notes and Comments" column: "It is doubtful that Oshawa can make much headway with a sea-serpent story. It has other claims to publicity, and, besides, Sault Ste. Marie has developed this sort of thing to such a fine point that it is useless for other municipalities to try to compare."

There are references here to champion swimmer George Young and the newly opened Welland Canal, as well as to famed Ogopogo, said to inhabit Lake Okanagan in the Interior of British Columbia.

Has Oshawa Sea Serpent Migrated from Lake Erie — Via New Welland Canal? — Description of Monster — Reported in Ontario — Waters Corresponds to — Port Dover's Famous — Reptile — Just George — Young Speeding, Says — Johnny Walker — (Special Despatch to **The Globe.***)*

Oshawa, July 20. — Although Oshawa's lakefront population has not taken seriously the story told by a party of campers that a sea serpent was seen in the lake just off Lakeview Park swimming beach on Saturday night, a hundred eager watchers lined the lake shore this evening, seeking a glimpse of the supposed monster of the deep, which is said to have struck terror into the hearts of bathers. "Curly" Rhue of Brantford, reported to have seen the sea serpent, states that the story, as published in Toronto evening papers, was greatly exaggerated.

"It was not a sea serpent at all that we saw," said Rhue, "but it was some kind of big fish."

At Least Thirty Feet Long

Bert Todd of Brantford, who is camping along with Rhue on the Oshawa beach, was more emphatic than his companion as to the size of the beast, and said that, judging from the common it was causing on the water, it must have been at least thirty feet long. Other campers think a school of several hundred of large carp were disporting in the lake, causing a commotion which led to the belief that some unusual animal was making for the unprotected bathers.

A second scare, however, was aroused last night by a report that the sea monster had been seen again, but no one could be located who has actually seen it.

Johnny Walker, whose swimming camp is quite close to the spot where the sea serpent is supposed to have been seen, laughed at the report, and advanced a new theory. "Why," he said, "all they saw was George Young out there flashing some of his old-time speed and making a splash in the water."

First Cousin of Ogopogo

There is a possibility that Lake Erie's famous serpent, which is reputed to be a first cousin of Ogopogo, world-renowned denizen of Okanagan Lake, in British Columbia, may have found its way through the new Welland Canal, large enough to accommodate it, into the lower lake.

C.D. Woolley, well-known Port Dover resident, yesterday recalled that some forty-two or forty-three years ago he was on a load of hay in the lake field of his father's farm, the banks being at least sixty feet high.

About half a mile out in the lake he saw a monster so hideous that he was so excited that he forgot to call his brother who was working in the same field. As described by Mr. Woolley, the reptile had about nine feet of its body out of the water. The head was carried in a reptilian manner and the portion of the body under water seemed to be at least thirty feet long. It was travelling at a very rapid rate in a southerly direction. Recovering from his stupefaction, he called his brother, Will, and they ran to the end of Woolley's Point, but the monster had disappeared.

Their Story Ridiculed

Some twenty years later the crew of the tug owned by Andy Forbeck, again saw the animal, this time off the end of Long Point. In spite of the protests of his crew, Forbeck, who feared nothing, set his tug in chase of the monster, which soon submerged. The animal is described by one of the survivors of that crew as having a head like a horse, which corresponds with the Oshawa description. Mr. Woolley states that the diameter of the neck of the creature appeared at that distance to be about sixteen or eighteen inches.

OSHAWA'S OGOPOGO?

"May Be Ogopogo" is the title of this commentary published in *The Globe* (Toronto), May 22, 1931. It was written in the wake of the paper's earlier story about the Oshawa sea serpent. Novelty seeking was common in the press in the 1930s, perhaps as an antidote to the psychological and financial burdens imposed by the Great Depression. The writer relates the season of the year to the sighting, spring, or tourist seasons being favourites, and also to the province's various waterways. He also alludes to the novelty value of the folklore and points his finger on the fact that the public seems to want "the" sea serpent and not a family of sea serpents.

May Be Ogopogo

Almost as certain as the sun in its course, the sea-serpent bobs up about this time of year. As with all other uncanny apparitions, there is shock in the suddenness of the appearance. By common consent, there is only one sea-serpent — "the" sea-serpent — and, judging by the widely separated scenes of its annual performances, it is gifted with considerable ability in the way of locomotion. This season it is "showing" in the waters of Lake Ontario, off Oshawa. Some time ago Port Dover folk saw it perform. Last year Californians were favoured with a visit; and next summer it may play an engagement off Capetown.

What is this sea-serpent? Not an animal; not a fish; not a snake. Each year sees some change in its make-up. For the Oshawa show it adopted a great hirsute head which was carried majestically above the water, and appeared to be bullet-proof. The only consistent feature of the reports is that the monster always is about thirty feet long. The old explanation of the scoffers does not hold in regard to the sea-serpent, as it has been seen under various liquor regulations.

It may be Ogopogo, which at intervals had terrified the people of British Columbia, and which, before the advent of the white man, was a tradition among the Indian tribes of the Pacific Coast. Ogopogo may have come East. Unless equipped with facilities for overland or air travel, he would have to come around by way of the Panama Canal, but he is reported to be a fast mover under his own power.

Perhaps he has been attracted by the [waters] of Beauharnois, and is bent on an inspection of other chief canals of the country. In that case the Sault should have him next summer — and that will be the end of Ogpogo.

Algoma will take this serpent to its bosom, feast him, make him a sort of social sea-lion, broadcast news of his every movement, kill him with kindness. With this in mind most people will cherish a secret hope that, after all, the creature seen at Oshawa may not be Ogopogo. He is worthy of a more dramatic fate; and, anyway, during the dog-days, the world and its newspapers need a fearsome sea-serpent.

THE SHAKING TENT

Here is a description of a performance of the rite of the Shaking Tent. The description is remarkable for its sense of high drama and its range of unusual details.

This eyewitness account was written by Chief Buffalo Child Long Lance and is reprinted from his highly readable book of memories titled *Long Lance* (New York, 1928). It is difficult to determine how much of Long Lance's description is remembered and how much of it is imagined. If the writer is describing the traditional manner in which the rite was practised by the Blackfoot Indians of Alberta in the early years of this century, it must be borne in mind that he was not there to observe the ceremony. As scholar and biographer Donald B. Smith has determined, Long Lance was an impostor and as such had much in common with the conservationist Grey Owl. Neither man was an Indian, yet both men were outstandingly successful in addressing issues of conservation and ecology to native and white alike.

Sylvestre Long (1890–1932) was an American of mixed Indian, white, and possibly black ancestry, who escaped segregation by "going native." He was adopted by the Blood as Buffalo Child in Alberta in 1922. He took his own life when his origins became common knowledge.

But the most weird and interesting part of the medicine-man's practices were the sensational rites which he would carry out when "getting in touch with the spirits." Whenever he wanted to get a forecast of the future, get the outcome of some future event, or cure some sick person who was lying at the point of death, he would hold this rite in the big medicine-teepee, and the entire tribe would be allowed to witness it. I often watched this as a youngster, and to this day I marvel over what I saw. I have never seen any old Indian who could explain it.

An hour or so preceding one of these medicine lodges the camp crier would go through the camp crying out the news that the "medicine-man was preparing to talk with the spirits." This caused great excitement in camp. The entire tribe would go early to the medicine lodge in order to get seats; for only about one hundred could get inside the lodge, and the rest had to stay outside and listen to the weird ceremony. Our mother would take us children with her and bundle us close to her on the women's side of the lodge.

As we sat and looked on with eyes agape, the medicine-man's assistant would erect four poles in the centre of the big lodge and tie them together at the top in tripod fashion. Under these poles there was an area about twelve feet across. In this area the assistant, with the help of four men, would drive into the ground a series of sharp pegs, placing them at intervals of about an inch apart until the entire area was covered. These pegs were so sharp at the top that they would go through a man's foot if stepped upon. In the centre of the twelve-foot area a little square was left clear, a place just large enough for a man to stand in. The only way one could reach this area over the sharp pegs was to jump into it, and that seemingly would mean serious injury or death.

The medicine-man would now enter with four men. These men would undress him, leaving only his breech-cloth on his body, and then lay him down on his back. They would place his two hands together, palm to palm, and with a strong rawhide thong they would bind his two thumbs together so tightly that they would sometimes bleed. They would place each pair of fingers together and bind them together in the same way. Then they would go down to his feet and tie his two big toes together, pulling with all their strength to bind them as tightly as they could.

Now they would take a hide about the size of a blanket, and roll it tightly around him head to foot, like a cigar wrapper. Around this wrapper they would twine him up from neck to ankles with a stout rawhide thong, winding it tightly around and around his body at intervals of each inch down the length of his form until he was securely bound. And still another hide was wrapped around him, and another rawhide thong was wound tightly around his motionless form. Now, as he lay helpless on the ground, he resembled a long brown cigar. Literally, he could not move a finger.

The assistants would now raise the medicine-man to a standing position and carefully balance him on the soles of his bare feet. He would stand there for a while like a post. Then gradually he would begin slightly to bend his knees and draw them up again, and after a while each bend of the knees would take the form of a short jump. These jumps would keep increasing in length until finally he would be leaping around and around the four poles with startling speed, resembling some ghostly post bobbing up and down through the air so fast that the eye could hardly follow them.

Then, suddenly, with a huge leap, so quickly executed that no one could see how he made it, he would dart through space and land with a thud in the one-foot clearing in the centre of the area of sharp pegs. He had leaped six feet over the dangerous spikes and landed safely in the little clearing, which was just big enough to hold his two feet — truly a remarkable exploit in itself.

But he has not yet started the really thrilling part of the ceremony.

As he stands there in the centre under the poles, still bound securely, he commences to sing his medicine song, accompanied by the throbbing boom of the big medicine-drum in the hands of his assistant.

What I am going to describe now may seem strange; it is strange, but it is exactly what happens. How and why, no one knows.

Presently, as the medicine-man stands there singing his weird chant to the spirits, voices from above are heard; voices which seem to emanate from the opening way up at the top of the big medicine-teepee. As everyone can see, there is nothing up there but the night air and the stars above. Where these voices come from no Indian has ever been able to explain. But, according to the medicine-man, they are the voices of the spirits — the spirits with whom he is trying to get in touch. The mystery of it is that no one has ever been able to prove that they were anything else.

These voices speak in a language which we cannot understand. Even the medicine-man cannot understand most of them. All he can say is that they are speaking in foreign tongues, and that they are not the spirits that he wants. There are only four spirits whom our medicine-man White Dog could understand. I remember the name of only one of them, and that was "First White Man." And that name had been with our medicine-men for years before our tribe knew that there was a white man on this earth.

As these voices kept chattering down into the lodge, the medicine-man rejects them one by one, and continues to ask for one of the four spirits whom he can understand. Sometimes it takes him many minutes to do this. I remember one or two times when he could not get hold of one of them at all, and he had to end the ceremony without accomplishing his aim.

But when he did get hold of the spirit whom he was seeking he would become excited and talk away so fast that he could hardly hear what he was saying. It seemed that he had to hurry to get in what he wanted to say before the spirit departed. If it was a cure he was after, the dying patient laying there in the medicine lodge would also become excited; and we have seen them get up and walk. If it was information the medicine-man was seeking, he would make his inquiries in short parables of his own, and he would be answered by the spirits in these same unintelligible parables, which later had to be explained to us. It was our language, but it was phrased in a way that we could not understand. And, furthermore, it was the ancient method of speaking our language — the way it was spoken a long time ago — and only our oldest men could understand some of the phraseology and old words.

But the part of the ceremony which made us young-sters afraid came at the conclusion of the medicine-man's interview with the spirits.

These interviews ended in many exciting ways, but always the final scene was accompanied by a howling wind, which would start to roar across the top of the lodge as the spirits ceased talking. The big medicine-teepee would rock and quiver under the strain of this wind, as it screeched through the poles at the top of the teepee and caused us to shake with fright. It was a startling climax. A chaotic med-ley of noise would come down to us from above — from the round opening at the top of the lodge where the teepee poles jutted out into the night air. Strange voices shrieking in weird pandemonium above the wailing of the winds; the clanking and jingling of unknown objects, and then a sud-den jerk of the entire lodge, a flicker of flames, a terrifying yell from the medicine-man, and then —

He would disappear right in front of our eyes. But in the same instant we would hear him yelling for help. And looking up in the direction of his voice, we would see him hanging precariously by one foot at the top of the lodge, stripped as naked as the day he was born. The only thing that held him from falling and breaking his neck was his foot, which seemed to be caught in between the skin cov-ering of the teepee and one of the slanting poles which supported it.

"*Kokenaytuksishpewow!* — Hurry!" he would yell frantically.

And the men would rush for long poles with which to remove him from his dangerous, dangling perch at the roof of the lodge, lest he should fall and break his neck.

How he got there, no one knows; but he said that the spirits left him there on their way out. But the greatest puzzle to us youngsters as how he got stripped of those stout bindings!

I have seen some miraculous things done by the old-time medicine-men, who have practically passed out of existence and taken all of their uncanny knowledge with them. I have seen them send messages for a distance of many miles merely by going into their teepee and sitting down, "thinking the message" to the other camp. There were quite a few old Indians who could "receive" these messages. I have seen them curing dying people, and I have seen them to foretell with accuracy the outcome of future events.

ABDUCTED BY THE SASQUATCHES

Here is an astonishing tale and the "classic case" of an abduction by a sasquatch. It is also an amazingly readable narrative. The characteristics that set it apart from other accounts of chance encounters between human beings and those hairy, ape-like creatures that are believed by some observers to inhabit the wild Interior of British Columbia are its detail, its sweep, its drama, and its verisimilitude.

Albert Ostman, a Canadian prospector with a Scandinavian background, was sixty-four years old in 1957 and living near Fort Langley, British Columbia. In longhand in a scribbler, he wrote out the account of his 1924 abduction. Before a Justice of the Peace on August 20, 1957, he swore as follows: "And I make this solemn Declaration conscientiously believing it to be true, and knowing that it is of the same force and effect as if made under oath and by virtue of the Canada Evidence Act."

There is a description of Ostman in the process of writing out his experiences by journalist John Green in his publication *On the Track of the Sasquatch* (1968): "When he was asked to recall all he could of his encounter with the Sasquatch back in 1924, he went about it by gathering whatever he could on hand from that period, including, among other things, a shopping list used in getting ready for one of his prospecting trips. Then he set about rebuilding the experience in detail, including his own actions prior to and following the actual encounter, in an attempt to re-enter, as much as possible, the scene of events that took place more than 30 years ago.

"When he was later asked if he would swear to the accuracy of the account, he made it clear that he could do so only as to the main elements of the story, not the surrounding detail. Here is the story that he wrote. Here is his account. It is in the hands of the reader to decide what to make of it."

I have always followed logging and construction work. This time I had worked over one year on a construction job, and thought a good vacation was in order. B.C. is famous for lost gold mines. One is supposed to be at the head of Toba Inlet — why not look for this mine and have a vacation at the same time? I took the Union Steamship boat to Lund, B.C. From there I hired an old Indian to take me to the head of Toba Inlet.

This old Indian was a very talkative old gentleman. He told me stories about gold brought out by a white man from this lost mine. This white man was a very heavy drinker — spent his money freely in saloons. But he had no trouble in getting more money. He would be away a few days, then come back with a bag of gold. But one time he went to his mine and never came back. Some people say a Sasquatch killed him.

At that time I had never heard of Sasquatch. So I asked what kind of animal he called a Sasquatch. The Indian said: "They have hair all over their bodies, but they are not animals. They are people. Big people living in the mountains. My uncle saw the tracks of one that were two feet long. One old Indian saw one over eight feet tall."

I told the Indian I didn't believe in their old fables about mountain giants. It might have been some thousands of years ago, but not nowadays.

The Indian said: "There may not be many, but they still exist."

We arrived at the head of the inlet about 4:00 p.m. I made camp at the mouth of a creek. The Indian was in no hurry — he had to wait for high tide to go back. That would be about 7:00 p.m. I tried to catch some trout in the creek — but no luck. The Indian had supper with me, and I told him to look out for me in about three weeks. I would be camping at the same spot when I came back. He promised to tell his friend to look out for me too.

Next morning I took my rifle with me, but left my equipment at the camp. I decided to look around for some deer trail to lead me up in the mountains. On the way up the inlet I had seen a pass in the mountain that I wanted to go through, to see what was on the other side.

I spent most of the forenoon looking for a trail but found none, except for a hog back running down to within about a hundred feet of the beach. So I swamped out a trail from there, got back to my camp about 3:00 p.m. that afternoon, and made up my pack to be ready in the morning. My equipment consisted of one 30-30 Winchester rifle. I had a special home-made prospecting pick, axe on one hand, and pick on the other. I had a leather case for this pick which fastened to my belt, also my sheath knife.

The storekeeper at Lund was co-operative. He gave me some cans for my sugar, salt and matches to keep them dry. My grub consisted mostly of canned stuff, except for a side of bacon, a bag of beans, four pounds of pancake flour and six packets Rye King hard tack, three rolls of snuff, one quarter sealer of butter and two one-pound cans of milk. I had two boxes of shells for my rifle.

The storekeeper gave me a biscuit tin. I put a few things in that and cached it under a windfall, so I would have it when I came back here waiting for a boat to bring me out. My sleeping bag I rolled up and tied on top of my packsack — together with my ground sheet, small frying pan, and one aluminum pot that held about a gallon. As my canned food was used, I would get plenty of empty cans to cook with.

The following morning I had an early breakfast, made up my pack, and started out up this hog back. My pack must have been at least eighty pounds, besides my rifle. After one hour, I had to rest. I kept resting and climbing all that morning. About 2:00 p.m. I came to a flat place below a rock bluff. There was a bunch of willow in one place. I made a wooden spade and started digging for water. About a foot down I got seepings of water, so I decided to camp here for the night, and scout around for the best way to get on from here.

I must have been up to near a thousand feet. There was a most beautiful view over the islands and the Strait — tug boats with log booms, and fishing boats going in all directions. A lovely spot. I spent the following day prospecting around. But no signs of minerals. I found a deer trail leading towards this pass that I had seen on my way up the inlet.

The following morning I started out early, while it was cool. It was steep climbing with my heavy pack. After a three hours climb, I was tired and stopped to rest. On the other side of a ravine from where I was resting was a yellow spot below some small trees. I moved over there and started digging for water.

I found a small spring and made a small trough from cedar bark and got a small amount of water, had my lunch and rested here till evening. That was not a good camping site, and I wanted to get over the pass. I saved all the water I got from this spring, as I might not find water on the other side of this pass. However, I made it over the pass late that night.

Now I had downhill and good going, but I was hungry and tired, so I camped at the first bunch of trees I came to. I had about a gallon of water so I was good for one day. Of course, I could see rough country ahead of me, and I was trying to size up the terrain — what direction would I take from here. Towards west would lead to low land and some other inlet, so I decided to go in a northeast direction, but I had to find a good way to get down.

I left my pack and went east along a ledge, but came to an abrupt end — was two or three hundred feet straight down. I came back, found a place only about fifty feet down to a ledge that looked like good going for as far as I could see. I got down on this ledge all right and had good going and slight down hill all day — I must have made ten miles when I came to a small spring and a big black hemlock tree.

This was a lovely campsite. I spent two days here

just resting and prospecting. There were some minerals but nothing interesting. The first night here I shot a small deer (buck) so I had plenty of good meat, and good water. The weather was very hot in the daytime, so I was in no hurry, as I had plenty of meat. When I finally left this camp, I got into plenty of trouble. First I got into a box canyon, and had to come back to almost where I started this morning, when I found a deer trail down to another ledge, and had about two miles of good going. Then I came to another canyon, on the other side was a yellow patch of grass that meant water. I made it down into this canyon, and up on the other side, but it was tough climbing. I was tired and when I finally got there I dug a pit for water and got plenty for my needs. I only stayed here one night, it was not a good camping site. Next day I had hard going. I made it over a well-timbered ridge into another canyon. This canyon was not so steep on the west side, but the east side was almost plumb. I would have to go down hill to find a way out. I was not well below timber line.

I found a fair campsite that night, but moved on next morning. It was a very hot day, not a breath of wind.

Late that day I found an exceptionally good campsite. It was two good-sized cypress trees growing close together and near a rock wall with a nice spring just below these trees. I intended to make this my permanent camp. I cut lots of brush for my bed between these trees. I rigged up a pole from this rock wall to hang my packsack on, and I arranged some flat rocks for my fireplace for cooking. I had a really classy setup. I shot a grouse just before I came to this place.

Too late to roast that tonight — I would do that tomorrow.

And that is when things began to happen.

I am a heavy sleeper, not much disturbs me after I go to sleep, especially on a good bed like I had now.

Next morning I noticed things had been disturbed during the night. But nothing missing that I could see.

I roasted my grouse on a stick for my breakfast — about 9:00 a.m. I started out prospecting. I always carried my rifle with me. Your rifle is your most important equipment.

I started out in a southwest direction below the way I had come in the night before. There were some signs (minerals) but nothing important. I shot a squirrel in the afternoon, and got back to camp at 7:00 p.m. I fried the squirrel on a stick, opened a can of peas and carrots for my supper, and gathered up dry branches from trees. There are always dead branches of fir and hemlock under trees, near the ground. They make good fuel and good heat.

That night I filled up the magazine of my rifle. I still had one full box of 20 shells in my coat pocket. That night I laid my rifle under the edge of my sleeping bag. I thought a porcupine had visited me the night before and porkies like leather, so I put my shoes in the bottom of my sleeping bag.

Next morning my packsack had been emptied out. Some one had turned the sack upside down. It was still hanging on the pole from the shoulder straps as I had hung it up. Then I noticed one half-pound package of prunes was missing. Also most of my pancake flour was missing, but my salt bag was not touched. Porkies always look for salt, so I decided it must be something else than porkies. I looked for tracks but found none. I did not think it was a bear, they always tear up and make a mess of things. I kept close to camp these days in case this visitor would come back.

I climbed up on a big rock where I had a good view of the camp, but nothing showed up. I was hoping it would be a porky, so I would get a good porky stew. These visits had now been going on for three nights.

I intended to make a new campsite the following day, but I hated to leave this place. I had fixed it up so nicely, and these two cypress trees were bushy. It would have to be a heavy rain before I would get wet, and I had good spring water and that is hard to find.

This night it was cloudy and looked like it might rain.

I took special notice of how everything was arranged. I closed my packsack, I did not undress, I only took off my shoes, put them in the bottom of my sleeping bag. I drove my prospecting stick into one of the cypress trees so I could reach it from my bed. I also put the rifle alongside me, inside my sleeping bag. I fully intended to stay awake all night to find out who my visitor was, but I must have fallen asleep.

I was awakened by something picking me up. I was half asleep and at first I did not remember where I was. As I began to get my wits together, I remembered I was on this prospecting trip, and in my sleeping bag.

My first thought was — it must be a snow slide, but there was no snow around my camp. Then it felt like I was tossed on horseback, but I could feel whoever it was, was walking.

I tried to reason out what kind of animal this could be. I tried to get at my sheath knife, and cut my way out, but I was in an almost sitting position, and the knife was under me. I could not get hold of it, but the rifle was in front of me, I had a good hold of that, and had no intention to let go of it. At times I could feel my packsack touching me, and I could feel the cans in the sack touching my back.

After what seemed like an hour, I could feel we were going up a steep hill. I could feel myself rise for every step. What was carrying me was breathing hard and sometimes gave a slight cough. Now, I knew this must be one of the mountain Sasquatch giants the Indians told me about.

I was in a very uncomfortable position — unable to move. I was sitting on my feet, and one of the boots in the bottom of the bag was crossways with the hobnail sole up across my foot. It hurt me terribly, but I could not move.

It was very hot inside. It was lucky for me this fellow's hand was not big enough to close up the whole bag when he picked me up — there was a small opening at the top, otherwise I would have choked to death.

Now he was going downhill. I could feel myself touching the ground at times and at one time he dragged me behind him and I could feel [what] was below me. Then he seemed to get on level ground and was going at a trot for a long time. By this time, I had cramps in my legs, the pain was terrible. I was wishing he would get to his destination soon. I cold not stand this type of transportation much longer.

Now he was going up hill again. It did not hurt me so bad. I tried to estimate distance and directions. As near as I could guess we were about three hours travelling. I had no idea when he started as I was asleep when he picked me up.

Finally he stopped and let me down. Then he dropped my packsack, I could hear the cans rattle. Then I heard chatter — some kind of talk I did not understand. The ground was sloping so when he let go of my sleeping bag, I rolled head first downhill. I got my head out, and got some air. I tried to straighten my legs and crawl out, but my legs were numb.

It was still dark, I could not see what my captors looked like. I tried to massage my legs to get some life in them, and get my shoes on. I could hear now it was at least four of them. They were standing around me, and continuously chattering. I had never heard of Sasquatch before the Indian told me about them. But I knew I was right among them.

But how to get away from them, that was another question. I got to see the outline of them now, as it began to get lighter though the sky was cloudy, and it looked like rain, in fact there was a slight sprinkle.

I now had circulation in my legs, but my left foot was very sore on top where it had been resting on my hobnail boots. I got my boots out from the sleeping bag and tried to stand up. I was wobbly on my feet but had a good hold of my rifle.

I asked, "What you fellows want from me?"

Only some more chatter.

It was getting lighter now, and I could see them quite clearly. I could make out forms of four people. Two big and two little ones. They were all covered with hair and no clothes on at all.

I could now make out mountains all around me. I looked at my watch. It was 4:25 a.m. It was getting lighter now and I could see the people clearly.

They look like a family, old man, old lady and two young ones, a boy and a girl. The boy and the girl seem to be scared of me. The old lady did not seem too pleased about what the old man dragged home. But the old man was waving his arms and telling them all what he had in mind. They all left me then.

I had my compass and my prospecting glass on strings around my neck. The compass in my left-hand shirt pocket and my glass in my right-hand pocket. I tried to reason our location, and where I was. I could see now that I was in a small valley or basin about eight or ten acres, surrounded by high mountains, on the southeast side there was a V-shaped opening about eight feet wide at the bottom and about twenty feet high at the highest point — that must be the way I came in. But how will I get out? The old man was now sitting near this opening.

I moved my belongings up close to the west wall. There were two small cypress trees there, and this will do for a shelter for the time being. Until I find out what these people want with me, and how to get away from here. I emptied out my packsack to see what I had left in the line of food. All my canned meat and vegetables were intact and I had one can of coffee. Also three small cans of milk — two packages of Rye King hard tack and my butter sealer half full of butter. But my prunes and macaroni were missing. Also my full box of shells for my rifle. I only had six shells beside what I had in the magazine of my rifle. I had my sheath knife but my prospecting pick was missing and my can of matches. I only had my safety box full and that held only about a dozen matches. That did not worry me — I can always start a fire with my prospecting glass when the sun is shining, if I got dry wood. I wanted hot coffee, but I had no wood, also nothing around here that looked like wood. I had a good look over the valley from where I was — but the boy and the girl were always watching me from behind some juniper bush. I decided there must be some water around here. The ground was leaning towards the opening in the wall. There must be water at the upper end of this valley, there is green grass and moss along the bottom.

All my utensils were left behind. I opened my coffee tin and emptied the coffee in a dishtowel and tied it with the metal strip from the can. I took my rifle and the can and went looking for water. Right at the head under a cliff there was a lovely spring that disappeared underground. I got a drink, and a full can of water. When I got back the young boy was looking over my belonging, but did not touch anything. On my way back I noticed where these people were sleeping. On the east side wall of this valley was a shelf in the mountain side, with overhanging rock, looking something like a bit undercut in a big tree about ten feet deep and thirty feet wide. The floor was covered with lots of dry moss, and they had some kind of blankets woven of narrow strips of cedar back, packed with dry moss. They looked very practical and warm — with no need of washing.

The first day not much happened. I had to eat my food cold. The young fellow was coming nearer me, and seemed curious about me. My one snuff box was empty, so I rolled it towards him. When he saw it coming, he sprang up quick as a cat, and grabbed it. He went over to his sister and showed her. They found out how to open and close it — they spent a long time playing with it — then he trotted over to the old man and showed him. They had a long chatter.

Next morning, I made up my mind to leave this place — if I had to shoot my way out. I could not stay much longer, I had only enough to last me till I got back to Toba Inlet. I did not know the direction but I would go down hill and I would come out near my packsack — packed the few cans I had — swung the sack on my back, injected shells in the barrel of my rifle and started for the opening in the wall. The old man got up, held up his hands as though he would push me back.

I pointed to the opening, I wanted to go out. But he stood there pushing towards me — and said something that sounded like "Soka, soka." Again I pointed outside. He only kept pushing with his hands saying "Soka, soka." I backed up to about sixty feet. I did not want to be too close, I thought, if I had to shoot my way out. A 30-30 might not have much effect on this fellow, it might make him mad. I only had six shells so I decided to wait. There must be a better way than killing him, in order to get out of here. I went back to my campsite to figure out some other way to get out.

If I could make friends with the young fellow or the girl, they might help me. If I only could talk to them. Then I thought of a fellow who saved himself from a mad bull by blinding him with snuff in his eyes. But how will I get near enough to this fellow to put the snuff in his eyes? So I decided next time to give the young fellow my snuff box to leave a few grains of snuff in it. He might give the old man a taste of it.

But the question is, in what direction will I go, if I should get out? I must have been near twenty-five miles northeast of Toba Inlet when I was kidnapped. This fellow must have travelled at least twenty-five miles in the three hours he carried me. If he went west we would be near salt water — same thing if he went south — therefore he must have gone northeast. If I then kept going south and over two mountains, I must hit salt water someplace between Lund and Vancouver.

The following day I did not see the old lady till about 4:00 p.m. She came home with her arms full of grass and twigs of all kinds from spruce and hemlock as well as some kind of nuts that grow in the ground. I have seen lots of them on Vancouver Island. The young fellow went up the mountain to the east every day, he could climb better than a mountain goat. He picked some kind of grass with long sweet roots. He gave me some one day — they tasted very sweet. I gave him another snuff box with about a teaspoon of snuff in it. He tasted it, then went to the old man — he licked it with his tongue. They had a long chat. I made a dipper from a milk can. I made many dippers — you can use them for pots too — you cut two slits near the top of any can — then cut a limb from any small tree — cut down on the limb — down the stem of the tree — then taper the part you cut from the stem. Then cut a hole in the tapered part, slide the tapered part in the slit you made in the can, and you have a good handle on your can. I threw one over to the young fellow that was playing near my camp, he picked it up and looked at it, then he went to the old man and showed it to him. They had a long chatter. Then he came to me, pointed at the dipper then at his sister. I could see that he wanted one for her too. I had other peas and carrots, so I made one for his sister. He was standing only eight feet away from me. When I had made the dipper, I dipped it in water and drank from it, he was very pleased, almost smiled at me. Then I took a chew of snuff, smacked my lips, said that's good.

The young fellow pointed to the old man, said some- thing that sounded like "Ook." I got the idea that the old man liked snuff, and the young fellow wanted a box for the old man. I shook my head. I motioned with my hands for the old man to come to me. I do not think the young fellow understood what I meant. He went to his sister and gave her the dipper I made for her. They did not come near me again that day. I had now been here six days, but I was sure I was making progress. If only I could get the old man to come over to me, get him to eat a full box of snuff that would kill him for sure, and that way kill himself, I wouldn't be guilty of murder.

The old lady was a meek old thing. The young fellow was by this time quite friendly. The girl would not hurt anybody. Her chest was flat like a boy — no development like young ladies. I am sure if I could get the old man out of the way, I could easily have brought this girl out with me to civilization. But what good would that have been? I would have to keep her in a cage for public display. I don't think we have any right to force our way of life on other people, and I don't think they would like it. (The noise and racket in a modern city they would not like any more than I do.)

The young fellow might have been between 11–18 years old, about seven feet tall and might weigh about 300 lbs. His chest would be 50–55 inches, his waist about 36–38 inches. He had wide jaws, narrow forehead, that slanted upward round at the back about four or five inches higher than the forehead. The hair on their heads was about six inches long. The hair on the rest of their body was short and thick in places. The women's hair was a bit longer on their heads and the hair on the forehead had an upward turn like some women have — they call it bangs, among women's hair-do's. Nowadays the old lady could have been anything between 40–70 years old. She was over seven feet tall. She would be about 500–600 pounds.

She had very wide hips, and a goose-like walk. She was not built for beauty or speed. Some of those lovable brassieres and uplifts would have been a great improvement on her looks and her figure. The man's eye teeth were longer than the rest of the teeth, but not long enough to be called tusks. The old man must have been near eight feet tall. Big barrel chest and big hump on his back — powerful shoulders, his biceps on upper arm were enormous and tapered down to his elbows. His forearms were longer than common people have, but well proportioned. His hands were wide, the palm was long and broad, and hollow like a scoop. His fingers were short in proportion to the rest of his hand. His fingernails were like chisels. The only place they had no hair was inside their hands and the soles of their feet and upper part of the nose and eyelids. I never did see their ears, they were covered with hair hanging over them.

If the old man were to wear a collar it would have to be at least thirty inches. I have no idea what size shoes they would need. I was watching the young fellow's foot one day when he was sitting down. The soles of his feet seemed to be padded like a dog's foot, and the big toe was longer than the rest and very strong. In mountain climbing all he needed was footing for his big toe. They were very agile. To sit down they turned their knees out and came straight down. To rise they came straight up without help of their hands and arms. I don't think this valley was their permanent home. I think they move from place to place, as food is available in different localities. They might eat meat, but I never saw them eat meat, or do any cooking.

I think this was probably a stopover place and the plants with sweet roots on the mountain side might have been in season this time of year. They seemed to be most interested in them. The roots have a very sweet and satisfying taste. They always seem to do everything for a reason, wasting no time on anything they did not need. When they were not looking for food, the old man and the old lady were resting, but the boy and the girl were always climbing something or some other exercise. His favourite position was to take hold of his feet with his hands and balance his rump, then bounce forward. The idea seems to be to see how far he could go without his feet or hands touching the ground. Sometimes he made it twenty feet.

But what do they want with me? They must understand I cannot stay here indefinitely. I will soon be out of grub, and so far I have seen no deer or other game. I will soon have to make a break for freedom. Not that I was mistreated in any way. One consolation was that the old man was coming closer each day, and was very interested in my snuff. Watching me when I take a pinch of snuff, he seems to think it useless to only put it inside my lips. One morning after I had my breakfast both the old man and the boy came and sat down only ten feet away from me. This morning I made coffee. I had saved up all dry branches I found and I had some dry moss and I used all the labels from cans to get a fire.

I got my coffee pot boiling and it was strong coffee too, and the aroma from boiling coffee was what brought them over. I was sitting eating hard-tack with plenty of butter on, and sipping coffee. And it sure tasted good. I was smacking my lips pretending it was better than it really was. I set the can down that was about half full. I intended to warm it up later. I pulled out a full box of snuff, took a big chew. Before I had time to close the box the old man reached for it. I was afraid he would waste it, and only had two more boxes. So I held on to the box intending him to take a pinch like I had just done. Instead he grabbed the box and emptied it in his mouth. Swallowed it in one gulp. Then he licked the box inside with his tongue.

After a few minutes his eyes began to roll over in his head, he was looking straight up. I could see he was sick. Then he grabbed my coffee can that was quite cold by this time, he emptied that in his mouth, grounds and all. That did no good. He stuck his head between his legs and rolled forwards a few times away from me. Then he began to squeal like a stuck pig. I grabbed my rifle. I said to myself, "This is it. If he comes for me I will shoot him plumb between his eyes." But he started for the spring, he wanted water. I packed my sleeping bag in my packsack with the few cans I had left. The young fellow ran over to his mother. Then she began to squeal. I started for the opening in the wall — and I just made it. The old lady was right behind me. I fired one shot at the rock over her head.

I guess she had never seen a rifle fired before. She turned and ran inside the wall. I injected another shell in the barrel of my rifle and started downhill, looking back over my shoulder every so often to see if they were coming. I was in a canyon, and good travelling and I made fast time. Must have made three miles in some world record time. I came to a turn in the canyon and I had the sun on my left, that meant I was going south, and the canyon turned west. I decided to climb the ridge ahead of me. I knew I must have two mountain ridges between me and salt water and by climbing this ridge I would have a good view of this canyon, so I could see if the Sasquatch were coming after me. I had a light pack and was soon making good time up this hill. I stopped soon after to look back to where I came from, but nobody followed me. As I came over the ridge I could see Mt. Baker, then I knew I was going in the right direction.

I was hungry and tired. I opened my packsack to see what I had to eat. I decided to rest here for a while. I had a good view of the mountain side, and if the old man was coming I had the advantage because I was up and above him. To get me he would have to come up a steep hill. And that might not be so easy after stopping a few 30-30 bullets. I had made up my mind this was my last chance, and this would be a fight to the finish. I ate some hard tack and I opened my last can of corned beef. I had no butter, I forgot to pick up my butter sealer I had buried near my camp to keep it cold. I did not dare to make a fire. I rested here for two hours. It was 3:00 p.m. when I started down the mountain side. It was nice going, not too steep, and not too much underbrush.

When I got near the bottom, I shot a big blue grouse. She was sitting on a windfall, looking right at me, only a few hundred feet away. I shot her neck right off.

I made it down the creek at the bottom of this canyon. I felt I was safe now. I made a fire between two big boulders, roasted the grouse, made some coffee and opened my can of milk. My first good meal for days. I spread out my sleeping bag under a big spruce tree and went to sleep. Next morning I woke up, I was feeling terrible. My feet were sore from dirty socks. My legs were sore, my stomach was upset from that grouse that I ate the night before. I was not too sure I was going to make it up that mountain. It was a cloudy day, no sun, but after some coffee and hard tack I felt a bit better. I started up the mountain side but had no energy. I only wanted to rest. My legs were shaking. I had to rest every hundred feet. I finally made the top, but it took me six hours to get there. It was cloudy, visibility about a mile.

I knew I had to go down hill. After about two hours I got down to the heavy timber and sat down to rest. I could hear a motor running hard at times, then stop. I listened to this for a while and decided the sound was from a gas donkey. Someone was logging in the neighbourhood. I made for this sound, for if only I can get to that donkey, I will be safe. After a while I heard someone holler "Timber" and a tree go down. Now I knew I was safe. When I came up to the fellows, I guess I was a sorry sight. I hadn't had a shave since I left Toba Inlet, and no good wash for days. When I came up out of the bushes, they kept staring at me. I asked where the place was and how far to the nearest town. The men said, "You look like a wild man, where did you come from?"

I told them I was a prospector and was lost. I had not had much to eat the last few weeks. I got sick from eating a grouse last night, and I am all in. The bucker called to his partner, "Pete, come over here a minute." Pete came over and looked at me and said this man is sick. We had better help him down to the landing, put him on a logging truck and send him down to the beach. I did not like to tell them I had been kidnapped by a Sasquatch, as if I had told them they would probably have said, he is crazy too. They were very helpful and they talked to the truck driver to give him a ride down to the beach. Pete helped me up into the truck cab, and said the first aid man will fix you up at the camp. The first aid man brought me to the cook and asked, "Have you a bowl of soup for this man?" The cook came and looked me over. He asked, "When did you eat last, and where did you come from?" I told him I had been lost in the wood. I ate a grouse last night and it made me sick.

After the cook had given me a first class meal, the first aid man took me to the first aid house. I asked, "Can you get me a clean suit of underwear and a pair of socks? I would like a bath, too." He said, "Sure thing, you take a rest and I will fix all that. I'll arrange for you to go down to Schelt when the timekeeper goes down for mail." After a session in the bathroom the first aid man gave me a shave and a hair trim, and I was back to my normal self. The

Bull of the Woods told me I was welcome to stay for a day and rest up if I liked. I told him I accepted his hospitality as I was not feeling any too good yet. I told him about my prospecting but nothing about being kidnapped by a Sasquatch.

The following day I went down from this camp on Salmon Arm Branch of Sechelt Inlet. From there I got the Union Boat back to Vancouver. That was my last prospecting trip, and my only experience with what is known as Sasquatches. I know that in 1924 there were four Sasquatches living, it might be only two now. The old man and the old lady might be dead by this time.

SASQUATCH

There is an entry for *sasquatch* in *The Canadian Encyclopedia* (1988) and its contributor explains that the word *sasquatch* means "wild man" or "hairy man" in the language of the Salish Indians of British Columbia. The contributor explains that it is "the name of the mysterious, ape-like creature said to inhabit the remoter regions of the Pacific Northwest. In northern California the giant creature is called 'Big Foot.' Evidence for the existence of the sasquatch in British Columbia and Alberta is based on references in Indian legend and myth, in passages from journals kept by early travellers and on modern sightings."

Credit for the first use of the word is accorded the Indian agent and writer J.W. Burns in an article that he wrote for *Maclean's* (when the publication was known as *MacLean's Magazine*). The article was titled "Introducing B.C.'s Hairy Giants" and it appeared in the issue of April 1, 1929. Sceptics have noted that the contribution was published on April Fool's Day, yet Burns is anything but a practical joker and the article is anything but foolish. The writer took pains to establish that the sasquatch is a race of hairy mountain men and not apes or bogeymen. He went on to ask the following question, "Are the vast mountain solitudes of British Columbia, of which but very few have been so far explored, populated by a hairy race of giants — men — not ape-like men?" He answers the question in the affirmative.

For the next thirty years the mysterious creature of the remote Interior has been known as the "hairy wild man of the mountains" or the sasquatch. The term *Bigfoot* (or *Big Foot*) did not appear in print until October 5, 1958, when it was coined by Andrew Genzoli, editor of the *Humbolt Times*, who used it to describe the plaster cast of a large hominid footprint found in the mud of Bluff Creek Valley, California. The American media immediately adopted the new name.

It was one year later, in 1959, that the term *cryptozoology* was coined to refer to "the scientific study of hidden animals, i.e., of still unknown animal forms about which only testimonial and circumstantial evidence is available, or material evidence considered insufficient by some." This is the definition of the Belgian-born researcher, investigator, and theorist Bernard Heuvelmans, who was recognized as the world's leading cryptozoologist with the publication of two trend-setting books: *On the Track of Unknown Animals* (1958) and *In the Wake of the Sea-Serpents* (1968).

What follow are narrative excerpts from J.W. Burns's landmark article from *Maclean's*. It will be appreciated that the sasquatches described by Burns resemble supersized, muscle-bound, hirsute human beings who were known to the Native population, but these are quite distinct from the ape-like aspects of creatures that one associates with Genzoli's word *Bigfoot*. In other words, the Canadian creatures are humans, the American creatures animals.

Peter's Encounter with the Giant

Peter Williams lives on the Chehalis Reserve. I believe that he is a reliable as well as an intelligent Indian. He gave me the following thrilling account of his experience with these people.

"One evening in the month of May twenty years ago," he said, "I was walking along the foot of the mountain about a mile from the Chehalis reserve. I thought I heard a noise something like a grunt nearby. Looking in the direction in which it came, I was startled to see what I took at first sight to be a huge bear crouched upon a boulder twenty or thirty feet away. I raised my rifle to shoot it, but, as I did, the creature stood up and let out a piercing yell. It was a man — a giant, no less than six and one-half feet in height, and covered with hair. He was in a rage and jumped from the boulder to the ground. I fled, but not before I felt his breath upon my cheek.

"I never ran so fast before or since — through bush and undergrowth toward the Statloo, or Chehalis River, where my dugout was moored. From time to time, I looked back over my shoulder. The giant was fast overtaking me — a hundred feet separated us; another look and the distance measured less than fifty — then the Chehalis and in a moment the dugout shot across the stream to the opposite bank. The swift river, however, did not in the least daunt the giant, for he began to wade it immediately.

"I arrived home almost worn out from running and I felt sick. Taking an anxious look around the house, I was relieved to find the wife and children inside. I bolted the door and barricaded it with everything at hand. Then with my rifle ready, I stood near the door and awaited his coming."

Peter added that if he had not been so much excited he could easily have shot the giant when he began to wade the river.

"After an anxious waiting of twenty minutes," resumed the Indian, "I heard a noise approaching the trampling of a horse. I looked through a crack in the old wall. It was the giant. Darkness had not yet set in and I had a good look at him. Except that he was covered with hair and twice the bulk of the average man, there was nothing to distinguish him from the rest of us. He pushed against the wall of the old house with such force that it shook back and forth. The old cedar shook and timbers creaked and groaned so much under the strain that I was afraid it would fall down and kill us. I whispered to the old woman to take the children under the bed."

Peter pointed out what remained of the old house in which he lived at the time, explaining that the giant treated it so roughly that it had to be abandoned the following winter.

"After prowling and grunting like an animal around the house," continued Peter, "he went away. We were glad, for the children and the wife were uncomfortable under the old bedstead. Next morning I found his tracks in the mud around the house, the biggest of either man or beast I had ever seen. The tracks measured twenty-two inches in length, but narrow in proportion to their length."

The following winter while shooting wild duck on that part of the reserve Indians call the "prairie," which is on the north side of the Harrison River and about two miles from the Chehalis village, Peter once more came face to face with the same hairy giant. The Indian ran for dear life, followed by the wild man, but after pursuing him for three or four hundred yards the giant gave up the chase.

Old village Indians, who called upon Peter to hear of his second encounter, nodded their heads sagely, shrugged their shoulders, and for some reason not quite clear, seemed not to wish the story to gain further publicity.

On the afternoon of the same day another Indian by the name of Paul was chased from the creek, where he was fishing for salmon, by the same individual. Paul was in a state of terror, for unlike Peter he had no gun. A short distance from his shack the giant suddenly quit and walked into the bush. Paul, exhausted from running, fell in the snow and had to be carried home by his mother and others of the family.

"The first and second time," went on Peter, "I was all alone when I met this strange mountain creature. Then, early in the spring of the following year, another man and myself were bear hunting near the place where I first met him. On this occasion we ran into two of these giants. They were sitting on the ground. At first we thought they were old tree stumps, but when we were within fifty feet or so, they suddenly stood up and we came to an immediate stop. Both were nude. We were close enough to know that they were man and woman. The woman was the smaller of the two, but neither of them as big or fierce-looking as the gent that chased me. We ran home, but they did not follow us."

One morning, some few weeks after this, Peter and his wife were fishing in a canoe on the Harrison River, near Harrison Bay. Paddling round a neck of land they saw, on the beach within a hundred feet of them, the giant Peter had met the previous year.

"We stood for a long time looking at him," said the Indian, "but he took no notice of us — that was the last time," concluded Peter.

Peter remarked that his father and numbers of old Indians knew that wild men lived in caves in the mountains — had often seen them. He wished to make it clear that these creatures were in no wise related to the Indian. He believes there are a few of them living at present in the mountains near Agassiz.

Charley Victor's Story

Charley Victor belongs to the Skwah Reserve near Chilliwack. In his younger days he was known as one of the best hunters in the province and had many thrilling adventures in his time.

Did he know anything about the hairy ape-like men who were supposed to inhabit the distant mountains? Charley smiled, and answered that he had had a slight acquaintance with them. He had been in what he thought was one of their houses. "And that is not all," said he. "I met and spoke to one of their women, and I shot ... " But let Charley tell the story himself.

"The strange people, of whom there are but few now — rarely seen and seldom met —" said the old hunter, "are known by the name of Sasquatch, or, 'the hairy mountain men.'

"The first time I came to know about these people," continued the old man, "I did not see anybody. Three young men and myself were picking salmon berries on a rocky mountain slope some five or six miles from the old town of Yale. In our search for berries we suddenly

stumbled upon a large opening in the side of the mountain. This discovery greatly surprised all of us, for we knew
every foot of the mountain, and never knew nor heard
there was a cave in the vicinity.

"Outside the mouth of the cave there was an enormous
boulder. We peered into the cavity but couldn't see anything.

"We gathered some pitch wood, lighted it and began
to explore. But before we got very far from the entrance
of the cave, we came upon a sort of stone house or enclo-
sure; it was a crude affair. We couldn't make a thorough
examination, for our pitch wood kept going out. We left,
intending to return in a couple of days and go on exploring. Old Indians, to whom we told the story of our discovery, warned us not to venture near the cave again, as it was
surely occupied by the Sasquatch. That was the first time
I heard about the hairy men that inhabit the mountains.
We, however, disregarded the advice of the old men and
sneaked off to explore the cave, but to our great disappointment found the boulder rolled back into its mouth
and fitting so nicely that you might suppose it had been
made for that purpose."

Charley intimated that he hoped to have enough
money some day to buy sufficient dynamite to blow
open the cave of the Sasquatch and see how far it extends
through the mountain.

The Indian then took up the thread of his story and
told of his first meeting with one of these men. A number of other Indians and himself were bathing in a small
lake near Yale. He was dressing, when suddenly out from
behind a rock, only a few feet away, stepped a nude hairy
man. "Oh! he was a big, big man!" continued the old
hunter. "He looked at me for a moment, his eyes were
so kind-looking that I was about speak to him, when he
turned about and walked into the forest."

At the same place two weeks later, Charley, together
with several of his companions, saw the giant, but this time
he ran toward the mountain. This was twenty years after the
discovery of the cave.

Charley Shoots a Sasquatch Boy

"I don't know if I should tell you or not about the awful experience I had with these wicked people about fifteen years ago in the mountains near Hatzie."

The old man rubbed his knee, and said he disliked recalling that disagreeable meeting — it was a tragedy from which he had not yet fully recovered.

"I was hunting in the mountains near Hatzie," he resumed. "I had my dog with me. I came out on a plateau where there were several big cedar trees. The dog stood before one of the trees and began to growl and bark at it. On looking up to see what excited him, I noticed a large hole in the tree seven feet from the ground. The dog pawed and leaped upon the trunk, and looked at me to raise him up, which I did, and he went into the hole. The next moment a muffled cry came from the hole. I said to myself, 'The dog is tearing into a bear,' and with my rifle ready, I urged the dog to drive him out, and out came something I took for a bear. I shot and it fell with a thud to the ground. 'Murder! Oh my!' I spoke to myself in surprise and alarm, for the thing I had shot looked at me like a white boy. He was nude. He was about twelve or fourteen years of age."

In his description of the boy, Charley said that his hair was black and woolly.

"Wounded and bleeding, the poor fellow sprawled upon the ground, but when I drew close to examine the extent of his injury, he let out a wild yell, or rather a call as if he were appealing for help. From across the mountain a long way off rolled a booming voice. Near and more near came the voice and every now and again the boy would return an answer as if directing the owner of the voice. Less than a half-hour, out from the depths of the forest came the strangest and wildest creature one could possibly see.

"I raised my rifle, not to shoot, but in case I would have to defend myself. The hairy creature, for that was what it was, walked toward me without the slightest fear. The wild person was a woman. Her face was almost negro black and her long straight hair fell to her waist. In height she would be about six feet, but her chest and shoulders were well above the average in breadth."

Charley remarked that he had met several wild people in his time, but had never seen anyone half so savage in appearance as this woman. The old brave confessed he was really afraid of her.

"In my time," said the old man, "and this is no boast, I have in more than one emergency strangled bear with my hands, but I'm sure if that wild woman laid hands on me, she'd break every bone in my body.

"She cast a hasty glance at the boy. Her face took on a demoniacal expression when she saw he was bleeding. She turned upon me savagely, and in the Douglas tongue said:

'You have shot my friend.'

"I explained in the same language — for I'm part Douglas myself — that I had mistaken the boy for a bear and that I was sorry. She did not reply, but began a sort of wild frisk or dance around the boy, chanting in a loud voice for a minute or two, and, as if in answer to her, from the distant woods came the same sort of chanting troll. In her hand she carried something like a snake, about six feet in length, but thinking over the matter since, I believe it was the intestine of some animal. But whatever it was, she constantly struck the ground with it. She picked up the boy with one hairy hand, and with as much ease as if he had been a wax doll."

At this point of the story, Charley began to make pictures in the sand with his maple stick, and paused or reflected so long that he thought he had come to the end of his narrative, when he suddenly looked up, and said with a grin: "Perhaps I better tell you the rest of it, although I know you'll not believe it. There was challenge of defiance in her black eyes and dark looks," went on Charley, "as she faced and spoke to me a second time and the dreadful words she used set me shaking."

"You remember them?" I asked.

"Remember them," he repeated, "they will ring round my old ears like the echo of a thunder-storm. She pointed the snake-like thing at me and said:

'Siwash, you'll never kill another bear.'"

The old hunter's eyes moistened when he admitted that he had not shot a bear or anything else since that fatal day.

"Her words, expression, and the savage avenging glint in her dark, fiery eyes filled me with fear," confessed the Indian, "and I felt so exhausted from her unwavering gaze that I was no longer able to keep her covered with my rifle. I let it drop."

Charley had been paralyzed for the last eight years, and he is inclined to think that the words of the wild woman had something to do with it.

The old man told how his "brave dog, that never turned from any bear nor cougar," lay whimpering and shivering at his feet while the Sasquatch woman was speaking, "just," said Charley, "as if he understood the meaning of her words."

The old man said that she spoke the words "Yahoo, yahoo" frequently in a loud voice, and always received a similar reply from the mountain.

The old hunter felt sure that the woman looked somewhat like the wild man he had seen at Yale many years before, although the woman was the darker of the two. He did not think the boy belonged to the Sasquatch people, "because he was white and she called him her friend," reasoned Charley. "They must have stolen him or run across him in some other way," he added.

"Indians," said Charley, "have always known that wild men lived in the distant mountains, within sixty and one hundred miles east of Vancouver, and of course they may live in other places throughout the province, but I have never heard of it. It is my own opinion since I met that wild woman fifteen years ago that because she spoke the Douglas tongue these creatures must be related to the Indians."

The Wild Man of Agassiz

At Agassiz, near the close of September, 1927, Indian hop-pickers were having their annual picnic. A few of the younger people volunteered to pick a mess of berries on a wooded hillside, a short way from the picnic grounds. They had only started to pick, when out of the bush stepped a naked hairy giant. He was first noticed by a girl of the party, who was so badly frightened that she fell unconscious to the ground. The girl's sudden collapse was seen by an Indian named Point, of Vancouver, and as he ran to her assistance, was astonished to see a giant a few feet away, who continued to walk with an easy gait across the wooded slope in the direction of the Canadian Pacific railway tracks.

Since the foregoing paragraph was written, Mr. Point, replying to an enquiry, has kindly forwarded the following letter to the writer, in which he tells of his experience with the hairy giant:

"Dear Sir: I have your letter asking is it true or not that I saw a hairy giant-man at Agassiz last September, while picking hops there. It is true and the facts are as follows: This happened at the close of September (1927) when we were having a feast. Adaline August and myself walked to her father's orchard, which is about four miles from the hop fields. We were walking on the railroad track and within a short distance of the orchard, when the girl noticed something walking along the track coming toward us. I looked up but paid no attention to it, as I thought it was some person on his way to Agassiz. But as he came closer we noticed that his appearance was very odd, and on coming still closer we stood still and were astonished — seeing that the creature was naked and covered with hair like an animal. We were almost paralyzed from fear. I picked up two stones with which I intended to hit him if he attempted to molest us, but within fifty feet or so he stood up and looked at us.

"He was twice as big as the average man, with hands so long that they almost touched the ground. It seemed to me that the eyes were very large and the lower part of his nose was wide and spread over the greater part of his face, which gave the creature such a frightful appearance that I ran away as fast as I could. After a minute or two I looked back and saw that he resumed his journey. The girl had fled before I left, and she ran so fast that I did not overtake her until I was close to Agassiz, where we told the story of our adventure to the Indians who were still enjoying themselves. Old Indians who were present said: the wild man was no doubt a 'Sasquatch,' a tribe of hairy people whom they claim have always lived in the mountains — in tunnels and caves."

Do hairy giants inhabit the mountain solitudes of British Columbia? Many Indians, besides those quoted, are sincerely convinced that the "Sasquatch," a few of them at least, still live in the little-known interior of the province.

MAYBE THIS WAS A SASQUATCH

Not much is recalled of William Roe except that he was a well-liked hunter and trapper and also a road worker on the highway near Tête Jaune Cache, British Columbia. One day in October 1955, he climbed Mica Mountain in the Monashee range, close to the Alberta border, to explore the site of an odd deserted mine. Instead of exploring the mine, he made a much, much more interesting discovery....

Roe felt it was necessary to prepare a sworn statement that he was telling the truth. So, two years later, on August 26, 1957, before a Commissioner of Oaths in Edmonton, he attested to the truth of this account of his strange encounter.

Roe's report of this encounter is reproduced here in its entirety, as it appeared in the publication *On the Track of the Sasquatch* (1968) by John Green. Green corresponded with Roe and from him gained the following additional information about the creature:

"The nails were not like a bear's, but short and heavy like a man's finger nails are. Its eyes were not light and large but small and black like a bear's. You couldn't see any knotted corded muscles. This animal seemed almost round. It was as deep through as it was wide, and I believe if this animal should have been seven feet tall, it would have weighed close to 500 pounds.

"We have to get away from the idea of comparing it to a human being as we know them."

Ever since I was a small boy back in the forest of Michigan, I have studied the lives and habits of wild animals. Later, when I supported my family in Northern Alberta by hunting and trapping, I spent many hours just observing the wild things. They fascinated me. But the most incredible experience I ever had with a wild creature occurred near a little town called Tête Jaune Cache, British Columbia, almost eighty miles west of Jasper, Alberta.

I had been working on the highway near Tête Jaune Cache for about two years. In October 1955, I decided to climb five miles up Mica Mountain to an old deserted mine, just for something to do. I came in sight of the mine about three o'clock in the afternoon after an easy climb. I had just come out of a patch of low brush into a clearing, when I saw what I thought was a grizzly bear, in the brush on the other side. I had shot a grizzly near that spot the year before. This one was only about seventy-five yards away, but I didn't want to shoot it, for I had no way of getting it out. So I sat down on a small rock and watched, my rifle in my hands.

I could just see part of the animal's head and the top of one shoulder. A moment later it raised up and stepped out into the opening. Then I saw it was not a bear.

This, to the best of my recollection, is what the creature looked like and how it acted as it came across the clearing directly toward me. My first impression was of a huge man, about six feet tall, almost three feet wide, and probably weighing somewhere near three hundred pounds. It was covered from head to foot with dark brown silver-tipped hair. But as it came closer I saw by its breasts that it was female.

And yet, its torso was not curved like a female's. Its broad frame was straight from shoulder to hip. Its arms were much thicker than a man's arms, and longer, reaching almost to its knees. Its feet were broader proportionately than a man's, about five inches wide at the front and tapering to much thinner heels. When it walked it placed the heel of its foot down first, and I could see the grey-brown skin or hide on the soles of its feet.

It came to the edge of the bush I was hiding in, within thirty feet of me, and squatted down on its haunches. Reaching out its hands it pulled the branches of bushes toward it and stripped the leaves with its teeth. Its lips curled flexibly around the leaves as it ate. I was close enough to see that its teeth were white and even.

The shape of this creature's head somewhat resembled a Negro's. The head was higher at the back than at the front. The nose was broad and flat. The lips and chin protruded farther than its nose. But the hair that covered it, leaving bare only the arts of its face around the mouth, nose and ears, made it resemble an animal as much as a human. None of this hair, even on the back of its head, was longer than an inch, and that on its face much shorter. Its ears were shaped like a human's ears. But its eyes were small and black like a bear's. And its neck also was unhuman. Thicker and shorter than any man's I had ever seen.

As I watched this creature, I wondered if some movie company was making a film at this place and that what I saw was an actor, made up to look partly human and partly animal. But as I observed it more, I decided it would be impossible to fake such a specimen. Anyway, I learned later there was no such company near that area. Nor, in fact, did anyone live up Mica Mountain, according to the people who lived in Tête Jaune Cache.

Finally, the wild thing must have got my scent, for it looked directly at me through an opening in the brush. A look of amazement crossed its face. It looked so comical at the moment I had to grin. Still in a crouched position, it backed up three or four short steps, then straightened up to its full height and started to walk rapidly back the way it had come. For a moment it watched me over its shoulder as it went, not exactly afraid, but as though it wanted no contact with anything strange.

The thought came to me that if I shot it, I would possibly have a specimen of great interest to scientists the world over. I had heard stories about the Sasquatch, the giant hairy Indians that live in the legends of British Columbia Indians and also, many claim, are still in fact alive today. Maybe this was a Sasquatch, I told myself.

I levelled my rifle. The creature was still walking rapidly away, again turning its head to look in my direction. Although I have called the creature "it," I felt now that it was a human being and I knew I would never forgive myself if I killed it.

Just as it came to the other patch of brush it threw its head back and made a peculiar noise that seemed to be half laugh and half language, and which I can only describe as a kind of a whinny. Then it walked from the small brush into a stand of lodge-pole pine.

I stepped out into the opening and looked across a small ridge just beyond the pine to see if I could see it again. It came out on the ridge a couple of hundred yards away from me, tipped its head back again, and again emitted the only sound I had heard it make, but what this half-laugh, half-language was meant to convey, I do not know. It disappeared then, and I never saw it again.

I wanted to find out if it lived on vegetation entirely or ate meat as well, so I went down and looked for signs. I found it in five different places, and although I examined it thoroughly, could find no hair or shells or bugs or insects. So I believe it was strictly a vegetarian.

I found one place where it had slept for a couple of nights under a tree. Now, the nights were cool up the mountain, at that time of year especially, and yet it had not used a fire. I found no sign that it possessed even the simplest of tools. Nor a single companion while in this place.

Whether this creature was a Sasquatch I do not know. It will always remain a mystery to me, unless another one is found.

I hereby declare the above statement to be in every part true, to the best of my powers of observation and recollection.

EVOLUTIONARY PRECURSOR

Don Hepworth and I met on the set of *The Shirley Show*, CTV's popular daily talk show that is now a happy memory. Shirley Solomon, the vivacious host of the show, had invited the two of us to be among the guests on the program that was devoted to the intriguing subject of "Canadian Monsters." When it came my turn to speak, I discussed about various monsters, including "the Monster of Meech Lake," Brian Mulroney!

On camera, Hepworth recounted for the studio and television audiences an experience that had taken place ten years earlier and had lasted all of eleven seconds. But that was long enough for him to see two creatures which could, for lack of a better name, be called sasquatches. As much as his event intrigued me, what impressed me even more was Don Hepworth himself. He is a no-nonsense kind of person, an accomplished gentleman, and a highly credible witness. He was born and raised in the Calder Valley of West Yorkshire, England. At the age of seventeen he enlisted in the British Army. He is a former member of the *élite* Special Branch. He also served with British Military Intelligence and the Metropolitan Police of London. After a stint with the British High Commission in Canada, he served as chief inspector for the Ontario Humane Society from 1973 to 1981. He resides in Mount Albert, Ontario and trains horses and riders for dressage and eventing. He is the author of *Gorilla in the Garage ... and Other Stories* (1987).

Hepworth and I chatted following the taping of the program. I encouraged him to prepare a written account of his experience and to send it to me, along with a photocopy of the drawing that he had prepared of the creature he had seen. Both the account and the photocopy arrived on January 30, 1991.

As he explained in the covering letter, "The phenomenon I encountered may be more common in other places and parts of the world than we thought. Although I don't believe we are overrun by primitive beings, I do think they are found in North and South America, Asia,

Russia and Africa, Malaya and some of the Pacific Islands (Sumatra for instance)."

It was early evening, on Monday, April 7th, 1980, as I drove southwest on U.S. Highway 95. I was heading towards the Idaho-Oregon border and, I hoped, accommodation for the night in the small town of Weiser.

With my wife Vickey, I spent the day in a leisurely drive through Moscow, the Salmon River Valley, and into the wild Snake River uplands. We had marvelled at the steep grades of the roadways, with their "runaway safety exits." Indeed, we had actually seen one large truck run away, its failed braking system smoking profusely, before coming to a halt on a boggy stretch of flat median.

We stopped to ascertain if all was well with the driver. (My wife is a registered nurse.) He assured us he was fine, but his elderly vehicle less so. It would require towing. He had summoned help on his CB radio. We chatted with him in the interval. We inquired if he knew of a motor inn nearby. "Oh, yes, New Meadows, some ten miles away, has a motel." The heavy-duty tow truck could be seen approaching, so we said farewell to our driver friend and drove on to New Meadows.

It may be we came in from the wrong direction or didn't explore the hamlet thoroughly, but in any event the only motel we saw looked well-used; battered would perhaps be a more appropriate description. We elected to drive on to Weiser, forty-odd miles distant.

The road wound its way through the Payett National Forest, climbing steadily upwards to semi-open range land, past the little village of Council and the hamlet of Mesa. Meanwhile, the sun was setting behind the Seven Devils Mountains west of Hell's Canyon, 7,900 feet deep. Wild country! Yes, you could say that.

As I drove along, I reflected on the events of the past week. I had completed a short seminar at Washington State University Veterinary College at Pullman. The subject had been Freeze Branding and Livestock Fraud. The week before that had found me in Vancouver, on loan to the Canadian Animal Welfare Association, completing a survey of slaughter-houses in B.C. I was at that time employed as the Chief Inspector of the Ontario Humane Society and was possibly the most experienced Humane Inspector in the whole of Canada.

Having completed my employer's business, I had taken time to study at Pullman, although initially I had decided to attend the course of study there on my own time and at my own expense. However, on learning my intention to visit the Pacific Northwest on leave, my employers asked me to advance my plans a week to assist the Animal Welfare Foundation. Since it would be a saving for me, I had agreed. My wife had joined me at the weekend. All was now completed. So now we were free to spend a few days exploring the wild areas of Idaho, Oregon, and Washington.

As I drove along at a steady sixty to seventy kilometres an hour, I was observing passing terrain. My wife dozed in the passenger seat beside me. Since she leads a high-pressure working life, she usually dozes off after thirty or so minutes on the road.

I suppose I was approaching the highest point of land on that stretch of highway, somewhere in the region of two thousand feet above sea level. The surrounding mountains loomed several thousand feet higher at their respective peaks. But that is when I noticed two figures walking towards the road-edge on my left. They were black in colour. My first thought was, "Two Negro kids from a nearby ranch, not as yet visible." Then I reflected that I hadn't seen any Negro persons all day. Only Nez Perce Indians and Caucasians like myself. And not too many of the latter.

The two dark forms seemed indifferent to my oncoming car lights. I slowed to a crawl, but drove closer so as to get the best possible illumination of the pair. I was aghast. At a distance of eight to ten yards, I could see they were both covered with short black hair, something like a Labrador retriever.

The smaller of the two walked one or two steps in front of the other. It was clearly female and appeared to be clutching something to its left upper torso. The one behind was a few inches taller than the female and more bulky. I guess it would be about five-foot-seven or eight in height. I estimated it would weigh between two hundred and two hundred and thirty pounds.

As the male crossed the road, it turned to look at the car. As its neck was extremely short, it had to turn from the waist. I saw the flash of white in its right eye, the bulge of its male genitalia. I noticed the hands on the loose-swinging arms. They were thick, elongated, and powerful. Their heads were low-set. The skulls were flat, back-sloping from heavy brow ridges to a top-knot, almost like the start of the sagittal crest of a young gorilla.

They walked bent forward slightly from the hips with feet and arms moving diagonally and arms swinging loosely. To the right of the road was a grass-covered bank about six feet high. The smaller creature paused on reaching the foot of this incline, flexing its legs and body. Then it sprang easily to the top and out of sight. The larger creature put its left foot flat against the slope and simply stepped up. I don't know anyone or anything that could duplicate this instance of locomotion.

"See that?" I exclaimed to my wife. She grunted, stirred, and said, "What is it?" She had missed seeing one of the most extraordinary sights of my life. I was too excited to explain.

About half an hour later, sitting in the warmth and comfort of a motel room in Weiser, I took a sheet of paper from my briefcase and tried to sketch what I had seen....

I am convinced that what I saw were young "teenagers" of this particular species of animal. I checked height later, by having my wife, who is five foot, five inches, stand roughly the same distance from the car as the creatures. She matched the height of the small one. So my estimate of height was correct.

What exactly were they? I don't know. I can't claim

to be a scientist. But during nine years of service with the Ontario Humane Society in the position of Chief Inspector, I have physically handled many species of exotic animals. Amongst them were black, brown, cinnamon, and grizzly bears.

I may well be the only Humane Official in North America, perhaps in the whole world, who has actually seized a male mountain gorilla. Oh, yes. He was five feet, eight inches, covered with black hair, and weighed four hundred pounds. So I know that the creatures I saw weren't gorillas. Nor would a pair of chimpanzees be suitable candidates. Their walk would not coincide with the walk of this primate.

For now, the matter rests. But one day, one day, I'm going back to the Pacific Northwest, to take my time and make a better effort at securing some really tangible evidence of this creature's existence. Perhaps I will find some hair, teeth, bones. They might turn up in some winter den where old age and general debility have caught up with an older specimen. Maybe the smaller forest scavengers have left something inedible to show the passing of this rare evolutionary precursor of ourselves.

I hope so. Shooting one would be out of the question.

GLIMPSING THE BUSHMAN

John Bernard Bourne, the author of this thoughtful and moving memoir, summers in Holland Landing, Ontario, where he was born, but spends the rest of the year in Gameti, Northwest Territories.

"Glimpsing the Bushman" originally appeared in *Maclean's*, March 3, 2003. It captures the essence of the contradictory thoughts and feelings that accompany a glimpse of an order of creation that is unexpected, undocumented, unreasonable, and inhuman.

I moved to Rae Lakes, this small, isolated community in the Northwest Territories, almost three years ago. In the parlance of the local population, I was a white man from Ontario coming to live amongst the Aboriginals. In this case it was a group of Aboriginals I had never heard of before — the Dogribs. At the time, I looked at myself as an anthropologist going to observe a unique and isolated culture.

When I first arrived, I was inundated with cultural orientation. I listened to the stories of the elders and observed some of the local customs. In those early days the story that stuck out to me the most was the one about the Bushman.

According to the Dogrib people there exists a creature known as the Bushman. It is tall and hairy and lurks in the bush ready to abduct anyone travelling alone. Those who have been taken by the Bushman are usually never seen again, and if they are, they are found mute and mentally deranged. As an outsider, this story sounded a lot like a cross between B.C.'s sasquatch and eastern Canada's windigo; but for the Dogribs it is something to be taken very seriously.

The Bushman story aside, I tried to leap into life in this Aboriginal community by embracing all of the rituals of their culture. I went on the caribou hunt, I attended the community feasts and I went every time there was a drum dance. Participating in the rituals was easy enough and I took it in as one would take in the symbols of any unique community and tradition. Although I felt detached and out of place most of the time, I still found it interesting.

The difficult part was adjusting to the challenges of everyday life. Many of the people in my village can only speak their native language, so the linguistic hurdle is the first one you have to overcome. Issues of illiteracy and substance abuse would also raise its ugly head and become an obstacle in trying to live and work with the people. There were many times when I would forget that I was still in Canada because I felt like such a foreigner. I had previously lived in South Korea for a couple of years, and I found that there was less culture shock living in that far away Asian nation than there was in the far north of the country I called home.

And then there is the darkness. Long and indescribable, the lack of sunlight creeps up on you at the end of October and stays until March. The phenomenon is fascinating at first, but the novelty soon wears off and you begin counting down the days until spring and the endless daylight that it brings.

It was when the daylight was beginning to reappear that I saw the Bushman. It was the middle of March and I was driving with my wife and a friend on the winter road (the ice road that is open about six weeks every year to bring in food and supplies). We were caught in a blizzard and our visibility had deteriorated to nothing. We were stuck on the frozen, endless white of Faber Lake, halfway between Gameti and Rae-Edzo (which means in the middle of nowhere). It was just a flash. In fact, I would have thought it was an illusion brought on by the snow, but the two other people with me saw it as well.

It was tall and hairy, running on its two hind legs. The hair was long and hung from its body in an unkempt and wild manner. It was gone before we could say anything. My friend who was driving shouted, "What was that?" But we all knew. We tried to push our original instinct away and rationalize it as something else. But we couldn't.

When I told my friends and family in Ontario about the experience, they thought I was making it up. Or worse, they tried to logically explain it ("It was probably a bear coming out of hibernation"). It was only the Dogrib people who did not treat the story with any type of condescension. They nodded solemnly and understood the story for what it was.

Shortly after, things began to make more sense to me in the community. The drum dance, which I initially perceived as being primitive and unsophisticated, became full of new meaning. I learned to drum. The hunt, which I had always thought was a little atavistic and barbaric, seemed almost spiritual. I became familiar with the various uses of the caribou, including the consumption of the unborn fetus by the elders because it is soft and easy to chew when you have no teeth.

This past fall, a story began circulating around our village. The wise ones were giving everybody fair warning — they had a premonition that the Bushman would be abducting somebody this year. We were warned to be careful and not to go walking by ourselves into the bush. I was surprised by how I reacted. Three years ago I would have laughed and made fun of it. Now, I just accepted the warning and kept it at the back of my mind.

Logically, I know there is no Bushman. It makes no sense and defies any type of scientific evidence. I know it is symbolic of other things, like the loneliness and darkness one feels when living in isolation in the Far North. It is a parable to understand a unique and distinct culture in the world.

But I did see something on that winter road.

Winter is here again, and the long darkness gives you time to think. Tales of the Bushman do not really pervade your thoughts during the times of daylight. But now, it almost seems plausible.

Every night, when I put my baby daughter to bed, I lie beside her, singing songs and telling stories. When she falls asleep, I used to creep out quietly and sit with my wife in the other room. Lately, however, I find myself staying longer, well after she has fallen into a deep slumber. I feel this subconscious urge to guard and watch over her, and protect her from the Bushman.

Just in case.

6

ALIENS FROM ELSEWHERE

It may seem an odd thing to do, at first, to include in a collection of ghostly hauntings these accounts of aliens who buzz the planet in their flying saucers or unidentified flying objects, land on Earth, and make contact with earthlings, where they sometimes merge into the population as "hybrids." After all, ghosts seem inseparable from ancient castles, log cabins, and long-established residences. Spirits seem to be presences that introduce themselves into the present from the past, whereas alien beings, identified with the sky rather than the earth, seem forces from the future as well as from faraway worlds unknown to us, domains among the stars, so to speak. Yet, when you come to think of it, the appearance of a ghostly being or an alien sends shivers up and down the spines of those earthlings who are startled by its unexpected appearance. Witness the frisson of fear created by the scary stuff in science-fiction films, like the *Alien* movies, alongside the traditional scary movies about monstrous creatures, like the seemingly endless *Friday the 13th* series, and it becomes obvious that as human beings we are geared to respond to the Unknown whether it emerges from fissures in the earth or from the far reaches of outer space.

THE MAN FROM THE SKY

The appearance of "the Skyman" is a traditional tale told by Jonas George, a Chippewa who lived on the Rama Reserve, Lake Couchiching. In 1917, he related the tale to the collector Colonel G.E. Laidlaw who printed the text in the *Ontario Sessional Papers* issued by the provincial government. The present text is reprinted from my book *Voices of Rama: Traditional Ojibwa Tales from the Rama Reserve, Lake Couchiching, Ontario* (1994).

At first glance this radiant tale may seem to be a description of the tradition of an encounter with an "ancient astronaut," *à la* the Swiss theorist Erich von Däniken. Yet it should be borne in mind that when this tale was collected by Colonel G.E. Laidlaw in the mid-1910s, the skies were full of airships. There were balloons and dirigibles aplenty. Pilots barnstormed from cleared farmers' fields. There was exhibition flying in August 1909 at Scarborough Beach in the east end of Toronto where, in 1915, the Curtiss School was established to train pilots for the war effort. Eyes were focused on the skies as never before.

At the same time, not all aerial phenomena are so easily explained. Awe and wonder was elicited by the procession of meteors that streaked across the skies of North America on the evening of February 9, 1913. Today the display is known as Chant's Meteors after C.A. Chant, professor of astronomy at the University of Toronto, who published the two definitive scientific papers on the subject. Between November 1896 and April 1897, there were sightings across North America of "mystery airships," as noted by Daniel Cohen in *The Great Airship Mystery* (1981).

Perhaps the Ojibwa informant Jonas George, whose myths and legends are "vague and mysterious, and have a local colouring to suit the expressions of the times," according to Colonel Laidlaw, had in mind "ancient astronauts" and what would later be called UFOs; then again, perhaps not.

> About four hundred years ago there were five or six hundred Indians living together somewhere south of Barrie on what is now called Pine Plains. These Indians had a big time at that place.
>
> Two Indians walked up and looked around those plains. They went a little ways and saw somebody sitting on the grass. This was a man, so they went to see. The man put up his hand to keep them back, so they stopped and looked. After a while the man spoke and said, "I don't belong to this land, I dropped down from above, yesterday, so I am here now."
>
> Those two men wanted him to go with them down home. "Yes," he said, "you go home and clean the place where I will stay, and come back again, then I will go with you for a few days."
>
> The two men went home and told the people about it.

They began to clean the place where they were to keep the Skyman for two days. Then they went to get him.

Skyman was a nice-looking man, clean and shining bright. Just at sundown, he looked up, just like he was watching. He spoke sometimes in a clear voice. Just after dark he spoke. He said, "Stay for two days. I'll go up, something will come down and get me to go up."

This wise man said that he was running from where he came. There was an open place and he could not stop running, so he got in and dropped. The next day he said, "It's a nice country where we live, everything good. Tomorrow noon, I am going up, I will leave you, and you people all be good. Every Indian must be home tomorrow to see me go up."

Just after noon the next day, he looked up and said, "It's coming." Everybody looked up but could see nothing for a long time. The man that kept Skyman at his home could see good and saw something like a bright star shining away up. The other people did not see anything till it came near the ground. This thing was the nicest thing ever seen in this world. Two men got hold of it and pulled down heavy, then Skyman got in and said, "All right," and away he went up happy.

SIGHTING AND WE ARE NOT ALONE

In the pages of *Mysterious Canada*, a large-scale study of supernatural and paranormal events and experiences that have taken place across the country from the beginning of time to the present, which appeared way back in 1988, I devoted a fair amount of space to the life and work of Wilbert B. Smith, Canada's first if not foremost exponent of the reality of flying saucers. Since then not much new information has emerged about the remarkable scientist, despite the publication of two books devoted to ufology. These are Palmiro Campagna's *The UFO Files: The Canadian Connection Exposed* (1997) and Chris Rutkowski and Geoff Dittman's *The Canadian UFO Report: The Best Cases Revealed* (2007). Let me summarize what is relevant.

Wilbert B. Smith (1910–62) was the country's leading proponent of flying saucers and unidentified flying objects. He was an electrical engineer with the Department of Transport and he had a special interest in radio-frequency allocation. At the time of his death he was DOT's superintendent of radio regulations engineering. When Kenneth Arnold described his epochal flying-saucer sighting in 1947, Smith was enraptured. Three years later he was able to convince his department to allow him to establish an "observation post" at Shirleys Bay, west of Ottawa. He also assisted with the department's Project Magnet and Project Second Storey which were formed to examine sightings, and ultimately discredit them as rumours in no way a threat to national security. Astrophysicist and colleague Peter M. Millman regarded Smith as a sensible and capable scientist who in his last years became convinced not only that flying saucers were buzzing the earth but also that their occupants were in telepathic communication with earthlings (that is, Canadians like Smith).

Here is an account of one of his own sightings followed by an expression of his personal philosophy titled "We Are Not Alone." Both texts come from *The Wilbert B. Smith Archives*, a CD compiled by UFO enthusiast Grant R. Cameron of Winnipeg, as it appeared on "The Presidents UFO Website," August 5, 2007.

If what Smith saw when he looked up was "not an ordinary aircraft," what was it? Smith was a positive person and he found that his flying-saucer interests and experiences widened and deepened his sense of the meaning of life. He writes, "It would appear that we are well along the way to becoming truly civilized." Would that it were so!

Sighting

On August 16, 1960, my wife, one son and myself were watching the sky for the passage of Echo 1 which was due about 9:00 p.m. About 10 minutes before the satellite was due we noticed a light in the south traveling north.

At first we thought it was the satellite even though the course was not right. However, as it came nearly overhead we realized that it was not the satellite because it was moving much too fast, about the speed of a aircraft at 5,000 feet, and because it carried, in addition to the steady white light, an intense blue light flashing at about 10 per second.

Through 7x35 glasses, the blue light was almost blinding, like a welding arc. As the object passed overhead the blue light slowed gradually to about 1 per second, and at about 60° above the horizon to the north, it made a sharp right-angle turn and headed west, where it eventually passed out of sight in the distance.

The entire operation was soundless. We are quite familiar with the many modern aircraft as our home is in line with, and about 3 miles from a major runway, and we see many craft flying overhead at about 5000-foot altitude, and we can say definitely that this object was not an ordinary aircraft.

We Are Not Alone

Our universe is a very large place, much larger than our minds are capable of understanding. There are several billions of stars in our own Milky Way galaxy alone, and there are millions of similar galaxies scattered throughout space and within the range of our large telescopes. The universe is also incredibly old. Our earth is estimated to be several billion years old, and it is presumed that the stars are much older. Maybe the universe doesn't even have an age; that it is eternal and ever passing through the cycle of energy to matter and matter to energy. The episode of man on this planet, so far as we can determine, is a relatively and extremely small portion of the larger time that the universe has existed, and the period of recorded history is relatively even shorter.

We consider the race of Man to be native to this planet and to have evolved here from lower life forms. We look upon our present civilization with pride and realize that we have accomplished much, particularly in the last few centuries. Even in the past few decades we have made tremendous progress in certain directions. Therefore, it is only natural that we should be egotistical about our position in the Universe. But are we alone? Are there not others in the Universe who, also, have progressed? The Universe is very large and has been here a long time.

In the past few years we have taken our first faltering steps out into the vastness of space, first through the Sputniks and now through manned space flight. There is no doubt that we can do it, and if we can restrain from blowing ourselves to glory with atomic bombs, we most certainly will do it. In the light of our present technology, and not allowing for any basic new discoveries, our timetable calls for interplanetary space travel well before the year 2,000 and a good possibility of inter-stellar trips being initiated shortly thereafter.

Our space travel plans include exploration, exploitation, and colonization, of other planets, so far as this might be possible, and there is no doubt that this thinking will be extended to the planets attached to other stars as soon as we can arrange to get there. Mankind has always been an adventurous creature, exploring, conquering, colonizing, and exploiting, and there is little reason to think that his future actions will be much different from those in his past.

Our large telescopes indicate low order perturbations in the positions of several of the inner stars, such as should be accounted for by the presence of large planets, and if there are large ones there will probably be smaller ones also. In fact, it is generally agreed now that the planets attached to the stars are more probably the rule than the exception, and that we will eventually find the heavens filled with all sorts of primary and secondary bodies.

When we consider the extent, the age, and the opportunity of the Universe, and the fact that we do have intelligent life here on this planet, it is only reasonable to speculate that somewhere else in the vastness of space and the eternity of time, other intelligent life could have blossomed forth. Since we have such rapid progress towards space travel in such a short time, a differential of only a few hundred or at the most a few thousand years between the development on some other planet and ours could easily have resulted in a race capable of doing right now what we plan to do in the future. Furthermore, it is quite possible that such a race may have reached this critical point eons ago, and to them space travel is as commonplace as the wheeled vehicle is to us.

Now, if this should be the case, and this alien race were anything like us, they would probably set forth to explore and colonize as rapidly as their means would permit. It is rather obvious that, even with the speeds of travel available to us, it would be much quicker to colonize the Universe than to wait for Nature to evolve separate races in each and every favorable environment. In fact, intelligent races might even set about accelerating environmental conditions to their liking, seeding and stocking planets with appropriate life forms, and watching over them as they develop.

The foregoing is not just idle speculation, since we have a great deal of evidence that something like this is actually happening. The Darwinian theory of evolution shows certain relationships between the various forms, which inhabit this planet, but there is very little evidence to indicate that they all evolved here. Maybe some of them did, but a more reasonable explanation is that they were brought here when the planet was in a suitable condition to receive them. Recent spectroscopic observations of the reflected light from Mars show the presence of vegetation, which synthesizes sugar, thus making it closely related to much terrestrial vegetation. Radio telescopes are picking up all sorts of radio noises from the sky, many of which are so systematic as to preclude natural origin. Peculiar markings, light flashes, and cloud and dust formations have been seen on Mars and our moon. And, most significant of all, the craft of these alien beings have been seen near, and on, this earth!

Legends and history abound in stories of visits to this earth by beings from the sky; beings which came in strange crafts capable of the most extraordinary performance, and who themselves possessed greats powers, or had at their command strange forces, and much beyond the understanding of the simple folk who witnessed those things. There is much evidence that this has gone on all through the ages, and is going on right now. With exceptional new gathering and disseminating means at our disposal, very little happens in the world which is not reported, and, if it is of sufficient interest, gets wide publicity. During the last ten years or more there has been much publicity about "Flying Saucers" and thousands of reports have been made of sightings of these strange objects in our skies. But this is not an exclusively recent phenomena; only publicity is recent. Ever since we have had newspapers there have been similar reports, but the absence of news services until recent times usually confirmed the details to a few local papers, and searches of old newspapers files confirm that flying saucers are old stuff.

The tense international situation in recent years has made everyone jittery, and anything in the skies that could not be established as known and friendly, was regarded with suspicion.

Consequently, procedures, projects, and publicity combined to make the whole subject of flying saucers appear quite out of perspective. Instead of recognizing them for what they probably were, they became a ward of the Military, and since the Military are charged only with the defense of a country, their interests waned when they established the fact that the saucers apparently were not hostile. But in order to arrive at this conclusion they collected much data, classified it, and buried it so effectively that no one else could get at it, and those who might have been able to sort the matter out found themselves deprived of the basic data and had to contend themselves with the bit which escaped the clutches of the Military. However, on the basis of this material some rather startling conclusions have been reached.

Thousands of people have seen lights and apparently solid objects in the sky that behaved as no light or object normally seen in the sky ought to behave. Thousands have seen these objects under circumstances, which enabled them to say definitely what they were not, even though they were not able to say what they were. Reliable photographs and movies have been taken, and bits of "hardware" collected which cannot be explained away without challenging the integrity of a great many cases, and there is quite a bit of evidence of physical contact with these strange craft.

In several instances reliable people have reported seeing the beings who ride about on these crafts, and they say they look just like us. There are quite a number of reported contacts between these people from "elsewhere" and people of this earth, and although this latter point may be hard to prove it is equally hard to disprove, and the results of these contacts are remarkably consistent and enlightening. At the present time there are quite a number of books, magazines, and bulletins devoted to the study of flying saucers, and anyone who wishes to establish for himself the validity of these things will find no dearth of material.

At this point we may summarize the position somewhat as follows. There is virtually no doubt that alien craft are visiting this earth, and that the beings who operate them are very much like us, probably our distant relatives. Considering the age and extent of the Universe, it is reasonable that space travel, exploration, and colonization, may be quite commonplace among races of mankind more advanced than we are. Information obtained through alleged "contacts" confirms the general nature of the picture as presented herewith, together with quite a bit of interesting side-lighting on the technology, customs, way-of-life, and philosophy of these people from "elsewhere." It would appear that we are well along the way to becoming truly civilized, and if we can refrain from committing racial suicide and learn to respect the dignity, divinity and brotherhood of man, we can expect eventually to be welcomed into the great cosmic fraternity of

advanced races that inhabit the regions beyond the limits
of this little planet.

THE FALCON LAKE ENCOUNTER

The Falcon Lake Encounter is the name given to the sighting of two
unidentified flying objects at Manitoba's Falcon Lake Provincial Park on
May 20, 1967. More information is available on this incident than on any
other UFO sighting reported in Canada. There is also about the episode
the suggestion of lingering menace.

The sole observer of the two UFOs was Stephen Michalak, a fifty-
one-year-old Polish-born Canadian. Later that year Michalak offered the
following account of himself: "In 1949 I came to Canada, and some years
later, settled in Winnipeg, Manitoba. I live with my wife, two sons and
a daughter in a modest home. I have a steady income from my job as a
mechanic at the Inland Cement Company. Two of my children attend the
University of Manitoba. We live a happy, satisfied life of average Canadians, fully enjoying all the blessings this country is offering us."

It was Michalak's passion for amateur prospecting that took him that
weekend to Falcon Lake. What he saw that Saturday is open to interpretation. What is laudable and sincere is his desire to tell others what he
witnessed and what he felt about the experience. His account appeared
in a privately printed, forty-page booklet titled *My Encounter with the
UFO* (1967). Michalak wrote about his experiences in Polish; the manu-
script was translated and printed for private distribution by his friend
Paul Pihichyn.

There were unexpected consequences from the sighting. The encounter left Michalak, as he wrote, "desperately in need of medical attention."
He suffered nausea and first-degree burns on his chest. He was admitted
to the Misericordia Hospital in Winnipeg, his first hospital treatment for
recurring, sighting-related health problems. This did not deter him from
leading investigators to the exact spot where the sighting had taken place.
"Landing traces" were found there. Earth analysis showed "some radiation but not enough to be dangerous."

The case was widely reported by the media. There were investigations
by the RCMP and the RCAF, by representatives of the National Research

Council and the Atomic Energy Commission, as well as by the Aerial Phenomena Research Organization. A question about the government's silence connected with the case was asked in the House of Commons by Ed Schreyer, then a Member of Parliament, not yet the Governor General. The Minister of National Defence replied, "It is not the intention of the Department of National Defence to make public the report of the alleged sighting."

The full story of the Falcon Lake Encounter will not be known until Chris Rutkowski, the Winnipeg-based UFO researcher and investigator, publishes his study of the episode. Even then there will be aspects of the story that will never be explained to everybody's satisfaction.

> It was 5:30 a.m. when I left the motel and started out on my geological trek. I took with me a hammer, a map, a compass, paper and pencil and a little food to see me through the day, — wearing a light jacket against the morning chill.
>
> The day was bright, sunny — not a cloud in the sky. It seemed like just another ordinary day, but events which were to take place within the next six hours were to change my entire life more than anyone could ever imagine. I will never forget May 20, 1967.
>
> Crossing the Trans-Canada Highway from the motel on the south side, I made my way into the bush and the pine forest on the north side. After travelling some distance I got out my map and compass and orientated myself.
>
> By 9 o'clock I had found an area that particularly fascinated me because of the rock formation near a bog along a stream flowing in the southward direction. I was searching for some specimens that I had found on my earlier expedition.
>
> My approach had startled a flock of geese, but before long they became accustomed to my presence, quieted down and went about their business.
>
> At 11:00 o'clock I began to feel the effects of the breakfast I did not eat that morning. I sat down and took out the lunch I had brought with me. Following a simple meal of smoked sausage, cheese and bread, an apple and two oranges washed down with a couple of cups of coffee, and after a short rest, I returned to the quartz vein I was

examining. It was 12:15, the sun was high in the sky and a few clouds were gathering in the west.

While chopping at quartz I was startled by the most uncanny cackle of the geese that were still in the area. Something had obviously frightened them far more than my presence earlier in the morning when they gave out with a mild protest.

Then I saw it. Two cigar-shaped objects with humps on them about half-way down from the sky. They appeared to be descending and glowing with an intense scarlet glare. As these "objects" came closer to the earth they became more oval-shaped.

They came down at the same speed keeping a constant distance between them, appearing to be as one inseparable unit, yet each one completely separate from the other.

Suddenly the farthest of the two objects — farthest from my point of vision — stopped dead in the air while its companion slipped down closer and closer to the ground and landed squarely on the flat top of a rock about 159 feet away from me.

The "object" that had remained in the air hovered approximately fifteen feet above me for about three minutes, then lifted up skyward again.

As it ascended its colour began to change from bright red to an orange shade, then to a grey tone. Finally, when it was just about to disappear behind the gathering clouds, it again turned bright orange.

The "craft," if I may be allowed to call it a craft, had appeared and disappeared in such a short time that it was impossible to estimate the length of the time it remained visible. My astonishment at and fear of [the] unusual sight that I had just witnessed dulled my senses and made me lose all realization of time.

I cannot describe or estimate the speed of the ascent because I have seen nothing in the world that moved so swiftly, noiselessly, without a sound.

Then my attention was drawn back to the craft that had landed on the rock. It too was changing in colour, turning from red to grey-red to light grey and then to the colour of hot stainless steel, with a golden glow around it.

I realized that I was still kneeling on the rock with my small pick hammer in my hand. I was still wearing goggles which I used to protect my eyes from the rock chips.

After recovering my composure and regaining my senses to some degree I began watching the craft intently, ready to record in my mind everything that happened.

I noticed an opening near the top of the craft and a brilliant purple light pouring out of [the] aperture. The light was so intense that it hurt my eyes when I looked at it directly. Gripped with fear and excitement, I was unable to move from the rock. I decided to wait and watch.

Soon I became aware of wafts of warm air that seemed to come out in waves from the craft, accompanied by [the] pungent smell of sulphur. I heard a soft murmur, like the whirl of a tiny electric motor running very fast. I also heard a hissing sound as if the air had been sucked into the interior of the craft.

It was now that I wanted a camera more than anything else, but, of course, there is no need for one on a geological expedition. Then I remembered the paper and pencil that I had brought with me. I made a sketch of what I saw.

By now some of the initial fear had left me and I managed to gather enough courage to get closer to the craft and to investigate. I fully expected someone to get out at any moment and survey the landing site.

Because I had never seen anything like this before, I thought it may have been an American space project of some sort. I checked for the markings of the United States Air Force on the hull of the craft, but found nothing. I was most interested in the flood of lights that poured out of the upper reaches of the craft. The light, distinctly purple, also cast out various other shades. In spite of the bright midday sun in the sky, the light cast a purple hue on the ground and eclipsed the sunlight in the immediate area.

I was forced to continually turn my eyes from the light which made red dots to appear before my eyes every time

I looked away.

I approached the object closer, coming to within sixty feet of the glowing mass of material. Then I heard voices. They sounded like humans, although somewhat muffled by the sounds of the motor and the rush of air that was continuously coming out from somewhere inside. I was able to make out two distinct voices, one with a higher pitch than the other.

This latest discovery added to my excitement and I was sure that the craft was of an earthly origin. I came even closer and beckoned to those inside:

"Okey, Yankee boys, having trouble? Come on out and we'll see what we can do about it."

There was no answer and no sign from within. I had prepared myself for some response and was taken aback when none came. I was at a loss, perplexed. I didn't know what to do next.

But then, more to encourage myself than anything else, I addressed the voices in Russian, asking them if they spoke Russian. No answer. I tried again in German, Italian, French and Ukrainian. Still no answer.

Then I spoke again in English and walked closer to the craft.

By now I found myself directly in front of it and decided to take a look inside. However, standing within the beam of light was too much for my eyes to bear. I was forced to turn away. Then, placing green lenses over my goggles, I stuck my head inside the opening.

The inside was a maze of lights. Direct beams running in horizontal and diagonal paths and a series of flashing lights, it seemed to me, were working in a random fashion, with no particular order or sequence.

Again I stepped back and awaited some reaction from the craft. As I did this I took note of the thickness of the walls of the craft. They were about twenty inches thick at the cross-section.

Then came the first sign of motion since the craft touched down.

Two panels slid over the opening and a third piece dropped over them from above. This completely closed off the opening in the side of the craft.

Then I noticed a small screen pattern on the side of the craft. It seemed to be some sort of ventilation system. The screen openings appeared to be about 3/16 of an inch in diameter.

I approached the craft once again and touched its side. It was hot to the touch. It appeared to be made of a stainless steel-like substance. There were no signs of welding or joints to be seen anywhere. The outer surface was highly polished and looked like coloured glass with light reflecting off it. It formed a spectrum with a silver background as the sunlight hit the sides.

I noticed that I had burned my glove I was wearing at the time, when I touched the side of the craft.

These most recent events occurred in less time than it takes to describe them.

All of a sudden the craft tilted slightly leftward. I turned and felt a scorching pain around my chest; my shirt and my undershirt were afire. A sharp beam of heat had shot from the craft.

I tore off my shirt and undershirt and threw them to the ground. My chest was severely burned.

When I looked back at the ship I felt a sudden rush of air around me. The craft was rising above the treetops. It began to change colour and shape, following much the same pattern as its sister ship when it had returned to the sky. Soon the craft had disappeared, gone without a trace.

CONTACT

Oscar Magocsi (1928–2002) was born in Hungary, came to Canada in 1957, and worked as an electronics technician. As a youngster he was interested in flying saucers (the term in the 1940s for what came to be called in the 1950s unidentified flying objects or UFOs). He claimed that he was contacted by alien beings in 1975, when he was taken aboard one of their flying saucers after it landed in Muskoka, Ontario. Then he was taken for a visit to the aliens' home planet "Argona" in the "Omm-Onn system, a member of the Psychean Federation Worlds." Magocsi's account of his travels appeared in his breathlessly written, 146-page memoir titled *My Space Odyssey in UFOs* (Toronto: Quest Group Publications, 1st ed., 1979; 2nd ed., 1980; 3rd ed., 1985). "Contact," the title of chapter three of that publication, is reproduced here.

What effect did the experience have on the contactee? A note attached to the publication explains it was all to the good: "Due to my experiences with the aliens and their effect on me, I became more spiritually oriented and psychically more aware, strongly life-affirming and as a result — better balanced, happier and luckier."

A discussion of Magocsi's contribution to contactee literature appears in my book *UFOs over Canada* (1991).

That summer of '75 I arranged to take two weeks' vacation starting with the end of July. I planned to spend most of that time at my Muskoka lot, in the hope of some revealing UFO encounters. Therefore, right after a friend's wedding, later Sunday afternoon, July 27, I was on my way driving towards Huntsville.

I arrived at my lot by sunset, when most cottagers for the weekend only had already left for Toronto. There was enough time left before darkness to unload my camping gear and to gather enough firewood for the night vigil. I was quite determined to be up all night till the "wee" hours of the morning. Then I could still sleep until noon, and go to some nearby beach if the day became too hot. It was good to be back in nature after a long winter and with half summer already gone. Somehow I never got around to come up here since last Fall, except for one short and uneventful trip in May.

It was already dark and the stars were shining brightly, when I finally lit up my campfire. The night was dry, but not too warm. I had to wear my long-sleeved sweater as I sat on the stool by the fire, at the pile of wood, stacked within arm's reach. Mentally, I recalled the whole chain of strange events that led me up to this point, making me trust a stranger's word for some UFO experiences about to come. I still wondered about it. I hadn't seen Quentin, or Steve, since. I hadn't had any new dramatic encounters either, not even dreams or hunches. The last few months this whole UFO topic had faded into insignificance, as if it was unreal somehow.

Nevertheless, I still enjoyed sitting out by the fire, the same way I had done it many times before. Around 02:30 hours though, I felt tiredness creeping up more and more on me. Since there were no UFOs about, not even a hint of a sensation, I decided to turn in for the night.

Next day, after sunset I walked up to the ridge to my "eerie" twilight magic spot. Barely five minutes after I got there, a wave of excitement hit me all of a sudden. I just knew positively that I would have a UFO experience that night!

I am at total loss to explain how this strong conviction came to me. One second I still felt pleasantly blank, the next second I knew "they" were on their way to transit into this dimension, and some time that night I'd be visited by a UFO. There wasn't even a pulsating glow in my mind, yet I knew they were coming and that there were only a few more hours left before actual show-up time.

I walked back slowly to my lot and lit the campfire. The vigil part ended, it was just a matter of some waiting.

It was shortly after midnight, when I began to feel that the UFO already was very close. Few minutes later, I thought I saw a faint pulsating orange glow briefly. Whether I saw it in the sky or in my mind, I wasn't sure. But I was sure that this signal was directed at me, as a form of making me aware. A strange notion struck me: if this was their first deliberate signal, then how did I know hours earlier about their coming? Was it possible that I became more sensitive, no more passive telepathic subject any longer, but an activated mind "sniffing" way ahead? Or had my "eerie" twilight spot something to do with it, like triggering my knowing somehow? It was all very intriguing, especially with this new angle added to it.

I stopped feeding the campfire, and backed away from it to probe the vast expanse of the sky overhead. Soon enough I perceived the approach pattern of some blinking orange light on a zig-zag course. It didn't behave like an aircraft, besides there was no engine noise. It kept disappearing, but kept converging on my hill. For a full two minutes it was blinked out of sight; then it got magically materialized out of nowhere, less than a few hundred feet away from me and close to the tree-top level, glowing orange, a disc-like shape.

I got on top of my observation deck, well away from the slowly dying campfire. From this vantage point I had an unobstructed view across the valley. Also, I was fully engulfed by the darkness, which made me invisible to any observer farther than a few feet away. Then I raised both my arms and waved towards the motionless distant glowing of the disc.

The glow blinked twice, as if to acknowledge my signal of being aware of it. Although I half expected the blinking response, it still surprised me that the UFO could see me in the darkness from that distance.

Now the UFO started to pulsate in a slow manner, and I sensed that I was being probed to the core of my mind. This went on for about ten minutes, while the cycling pulsations nearly put me into a pleasant drowsiness of some hypnotic trance. To check if my conscious will was still functioning, I climbed down to the smouldering campfire momentarily, then climbed back on the platform. Well, it worked, but I don't know if it really proved anything.

Soon after my exercise, the disc stopped its pulsations, changed its colour into steady greenish and started moving in my general direction. Rising up higher, it swam slowly past me almost overhead with a faint purring sound, heading somewhere beyond the ridge towards "no man's land"! My eyes kept following it, trying to make out its detail. But all I could see was just a hazy glow of an oval shape that became circular when passing overhead. I couldn't detect its source of illumination: the whole disc was just one big blob of yellow-green luminous glow. Only the centre core of its underbelly, like a hole in a doughnut, pulsated with some blue light.

After the disc went out of sight beyond the ridge, I stayed another few minutes in the dark, in case it came back again. But somehow I knew it wouldn't, for it just must have landed in "no man's land," possibly waiting there for my move. Even though I became aware of a gentle pull in that direction as if telepathically induced, I was quite ready to go and see on my own, too.

I put the dying fire out, grabbed my flashlight and took off on foot for the logging road that led into "no man's land." The night was quiet, the few cottages this side of the turn-off were dark. No one seemed to be up. Other than me, perhaps no one even saw the UFO.

It took me a good minute's walk to reach the general area where the UFO might have landed. At a familiar turn of the logging road, I came up on a big clearing, close to my "power" magic spot.

And there it was! What a dramatic moment! Not more than about sixty feet from me, a real flying saucer was moving in the air just a few feet above the ground. I guessed its size for roughly thirty feet in diameter and ten feet in "thickness." It was bathed in a diffused, greenish-blush and soft-glowing luminosity that was radiating from its entire surface rather than coming from points of light. There were two porthole-like, dark oval spots resembling a pair of eyes. On its top there was a bubble-dome-like turret, on its underside there were some ball-like bulges that suggested a landing gear.

There I stood frozen in my tracks, by a clump of trees in the darkness. I was very much excited, but also very nervous with unknown fears. What a magnificently thrilling sight I beheld! This was the living proof of intelligent, extraterrestrial life. For I had no doubt that this flying saucer was from outer space. Possibly even from another dimension, as Quentin claimed, but certainly not of earthly origin.

At this moment, as if trying to prove the point, the saucer started to fade away without moving its position. Then "presto!" and it was gone with a peculiar sighing sound as if the air moved into its place. I shone my flashlight through the spot, but found nothing. The saucer went totally invisible....

Then, within a few moments, a very faint glow came from the same empty space, solidifying slowly back into the flying saucer again. It was very dramatic! After all, it was quite true about fading out of this dimension and fading back again.

This time the saucer gently lowered itself to the ground, into a real landed position. Then it stood there motionless, soundless — just like I stood farther away, frozen and breathless. No one came out of the saucer; it just sat there patiently, as if waiting for me. Somehow I knew that it actually was waiting for me, but I just could not make myself move. I was simply terrified to go near, that's all. Recalling a few speculations I read of sinister alien motives, my mind was working overtime. I guessed if the saucer wanted to, it could have attempted to draw me hypnotically towards itself. But there were no such indications; it seemed my move had to be made entirely of my own free will. For without my moving, there was no other way to learn more. It was as simple as that.

Finally, I decided to take the risk: with cold sweat breaking out all over me, I walked up to the saucer!

After some hesitation, I poked at its hull with my rubberized flashlight. The hull felt more like fiberglass than metal, yet emanating some heat like the hood of a car in hot summer. Next, I pressed my cigarette paper back to the pull for a second to guess at the surface temperature. My pack just got warmer, but did not get burned; yet I didn't feel like touching it with my bare hand.

I found the saucer's actual size to be about thirty-five feet in diameter, ten feet high from top to bottom, plus another two feet perhaps for the upper dome. I guessed its true colour for light grey. I walked around it a few times, looking for some door, or some indication of an opening. There were none. Equally set apart around the circumference, there were three oval-shaped portholes. I couldn't peek through them, for they were above my eye-level, as the saucer squatted on three ball-like protrusions that raised its bottom about three feet from the rocky ground. There would be no marks left by the landing gear on that rock; so far I didn't detect any burn marks, either. Yet there was the definite smell of ozone, as if some high-voltage corona discharge was being produced by the saucer's hull. Maybe it was wise not to touch.

By now I was considerably calmer, although still on the jittery side. Satisfied with my close-up survey of the exterior, I backed away thirty feet or so, wondering about further developments — if any.

Less than a minute, there came the new development, and a rather dramatic one at that! A three-foot-long horizontal crack appeared and widened into a closed-mouth-like slot, well under the line of portholes and between two of them. Then the slot started to widen vertically, as if a gigantic mouth was opening up. Finally, it formed itself into a man-sized open doorway, while a short walk-up ramp got lowered from it to the ground. Soft yellow light spilled out from the interior, invitingly.

I nearly took to my feet in a momentary panic. Then I took a grip on myself, and decided facing the aliens to come out of the saucer. Or else I'd never see one. This venture wasn't exactly for faint hearts, I thought. So I braced myself for my first alien encounter, and waited....

Finally, I realized that there would be no aliens coming out. There were no telepathic proddings or hints coming, either. The saucer was just sitting there, blankly. Were the occupants incapacitated? Or were they some immobile life-form? Somebody had to be there inside; otherwise who did all the signalling, the telepathic probing earlier, not mentioning the piloting of the craft itself, the fade-out, the door-opening? I felt rather confused.

I edged up near the doorway for a peek inside. But

this didn't give me a clue, for a partition behind the door prevented my looking into the interior. Obviously, I had to take another risk, and a tremendous risk this time: Since no one was coming out, I should go in and see for myself. Yet, only heaven knew what manner of alien monsters could be waiting in there! Besides, what about radiation, toxic air, or other harmful substances? Well, there was only one way to find it out....

I summoned up my courage, and with a deep breath, I went up the ramp. Then I stepped onto the inner platform within the doorway, finding that there was no partition at all. It was only a curtain of yellow light, which had created the illusion of a wall from the ground at that angle. The square of the platform was illuminated, but the interior was shrouded in darkness. I tried my flashlight — it didn't work.

I hesitated for a moment, then took a couple of steps into the unlit area. My weight on the floor must have activated built-in sensors, for some blue-green glow sprang up all around me, illuminating most of the interior.

At first glance everything looked incomprehensibly alien. But I had no time to look more, for a subtle noise behind made me turn around fast. It was the doorway closing down. Sudden panic seized me, it was a wonder I didn't have a heart attack! Good heavens, I was captive. The closing crack sealed itself into one seamless wall, making me stare paralyzed at it.

Then I tried to calm down. Perhaps this was just another automatic piece of function — once the occupant was inside, the door just got shut by itself. I stepped back on the platform and waited. Nothing. Meanwhile, I noticed one shaft of white light shooting down vertically from the ceiling, slightly to the left. I had a hunch this could be the door-opening activator. So I stuck my insulated rubber flashlight through the beam, and it did the trick — the door started to open up.

Just to make sure, I stepped out momentarily into the night, then back again, making the door close. I repeated the procedure to put my mind at ease. Then I started to look for some manual back-up system for the door-opener, in case something went wrong with the light. I never trusted a fully automatic gadget, and felt safer if I found some manual override. Slightly to the right where the door should have been, I found a fist-sized indentation in the wall. I poked my flashlight into it, which made the door open again. It had to be similar to a spring-loaded activator, which was the next best thing to a manual crank. I just wondered who or what made the door open in the first place, while I still had been outside, for I had the feeling that the saucer was devoid of any creatures.

Feeling much calmer now, I turned back to the interior for a close examination. My eyes were first attracted to a three-foot diameter globe hanging at eye-level. It was suspended in the saucer's centre, inside a transparent vertical tubing that connected the domed porthole in the ceiling to an identically shaped porthole in the floor.

The synthetic material of the floor was pearl-greyish and honeycomb patterned, as if a conglomeration of battery cells. Three curved sections of benches that resembled soap-stone Eskimo sculptures were ringing the vertical tube. There was a circular railing of bone-like material that girdled the tube, convenient to grip if one was seated on the bench. Very handy in a turbulent flight for humanoids, or even for any creature with arm-like appendages. At least the saucer's interior walls were designed for transporting some manner of creatures. This seemed a reassuring thought, even if there was nobody home momentarily. Or maybe the occupants were just out on some business, liable to return soon; though somehow this line of thought did not make sense in view of the events that got me inside here.

All this left only one possibility — the saucer was a robot vehicle, an unmanned probe, or rather "manned" by some kind of a programmed computer — or remote-controlled by some unseen intelligence, perhaps through a built-in computerized system. I found nothing, though, that would even vaguely resemble some computer system.

Unless if it was built in a completely alien manner, inconceivable to my earthly framework of possible technologies. There was no electronic gear or other gadgetry in sight. Therefore, it had to be a vastly different type of technology behind all this — if it was technology at all!

That thought gave me a shiver, as I was scrutinizing the "suspended" huge ball in a vertical plastic tubing. Inside the globe itself, there were myriads of flickering lights in swirling patches of multi-coloured mists, as if some artist's conception to show a three-dimensional visual model of a supermind's functioning. Of which I had no doubt it was — either a living intelligence, or the strangest computer.

I tried to poke my flashlight through the plastic tubing-like shaft of light. I met a soft, but firm resistance of a flexible shield, which would yield only so far. Apparently, it was a force-field that acted like a protective tubing. And inside it, perhaps the shaft of light was what held the globe suspended at my eye level. I noticed some very faint vertical "*flow lines*," or traces of energy flow taking place within the shaft. As I turned away, my left hand accidentally bumped into the force-field. Much to my relief, there was no adverse effect, just a touch of silky but firm resistance.

I looked up on the gently domed ceiling — there was a wall-to-wall spiral that centered on the tubing like a gigantic heating element, made of shiny gold-looking material. Another energy device, I guessed, perhaps in conjunction with the vertical tube that centred on the globe. Or vice-versa. Who knows?

I turned my attention to the circular wall. The blank space for the sealed doorway was flanked on both sides by huge, semi-curved bulges from floor to ceiling — perhaps some storage tanks or cabinets that I could see no doors for. Each bulge was followed by one porthole, with the third porthole being on the opposite wall section. They were equally spaced apart, slightly oval and about three feet in diameter. Then there were two towering "instrument" slabs jutting out from blank wall spaces — one to my left and one to my right, each flanked by a gigantic 6 x 4 foot screen with some sofa under them. And that brought my survey around the wall to its completion....

Matter of fact, that completed my first preliminary survey of the whole interior, for the time being. All of a sudden, I felt the exhaustion, caused by my nervous tension weighing down on me. I wondered if I should get into a much more detailed scrutiny, or just ...

At that moment, the ceiling spiral glowed up to an intense orange hue, and started to pulsate slowly. Panic seized me again — I felt a drastic change to come in the "*status quo*," which I wasn't sure I wanted to face. Now, the shaft had energized, too — there was a strong downward flow of some currents taking place in it.

Maybe I'd better beat it, I thought, before this darned thing takes off with me, or brainwashes me, or disintegrates me, or who knows what. Fear won over the spirit of adventure — in a hurry, I activated the door opener — and it worked! I scrambled down the ramp, retreating to the edge of the clearing like a frightened deer. Or rather like a dumb bunny — but I just couldn't help my reaction. I thought it would be wildly humorous, if a hidden onlooker now took me for a scary alien out to eat him, or something.

But there was nothing out there (or ran away and dropped dead since), except the darkness and the bush. I stopped and turned around.

The saucer glowed orange pulsatingly for a short while. Then it retracted the ramp and sealed its door. Now it changed its light into a steady greenish-blue, and started to lift off the ground. It rose slowly up and up, to a few hundred feet. I wondered what could be its driving force. Some kind of anti-gravity device? For I did not detect flame exhaust, compressed air, not even sound except a faint whirring noise.

Now the saucer blinked twice and flew away rapidly into a rising arc, soon going out of sight.

It seemed that my encounter was over. Yet, I stood

there for quite a while in the completely dark woods, filled with awe and wonder, relief and regret, pride over my bold adventure, but shame over my cowardly running away. And also, I felt terribly tired, drained.

Time to turn in, I thought. So I slowly walked back through the woods to my lot...

LETTER FROM SIMSON

I find I have been corresponding with Simson for close to forty years. It is one of those on-again, off-again correspondences that waxes and wanes, not on a monthly basis like the cycles of the moon, but on the basis of decades. Simson Najovits is his full name. He was born in Montreal, graduated from Concordia University, served with the RCAF, and (his French being excellent) decided he preferred life in the various *arrondissements* of Paris to life in Montreal. (Life in Toronto was never an option for Simson.) Until his recent retirement from the French radio network, where he headed a broadcast department, he had less time to correspond (in those days it was by snail mail) than he does these days (by email). We exchange long admiring letters followed by short, snappy letters in a *rubato* fashion that neither of us fully understands. So far he is known to the world of letters for his splendidly researched, two-volume history of Ancient Egypt. Some of his short fiction has appeared in literary magazines, but as yet no mainstream publishing house has been willing to accept for publication of his series of long novels (written in the evocative manner of the two novels *Place d'Armes* and *Civic Square* by writer Scott Symons). Simson and I have met face to face five times in four decades: twice in Toronto and three times in Paris (where we dined splendidly at La Coupole). Yet it was not until last year that I learned that Simson had once seen an unidentified flying object in the days when they were still called flying saucers. This fact came out in correspondence, and I can do no better than to print his letter to me about the experience. Here it is.

From: Simson Najovits
To: John Robert Colombo
Subject: UFOs and all that jazz
Date: Wednesday, November 19, 2008 4:42 AM

Dear John,

Well, I can see that you take UFOs very seriously. Really, it's not such a big deal, it's not peanuts, but it's not such a big deal ... and that doesn't imply that there are no mysterious aspects to it. Here's my story:

I was an RCAF Flying Officer during my university years (the recruiters didn't realize that I was already a Beatnik in the making) and as such was cleared to secret and one summer I was posted to a very strategic airbase and there for a time my job was managing the office which handled confidential and secret files.

It wasn't much of a job, all I had to do was to examine the credentials of the officers who requested to consult certain files, but not only was it boring, business was slow, not many customers ... so to pass the time of day I began dipping into the confidential files, mainly those of my pals, and one of these files, of a macho pilot friend of mine, was a jewel, the Air Force had hesitated to authorize him for pilot training because he had only one ball. A medical and psychological committee was convened and they put him through a battery of tests and produced a 50-page report whose final paragraph, written in medical jargon, came down to this: This man with one ball is as good as a man with two balls.

Well, I'm sure that you'll understand that after coming across such edifying reading I wasn't going to stop my dipping into the files and so I dipped into the secret files and there I found photographs of what today would be called flying saucers with RCAF markings. The conclusion is that as early as the late '50s, the RCAF, and so, of course, all the major air forces in the world, were secretly experimenting with flying saucers, probably because of certain of their supposed aerodynamic characteristics. And so what I conclude is that some, and maybe many, UFO sightings were Air Force flying saucers.

About the ghost business — it's not that I begrudge

the so-called quidam their ghost experiences, it's rather
that I think literary and mythological and fairy-tale ghosts
are better. It's like John Dewey used to say — there's no
metaphysics and there's no absolute truth but there are
least imperfect answers ... and literary ghosts are the least
imperfect ghosts. For me, the so-called serious people who
take ghosts and monsters and giants and demons seriously
and weave immense serious theories about them are the
worst offenders.

The title of my new book is Modern ... and while all
my books contain ghosts and demons and angels and elves
and what-not, this one — so far anyway — doesn't.

Regards,
Simson

JRC's Postscript: The reader will be aware of the fact that in our letters we were discussing the status or the service supplied by ghosts or by
ghostly experiences. Into this correspondence Simson dropped his "time-
bomb" about the flying saucer. My reply was "Now I am worried." His
reply to that was, "I'm not pulling your leg!" I continued:

We disagree on whether or not "ghosts are good for
you" because you want to reserve the goodness for literary and folkloristic ghost stories and I want to extend it
to the experiences that people report which may or may
not be caused by ghosts or spirits. The people I meet
and quote do not necessarily "believe in" spirits but
they have had *anomalous experiences* and they do not
doubt that these are a reality for them. You would deny
them their own experiences, it seems. This reminds me
of the aphorism, "You can tell a woman what to think,
but not what to feel."

I spent about five years meeting with UFO types and
all of them — with one exception, a brilliant man and a
psychiatrist — came to bad ends, in the sense that they
lost their perspectives on the field and began to make
semi-oracular pronouncements (as Colin Wilson does in

his book *Alien Dawn* which does him no credit). They began to confuse their researches with their belief-systems. So your final sentence sends chills up and down my spine: "Believe me, I do know, but it's classified as Top Secret information...." I assume you are pulling my leg. Do you have a title for your work of philosophy?

"GEORGE ADAMSKI-LAND"

You meet the darndest people when you collect stories of strange and incredible sights and experiences. The morning of February 19, 2008, was enlivened with the appearance of the following email on my monitor. I am reproducing it here as I received it except for setting it forth in paragraphs for ease of reading. The correspondent, James Pfleeger, sounds like a lively guy! I'll allow him to tell his story in his own inimitable way, which he would do anyway!

Dear Mr. Colombo,

I happened upon your book last year while browsing at Chapters. I'm 62, retired, and have a lot of "unpublished nostalgia" about UFOs. After reflecting for some time, I decided to take the leap of faith and contact you.

Much like you, I'm not a one-horse cowboy. As a young Catholic schoolboy, I was fascinated by the paranormal stories accounted in the lives of the saints. I was living in a quiet New England town called East Aurora, N.Y., until the age of nine. Something odd happened to me then that defies explanation. I was nearly seven, and my little friend, Chuckie, and I were allowed to run to the fair in the park, unescorted. In 1953 kids were safe running around a small town.

When we arrived at the park, I was so excited that I screamed back at Chuckie behind me to "hurry up and catch up with me, darn it!" Then, suddenly, everything seemed like a dream, then oblivion. It was about noon when we entered the park. About six and a half hours later, I found myself standing alone, unharmed, at the other end of the park, across the street on the sidewalk, struggling mentally to remember my name and where I lived. After a terrifying moment or two, my memory returned, and I happily set out for home and the spanking of my life from my hysterical mother.

Chuckie's father was the Chief of Police, and a frantic city-wide manhunt had failed to locate me. My exasperated parents listened to me say over and over, "but I don't know where I've been." Chuckie had explained to everyone, "He was right in front of me, and then he disappeared." Somebody explain it to me.

I spent high school studying earnestly to be a Franciscan priest at St. Anthony's Seminary in Santa Barbara, CA. I spent my days pouring over theology texts in the library and much of my night praying. The spiritual life was all that mattered to me. However, my overall scholastic achievement did not permit me to remain into my senior year. Sadly, I returned to home to Vista, CA (home of The George Adamski Foundation) where I had witnessed my first multiple UFO sighting.

It happened in January 1958, I believe. I witnessed a huge, orange "mother ship" and five or six scout ships in the sky over northern San Diego County. It was visible for miles around, and thousands of people reported seeing it, according to the *San Diego Union* newspaper the next day. Two interceptor jets were scrambled to shoot the UFOs out of the sky, and I watched as the "visitors" streaked across the entire expanse of blue sky faster than the eye could follow. My parents were tolerant of me, then.

I didn't know then that I was living in "George Adamski-Land." My father reported to me two weeks later that a certain George Williams had been lecturing nearby in Fallsbrook, CA, on the subject of UFOs, and that when he and his audience had left the meeting hall, they were treated to a 35-minute UFO display in the night sky, and that this had happened in three other instances as he lectured from Seattle on down the coast. Weren't the 1950s great? Wide open!

I was drafted by the United States Marine Corps on Feb. 16, 1966, while living in Yuma, AZ. My dad was a Gunnery Sergeant, like his father, all USMC, and I had just applied to San Luis Rey to return to the religious life as a Franciscan Brother to teach English and Creative Writing. Selective Service claimed me first. Dad was relieved, but I had other ideas. I finished "basic training" #8 over all, then six months in the brig.

I'm now a Canadian / American dual citizen, and a Conscientious Objector.

Montreal is "home" now for the past 42 years. No sooner had I arrived, than I read *A Search for the Truth* by Ruth Montgomery. Then began the odyssey. I joined the First Spiritualist Church of Montreal, witnessed trance mediumship, and trained with a group of gifted college students who formed a "teaching circle." I'm still in touch with chief medium, Paul Biscop, who has just formed the Two Worlds Church in Nanaimo, BC. Theosophy, TM, Rosicrucianism, and Free Masonry are just a few of the major traditions that I joined in the ensuing years, juggling marriage and three sons in the mix.

During the Paul Biscop teaching circle, it happened that one Saturday in October I awoke with an absolute certainty out of thin air that I MUST fast all day. As anti-intuitive as that is for a 22-year-old, I persevered throughout my evening shift at the hotel Chateau Champlain, where I was a theatre tech with the "Caf'Conc" show. When I finished my shift at 1:00 a.m., I was "drawn" somehow to climb Mount Royal in the dark to a point just to the south and below the Chalet.

The radio tower to the left was shrouded in a mist with no stars in evidence in that area above it. I felt "paranoid" but calm, wondering what madness led me to such outrageous behaviour. I kept wondering if there was something I could not see above the radio tower, as I imagined that I was being viewed, like an x-ray exam. Losing patience with myself, I started back down the mountain path in disgust.

Halfway down the path, I decided to challenge my own madness with greater madness. I turned to the dark mass above the radio tower, believing by now that it might well be a UFO blocking my view of the stars, and I mentally commanded that "they" dim the lights of the radio tower to prove me right. Instantly, the lights dimmed! I knew that UFOs can "mess with electricity" and communicate telepathically, but were my eyes simply deceiving me? So, I commanded that the lights be dimmed even more. Again, the lights were nearly dimmed out completely. I ran!

I hurried to another area of the mountain to view the shadowy object from a different perspective. Yes, there was a definite outline in the night sky. Just then, as I ascended on another path, I panicked as I sensed a strong invisible presence in front of me. I pleaded silently, "Don't you dare appear in front of me! I'm not ready for this!" When I opened my eyes, I noticed that the first light of morning was beginning to show itself. I could see the great dome of St. Joseph's Oratory just across the crest of the mountain. I wondered what the rest of my college friends would think of my self-induced psychosis. I decided to go check in with Paul right then and there.

When I arrived at Paul's apartment, to my astonishment, the entire teaching circle group was assembled, patiently finishing a night-long vigil awaiting my return. All of us, apparently, had awakened Saturday morning with the same absolute conviction of fasting all day. All of us had felt the inexplicable urge to climb the mountain late that same evening. All of us had encountered one or more invisible presences! In the case of my more "gifted" counterparts, they had all called Paul and gone up the mountain in a group. I was still at work, and no one suspected I'd be doing the same thing later.

The group had encountered tall beings surrounded by a brilliant, turquoise auric light. The beings communicated warnings of global tribulation, if mankind were not to drastically change direction from the "cold war" footing. They had all broken down and cried from what they were "told." I related my x-ray exam and the shadow UFO that I had commanded to prove itself by dimming the lights, plus my dread of something about to material-ize before my eyes. I was asked what time I thought it was when about to be confronted by "something." I answered, "About 3:00 a.m."

"So, where have you been exactly for the three past hours? It's only a short walk down the mountain to where we are, and it's almost 6:00 a.m. What happened to you?"

I was speechless. It had been pitch dark when I had asked the "thing" not to appear. Suddenly, the sun was on the horizon. Oh, my God. They're right. This was 1969, and Budd Hopkins had not published *Missing Time*. Years later I would read his book and wonder about my experi-ence on Mount Royal that October night.

As some weeks passed, Paul began having strange dreams of aliens disguised in police uniforms, often giving him chase. Although it was a bit disturbing and implau-sible, Paul had kept it to himself. That December, a friend of mine picked me up after work on a Saturday. Again, it was quite late after leaving the restaurant, and we drove up over Mount Royal to enjoy the lights from the look-out. No sooner had we passed Beaver Lake (Lac au Cas-tor), then we saw what I can only describe as a "house on fire" just over the top of the mountain. Orange and white licks of flame seemed to be rotating in a circular motion, stretching dramatically skyward. What was happening?

We raced to the lookout, knowing that there was a staircase of stone which we could run up and try to get a look at whatever this fiery spectacle could be. By the time we had reached the mountain top, nothing remained of any fiery light. What we did encounter was a force-field energy that robbed us of our breath and made us feel like we were running in slow motion. We thought we heard a faint high-pitched sound.

Then my friend looked up suddenly and saw a blue flame streak through the sky toward Quebec City. Then all was silent. We looked around and realized that the famous landmark cross on the mountain was in darkness, as well as all other lighting.

Best of all, just a little further ahead near a security booth, was an abandoned police car with the door still ajar — the only eery source of light on the mountain. Later, Paul would relate his dream of aliens wearing police uniforms. We were all very uneasy.

I would travel to Vancouver during the next two years, meeting Herb Clark, who was President and UFO savant of the UFO society there, and Dr. Bill Allen, a notable physics professor and UFO researcher in Calgary, as well as Bill Knight, who had a UFO call-in radio show, and H. David Linnen, ex-Anglican priest, healer and UFO lecturer on the place of UFOs in the Bible. This was followed by a memorable trip to Giant Rock Airport in the California desert and a two-hour interview with the great George Van Tassel. I saw several UFOs during those two years. Little did I know then that this phenomenon would be passed on to my children, my three sons, right in the middle of Lachine, Qc on two occasions: Dec. 1986 and Dec. 1988. After I told a few too many people about it all, I received a sobering call from the US photographic expert on the Golf Breeze UFO Study, Bob Ouechsler, who phoned me at my home at 10:30 one night to inquire if I was sure that the UFO my sons had seen in 1988 was identical to the UFOs in Gulf Breeze. I said it was exactly that kind.

Bob thanked me and suggested that I "keep these matters more to myself if I didn't want to end up on the cover of the *National Enquirer*." I said I appreciated his advice.

Getting late. I didn't mean to talk your ear off. I just know that your interests are very much mine, and I thank you for all that you have accomplished for your readers.

Good-night,
James Pfleeger

IT SUDDENLY GLOWED VERY BRIGHTLY

Hi John —

You've been in contact with my old friend James Pfleeger and his story occurred in Montreal. This story, though not so amazing perhaps, also occurred in Montreal. If you can use it, you may use my name and title, since I have told the story to many of my cultural anthropology classes at Douglas College, New Westminster, B.C., as well as in classes at Simon Fraser University and U.N.B. Let's call it:

A High Rise Encounter

The autumn of 1970 in Montreal, Que., was a tension-filled one, what with the FLQ and the October Crisis and the implementation of the War Measures Act by Prime Minister P.E. Trudeau as a means to calm people down after the *separatistes'* bombings and the threats.

Early in November of 1970 my two room-mates and another friend and I had been meditating in the living-room of our shared apartment on the tenth floor of a high rise near McGill University, where I was a part-time student and one of my roomies was a full-time graduate student. He was American; I, a Maritimer anglophone, and our other room-mate was a francophone. So we represented a good section of North American society!

After meditating, I went behind the couch to pull the drapery cord and open the window to the city nightscape and lights; my mates had gone to the back of the suite to put on some coffee, etc., and our friend was sitting facing the living-room window. As I was drawing the drapes, he suddenly jumped up and yelled, "My God! Look at that!" I stopped pulling the drapes and stuck my face to the window. At the same time my mates came running out as Val had gotten so excited. We all saw the same thing: about a foot away from the window pane there was a round saucer-to-saucer shaped object, about 18'24" in diameter, with lights around the central portion. The object appeared metallic and was smooth-surfaced except for the lighted area. We stood there watching it agape for easily 30 seconds. Then it suddenly moved down at an angle toward the ground at great speed. As it approached the other side of the street, it suddenly glowed very brightly, the flash lighting up the side of the high rise across the street. It changed direction just as fast, to speed up into the night sky and disappear from out of sight. Absolutely nothing we knew of could move and change direction in the air like that object. We had no idea how long the object had been there, nor what its purpose was. We felt at the time it was an extraterrestrial object of some kind, possibly a reconnaissance device of some sort. We did not see any "little green men" of any sort. In retrospect, I suppose it could have been a CIA device of some sort, since it was known that the CIA had a strong presence in Quebec at that time. If so, it was advanced beyond our wildest imagination. All four of us believed it came from elsewhere rather than being human made. End.

Reading James's account of our experiences a year or so earlier, I am stunned by the details that I had repressed from my memory over the years. No wonder. Even earlier than October 1969, one of that group and I had an experience on Mt. Royal, as well, that was extremely strange but did not obviously involve UFOs or ETs, though we believed so at the time. Even with my spiritual involvements and beliefs, I am still a social scientist and generally sceptical of paraphenomena and much that is accepted as ufology. Nonetheless, I also know that the nature of *anomalous experience* is such that a great deal is repressed from memory as a means of dealing with something that does not fit our ordinary paradigms of reality. And I strongly suspect there's a lot more going on than meets the eye. Back in the 60's I was a member of the Aerial Phenomena Research Organization (APRO), and interviewed a number of people in Saint John, N.B., and

Halifax, N.S., for their UFO encounter stories. Wish I had kept the records!

Cheers,
Dr. Paul Biscop

WHY SEVEN?

I received this *memorate* (to press into service the term I use for a first-person account of an incredible experience that is described as true) from Benoît Racine. When I saw the French name, I thought, "Here is a correspondent from Quebec." But when I read his email, dated August 19, 2007, I learned that he is writing from my own city, Toronto. Here is what M. Racine wrote:

> Dear Mr. Colombo,
>
> I am reading your excellent *True Canadian UFO Stories* and I am happy to share the enclosed memorate with you.
>
> Benoît A. Racine

What he has sent is a classic account of "aerial phenomena" not easily summarized or interpreted. M. Racine unexpectedly — and inexplicably — enjoyed a rich visual experience against the starry sky. Who could have prepared for it? A number of points could be made. The "sighting" occurred more than forty years ago yet it remains vivid in memory and continues to pique the intelligence. There is the irresistible and perhaps automatic temptation to relate the lights to something concrete, lights in the sky = years of one's life, and see them in terms of one's own future. A very rich sighting, a very complex experience.

> My UFO story happened on the third Saturday of August 1968. I was 18 years old and very lonely in St-Lambert (Québec), a South Shore suburb of Montreal. I had just completed my classical course at a Jesuit college while

living at home with my parents and deciding on a possible university education.

On weekend nights I would regularly walk to the band of grass that lay between the riverside highway and the St. Lawrence Seaway canal facing the Expo grounds. In 1968, Expo 67 was over but the lights and activity went on as Man and His World, a permanent exhibition. I went there to watch ships from all over the world parade down the canal.

That Saturday night, around 10:00 p.m., I lay on the grass, my feet to the west (i.e., the canal, the Expo grounds and Montreal) and my head to the east (i.e., the highway and St-Lambert) looking straight up at the sky which was clear but hazy.

I concentrated on a flat triangle of stars right above me which I believe is known as the Summer Triangle and which was practically the only celestial feature to shine through the surrounding light pollution, when right in the middle of it I saw a tiny concentration of light materialize and start moving slowly but regularly to the south (i.e., my left as I laid flat on the grass). On closer inspection, this light appeared to be composed of three distinct smaller lights which seemed to be circling one another or regularly changing places with each other according to a complex but regular pattern. This was difficult to see as, despite my glasses, details were hard to ascertain, one look at a highway streetlight behind me being enough to blind me to the phenomenon for several seconds.

Despite the haziness, I managed to watch this little threesome of playful lights as they followed a very straight line to the southern horizon where they disappeared. Less than five minutes had elapsed during that whole process.

Immediately after that, a second group of three lights of the same description materialized right in the middle of the Summer Triangle immediately above my head, with exactly the same aspect, behaviour, speed, and direction and it too disappeared in the southern horizon. This whole ballet was repeated exactly six times in 25 minutes until a seventh group, exactly like the ones preceding it, appeared and repeated the same movement, except for the fact that, having reached the southern horizon, it decided to change its course and started to hug the horizon in a northward direction, floating over Montreal and the Expo grounds and in turn disappearing to the north (my right-hand side). No more lights appeared after that.

Being very conscious of having seen what can only be termed 21 "UFOs," I remember being somewhat disappointed that they had only been of the "luminous points in the sky" variety and extremely tiny at that — to the point where they could have been mistaken for mosquitoes — but I was disquieted just the same. I had to wonder if this very unspectacular display had been put on uniquely for my benefit. After all, why did it apparently start only after I had lain down my head on the grass to look up at the stars, and why did it start directly over my head in the only part of the sky still visible through the light pollution? There were many more questions. What had I seen exactly? Was it some kind of extraterrestrial cargo entry into our atmosphere following established routes that coincidentally followed our St. Lawrence Seaway, a phenomenon I wasn't meant to see? And if so, why the parallelism to the St. Lawrence Seaway itself? Had I come to watch ships pass in the night and been rewarded instead by spaceships in the stratosphere? Was it, perhaps, a heretofore unknown or unnoticed natural phenomenon of light activity having to do with the magnetic envelope surrounding the Earth? Or was it a symbolic representation of some kind? I remember associating the fact that I had seen three times six UFOs going south with my age of 18 years at the time and wondering if the change of direction of the last group of three lights indicated a positive change in my immediate future. Whatever may be said about that, I know this is how I managed to remember the details of this incident for so many years afterward.

FASCINATED BY THE SKIES

Deep River is the home of Leslie Moore who has contributed this detailed account of her multiple sightings of unidentified flying objects. Her Ontario home is the residential community close to Chalk River which has played an important part in the development of Canada's atomic and nuclear reactors. Here, dated March 2, 2008, Ms. Moore identifies herself and tells her story, in two parts.

Introduction

I have always been fascinated by the skies. My father took us to the hilltop to see the first Sputnik back in the '50s. Dad taught me the location and names of constellations and planets. I used to sleep out in the back yard and watch our many different satellites. Some rolled and reflected the sunlight so that they appeared to turn on and off. I once watched one that must have bumped a piece of junk, then veered slightly off course, then corrected itself.

I was raised in the scientific town of Deep River by a botanist Mom who worked at the Petawawa Forestry Experimental Station and a biochemist Dad who worked at the Chalk River Nuclear Laboratories. I taught school a few years and worked eighteen years as a grocery cashier. At fifty-nine years of age, I still spend lots of time in the outdoors and enjoy watching nature.

In the mid-sixties, I saw out my bedroom a large black and red meteor falling like a huge coal (no shootings star trail or white glow) straight downward up past MacDonald Street making it appear to fall beyond the highway in toward Algonquin Park. As it fell one smaller piece broke off.

Betty Cooper, my friend of some twenty-nine years, told me on Friday, Dec. 1, 1989, that she saw, over the Deep River golf course about 6:30 p.m., what appeared to be a "plane" of too many red lights being chased by a normally lit small plane! She also noted that the sky was twilight and clear. She joked about Santa's sleigh and Christmas lights on a plane.

Jan. 18, 2008, on our way back from Pembroke the night my Mother died, Betty also saw a strange bright white light above the trees as we turned onto Wylie Rd. I missed it. She said it looked like a huge street light. There are no roads or houses in that direction, just woods.

According to the records of Environment Canada, Nov. 29, 1989, was clear with about -13' c 100kPa, 7 kph southeast breeze and ~ 70% humidity at Ottawa. I did note that at North Bay, about an hour and a half drive north-west of Deep River on Hwy 17, it had actually started to snow a little. This agrees with my memory that it was a clear early twilight cold sky in late November.

Story

Dear Mr. Colombo:

Wednesday, November 19, 1989, I drove alone to Chalk River Laboratories to pick up someone at 7:30 p.m. About 7:40 p.m., as we entered the straight stretch of Hwy 17 west of Chalk River along Black Duck Lake, we both spied what at first looked like a plane (a military *Hercules*) flying very slow above and beyond the homes and trees on the north side of the highway.

Since we live about 15 km west of the CFB Petawawa (military base) and Deep River is 7 km west of Chalk River, I am quite used to hearing and seeing these planes as they fly low, and I am used to their size and speed. They are quite loud even when you are inside the house.

Odd thing was the number of red lights outlining the shape. I remarked repeatedly that it had only red lights and too many. I was trying to find a light for each wing, perhaps a light up on the tail and one at the nose (front end) but instead I saw about 6 or 8 lights outlining a shape — red only!

I assumed it was banking a turn over King Road North, so as we turned the corner of the highway I was surprised to see a fairly large mess of scattered red lights above the big pine tree. It was like a string of Christmas lights had been tossed in the air — no logical shape.

I checked traffic and took a long look out my left window. Over the swamp across the road I saw a house-sized triangle, pointing down, with big round red lights in each of the points and about two softer red ones along the edges in between.

It just didn't fit the lighting of a heavy slightly tiled plane because of the shape, and there were no lights typical of an aircraft for the wings.

I quickly parked the Volvo half way between the corner and the next house and stepped out leaving the engine running and the door shut to silence the buzzer.

What a sight it was. I did not hear any sound coming from it. I knew it wasn't a plane because a tilted plane, banking a turn, would have to show both wings and make noise.

Assuming that it was of that shape — a triangle — banking on its side, it looked flatter as it drifted over Black Duck Lake, a marshy wetland at best, heading towards the railway tracks and the woods southwest of Chalk River. This would be similar to watching a plane finish banking a left turn.

The thrill at this point was that a band of whitish blue light came out from the centre bottom, spread a little without fading with distance and pointed straight down to the lake. It appeared like a search light (or how about sucking in marsh gasses for fuel!).

We left with the car still working fine and chatted our way home.

7

EMAIL ENCOUNTERS

In many ways this section is the heart and soul of this book. It is also the longest section in terms of numbers of contributions, though the contributions are inclined to be shorter than those in the other sections of the book. Here is how they come to me.

I call these contributions *memorates*, for they consist of first-person accounts of odd and unusual experiences. I occasionally appear on radio and television, and listeners and viewers often contact me care of the station or program or through my publisher. Or a reader will find one of my books in a bookstore or a public library, read the accounts included in it, and then decide to contact me. Some people send queries: "Would you be interested in reading my account of the sighting of a ghost?" Obviously I answer yes. Other people have been retelling their stories for months or years, even decades, and find a sense of relief in sharing their accounts with sympathetic souls. So they send their stories along. I think I have a "green thumb" where accounts of mysterious events and experiences are concerned, as they "come to me."

When I have an account on paper or on screen, I examine it and then begin to conduct a correspondence with the contributor. I often ask for more details. Can you recall the precise date the event occurred? If not the day, then the month or the season? What were your feelings about the experience at the time? What are your feelings about it now? Were there any other witnesses? Do you have a "history" of such experiences? (The answer to that question is often a history of years.) From time to time I ask a witness to fill out a statement that says, in effect, nothing relevant has been ignored, nothing irrelevant has been included, and it constitutes the full truth of the event or experience. From time to time a contributor will decide to withdraw the account and not want it to be published, at least at this time. I honour that request, of course, but the greater number of accounts are published without a hitch. When the collection of these appears, usually a year or so later, I often receive letters of thanks. I believe publishing these accounts is a way of dealing with the issues behind them. In addition to being a way to bring about "closure," it is a way to "fix" the details in print in a way that is not possible in oral communication, and that is to the good.

Contributors frequently ask me, "What do you yourself think?" I try not to judge the content of the communications as they quite often seen laden with a feeling of emotion or a sense of wonder. Like a defence attorney I test the stories from time to time, but I do not question the veracity of the contributors whose works appear in print. (The stories of a number of contributors I quietly shelve.) As for my own explanations for the phenomena being recorded, I have no ready answers, though I often see patterns unfolding that permit me to discern in the accounts their common characteristics as well as their wealth of individual differences.

Here, then, are my email encounters.

I AM NOT SUPERNATURALLY GIFTED

True Canadian Haunting Stories is the reprint title of a compilation of "told-as-true" ghost stories originally published as *More True Canadian Ghost Stories* which I compiled for Key Porter Books. The publisher supplies copies of these books to the Indigo-Classics chain of bookstores, and book browsers, eager to read Canadian rather than American or British mysteries, gobble them up! On August 22, 2008, I received the following email from a buyer of that book. He wishes to be known as "Ace." (I have his full name and address on file but, at his request, am safeguarding the biographical details.) I am pleased to have Ace's account of the peculiar experiences that occurred to him at early stages in his life. I have come to hold that such experiences are commoner than is generally believed. In other words, many readers of the present book may have had experiences similar to Ace's. I usually copy-edit accounts like this one, for ease of reading, but as Ace is writing "off the cuff," so to speak, I think the flavour of the original email text is retained by reproducing it as it arrived. I am omitting only an explanatory passage in which "Ace" requests anonymity.

Ace is probably right when he makes the following declaration: "I am not supernaturally gifted." But what can account for these experiences?

Hello Mr. Colombo,

I have just finished reading your book *True Canadian Haunting Stories* and liked it very much. I have had a few paranormal experiences.

I was very young at the time perhaps 1 or 2 and did not remember this but my mother has told me about it. First off before i was born my great great uncle passed away. so when i was asleep i would wake up in the middle of the night and see a figure standing over me i would describe him to my mother as tall and bald which fit the description of my uncle this happened several times until he left cause i got scared a lot from seeing it so my uncle must have left me alone. when i was about 10 i was more open minded about spirits and i still can see to this day a hazy figure not like when I was a child but a hazy figure watching over me at night.

Another story is that I had moved to Kingston Ontario and had been living there for 10 years when I decided to take one of the 2 haunted walks of Kingston offered. i choose the Fort Henry one. Fort Henry was built by the British army in the early 1800's to defend the St. Lawrence seaway from American attacks. Well anyway i was there and was in the lower fort when i thought i felt someone right behind me i turned around and there was nothing. I continued on my way and until we got to the bottom of Fort Henry Hill felt someone watching me.

My last story is not paranormal but rather an alien sighting I was lying in bed and staring out the window when I saw a large light move across the sky. It turned and turned and turned in maneuvers no modern day jet could perform. it would loop the loop twist turn stop in flight hover and whip around again in the other direction. This lasted for about 20 seconds then the U.F.O. flew across my window at a fast speed. I ran to the window and saw another glimpse of it flitting away across the sky.

These are my stories. while i am not supernaturally gifted seeing many ghost i have had theses experiences you may edit this anyway you want just as long as you keep the facts.

WE COULDN'T STOP THINKING ABOUT THEM

Television programs which are devoted to accounts of hauntings and other psychical encounters often give their viewers the mistaken impression that ghosts and phantoms, demons and spectres, infest a given site and pose a genuine threat to the living. The truth of the matter is that most reports of psychical events and experiences stress their low-key nature: the spirits are gentle, they reassure rather than harass the living, and the effects are minor.

That has certainly been the experience of Julianna Brzezicki, who sent me this email on June 30, 2008. The experiences that she reports are subdued and benign and open to a variety of interpretations. The events occurred not too long ago in Glenburnie, Ontario.

> Dear Mr. Colombo, I'm not sure if you need any stories right now but I'll share mine with you.
>
> It was July of 2007. My Mom, Grandmother, my 15-year-old sister, F., and I were going to put new flowers by my Grandfather's grave.
>
> Whenever we go to the cemetery my sister and I wander off and look for really old graves. After a bit of searching we found a family, the Brownes. The parents had lost both of their children, James (1873–1884) and Thomas Joseph (1877–1883), at young ages. Their mother died a few years later. We left some flowers on each of their graves because no one visits them anymore.
>
> For the rest of the day we couldn't stop thinking about them.
>
> That night, after I said good-night to everyone, I climbed into bed. I had only had been lying there a couple

of minutes when I heard the sound of a plastic bucket dropping. I thought my Mom was doing something out in the kitchen and had dropped a bucket. A few moments later the sound came again. It sounded much closer this time. Every time it got closer, and one time it was right outside my bedroom door. The sounds went on for an hour or so.

In the morning I asked Mom if she had been doing anything in the kitchen. She said no. She had been getting my Grandma ready for bed (she lives with us).

Francesca said she had heard the noises too, and when she woke up a picture had flashed in her mind of a boy wearing a black velvet suit sitting on a gravestone with a very sad expression on his face.

I think the boys wanted to say "thank you" for the flowers, by making those noises. Little boys can be very loud.

The bucket sounds never happened again, but every once in a while there is an odd experience. I often notice a weird smell. It is most often like the scent of flowers.

I often wonder if those little boys followed us home. Maybe they want to see what life has been like since they passed on 125 years before.

I sent Julianna Brzezicki a printout of the account that she sent me. I always do this regularly for contributors, to allow them to reconsider what they have written and also to review what slight editorial changes that I make in their texts to ensure fluency of reading and consistency in style.

It was not until June 30, 2008 that I had a reply. Usually people with paranormal experiences to recall and record respond right away; not in this case. Here is what Julianna wrote on that day:

Sorry, I haven't checked my email in a very long time. The copy of the story you tried to send me didn't come. You'll have to try again. The happening takes place Kingston, Ontario, more specifically outside Glenburnie. In case you're interested, we have a few other things that have happened:

Hello Mr. Colombo! I am Francesca Brzezicki, Julianna (the sender)'s sister, and a very avid reader of ghost stories, particularly your books. I've been reading them since I was pretty young!

Anyway, I had always wanted to have some sort of paranormal experience (despite the fact that I was sure I would spend most of it quietly wetting myself in terror!). So I finally got to.... I was about eight, and sleeping over at my grandma's house, which I often did. At some point during the night my grandma got up to go to the bathroom, and I woke up in the process. She told me to go back to sleep, so I rolled over, facing the wall. There is about a foot-wide space from the bed to the wall.

Suddenly, I heard the distinctive noise of a cat scratching the carpet beside the bed. I know that sound because I have a cat. Now, at this point I was very groggy still, and I immediately thought, "My cat is so annoying!" And then I realized I wasn't at home! I was really scared, too scared to look down. The scratching noises lasted about 15 seconds, and stopped when my grandma came back in the room.

Later on when I told my family, my mom (ever the skeptic) laughed and told me it was just the pipes. But I am positive they were cat noises. My grandma doesn't have a cat now, but used to. It died about 12 years before the incident took place, before I was born, and was well-loved. The experience doesn't sound very scary, but believe me, it was.

Another experience happened on the second floor of my grandma's house. At the end of this past April I was trying on a skirt I had just bought in the same room the cat incident had happened in. No one else was upstairs, but my grandma, sister, and mother were downstairs. I had been up there a while, and when I was about ready to change back, I heard very, very soft footsteps come up the stairs and walk into one of the rooms across the one I was in. I automatically assumed it was my mom or sister and quickly changed. However, I heard no other noises coming from the other room. I got a little nervous and stepped out, but all the other rooms were dark. And as I flew down the stairs (really scared again), I heard a door bang shut behind me, I'm not sure which one. I asked every one who was downstairs whether they had been up there, but every one said no.

There have been other weird sights and sounds in this house, for example, my grandma once saw legs (no body, apparently) walking down the stairs, and refuses to eat in the living room now.

As for me ... the rest of my life so far has been fairly normal, except that I and my sister seem to be unusually "in tune." For instance, one of us will comment on something, and the other one will say, "I was just thinking that!" I've also had things mysteriously move around my room. Once, when I was thinking I needed to get my purse from across the room, I looked down, and there it was ... no idea how that had happened!

Sorry I write so much ... bad habit. I hope this helps!

Francesca

Julianna added the following postscript to Francesca's email:

A few days after I sent you my account, I was following Francesca into her room (which is at the beginning of the hall), and I happened to look to the very end of the hall where my bedroom is located, and I saw a pre-teen boy wearing a newsboy hat and some old-fashioned clothes come out of my Mom and Dad's room and go into mine. I was looking *straight* at my room. I know I saw him. Francesca and I are pretty sure that whatever is in this house stays in my room for the night. Julianna

I WAS COMPLETELY AMAZED

I received the text of this email on November 9, 2008, from Corinne Boudreau who is a contributor of an experience that she describes in my previous collection, *The Big Book of Canadian Ghost Stories*. In that book I argue that it is people rather than places that are haunted, using the word *haunted* in the sense of reporting experiences that are regarded as more extraordinary than simply out-of-the-ordinary. Here is an event that takes place in the context of a family despite a change of dwelling place. I queried Ms. Boudreau about the time and place. She wrote back as follows: "The first incident took place at my mother's house on Acorn Rd. in Halifax. The second took place in my new house on Arvida Ave. in Halifax as well. The events took place in October of 2008 and my daughter is only two years old and I am twenty-eight." The account is very believable.

> Last month when my daughter and I were visiting my parents, my daughter was laughing and talking away to the door of my Nana's old room, and when I asked her to whom she was talking, she replied, "My Nanny!"
>
> I didn't really give it any thought and went back to what I was doing. I had recently moved (on Halloween!) and, as I was in the process of moving, my two-year-old daughter was staying with my Mom. After the move was complete and I had my daughter back home, I was digging through a box and found a picture of my Grandmother. I put it on my shelf. Then my daughter came running over yelling, "My Nanny!"
>
> I was shocked when I heard her and asked her where she had seen her picture. (Before the move, the picture had been in a box for a long time before my daughter was born, also there are no pictures of her in the house where I had grown up, aka my Mom's where my daughter had been staying.) She just looked at me rather strangely and said, "At Grandma's house, silly!"
>
> I was completely amazed! Nanny is what I had called my Grandmother when I was young, and she does not refer to either of her Grandmothers in that manner. I felt all the hair on my neck and arms stand on end, as my daughter proceeded to tell me about my Nanny and her rocking chair! (This too was something she would have not known about unless she had seen it because the chair is not even at my Mother's house anymore!)
>
> So I have concluded that my Nanny is still roaming the

house where we grew up, now she is looking out for my daughter the way she looked out for me!

THE OPEN WINDOW

Another contributor to this collection of eerie experiences suggested that I write to a woman of European background whom she had met by chance, who had said that she had an inexplicable experience, not just one of them but a string of them. Naturally I followed up this suggestion and wrote to "Tina" (whose last name is known to me). She lives in Northern Ontario and at my invitation sent me this charming account of a peculiar experience. It arrived November 25, 2008.

Many *anomalous experiences* occur at dusk and at dawn, when the mind is entering a secondary state, and others occur during interrupted sleep. This seems to have been the case with "Tina." She had a "night terror." Two features of her account make it of special interest. The first feature is the "footprints" that run up the outside of the house. The second feature is the surprising identification of the guitar-wielding, yodeling nighttime visitor.

Make of it what you will. It certainly affected "Tina," and I believe it will affect you too.

> My name is Tina. I've been asked to write about some of my experiences that I've had with the paranormal.
>
> First I will give you some information about myself. I come from a European home. I'm actually a little Dutch girl. I was raised very strictly. It was back in the days when little children were to be seen and not heard. I'm sure everyone has heard of that expression at one time or another. My father was a user of that statement. My parents were raised in the old way, the old way being that psychical or unexplainable things were from the devil. So obviously I didn't talk too much about the experiences I was having. But every now and then I would talk to my Mom and mention the odd thing.
>
> This particular experience I'm going to talk about

involved my mother and my husband. I lived in a subdivision in Southern Ontario. It was a two-story home with bay windows in the living room and the upstairs bedroom. I had three children at the time, all in bed, and my husband also. I always slept with the windows open at night. I love the fresh air at night coming into the bedroom. So, of course, I slept on the side of the bed near the window.

I remember this event so well. It happened on a Friday night during the month of July, 1993. It was a nice summer night, warm, with just a nice breeze. I was trying to sleep in my bed, and was having a restless night's sleep. This is a normal thing for me, not sleeping well. I'm sure it's because so many things happen at night.

As I was sleeping something woke me up suddenly. I looked around my room. I didn't see anything at first. No child awake, I thought, maybe one of them is sick. But the children were all in their beds, sound asleep. I looked at my husband. He was snoring away. Then I lay back down and looked at the clock and it was 2:35 a.m. I thought to myself, "I must have been dreaming." Lying on my side, I watched the curtains in my room blow around with the nice breeze. I heard something again. All of a sudden I saw a man!

I blinked, and I was shocked. This man came through my upstairs window. As he came into my bedroom, I watched him. He stopped at the end of my bed and looked at me. He had long red hair down to his shoulders, a long thin face, and he was wearing a trench coat. In his hands he was carrying a guitar case. As he was looking at me, he was yodeling. I couldn't believe my eyes. My heart was pounding so hard, I was speechless. I couldn't say or do anything. I just watched him. I'm sure people in the house next door could have heard my heart beating.

He didn't say a word to me ... nothing. He just yodeled. Then he walked straight out of my bedroom. I watched him with the guitar case in hand. I thought to myself, "Was this real?" After a moment I realized, "Yes, it was, and I'm awake." So I got out of bed. I checked every room. Nothing was gone.

So I went into the kitchen and made myself a cup of coffee, trying to figure out what had just happened. I couldn't think of who it may have been. So I went to bed and back to sleep. In the morning I didn't mention the incident to my husband until my Mom came over.

Mom arrived around ten-thirty in the morning for coffee. The three of us were Mom, me, and my husband, and we were sitting in the living room. I waited a few minutes and then told them about the experience I had had the night before. I explained how the man looked and how he yodeled. I told them how he came through my bedroom window. Mom listened so patiently.

My husband got scared. He ran outside and looked at the window upstairs. He came running into the house and told us there were footprints all the way up the wall to the window of the bedroom. He was as white as a ghost. He said, "There is no way someone can have footprints that high into our window. Mom and I got up and went outside to see the footprints. Amazingly, they were there. Mom and I were speechless for a moment. We just looked at the prints so high up to the window. My husband was so freaked out that he got the garden hose and proceeded to wash the front of the house to remove the footprints. So Mom and I went back into the house while was doing this.

While my husband was outside, my Mom explained to me that it was my father. The man I had described to her was my father when he was young. My father played the guitar, yodeled, and that's how he dressed when he was young. Mom explained to me that my Dad was checking on us. She said that she too was having visits from my Dad at her home.

I was relieved to know who it was coming into my house, singing and checking on us. As for my husband, he wouldn't let me sleep with the window open any more. Closing the window didn't change anything for me, as I was used to unexplainable events in the night.

THE CORNER BROOK SIGHTING

I received an email from a correspondent otherwise unknown to me on June 19, 2008. It was short. It consisted of a greeting, a question, and two sentences. Here it is:

> Hi John:
>
> Are you still compiling UFO reports? I would like to report a sighting that occurred last week. If not, would you please point me in the right direction.
>
> Thank you.
> Wayne Elford

Here is my reply:

> Dear Wayne:
>
> I continue to collect reports of UFOs, so if you want to send yours to me, I would be pleased to have it. I will acknowledge receipt of it right away. Make the report as detailed as possible — time of day or night, weather conditions, state of mind of observers, effect on observers both short-term and long-term, etc.
>
> Hoping to hear from you,
>
> John

Later that day — such are the wonders of email! — I received the following report from Wayne. What distinguishes it from most reports of sights in the skies that I have received in the past is that in this instance the observer is objective and reportorial rather than interpretive or judgmental in nature. It is obvious that Wayne is a conscientious person and does not know what to make of this sighting of an object or of an effect in the sky over Summerside, and neither do I. There are people who will jump to one conclusion or other — it is Venus or swamp gas or reflection or refraction; it is Venusians or alien beings from outer space. The chances are that what Wayne saw was none of these. The delicious thought that I have is that precisely what it was he did see will never, ever be determined.

This sighting occurred sometime between June 10–12, 2008. I was returning from my workplace at approx. 1:30 a.m. and proceeded on O'Connell Drive in Corner Brook, NL, towards the Lewin Parkway. Upon reaching the Parkway (turning right and heading East), I immediately noticed a bright formation of lights in the sky over the harbour (Bay of Islands). I first thought that is was a plane as there are regularly scheduled flights around that time into Deer Lake, NL.

Because I was driving, I couldn't tell whether the lights were moving, but I could see them constantly on my drive home (approx. 5 minute drive). I then turned left onto Curling Street and I could still see the lights directly to my north.

I was home within a couple of minutes from there, and upon exiting the car I stood outside of the house looking directly north. The object was hovering motionless directly over Summerside, which is located on the north shore of the Bay of Islands. The object was several thousand feet in the air and must have been huge according to the detail that I could see in the light formation. The object was a "V" shape with very bright red and blue lights at the end of each "V". On the bottom of the "V" were very bright white and blue lights, changing colour on regular intervals. At times there were "beams" of white and blue light that shone down from the bottom of the object.

I was alone at the time of the sighting, not impaired in any way. The weather was totally clear and starry. (If I recall correctly, there was no moon.) While I was watching the object, I noticed what appeared to be a satellite fly overhead slightly to my right, heading directly toward the lights (probably just a coincidence but it was worth observing). I couldn't track the exact path of the satellite because it faded from view before it reached the object's location.

I stayed outside for approx. 30 minutes and the object remained in the same area. Upon going into the house, I looked outside from the staircase landing (the window faces north) and the object was still there. I was awake until about 3:30 a.m. and it was still there when I retired for the night.

It definitely was not a cluster of stars, as I am an avid night-sky watcher. I did set a reference point on the ground by noticing lights that are on the ground in Summerside. If it had been a cluster of stars, they would have moved away from their original position during the length of time that I viewed them.

I am 46 years old, well educated, and have had an interest in UFOs and the paranormal since I was a child. This is only one of many sightings that I have had, and it is only now that I have been telling people about them (with the exception of family and a couple of close friends). I have never officially filed a report, but I think it's time to remain silent no more about these events.

I will contact you in the near future with the details of other events.

I appreciate you taking the time to read my report and I look forward to contacting you in the near future.

Cheers!
Wayne Elford

A WOMAN WALKING BY THE DOOR

I enjoy receiving unsolicited emails, especially when they touch upon the paranormal. I received this one on September 4, 2008. I would like to say that "it speaks for itself," but there is always room for a comment or a commentary, an observation or an aside.

I replied to Derek Honeyman and thanked him for the courtesy of sending me these accounts of his two extraordinary experiences. As he has been trained in anthropology and teaches the subject, or at least the

approach to the discipline, he is aware that his personal accounts constitute *prime-face* evidence of experiences or events that seem to defy logic.
They may not necessarily do that, but they seem to do that, and that is
what is most important.

There is no ready explanation for his experiences, except to note that
they both involve phantom women. Freud or Jung could offer interpretations based on childhood memories or ancestral archetypes, but the
experiences themselves are what count. So in my email to Mr. Honeyman, I asked for some further details — specifically, when these events had
occurred, the season or the weather if not the specific date. Here is what
he replied the following day under the heading "Thoughts."

"For the first experience, I was never frightened by what I saw; either
because I rationalized it so well or because I felt a nurturing presence from
whatever it was. Or a combination of both.

"The second experience, I think, can tell us a lot about potential environmental and climatic influences on sightings. As I indicated before, I hold
a graduate degree in anthropology and I am working on furthering that here
in Tucson. I've taught a few university-level courses, some of them have been
on Mexican American Culture, and when we get to the section on folklore,
ghosts, etc., I'm always amazed by how many students have had either a personal experience or know someone who has. My training in anthropology has
provided me with: (1) a sense of respect and cultural sensitivity when hearing
of such accounts, and (2) objectivity, one would hope, and the need to investigate further. I am still not sure whether or not I saw a ghost."

Mr. Honeyman is astute. He has observed that, far from being atypi-
cal, anomalous states of consciousness are surprisingly common and are
reported by a great many people. Even people who have not reported
them, or who do not admit to having them, often know someone who has
whom they believe to be truthful.

Dear Mr. Colombo,

I'm in the process of finishing *More True Canadian Ghost
Stories*.... I thought I would finally share some of my own
experiences.

You'll see one thread throughout.... I can rationalize
almost anything. In two of the following examples, you
will see that.

1. I had just moved into my apartment in Edmonton in the fall of 1996. It was an older building, located in an older area of the city, near the University. I loved it; hardwood floors, non-functioning fireplace that used to hold a heater, built-in cabinets. And the location ... only a few blocks from the campus. It was very small, though. The bedroom was roughly five feet wide and eight feet long, forcing the bed to be up against one wall. The bedroom door had been taken off, because when it was open, it took more room. Living alone, I really didn't see the need for a bedroom door anyway.

One night I woke up to see a woman walking by my door. I seem to recall she was wearing an older dress. She stopped by my door, looked in on me, and proceeded to walk through a rocking chair towards the main door of the apartment. I remember thinking it was odd, but as I did not sense any malevolence from her, quite the opposite, I went back to sleep. If anything, I got the sense that she was looking in on me and once she was satisfied that all was well, took her leave. I also remember thinking it was so dark, that we have a tendency to see movement when it's completely black and that was what it was. It was very dark that night. My unit overlooked the back alley, so there were no street lights, and I never sleep with any lights on.

Over the years, small things occurred that I easily brushed aside. One night I found the picture frame over my bed vibrating, loud enough to wake me up. But as the apartment was mainly populated by students, and I was neighboured by two fraternity houses, I assumed it was the bass from someone's stereo. However, there wasn't any noise coming from anywhere that I could hear. Again, I thought perhaps that the bass (if that's what it was) was too low for me to hear, yet enough to cause vibrations.

2. I was driving to work one summer morning in 1997. I was commuting from Edmonton to my job about a half

hour away. In order to get to work, I had to drive through the town in which my parents lived. There is a cemetery next to the highway right outside the town. What I saw happened so fast that I will attempt to relay my bafflement as clearly as possible.

I remember driving past and glancing into the cemetery as I saw three individuals. Two of them were mowing the lawn, and another, a female, was sitting on a tombstone with her face up, seemingly absorbing the morning sun. The sun was rising, and it seemed to me she was taking a break, unlike her co-workers, and simply enjoying the sun.

After I had driven past, the thought occurred to me that the two males mowing the lawn were oblivious of her presence ... that they didn't know she was there. It was something about their manner regarding her presence. Of course, I started thinking about it and came to the conclusion that I had finally seen a ghost.

After work, I went to my parents' for dinner and then began the drive back to the city. It wasn't dark yet, and my morning sight had been bugging me all day. I drove to the cemetery, parked my car, and walked in.

Sure enough ... where I thought I saw the young woman, I found a monument dedicated to women who had lost their children (Martha, I believe, from the Bible).... The weird thing is, the statue was kneeling on a base, face slightly lifted, and was quite small. When I saw the future that morning, she appeared to be a normal-sized young girl, sitting, with her face up. Instead, what I now saw was a smallish statue, kneeling, and made of a bronze-copperish metal.

Combined with my speeding past and the sunlight shining on it, she appeared larger and different. But as I said earlier, all things may be rationalized.

I don't know if these experiences can be of use. I am a graduate student in Anthropology in Tucson. One of the classes that I teach is on the Anthropology of Religion and I always spend time on ghosts, ancestral spirits, and folklore.

If you need more information, please do not hesitate to ask. I hope you are planning a new book.

Best, Derek

FINALLY ONE DAY I SAW A GHOST

I received this email on August 3, 2008, and I particularly enjoyed receiving it when I did as it supplied diversion over a long weekend. It came from Jody and she has asked me to withhold her last name, which I have in my files, and to be vague about the locale of the "haunted inn." It is okay to say it is located not in Newfoundland but in Southern Ontario. I asked for some more particulars to share with my readers. Here is what she sent me the next day:

"Thank you so much for your prompt reply, and please call me Jody. I'm glad that you liked my stories. I am very honored that you would like to include them in a book. I am not a great writer so please feel free to fix whatever you like.

"I am currently living in Kingston, ON, but my heart is still back east, so I hope to return there one day. I have two jobs. I'm a youth councilor and a house keeper at the haunted inn. For my first two years there I experienced a lot of things, but the activities have slowed down there now. To date I have only seen the ghost once, but I hope that I will see it again.

"As for the question you asked about whether anyone in my family is psychic, the answer is definitely not. My mother can't even watch *Casper* without screaming, and I have never heard my grandparents say anything about ghosts. I also don't look at myself as being 'a psychic.' I think I was just in the right place at the right time."

What I find particularly enjoyable about Jody's accounts of the weird happenings in her life is that she is so robust and energetic and lively and unflappably positive about it all. Other witnesses might be frightened to within an inch of their lives! Not Jody!

Dear Mr. Colombo,

My name is Jody and I have become a big fan of your

books. I have always been interested in the paranormal. I'm a big fan of both ghost books and the TV shows. I especially like *Ghost Hunters* because they try to disprove hauntings. I'm the same way. I won't believe something till there is no other explanation for it. That would be my "dream job," being a ghost hunter. Sadly I haven't had many experiences, but there were a few. I hope you enjoy reading them.

My first ghost story took place in 1998 or 1999, when I was in high school and living in a very small town in Newfoundland (1,500 people). It's the kind of town where everyone knows everyone. I lived with my grandparents in an area that had many seniors and I became close to many of them. Sadly one senior couple, Mr. and Mrs. Ingram, locked up their house and moved to a city that was over two hours away. My grandparents kept in touch with them.

One summer night my grandparents received a phone call from Mr. and Mrs. Ingram's daughter, letting them know that Mr. Ingram was in the hospital and the doctors told her to inform family and friends that he might not last the night. All of the Ingram family that were still in my hometown left that day to be with Mr. Ingram. After the phone call I went out doors with my friends for the night. At 1:00 or 2:00 a.m., I left my friends and walked home. Mr. Ingram's house is at the bottom of the hill that I live on. When I reached the hill I noticed that there was someone standing on Mr. Ingram's porch. It looked like there was a tall skinny man with an old fashion salt and pepper hat on standing there trying to put a key in the door. All I could see was a solid black figure. I walked closer to see who it was. Again all I could see was a solid black figure even though I could see the green siding of the house behind him. Being from a small town, I know that only two men wore an old-fashioned, salt-and-pepper hat like the one I saw on the black figure. One of those men is short and stocky and the other is tall and skinny, Mr. Ingram!

When I got home my grandmother told me that Mr. Ingram died that night and that all of the family was there with him. None of his family was in town that night and if someone were to have broken into his house we would have heard about it. (Small towns know everything.) Also, there was the fact that I was able to see the colour and lines of the green siding behind the figure, yet I wasn't able to see any details on the figure itself. I believe that Mr. Ingram came back to his home one last time.

Growing up, not only was I lucky enough to live with my grandparents but my closest neighbours were my great-grandparents. I was very close to them both. I would go over to their house every day and they would come over to mine every night . In November of 1997 my great-grandmother passed away. This hit me hard. Not only was it the first death that I experienced in my family, but it was the death of someone whom I was with every day of my life. My great-grandfather couldn't bear to live in their house any more, so he moved to be with his daughter in another local community.

About a month after he moved, I started to experience something weird. I would smell my great-grandmother! She had a certain smell. A mix of Newfoundland home-cooking and mint. She always had some kind of mint-smelling liquid in an old bottle near her when at home.

The first time I experienced it was one day when I was walking around my house and it just hit me. It always leaves just as fast as it comes. I have smelled her at home, in school, outdoors, anywhere. Each time I would feel happy, I would feel like she's watching over me.

In 2001, I went on a trip to Nova Scotia as part of a field trip at college. The first day of the trip we were getting a tour of Acadia University. My classmate Kim and I were apart from the rest of the class during the end of the tour. While we were walking, all of a sudden I stopped. I could smell my great-grandmother, but this time it was different. It was not the happy feeling like the other times. This time all I could think of was, "There is something wrong with my great-grandfather." Kim knew there was something wrong with me from the look on my face. I said I was fine and tried to act as normal as possible. We caught up with the rest of the class and headed back to the hotel.

As soon as I got there I called my mother. I asked her if my great-grandfather was okay. She paused and said that he was. I asked her if she was sure and she said yes, she was just been talking to him. After hearing this, I felt a little better, but I still had a feeling that there was something wrong. A week later, when I got back to Newfoundland, my mother called and asked why I had asked her about my great-grandfather. I didn't want to tell her what had happened, so I just said that I was thinking about him. She then informed me that he wasn't okay. She told me that he had cancer. He got the call from the doctor the same day that I called her. She didn't want to tell me at that time because she knew I would have come back that day. My great-grandfather passed away two months after being diagnosed with cancer.

I believe that my great-grandmother was trying to give me a warning. She was letting me know that my great-grandfather would be leaving me soon. Since my great-grandfather died, I haven't smelled my grandmother much. Before the scent was around once every two months, and now it's there about twice a year. I liked having the "heads up" from her, and I hope I get them in the future.

I now live in Kingston, Ontario, and I have two jobs, one of which is working at a haunted inn. The owners don't like their guest knowing that the place is haunted, so I can't give the name of it. I been working here for three years now and have had many different experiences. The first one was about two weeks after I started.

I was cleaning the kitchen one day when my bosses — I'll call them June and Barry — told me they were leaving for a few hours. After they left I knew that the only people in the building was the maintenance man and myself. Shortly after they left, I heard footsteps right above me. I could hear someone walking around to the different rooms. I didn't think much of it, assuming it was the maintenance man. When I was thinking this, he came around the corner and went into the room next to me. So there went the maintenance-man idea! I knew it wasn't a guest because no one had checked in yet and the main door is always locked. There was only one explanation, Barry must have changed his mind and stayed behind. About an hour later the walking stopped and I heard the main door open. June walked in, I asked her why Barry hadn't gone with her. She informed me that he did go; in fact, he was outside taking things out of the car. I told her what had happened and she said that some people believed the place was haunted.

I had many different things happen, mostly smaller things. Then finally one day I saw a ghost. I was in one of the rooms cleaning the floor. I was about two feet away from the doorway leading into the room. The door was kept ajar with my basket. I was on to the door cleaning when out of the corner of my eye I saw a very tall man dressed in a black or dark blue suit walking very fast passed the door. It was a solid figure. I remember seeing the end of his sleeve when he passed by and the stairway between his legs from his wide steps. I went outside as soon as I saw him to see who it was and there was no one there. No one was walking down the stairs and no one was in the hallway. The only other place he could be was in the only other room in that area. I checked and there was also no one in there. So not only did I see a ghost but he was only about three feet away from me!

Many other little things happen such as hearing plates and glasses in the kitchen. I would go in and check and there would be no one in there and nothing had moved. This happened a few times. In the same room where I had seen the ghost, there is a fireplace. Once the fire turned on, all by itself. I tried to turn it off several times but it wouldn't go off. I also noticed that the flames were bigger than they normally were. The fire can only go so high, but this time it was at least 50% bigger. I stood in the door-way and asked my boss to come and fix it. As soon as he stepped into the room, the fire went out and there wasn't any heat coming from it.

Another housekeeper saw a ghost exit a washroom and walk into the hallway. I then came right through the door and yet I didn't see anyone pass me. The fireplace in this room has also been known to come on by itself.

Then there were things being moved in rooms after we just cleaned them. One day I found a room key in the dryer with the towels. I took it out and put it away with the other keys. I went to the laundry room again thirty minutes later and put a new load into the dryers. I heard something hard tumble in the dryer, and it was the same key as before.

One day there were red stains on the floors and carpets leading to different parts of the inn, like a trail. The stains were hard to get out (leading me to think that they were either blood or wine). They were placed weirdly. Each drop was also a perfect circle. None were oval or had a splattered look to it. They were perfectly round.

One light bulb came out of its socket four times in one night, hitting the floor but not breaking. Lights turned off on their own. The TV turned on, on its own.

One day I put mini containers of shampoo, conditioner, and soap in my pocket. When I pulled them out, I had containers of shampoo, soap, and shower gel. The weird thing is that not only am I 100% sure I had conditioner, but we haven't had shower gel for about two years at that point.

I am sure there are more things that happened about the inn, but that is all I can think of, off-hand. Sorry this email is so long, but if you're like me you will love reading anything that has to do with ghosts.

I hope you enjoyed these happenings. I know I can't wait to read more of yours.

Take care.

I HEARD FOOTSTEPS IN THE LIVING ROOM

A correspondent known to me as K.J.M. sent me this long account of multiple hauntings. It arrived by email on August 7, 2008, and it appears here as it arrived. It is written with great fluency and it documents a series of "odd experiences" that occurred to the writer when she was a young girl and woman in Edmonton a number of years ago. I marvel at how well written this account is. Its author is deeply puzzled by these events and experiences; I am sure the reader will be as puzzled as well. There is no ready explanation for these occurrences, otherwise they would have occurred to K.J.M. or to her sister. It is possible that she is "suggestible" and that her imagination has been set in motion for reasons unknown. But that does not account for such poltergeist-like occurrences as computers turning themselves on. When you think about it, the account describes *creepy* experiences! I am grateful to K.J.M. for taking the time to write out this highly readable account and share it with me and my readers. She concludes, "I'm sorry if it's long — I thought it would be shorter!" I disagree: it is not too long — it is the right length — and I would not sacrifice a single word.

Dear Mr. Colombo:

After reading your book *True Canadian Haunting Stories,* I finally mustered the courage to tell someone about my odd experiences as a child. I was quite relieved to discover that other people across the country have been subjected to peculiar occurrences and decided that it was about time I related my events to someone who knew a thing or two about the paranormal.

I've lived in Edmonton all my life, although my family and I have moved from house to house across the north side of the river several times since I was young. I have two sisters (one who is older than me and one who is younger) and the three of us have lived with our mother since my parents' divorce four years ago.

The first house we resided in is where most of my adventures occurred. It was a large place that was situated on the far northwest side of Edmonton in a small community called Lego Lindo. At that time, the surrounding area was just beginning to be developed (there was still a small ranch located across the road from where I lived) but I was told that our new house was built on native ground. Despite this fact, I've always had an odd sensation that the entities "visiting" us were not aboriginal.

Our house was two stories tall, but the front living room, main entrance, and dining room all had high ceilings. The second floor was stretched out above the kitchen, the family room, den (which later became my older sister's room), and a long stretch of hallway that led to the laundry room, a washroom, and the entrance to the basement. My first experience, as I've been told by my mother, occurred in the dining room where a large crucifix is nailed to the wall high above the table. She said she used to hear little girls giggling in there when she was cooking in the kitchen (which is divided from it by a wall), and that she knew it couldn't have been me or my older sister since we were away at school. My little sister was still a baby back then and she was either in the kitchen with my mother or asleep in the family room, which, in good sense, meant someone else was home with her. Sometimes, she said, either I or my older sister would come to her and say we heard little girls in the dining room. We called them "angels" and, despite all the creepy occurrences that happened in that house, the dining room always felt like the safest place to be. Sometimes, my mother would even smell cigarette smoke — since no one in our family smoked, she always assumed it was my paternal grandfather who died before my parents were married. He died of lung cancer from smoking. My mother believed he hung around when we were younger just because he wanted to see his granddaughters. Like the angels, the smell of smoke only appeared in the dining room.

Other places in the house, however, sometimes frightened both me and my sisters senseless. When my little sister was old enough to sleep in a bed of her own (at the age of three or four), I was moved into my older sister's room so that E (my younger sister) could have mine. My old room was situated next to ours (the master bedroom being across the hall), but I always felt agitated after my mother left E's room. I would spend hours at night staring at the ceiling or the wall, haunted by the image of a strange man pacing back and forth across my old room. I could envision my sister being paralyzed by an unseen force, smothered by something she couldn't see. Sometimes he would speak to her in low tones. At first I thought I was hearing sounds from the television downstairs, but after a while I noticed that the light from my little sister's nightlight would flicker a few times in the hallway before shutting off completely. It wasn't until I collected enough wits to get out of bed and turn it back on that I noticed that she was still awake, frightened by something moving around in the dark. I offered to sit in the doorway until she fell asleep and, many nights later, she was no longer disturbed in her room. She became a very hard sleeper after that experience.

Another experience she suffered was directly related to one that my older sister was plagued by as well. When my older sister, A, was in junior high, my father moved his office out of the den and into the basement so that we could each have our own room. The den was painted, refurnished, and A was moved downstairs to "have a space of her own." She thought it was a great idea at first until, a few nights after moving in, she noticed that she heard someone walking up and down the hall located next to the den. Sometimes she would be too afraid to get up to use the washroom because it was located at the far end with the laundry room. The footsteps would fade and then return until the "entity" reached the door to the den. Across the hall from her new room was the entrance to the basement and, after a moment of silence, the entity would turn and climb down the stairs. At first she thought it was our father since he worked late into the evening sometimes and his office was located down in the basement. However, there was a bolt on the basement door (to this day, I don't know why) that could only be opened from the hallway. Upon peeking outside her door to see if the coast was clear, A noted that the bolt was still done up. Whatever had gone downstairs obviously hadn't used the door and some nights she would be too terrified to sleep, worried that the entity would suddenly decide to enter her room instead of the basement.

This "entity," we believed, was the same one that bothered my younger sister in her room. She told me once that at times she felt as though someone was shoving past her (or against her) as she was walking up or down the stairs. Many times she would hit the railing, but as soon as she stepped onto the first landing of the stairs (which reached over the dining room) the feeling would disappear and she would find herself at ease. We believe it was the angels that stopped the entity since we never heard or felt its presence in that room, and that the entity probably resided in our basement. I know it's common to be frightened of the basement (since it's usually dark and cold), but we had reason enough to believe it dwelled in that area.

One of the few experiences I could remember of the entity was actually in the basement. One day, after walking home after school (I was still in elementary), I found a note from my mother saying that she was leaving late to pick up E from play school and probably wouldn't be home for a while. She also asked me to go into the basement to pull out a loaf of bread from the freezer so that it could thaw for breakfast tomorrow morning.

My sisters and I, as I've already mentioned, were terrified of the basement. Sometimes my father's computer would turn on by itself if we stayed down there too long. My father was very careful to leave everything off in his new office since he didn't want us to mess around with his stuff, and we could never explain to him how it happened. Well, upon steeling myself to run down there, I unbolted the basement door and turned on the lights. I originally planned to dash down there, grab the bread, and run back up, but, quite often, I would fall on the stairs and bruise my knees. Deciding to be cautious, I descended slowly for once into the basement.

I was only halfway down the stairs when I heard a loud bang above me. It sounded as though something large had fallen in the living room and I thought it was my knapsack (which I left on one of the couches). Both curious and terrified, I froze on the stairway and listened as I heard footsteps in the living room. I first thought it was my mother (since the footsteps were quite heavy), but usually a person can hear the door slamming shut whenever someone arrives home. Still terrified, I waited for my mother to call my name.

After a while, I heard nothing. Blaming my imagination (and cowardliness), I took a few more steps down into the basement. Above me, I heard another thud, followed shortly by the sound of someone running up the stairs toward the first landing. The noise ended abruptly where the "person" should've entered the dining room before suddenly continuing in the kitchen — almost as though my uninvited guest had jumped clear over the room in which our angels resided. It wasn't until then that it occurred to me that this was the entity that had been bothering my sisters.

The footsteps continued through the kitchen and into the family room before stopping at the top of the basement stairs. I had only left the door open a crack behind me and now I was afraid the entity would lock me down there with the bolt. Terrified, I scrambled atop the freezer and sat there, knees huddled close under my chin for what felt like an hour until my older sister arrived home from junior high. When she called my name, I jumped off the freezer, grabbed the bread, and darted up the stairs as though the hounds of hell were on my heels. Since then, I never ventured into the basement on my own unless someone else was at home (bread be damned!).

My final experience occurred in our second home, a new townhouse that was built in the Clareview community of Edmonton, and I can describe it better as a "sensation" than an actual event. The upstairs bathroom was long. It had a bathtub and walk-in shower with translucent glass doors on one side, and a long counter that had two sinks next to the toilet along the opposite wall. There was a mirror above the sinks that stretched the length of the room and allowed a person to see every little bit of the washroom no matter where they stood. Being in junior high (and being free of our old "haunted" house), I was accustomed to spending time alone at home while my sisters were at school and my parents were at work. Nothing strange happened to me when I was alone, but, even if I had one of my sisters with me, I hated using the upstairs bathroom. Washing my hands, I could see a shadow moving behind the translucent glass doors of the shower. It "creeped" me out but I always told myself that I was seeing things — it was a trick of the light! It wasn't until a few months after we moved in that the strange presence decided to be a bit bolder.

Washing my face before bed, sometimes I would feel as though a man was standing in front of the bathroom door, watching me. As soon as I closed my eyes to splash water on my face, I could see the pale shadow of this man in the back of my mind, moving his mouth as though he were trying to say something. I tried to ignore it, but one night I felt as though he was moving toward me. It wasn't until I felt a small brush of air against the small of my back that I freaked out and yelled that I wanted him to leave me alone.

The following evening, I fell off a ladder and injured the lower muscles in my back. After being taken to the emergency room by my mother, I spent two weeks at home from school trying to recover and several weeks after that in physiotherapy trying to correct my back. I'm much better now (better than new!), but I can't help but wonder if the strange spirit was trying to warn me about the fall or if he was the one that caused it. Since the incident, I never felt the strange presence again, but I always wondered who it was that was lingering in the washroom.

Other people had moved in and out of the surrounding townhouses several times and soon, after my parents began splitting up, we moved out as well. A month after we left, the apartment complex located next to the townhouses burned down without explanation. Everything was ruined.

Well, that's my bit for now. I'm sorry if it's long — I thought it would be shorter! Thanks anyway for lending me your ear.

Yours truly,
K.J.M.

FAMILY STORIES

I received this email from Tia Kingshott, a correspondent new to me, who identified herself as a reader of the book *True Canadian Haunting Stories*. (This is one of my many compilations, and it is also a good place for me to note that for collectors of these "ghost books," this one, published by Prospero Books, is really a repackaged second printing of the first edition which bore the original title, *True Canadian Ghost Stories*. Some industrious person at Prospero or Indigo Books, pondering the book's first title, came to the conclusion that the word *Haunting* was more haunting than the word *Ghost* and then changed it. Small matter!)

This email arrived January, 2009. I read it immediately and enjoyed doing so because it is written in a friendly fashion and because it focuses on the correspondent's family and friends. It captures some of the stories that family members tell, and it also conveys the correspondent's early adolescent experience with a makeshift "seance." The use of candles and the holding of hands is a fairly common pastime, though I had expected that one of the girls would discover an Ouija board in the closet and use it. No need for that, as "Bop-It" began to react like mad! Psychologists are familiar with such reactions and call them *psychomotor*, though in this instance I am not sure that the word applies, as no one was touching the toy at the time.

Curious about my correspondent, when I emailed a slightly edited version of her original text, I asked her about herself. Here is what she replied the following day:

"Hi again, Mr. Colombo. I'm not sure of anything I would change in my letter, I think it sounds pretty good after having you edit it. I was born in Bracebridge, Ontario, in 1990, and I'm still living here today. I live with my parents still, seeing as I'm still 18. I am currently a cashier at the Bargain Shop here in Bracebridge, until I decide where and for what i want to do my post secondary schooling.

"I do believe in the paranormal; I watch a lot of the *Haunted Canada* and *Ghostly Encounter* shows, and every time I do, I think it makes me believe a little more. I'm also afraid of the dark, which sounds kind of silly and immature, but it's the truth that I can't really change. So I guess you could say that, yeah, I am really afraid of having any encounters with the paranormal or the supernatural, although it still would never stop me from experiencing it if I had the chance.

"If people around the world, including people who are close to me, have had or think they have had encounters with the paranormal, there is no doubt in my mind that it's true. I hope some or any of this information helps; feel free to use any bits and pieces you need. If you need anything else, don't hesitate to contact me. Thanks again."

Dear Mr. Colombo,

I know you're never supposed to judge a book by its cover, but I recently purchased one of your books, *Haunting Stories*, as the title drew my curiosity. I have always been a fan of ghost stories; just like anyone else, I like to be a little spooked sometimes. Although I have never had any real encounters with the paranormal or the supernatural, I have had some weird experiences and I have heard some scary and unexplainable stories from friends and relatives. I'm not sure if you have time to read over my stories, but if ever you can spare a minute or so, feel free to indulge.

When I was about 12 or 13 years old, my friend and I were staying the night at her place in Bracebridge, Ontario. We were down in her basement playing around and exchanging scary stories, and being young we were easily getting scared. We lit candles and held hands and tried to create a "seance." We tried contacting her late family members and mine, not really knowing what we were doing.

We asked the "spirits" to move something, so we know "you are here with us." The candles flickered but that wasn't enough to satisfy our curiosity. So we kept trying when all of a sudden one of her toys, called "Bop-It" which we were playing with earlier, started playing, as if the buttons were being pressed in by a player and they were not letting go. The noise this toy made was so constant, and it seemed as if it was getting louder and louder and we couldn't get it to stop. We were so scared that we ran out of her room and called for her Mom to help us get rid of it. I never tried having a seance after that. That one totally freaked me out. It could easily have been the batteries running low that made the noise stick, but the toy was sitting on the floor about 10 feet away, and neither of us had touched it! I was convinced that something weird was really going on, so we both ending up sleeping upstairs.

My uncle Ken passed away Halloween 2008 at the Huronia District Hospital in Midland, Ontario. The next day his wife, my aunt, Nancy's family, came to visit and attended the funeral services later that week. As they stood around talking in the kitchen, my aunt's sister noticed an older woman standing behind her. Feeling rude not have noticed or being introduced to this lady earlier, she asked my aunt who this lady was. When my aunt turned around, there was nobody there. My aunt asked what she looked like, and what her sister described apparently sent chills through my aunt. She took her sister upstairs and showed her some pictures of Kenneth's Mother (my grandmother, whom I never had the chance to meet). Her sister told my aunt that those pictures very much resembled the woman she had seen standing behind her. My aunt told her that this lady was Ken's Mother who had died in 1982. Her sister was very surprise and never could understand why she had see Ken's mother, someone she had never met before. My aunt knows not to be scared at all by the noises that still come from my late uncle's room, and that the sighting of her mother-in-law was just her way of letting her know she was watching over her; making sure she was all right.

Another story is one I heard from my Mom. A while back in her life, she moved into an apartment in Toronto with her first son and her boyfriend. My Mom and her boyfriend had a fight, and she ended up sleeping on the couch that night. While her boyfriend was asleep in their bedroom, she stayed up and watched TV. A while later he came and stood in the doorway and asked her what her deal was, why she would come to bed and then leave again. She told him she has been sitting on this couch watching TV ever since he had left for bed. He called her a liar because he claimed that he felt her get right into the bed then leave before he had a chance to turn over or talk to her. She again told him she never even went into the bedroom and that's that. What was it that he was feeling? He could have been dreaming, or feeling something else. My Mom still doesn't have a clue.

Hope you enjoyed my stories. They're nothing much, but they're still kind of freaky!

I'd love to hear back.

Sincerly,
Tia Kingshott

I corresponded with Ms. Kingshott and then I was treated to a surprise. On January 31, 2009, I received this interesting email, a postscript to the above accounts.

Mr. Colombo! I cannot believe I have written you twice already and ended up never telling you one of the stories that has scared me for years! It must have totally slipped my mind, although I'm not sure how this happened, since it was a bone-chilling experience. My Mom reminded me of it today, when I told her about sending you those stories. It didn't exactly involve me, but I was just as scared.

Okay, a long while back, I can't really remember what year, it was Halloween night though, and my brother T.J. and I had already gone out trick-or-treating and I had gone to bed. I don't believe it was that late in the night, around 9:00 or 9:30 (well past my bed time anyway), when I heard T.J. bawling his eyes out. He was hysterical. It obviously woke me up. (I always slept with my door open, so I could hear him clearly.)

I looked out my door and T.J.'s bedroom lights were on. I got up to see what was wrong, and I remember not even getting completely into the living room when my Mom, holding my brother in her arms as he was weeping, kept telling me to go back to bed. "Just go, Tia; your brother just had a bad dream," or something along those lines. (Bear with me, it's been years now.) I didn't believe it; I knew something was wrong. I kept asking her to please, please, please tell me! I believed I was getting scared by this point; it was Halloween after all.

I didn't go back to bed until she told me what had happened. She said my brother had seen a man standing in his doorway, and then he disappeared down the hall. I was *terrified*, being so young, and hearing that, I didn't understand. Could you blame me, though? Being scared of the dark already and now having some strange man seen right in front of my door as well. (Our rooms were directly across from each other's.) I was a mess. I refused to go back to bed. Of course, it ended up that I had to, but I don't think I slept for long hours after, though; I was too scared to sleep, to close my eyes. I was curious but I definitely wasn't in the right state of mind to see a ghost.

Anyway, Mr. Colombo, I forgot to mention this story in my last letter yesterday, so I thought that you might like this one, as well. You can thank my Mom for reminding me of this story, seeing as I didn't remember it at the time.

P.S. This happened in the house we are still living in now.

Thank you
Tia

8

MORE EMAIL ENCOUNTERS

Earlier I mentioned that I consider email encounters like the ones in this section and the ones in the previous section to be unusually interesting because they make no claims about the reality of psychical phenomena and yet they attest to the fact that something unusual or at least unexpected is occurring. It is possible to find, in the many pages of the *Diagnostic and Statistical Manual* consulted by psychiatrists, descriptions of many of the psychological states recounted in these contributions. That does not mean that there is no other explanation for their causation. Many odd and unusual things do occur during the course of everyday life — statistical anomalies, freak weather conditions, a sense of presence, states of deep reflection, et cetera — so we should not automatically conclude that "such things do not occur." Anyway, here are some more email encounters — and some opportunities to meet such mightily interesting people!

A DREAM THAT I HAD HAD

I received this email from Ernie Lacasse, a resident of Toronto, on October 25, 2008. It describes a prophetic dream that occurred to him while he was working in Brisbane, Australia.

I would not describe such dreams as common, but neither would I describe them as uncommon. They seem to occur from time to time and they are deeply meaningful to the people involved. But a dream is a tricky state of mind. The content of a dream is hard to recall, it seems at the time to be nonsensical and open to a range of interpretations, and it is seldom documented at the time that it occurs (upon waking, for instance) but is recalled once the details have proven (in the life of the dreamer) to be prophetic. Yet they are undeniably powerful and they do occur.

One characteristic of a prophetic dream is that it is tightly bound to an event, and it defines a phase in the life of the dreamer. Here is a dream that occurred way back in 1965, being recollected in 2008. Obviously the forty-two years between the occurrence and the recollection today have not dimmed what was revealed in the least. Curious about Mr. Lacasse, as well as curious about his experiences in Australia (a most remarkable country on a most remarkable continent), I asked him for a few more biographical details. Here is what he supplied:

"In the 1950s and 1960s it was quite common for Commonwealth youth to travel to other Commonwealth countries on 'working holidays.' I had been in Australia for slightly more than five years at the time of this incident — and had been living in Brisbane, Queensland, for two and a half years. I was living in a large and well-run boarding-house but, when I first arrived in that city I had spent a few weeks with the family who lived in the house where this dream was situated. I had been back to visit that family a number of times in the interim. My occupation was as a clerk in the office of a large rubber products wholesaler situated in downtown Brisbane."

Mr. Colombo, I have had a fascination for ghost stories and, at present, I am reading *True Canadian Ghost Stories*.

I never have encountered a "haunting" myself (although I attend a church — the Metropolitan Community Church of Toronto, formerly Simpson Avenue Methodist — and then United — Church, which is rumoured to have at least one resident ghost).

However, I did have an experience in November, 1965, which is forever etched upon my memory.

In September 1960, I had left the family home in Coquitlam, B.C., to go on a "working holiday" to Australia. In November 1965, I was living and working in Brisbane. One day, while at work, my landlord telephoned to say that I had received a telegram. It was from my mother to tell me that my father had died in his sleep. He had suffered an aneurysm.

Upon hearing the news, a dream that I had had the previous night came back into my memory. In the dream

I had gone to visit a family that I had been friends with for a while. In the dream a knock came to the front door. (Curiously, while the front door faced the street, all regular visitors walked down the driveway and then climbed a back staircase to the kitchen door for entry.)

In the dream I was the only one in the living room, so I opened the door to find Dad standing on the stoop. Wordlessly he gave me a hug and the dream ended.

Just as you are quoted on the back cover of your book, "I neither believe in ghosts nor disbelieve in ghosts...."

Ernie Lacasse

THE ALGONQUIN PARK HAUNTING

I received this lively email on March 26, 2008, and immediately replied to its sender, Axy Leighl, to assure her that I liked her account of seeing the old man in Algonquin Park and that it constitutes a first, as I had no other such stories from this provincial park, one of the largest and oldest in the country. More than a century ago, Algernon Blackwood, the English author of stories of horror and terror, composed his first stories in a cabin on secluded Bohemia Island in Algonquin Park, but those stories are works of fiction, fine horror fiction at that! There are also those campfire stories, tales told by camp counselors at summer camps to impressionable youngsters — stories about Anson Minor, the hermit or recluse who stalks the woods at night and spies on little kids. Perhaps Axy saw Anson Minor! What is interesting to ponder is why this experience, which occurred some thirty-three years ago, remains so vivid in Axy's memory. The power of fright!

Hi, John (I hope you don't mind me being informal):

My name is Axy (pronounced "Axe'ee") Leighl ("lay'el"). I'm 41 years old and have lived in the GTA since I was about 3 years old. I emigrated here with my parents from Fiji.

My parents made friends with a 2 couples when they first came to the GTA and have been life-long friends with them since. The first couple, "Phillippa" and "Alex" (the Haijdu's) introduced us to camping and Algonquin Park. My parents would take us (my sister and me) camping in Algonquin, borrowing the Haijdu's tent trailer.

On one of these trips, something really strange happened to me that has remained vivid in my mind. I was 8 years old at the time. My parents had put my sister and me to sleep — she was about 4 years old at the time.

Some time after my parents had fallen asleep, I awoke in my bunk which I shared with my father. I was gripped by a paralyzing fear ... I slowly moved my head to the right so I could see the tent's vent window ... peering in at me was a man with a white beard and a moustache, much like Santa Claus. He was wearing a red raincoat and hat ... my recollection was that it was raining ... unlike Santa Claus, he appeared menacing ... at 8 years of age, I told myself that this was just a dream ... that it wasn't happening ... I was too terrified to awaken my father ... the image was there even when I looked away and looked back ... at some point, even the fear couldn't keep me awake and I fell back to sleep.

While I remembered the event and told a few people about it through the years — it made that big an impact / impression on my mind — the fear never struck me again. And I never felt that the image was a ghost until almost 15 years later when I visited Algonquin Park again with a girl friend.

On this trip, we visited a small museum, and while wandering around the museum, I came face to face with the image of my childhood in a black-and-white photo or drawing (I can't recall which). The posting with the image told the story of how the park is haunted by an old woodsman who can be seen wearing a red raincoat.

I must add, that my parents had never taken me to this museum in the park, and I had never heard the story of the woodsman haunting the park before that last visit.

Do you know of any other stories involving the woodsman in Algonquin Park?

Axy Leighl

WEIRD AND STRANGE MEMORIES

"Weird and Strange Memories" is the phrase that appeared in the subject-line of an email that I received on July 13, 2008. The words describe succinctly the contents of this email sent by Elizabeth Livingstone, a correspondent hitherto unknown to me. My correspondent lives near Westville, Nova Scotia, and is obviously a very sensitive person. She has access to her feelings and sensations and some of these are quite spontaneous and overpowering. She has no hesitation sharing her memories of them with other people. An earlier generation of readers would be inclined to describe Ms. Livingstone as "psychic," but that label is misleading because everyone is to some degree psychic in that he or she has experiences that are difficult to categorize or explain. Most people simply ignore what they cannot readily explain. Ms. Livingstone is a curious person who is interested in her memories. A few people admit to a genuine interest in anomalous phenomena.

One experience that she describes might be categorized as "the old hag" phenomenon. It occurred in an old house at Telford, outside New Glasgow, Nova Scotia. The phenomenon is known in Nova Scotia and quite well known in Newfoundland, and indeed the folklorist David Hufford, who founded the Folklore Department of Memorial University in St. John's, has written an impressive book on the subject. The sensation is one of being attacked while helpless during deep sleep by a succubus or an incubus. The sensation is related to "sleep paralysis," a response to dreaming that has been well documented by psychologists. Children commonly report the sensation of being unable to move before awakening from a deep sleep. It creates a short-lived panic. The sensation is reported by adults as well as children perhaps for the reason that nothing that has been experienced by the child is ever forgotten by the adult. The mind, having learned a trick or two, like riding a bike, never forgets.

I do not know why Ms. Livingstone has experienced these feelings and sensations. All I know is that I do not doubt that these experiences overcame her and terrified her at the time and that they continue to puzzle her to this day.

> Dear Mr. Colombo: Hello, my name is Elizabeth, I am a 42-year-old Mom of two wonderful children. I work with and teach disabled children / teens / adults. I recently bought a book titled *More True Canadian Ghost Stories*. It encouraged me to write to you. I have a few stories that have baffled me for quite a long time. Sometimes, when I am driving, I think about them, and I wonder who in the heck would ever believe me? When I read your book (in one day, I couldn't put it down) I thought, what do I have to lose, you might read my stories and think me a quack, or maybe you would be interested. If you would humour me with your attention, the following stories are true to me.
>
> Story One: When I was around 6 years old (1971–72), my Dad and Mom moved our house about 3–4 miles down the road. While getting settled my Dad made a makeshift swing-set out of a log between two trees, a rope, a wooden seat with "V"-cut slats on the sides to hold the seat onto the rope. My older sister and I spent hours on the swing, and my parents were happy to see us busy, and somewhat out of their way. As time went on my older sister lost interest, and so many times I would go out to the swing and swing for hours alone. I'd swing and sing, until supper-time. One particular day, in early June, during the morning, about 10:00–11:00 a.m., I was swinging and not paying attention. I looked up, it was as if the day stood still, like the kind of day where even the leaves on the trees didn't move. The sky was gray and appeared to look still. It was like the clouds were not drifting across the sky. There were no bird sounds, no bug sounds, or frogs chirping, not even a sound coming from my Dad who was underneath the hood of our car. (When my Dad was fixing something, you could hear him, swear words and all.) I looked at our kitchen window to see if my Mom was there.

She wasn't. I got up from my swing and walked over to the side of our house, and then I heard it. It sounded like a dull whistle. I looked up at this object about a foot above me. It was just hanging there. I reached up and grasp this rail thing and held onto it. I was being lifted quite far off the ground. I got scared and I let go, but not before I had a good look at the underside. There were little lights in one row, right down the center of it, white ones, yellow ones, and some red ones that actually looked orange. The rail I was holding was very cold, like the outside of your car in the winter. Everything was very plain. It was brushed silver, charcoal gray. It felt very inviting. I felt as though I wanted to crawl up inside of it, but there was no door or hole of any sorts. I was curious just to see what was inside. When I fell to the ground, on my feet standing straight up, I though for sure I might have fell quite a distance. But if I had fallen a long ways I would have hurt myself. I was perfectly fine. I do not know why I thought that I knew I was so far up. I felt the opposite, like I was only a few feet off the ground. Then in a split second it was gone, no smoke from an engine or fire or dust or anything. It just disappeared. I stood there looking around to see if it went anywhere, but to no avail. I then ran over to my Dad and began excitedly telling him about what happened, I asked, "Did you see that, Dad? Did you see it? Did you see me get lifted off the ground? Did you see it?" He looked at me and told me, "Go and tell your Mother," and he added he was too busy to listen. I ran into the house and told my Mom, and she told me to go outside and play. No one would listen to me. Later, many years down the road, right out of the blue, my father asked me to tell him about what had happened. I told him and he told me that there are things in this world that are truly unexplained, and not to dig too far. "You might be very disappointed in what you find, or it might scare the hell outta ya!" To this day I still feel the same, as though it just happened. I try to shake the feeling, or try to make up explanations for what I experienced. But nothing can change what I saw.

Story Two: This story is most recent. About 5 years ago (2003–04) I was at my boyfriend's home. His home is over a hundred years old and it has its own story. Sometime through the night while sleeping, I would wake up abruptly, screaming, "Get it off me, I can't breath, just get it off me." My entire body was being pressed down into the waterbed, which is kind of difficult when you think of it. If you have ever been in a waterbed, you know that it can be a little impossible to be pushed down flat into it, especially when there are two people in it. The water in the bladder keeps you afloat, so to speak. I could not move a single part of my body. In my thoughts it felt as though it was someone pushing down on me. It felt male, perhaps because of its strength. But it wanted to purposely do this, as if to keep me still, like it was funny or a trick. It was covering my mouth, not with a hand but with a cheek or a mouth, so I could not make noises or yell out. It was not sexual at all. As I said before, it was as if a trick was being played on me, and it was telling me it was funny. I had washes of not being afraid to being absolutely terrified. It felt harmless, then pure evil. My boyfriend woke me, he told me what had happened and I lay there for the rest of the night feeling the same feeling. What the hell was that? I heard recently about "sleep paralysis." Maybe this is a real medical explanation, but not when you "know" there is someone there, telling you they are funning with you.

Part Two of Story Two: About 2–3 months later it was around eight o'clock in the evening. I was watching a movie, while lying at the end of my boyfriend's waterbed. Arms propped up under my chin, I became engrossed, not really paying attention to my surroundings. Then out of the blue I am flat on my back with the same pressure on top of me. This "being" was laughing. Not like you or me, but as if it was making fun of me for someone else with him. My boyfriend was in the bathroom taking a bath. When he was finished, he came into the bedroom and the pressure was stopped and was gone in a flash. At this point I am totally freaked out. I told my boyfriend and he was confused. I can't believe it happened again. The difference this time was that it did not last long and it did not feel evil. What are your thoughts on sleep paralysis?

I have a few more interesting stories if you would like to hear / read them. Here are a few things about me: My name is Elizabeth, I live in Gairloch, Nova Scotia, just outside Westville. I have never really been a believer of ghosts or goblins, but it sure does put a squint in your eye when you can not explain certain things. I look forward to hearing from you.

Sincerely,
Elizabeth

INTERESTING MAIL

I receive the most interesting mail and email, as well as the most intriguing phone calls and courier-delivered packages. I try to respond to every communication I receive within twenty-four hours. The following letter arrived on January 6, 2009. I am reproducing its text here as it arrived from my service provider, followed by the text my immediate response.

Hi, Mr. Colombo. My name is Maxwell Falletta-Ehler. I'm 15 years old and reside in Hamilton, Ontario.

I bought your book *Ghost Stories of Canada* a few years ago. I remember reading on it that you were a master compiler of different sorts in your books. I can believe that, *Ghost Stories* was a very impressive collection.

I'm writing to you to tell you of a friend of my mom's. She used to work with him. His name is Merv. Apologies, I forget his last name, but if you are truly interested, I'll make sure his last name gets to you. Merv is an electrician. He works with many types of home construction. It wasn't until about one month ago that I found out that he makes time capsules and puts them into the walls of the homes he works on, to provide accurate histories of what's going on for the people of the future to stumble upon.

Merv usually puts bits and pieces of crazy news stories, jokes, and otherwise pack-rat-esque stuffings into these time capsules. He's found the most interesting things in the homes he's worked on (he once found an 80-year-old pack of condoms in a house's cellar) and in turn, he puts interesting tidbits of his own into the walls.

He does the most incredible things, the time capsules he creates are true treasures, and if that's not a brilliant achievement, letting the future generations see what we saw, I don't know what is. I thought you might want to be notified that he also is a master compiler, and one of the nicest, most intelligent, and most interesting people one could ever meet.

I'm not sure why, but I thought you might be interested in hearing of him.

Sincerely,
Max Falletta-Ehler

I was intrigued with this letter from this youthful correspondent unknown to me until this moment. So it was with enthusiasm (coupled with a sense of wonder) that I sent the following reply, within the above-stated period of twenty-four hours:

Dear Mr. Falletta-Ehler:

You are right. Your instinct is correct. I am interested in Merv and his interest in time-capsules. (I find myself wondering if his employers know what he is doing.) You have a good eye for an intriguing oddity and also a lively writing style.

Tell me a little about yourself. You are obviously a student and will proceed to college or university. What will you study?

Have you read the books of Charles Fort, who collects oddities, rather in the manner of Ripley's "Believe It or Not!" (The movie *Magnolia* was inspired by "Fortean" phenomena.) You can check Charles Fort through Google, if interested.

Hoping to hear from you,

Best,
JR

I did not have long to wait. Later that day I received the following email from my young correspondent.

Dear Mr. Colombo,

I'll make sure I get Merv's last name to you later tonight.

Yes, I am a student. I'm flattered by your compliments on my writing style. I try my best when I write to authors.

I am pursuing musical composition as my career path. Playing music, writing music, listening to music. It's what I do best. I am a connoisseur of fine music.

I have not read the works of Charles Fort. I'll look him up, though. His work definitely sounds like something I can get into.

Thanks for replying, and keep watching the skies!

Sincerely,
Max Falletta-Ehler

Max is sure-footed, ending his email to me with the injunction "Keep watching the skies!" That is the way I quite often end essays or books on flying saucers or unidentified flying objects. It obviously appeals to him.

In the back of my mind is the fact that Max is only fifteen years old. I began to think: does he have a web presence? So when I checked his name through Google, and I was not surprised to discover there are twenty-five sites that mention him. One of these shows him discussing how he makes music videos. This appears on YouTube.

I have no doubt that Max has a great future ahead of him, writing to authors, sharing oddities with like-minded people, making videos, and studying, performing, and composing music.

I sent the above copy to Max and the next day, January 7, 2009, received the following cheery reply.

Dear J.R.,

I just printed it off for my mom. I would be flattered if you used the emails in a book. Merv's surname is Nelson. He is a self-employed handyman, so the time capsules are never an issue. The odd twist he has added to his job has been written about by Paul Wilson in *The Hamilton Spectator*.

My last name is hyphenated because my mom and dad never married. Falletta is my mom's last name, and Ehler is my dad's. Falletta is Italian, specifically Sicilian, and Ehler is German. I have yet to discover what either of my surnames mean. My mom is the manager of a brick company in Burlington. My dad drives a taxi.

Thanks for finding me so interesting!

Sincerely,
Max Falletta-Ehler

I FROZE! I WAS TERRIFIED!

Are some families more psychic than others? Are there "psychical genes" that are inherited? It seems unlikely, yet both Corinne Boudreau and her sister Tricia Boudreau have recorded odd experiences. Corinne sent me "Ghosts of Both My Parents" and urged me to contact Tricia and ask her if she had any ghost stories to relate connected with the family residence. She emailed back to say no, but that she did have some other experiences to share. So I urged her to do so. This account, the first in a series, arrived on December 3, 2007, along with the first snowfall and the start of the Christmas season. What I like about it is the fact that it captures the spirit of a young child as she has begun to experience the sensation of fear.

Dear Mr. Colombo,

I must apologize for the lapse in time since my last email, 'tis the season. To keep with your original inquiry, I will begin with the frightening childhood experience that taught me not to tap on the headboard of my bed. I was about four, maybe five years old, and still sleeping in my grandmother's bed at night to "warm it up" before she went to bed. I moved to my own bed at this time. This one particular night my father was away, working on a tug boat. Just my mother and grandmother remained in the house watching television after they put me to bed. My little sister, Corinne was only a toddler, and already sleeping. I lay there restless, unable to sleep. I wanted to be in the living room watching t.v. too. On the headboard of my grandmother's bed there was a sliding door. I lay there sliding it back and forth, and playing with the contents inside. I closed the door and knocked on it. Three little taps ... tap, tap, tap. The door knocked back! Three more taps, louder than mine. I froze! I was terrified! I remember thinking, "It's a *ghost*!" I ran from the room looking for an explanation. My mother and grandmother were surprised to see I was still awake. When I told them what happened, they told me not to be silly and go back to bed. I slept in my own bed that night, and never tapped on the headboard ever again. I will write again in the next couple of days with the account of my re-occurring nightmare.

Thanks for your time,
Patricia Boudreau

THIS DAMN CRAZY STORY

I received the following email on February 10, 2008. It came unbidden from Tauscha Gove, a reader of one of my books who lives in Calgary. I am pleased to offer it to my readers. I am not sure what to make of this account of seeing a "devil" (with or without scare quotes!) except that the account is quite unusual. Visions of demonic beings are not all that common in this day and age in this country, but they do occur from time to time. I am not sure how the Ojibway shaman fits in, except that the person seems a font of psychical knowledge.

Dear jrc,

My story, is this:

One evening at a house in the Woodbine area of Calgary, I saw what must have been "the devil"! It was quite large, slimy, hunched over, and dark greenish black in colour, like a horny toad, sort of ... is what it seemed to be in the darkness of that corner room.

Yet I recall that I saw different tones and colours on the creepy skin in the dark room as a low light filtered from the hallway behind me.

Let me say right here that I have never believed in a devil, and to this day do not. But what I saw in that room that night was indescribable in any manner other than "the devil."

I am curious still.

For whatever reason, some years back I was introduced to an Ojibway at a barbeque party who gave me an owl-wing right on the spot and claimed that it was a gift from the Creator to me.

Well, needless to say this wing has taken me on quite a journey. I have learned much about life and death. As a child I saw the future, illness, lies, and the deceased, as well as many written untruths.

I went to the "other side" and came back for my father and also because I was told that I had to come back! So what that means to me today is a memory. I still see the departed sometimes and my intuition is sound and expanding by the week.

However, that night in the Woodbine area, when the Ojibway touched my arm and said, "Look," I saw what I guess would be called a demon. Right there before my eyes! It looked right at me and taunted me with its eyes, and for some reason I had no fear whatsoever, but simply a firm stand and curiosity.

The Ojibway said to me later, when I questioned why he walked away after touching my arm, that he could not go to the "other side" and come back, but that I could. Perhaps my disbelief saved me! Perhaps no fear saved me! And, saved me from what? It wanted to scare me and it didn't get its wish.

But there is some reason that I saw that thing. I heard later that the demon was still there in their house after we left. It seemed logical to me because it was attached to one of the family members, not the house.

Well! It is still a mystery to me, and after picking up your book called *Strange but True*, I thought I might share this damn crazy story and get it out of my head into the light of day!

I would be interested to hear what you have to say and if you have heard of something like this before. A devil?

This same night I was shown a picture of a devil in a photograph but I dismissed it as only thought-forms in the church where it was taken.

Regards,
T.

THE UNMISTAKABLE BRIGHTNESS OF HIS EYES

Readers of my books know that I include both my email address and my website address in my books and that I encourage readers to share their odd or eerie experiences with me and my readers. (For readers who do not use computers, I also include a mailing address, generally that of my publisher. But most people now have access to personal computers and email.)

On April 26, 2008, I received a query from Lorraine S. Waller of Guelph, Ontario, who wrote to check to see if the email address that she had was still valid. I immediately wrote back to assure her that it was and that I would be interested in receiving an account of her experiences.

Here is Mrs. Waller's response. It arrived later that day, such is the speed of the genie of electronic mail! In it she wonders if I have an opinion to add to her account. As it happens, I do! I have no doubt that the description of the appearance of the phantom child is accurate in terms of physical accuracy and especially in terms of psychological authenticity. In other words, Mrs. Waller is faithful to the facts and to the experience. She is a careful observer of sensations and emotions.

What to make of the experience itself? I wonder if she had heard about the little boy's suicide *before* she had experienced the apparition. If before, then she might have been prepared to interpret some optical effects caused by the flash of lightning in terms of a child; if *after*, then not, and so it would be independent corroboration that something indeed odd had taken place.

In either case, the experience, so well described here, is unforgettable. My strongest feeling is that something unusual occurred, precipitated by the lightning-bolt, and wonder that an experience that lasted a mere three seconds in time is so vivid in her memory two years later. I will safely predict that she will continue to recall it — and puzzle over it — for the rest of her life, so powerful are these effects.

No ready explanation comes to mind.

Dear Mr. Colombo:

Thanks for your quick response to my email!

Before I begin my story, I just wanted you to know that I received your book *Strange but True* as a 53rd birthday present from my son, on December 23rd, 2007.

My children know how much I love reading, and researching the paranormal, and although I have from time-to-time briefly delved into your other books — this one had me extremely intrigued.

So I started from page 1, and only read it in the day, not at night! — as it tends to make the imagination wander after reading some particularly frightening chapters, even though I am fascinated with the world of the supernatural ... even you must admit, some events are chilling!

My experience dates back two years ago — April 26th, 2006. I had moved into an apartment with my daughter. We had only lived there nine months, and nothing out of the ordinary had happened — although we were both dismayed by apartment living. We had always lived in a house, so sadness, and regret lingered on as my daughter Madeleine and I realized that we were not comfortable with this type of home.

That late April night was a stormy one. A thunder storm had erupted in the skies, and the lightning was ter-rifying, followed by big booms. The weather report had warned of an "electrical" occurrence over our area.

It had been very hard to calm my daughter enough for her to go to sleep. She has a fear of thunderstorms. They just scare her to death. As for myself — I love them! The scarier the better.

My daughter was finally asleep. We had held each other tightly after every crack of thunder, and the storm finally subsided enough for her to nod off.

I crept out of her room, and walked down the hall to the kitchen. I opened the fridge to pour myself a cold glass of ice water, and as I shut the fridge door, I came face-to-face with a boy hovering about 3 feet in the air. Never in my entire life have I been so shocked. I remember I gasped, and my mouth must have been agape.

He appeared to be around 14 or 15 years of age — with big blue eyes, and blonde curly hair. I still do not understand to this day, why I did not drop my glass, but I was all at once astonished, but also thrilled that I knew I was finally viewing my very first apparition.

The boy was surrounded by a misty white image, but what he was wearing was quite brilliant. His pin-striped shirt was blue and white — very crisp and neat and quite possibly dark blue or black pants. I only witnessed the upper half. In about three seconds he was gone.

Those brilliant baby-blue eyes were fixed on me, but I could see that they were also looking "through" me — not at me directly. I can only describe it as if I saw into the boy's soul, and the instant feeling was one of unbelievable sadness and sorrow. I have never before witnessed such sadness.

It was a look of complete and utter regret. Quite possibly his feeling at the moment of death.

It took me a minute or so to collect myself, but I did smile, and I said to nobody in particular, "Oh my God! Finally!"

This has been the most remarkable experience of my life. Can one feel honoured to witness such an event? Well I did and I felt honoured.

It wasn't until I had the nerve to leave the kitchen that a chill came over me, and I became very frightened.

I stayed in my room all night, and didn't sleep too well.

There was no way I would venture into the kitchen late at night anymore. I was petrified he would do it again.

So after 11:00 p.m., I would race into the kitchen, get my water, and race out. This went on for a complete year before I felt comfortable enough to linger in the kitchen at night.

At the precise moment I had opened the fridge door, the shocking electrical bolt of lightning illuminated the living-room and dining-room, and suddenly the boy appeared. His head was level to the freezer door, which would make his apparition about 3 feet off the floor.

I remember the unmistakable blueness of his eyes, and I felt such pity for the poor soul. He looked out to utter desolation.

A gossipy neighbour had revealed to me that a boy on the 8th floor had hanged himself. It happened around two years before I moved in, but I lived on the 2nd floor.

He was in his mid-teens, and was just trying to get his mother's attention, only it went too far. When he was cut down, it was too late.

So, dear Mr. Colombo, if you have an opinion on this, I would love to hear it. Yours truly, and with kindest regards, Lorraine S. Waller

TWO EXPERIENCES

I meet such interesting people through the mail, the email. On March 5, 2009, I received the following communication from Lee Bice-Matheson, who is most courteous and complimentary. Here is what she wrote.

Good afternoon, Mr. Colombo:

My husband, son, and I have read your books on ghost stories over the years. You have provided many hours of lively reading and conversations around our fireside. Thank you for that.

I was wondering if you are compiling true stories of relatives visiting after their death. I have had the privilege on several occasions after both of my parents died. There is no question in my mind that it was my mom and my dad. I stood by my mom's bedside and held her hand as she passed and had a most wonderful experience as she drew her last breath. On the other hand, when my dad died, I was absent. He and I were close since he had undergone a bankruptcy and I lived with my parents and helped them through this time. We experienced things most parent / child relationships do not. I understood him and loved him very much.

After he passed, he came back to visit with me on and off for six months. For two years after my mother's death, I experienced a lot of activity in our home; my son did as well. Finally, I called in a psychic who told me that what I perceived is what he does for a living — goes around the country and proves to people spirits are around. His name is Robbie Thomas and his website is www.robbiethomas.net

I wrote a story about my dad, called "Paranormal Dad" and the rest of my experiences are yet to be written down. I would not write under my real name as I work with my husband in a small town with patients and really do not want to open up communication on this topic. But I would be willing to submit a story if you are interested.

I admire your sensitive and professional manner in which you portray your subjects and their stories. I have a Master's degree in Library and Information Science and have taken a post-graduate writing course. I work with my husband in a clinical setting now helping patients overcome the negativity in their life and provide moral support to many. My other worldly experiences are kept private but if I used a pseudonym I would love to write the experiences. I am one of the lucky ones to know first hand there is life beyond our human form.

Thank you for your time.

Sincerely,
Lee Bice-Matheson

I am reproducing Ms. Bice-Matheson's letter with her permission because it places in context the accounts of the two experiences that she has written. I encourage men and women who are witnesses to extraordinary events or eerie experiences to set their impressions and feelings down on paper, or up on a computer screen. By doing this they "fix" the details — as hypo fixes photographic images — which, otherwise, like dreams, would likely dissipate or change over time prior to entirely disappearing! Ms. Bice-Matheson did so and in the process decided to attach her name to the account.

I have no explanation for the experiences that she has had, other than to suggest that they are carefully recalled, honestly described, sincerely held, and in keeping with the experiences that have been recorded by other sensitive witnesses over the centuries. Our society thinks it carefully distinguishes between what is "real" and what is "unreal," but "reality" is a term that applies to what we sense, feel, and think. We may be mistaken in finding a casual connection between Feeling A and Thought B, but unless we record them and ponder them, we will never know about the connection. Ms. Bice-Matheson gives us a lot to think about, and experience along with her.

Paranormal Dad

I wouldn't believe what you are about to read if I hadn't experienced it myself. I can assure you that it truly did occur, and of course, you are entitled to your own interpretation.

My father passed away rather suddenly on November 30th, 2004. He was diagnosed with gastric (stomach) cancer six weeks prior to his death, and really did not experience a lot of pain until weeks before he died. Some rib pain was a subtle indicator of an underlying problem, but many passed it off as "he was golfing too much." His doctor had just given him good news that with some chemotherapy treatments he would be fine. A few days later he was sent up for a rather routine test that went awry and he died. My husband, my mom, one of my sisters and her husband were all with him on that day.

I was not. I was home sick in bed. I did not get the chance to say good-bye. I truly loved my dad. I am the youngest of three daughters and was often spoiled with his attention. As an adult, with my own small family consisting of my husband and son, I was often at odds with my father for nothing other than just growing up. Sometimes, parents find it hard to let go of their children and acknowledge that they're adults now with their own families and lives to look after. Nonetheless, it did not change the love I felt for him.

On Wednesday, May 25th, I walked downstairs to our work-out room, located in our basement, for my daily bout of exercise. We have only two small windows and on that particular day, I could see the clear skies and feel the warmth of the sunshine filtering in.

My husband had pictures of my dad blown up and hung on the wall for my benefit. One of my favourite pictures was taken in Florida, of my dad with our young son standing on either side of a sign, with a picture of an alligator and an "X" through it. It is illustrating the phrase, "Please do not feed the alligators." I walked over to the picture, squatted, smiling with pure love in my heart, and kissed my index finger and touched it to my dad's face. I told him I loved him and walked away to put on my favourite CD, the LCBO's *Summer Grill, Volume Two*.

I proceeded to step onto the elliptical trainer to work-out. The third song on this particular CD is the famous "Chain of Fools" by Aretha Franklin. The song played, then suddenly stopped and replayed a chorus of the song — three different times.

It was at this moment that I smelled something really foul, something I was sort of familiar with, and yet, not really. It started as a faint smell of musty soil, then urine mixed with feces and then something rather rotten. Considering I have asthma, it was immediately noticeable. At the same time, my fingers and hands went cold while holding onto the elliptical bars. The freezing cold shot up my arms to my head and then through my body down to my toes. I had never experienced anything like this in my life. I stopped exercising and said out loud, rather foolishly, "Okay what are you trying to tell me?"

The CD played the chorus for the third time. It was playing "... and my daddy told me to go home, and take it easy." I said aloud, "Okay, I get the message, I'll slow down. And Dad, if it's really you, please don't show yourself. I couldn't handle that but I want to tell you I love you and I will always miss you each and every day. I'm sorry I didn't get a chance to say good-bye. But now I can. You don't have to hang around, I'll be fine. We'll all be fine."

Without even realizing it, I had acknowledged to myself: it was my father telling me to take it easy, as he had said time and again when he was alive. His words were, "Take it easy. You've got to settle down." Being a rather rambunctious child and passionate adult, I heard those words often. I went over to the CD player, stopped the CD, took it out, put it back in and pressed play. The CD never skipped again.

I feel fortunate to have had a visit from my dad. I was working out that day to relieve the pain I felt because now my mother was sick and in the hospital. Anyone who has ever supported a parent in the last stages of their life will understand that this is an exhausting process for all involved. But, not one I wanted to miss out on. I loved her so.

I believe my dad was telling me I cannot solve all of my mother's troubles and to remember to look after myself and my family. I knew I felt ill at this time but didn't realize until a year later just how sick I was. His visit prompted me to see a medical doctor in New York City to diagnose and treat my health problems.

I think of that day and smile. My dad was always trying to boss me around all of my life and now he was trying to do so from beyond the grave. It's okay with me and he can visit anytime.

A Spiritual Bond

The weather in Southwestern Ontario can be very hot and humid in the summer months and, unfortunately, accompanying that can be the dreaded fine particulate, or bad air. On days like this, my asthma prevents me from living a regular lifestyle, and I have been ordered by my doctor to stay indoors in the air conditioning. Not something an outdoor person wants to hear.

One particularly bad air day, I could not go to visit my mother in the hospital. She had been ill for some time. She was in a fragile state and not being able to go to her was unbearable for me. In fact, I paced the floor and spoke to her out loud as if she was in the room. I said, "Mom, I'm so sorry I cannot be with you today. I'm so angry. You know it's my asthma preventing me. I have to stay inside in the air conditioning. The FP is so high today, I couldn't even risk going to the car and running into the hospital. I'm so sorry!" And as this was spoken, my fists were folded and I waved them all about. I felt this energy, or force, coming from me — it filled the room.

Later that afternoon, my sister, who was with my mom all day, dropped by and asked, "Were you talking to mom today when you were at home?" I admitted I was. I recounted what I said. My sister's eyes went wide as she slowly collapsed onto the couch and said, "Oh my God, mom was answering you, telling you it's all right." I will never forget the look on her face nor my goose bumps from hearing what I had intended to happen in fact did.

Several weeks later it was obvious to all that my mom was going to die. She had the best of care and as many family members as she could bear around her, offering their support. On the day of her passing, August 25th, 2005, my sisters and I and our partners were all at the hospital. I asked a nurse what happens when a person is about to die. The reason being I knew my mom did not want to be alone at that particular moment. My father had died nine months previously and I felt vigilant that if I could be there, I would not leave her side to face this moment alone. The nurse said quietly, "When someone is soon to pass their breathing becomes shallow," and then she said, "You'll know."

We were all supporting our mother, best we knew how. It was early afternoon; my husband and I were in the room. I was holding her hand. I would not let go. I quietly spoke to her telling her how much I loved her and how much we all do. She was a great mother, grandmother, and all the things you want to say to someone so special that you loved dearly.

Suddenly, her breathing grew shallow. I asked my husband to run and tell my sisters to come in the room, immediately. The four of us were by her bedside, my husband and I on one, my sisters on the other. As hard as it is to let your mother go, we knew she had to. She had suffered greatly in her last several months of her life. When she drew her last breath, I felt this most awesome feeling emanating from my mother. It was like her energy, or spirit, bolted from her body and ran up and down mine. I felt it so vividly. It was the most exhilarating feeling I had ever experienced. She was beside herself with euphoria to be free from her body that had been holding her hostage. It only lasted a second and then she shot up alongside my body and disappeared. I felt joy like I'd never felt before: her joy. I honoured my commitment to my mom; we all did. She was not alone when she died. And she was so happy and grateful to all of us for standing by her side for so long.

It is wonderful to see a family that pulls together in the face of something so dreadful, the death of a loved one. Our family supported each other to help our mother through the most difficult time of her life. She was thrilled!

AFTERWORD

The distinguished New England psychologist William James dedicated twenty-five years to the study of paranormal phenomena, even serving as president of the Society for Psychical Research as well as the American Society for Psychical Research. In the essay "The Final Impressions of a Psychical Researcher" (1909), he sums up his thoughts and experiences and admits to a quarter-century of bafflement. He found the work worthwhile and rich in the study of human nature, with a few deeply puzzling episodes, but overall he admitted it is not a field for strong opinions. This essay, along with numerous others written in the same vein, may be found in *William James on Psychical Research* (New York: The Viking Press, 1960) edited by Gardner Murphy and Robert O. Ballou. Here are James's final words.

> Yet I am theoretically no "further" than I was at the beginning; and I confess that at times I have been tempted to believe that the Creator has eternally intended this department of nature to remain *baffling*, to prompt our curiosities and hopes and suspicions in all equal measure, so that, although ghosts and clairvoyances, and raps, and messages from spirits, are always seeming to exist and can never be fully explained away, they also can never be susceptible of full collaboration.

ACKNOWLEDGEMENTS

Over the last forty years I have been ably assisted by a whole host of men and women who have helped me to collect accounts like the ones that appear in this collection. Alice Mary Neal for many years served as my research assistant. Philip Singer has proved to be a fine friend and excellent librarian, resourceful in ferreting out information. Tony Hawke, publisher, editor, and friend has done double duty along the way. Publisher Kirk Howard and vice-president of marketing and sales Beth Bruder of Dundurn Press encouraged me to work on this book and on previous ones. The editing was expertly handled by Jason Karp, and Erin Mallory contributed the cover and the design of the pages. Independent researchers Dwight Whalen, E. Ritchie Benedict, and Ed Butts have shared with me many of their insights and discoveries. I have discussed the matters and issues raised in this book with knowledgeable, long-time associates who include Cyril Greenland, David A. Gotlib, and Daniel Bursten. I very much miss Marcello Truzzi, the sociologist with a special understanding of the operations of the mind — he would have really enjoyed the account of the psychic Langsner — but his wife, Pat, yet lives and has offered many insights and courtesies of her own over the years. I cherish my memories of the late Edith Fowke, enthusiastic folklorist *par excellence*, and I have intermittently corresponded with Hilary Evans, a fine researcher, as well as with historian-of-rejected-knowledge Ted Davy of Calgary and Denise Bonds and Christian R. Page of the television series *Dossiers mystère* aka *Missing Link*. George A. Vanderburgh and Bill Anderson supplied technical assistance. My wife, Ruth Colombo, made many invaluable suggestions along the way. Surveying the scene, I have come to the conclusion that I am yet again most indebted to the innumerable men and women who in the past have accepted my invitation to recount their experiences, this time for posterity in the form of narrative accounts.

NOTE FROM AUTHOR

I am always grateful to hear from readers!

The fields of the psychical, the parapsychological, and the paranormal continue to be of great interest to me. They are ongoing concerns, so I enjoy receiving letters or emails from readers about their unique or unusual experiences. The collection at hand consists of "hauntings of the past" and "hauntings of the present." If there are to be "hauntings of the future," they will derive from the contributions from readers like you. Keep in touch!

You may send me a letter care of the publisher: The Editorial Department, Dundurn Press, 3 Church Street, Suite 500, Toronto, Ontario M5E 1M2, Canada. My email address is *jrc@ca.inter.net*. I have two websites: *www.colombo.ca* and *www.colombo-plus.ca*. The latter site includes a longish essay on the unknown, with special reference to Canadian mysteries of the past, the present, and the future.

Chimo!

Also by John Robert Colombo

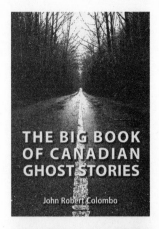

THE BIG BOOK OF CANADIAN GHOST STORIES
978-1-55002-844-7 / $29.99

This fascinating, scary book brings together the most notable stories from the archives of John Robert Colombo, Canada's "Mr. Mystery." Whatever your views are about the supernatural and the paranormal — skeptic, believer, middle-of-the-road — this huge collection of stories filled with thrills and chills will cause you to wonder about the nature of human life and the afterlife.

STRANGE BUT TRUE
Canadian Stories of Horror and Terror
978-1-55002-735-8 / $22.99

This is a chilling collection of fifty accounts of truly unusual events and experiences that are told by the people who experienced them. Ghosts, strange coincidences, strange creatures — these horrors and more are told through fascinating first-person accounts, originating in the columns of old newspapers and in the highly readable narratives derived from correspondence conducted by the author with present-day witnesses.

TERRORS OF THE NIGHT
Canadian Accounts of Eerie Events and Weird Experiences
978-1-55002-576-7 / $22.99

Terrors of the Night is a collection of more than one hundred accounts of eerie events and weird experiences that have been recorded by Canadians over the past four hundred years. These incredible accounts come from all parts of the country and concern witchcraft, peculiar weather conditions, wild beasts, hardly human creatures, omens, prophecies, powers beyond ours, miraculous cures, and other such instances of bizarre behaviour.

Available at your favourite bookseller.

DUNDURN

www.dundurn.com

TELL US YOUR STORY!
What did you think of this book?

Join the conversation at

www.definingcanada.ca/tell-your-story

by telling us what you think.